AQA Geography

Exclusively endorsed by AQA

AS

John Smith
Roger Knill

 Nelson Thornes

Published in 2008 by:
Nelson Thornes Ltd
Delta Place
27 Bath Road
CHELTENHAM
GL53 7TH
United Kingdom

08 09 10 11 12 / 10 9 8 7 6 5 4 3

A catalogue record for this book is available from the British Library

ISBN 978 0 7487 8258 1

Cover photograph: Getty/Monica Delmasso
Page make-up by Pantek Arts Ltd, Maidstone
Printed in Croatia by Zrinski

Acknowledgements

ActionAid: 217; Alamy/ Chris Gomershall: 125; Alamy/ Photofusion Picture Library: 185c; Alamy/ Pixel Youth Movement: 33a; Alamy/ Richard Coulam: 18 (top); AP/ Benny Gool: 267; Assured Food Standards: 226; Collections/ Ashley Cooper: 47; Corbis/ Barry Lewis: 173; Corbis/ Cheryl Ravelo/ Reuters: 207; Corbis/ Chris Sattlberger: 256; Corbis/ Digitalglobe via CNP/ CNP: 112; Corbis/ Ecoscene/ Peter Hulme: 94; Corbis/ Jayanta Shaw/ Reuters: 41; Dartmouth Flood Observatory 2007: 42; 2005 DMCii, From NigeriaSat-1 of the Disaster Monitoring Constellation: 1; epicscotland/ Geoge Logan: 17 (bottom); Environment Agency: 35; Dan Frater: 33c; Geoperspectives: 28, 58; Geophotos Picture Library/ Dr Tony Waltham: 90; Geoscience Features Picture Library/ K. Gardner: 17 (top), 18 (bottom); Geoscience Features Picture Library/ K. Thomson: 20; Getty Images/ Colin Monteath/ Hedgehog House/ Minden Pictures: 51; Istockphoto: 246; Juerg Alean, Glaciers online (www.glaciers-online.net) Eglisau, Switzerland: 50; C.J. Knill: 23; R.A. Knill: 29a, b; Mary Evans Picture Library: 185d; Nigel Press Associates Ltd: 130; PA/ Empics: 6, 33b; PA Photos: 24; Panos/ Fred Hoogervorst: 251; Panos/ Mark Henley: 185a; Paul Paris Les Images: 19; Rex Features/ Richard Austin: 118; Robert Harding Picture Library: 56; Rachel Smith: 127 (left), 133, 134, 135, 140 (right), 141, 142 (top), 143; Still Pictures: 185c; Still Pictures/ Martin Bond: 255; TerraMetrics www.truearth.com: 71; David Waugh: 62; World AIDS Campaign: 268.

p24: Excerpt from 'Dry Savages' in Four Quartets by T S Eliot reprinted with permission from Faber & Faber Ltd; p27: 'Flood risk rises as gardens disappear' by John Vidal, 3 September 2005. Reprinted by permission of Guardian News & Media Ltd © 2005; p73: Arctic Borderlands Ecological Knowledge Co-op excerpt reprinted from http:// www.taiga.net/coop/indics/pchpop.html; p73: Mary Jane Moses item reprinted from http://www.oldcrow.ca/ccpage3.htm; p73: Yukon Community Profiles item reprinted from http://www.yukoncommunities.yk.ca/communities/oldcrow/economy/; p101: Cliff-top couple living on the edge – by kind permission of Mail News & Media; p174: Population control in China item reprinted from People's Daily June 2000; p175: http://www.unfpa.org/countryfocus/iran/demographic.htm by kind permission of UNFPA; p179: Julian Simon quote reprinted from http://www.juliansimon.com/; p180–181: Extract from 'The limits to growth' reprinted from http://www.clubofrome.org/; p207: World Trade Organization (WTO) reprinted from http://www.wto.org/English/thewto_e/whatis_e/tif_e/fact1_e.htm; p213: http://www.ifpri.org/pubs/ib/ib11.pdf reprinted by kind permission of (c) International Food Policy Research Institute; p216: From Rights to End Poverty – a policy statement by ActionAid India (2003); p221: http://www. naturalengland.org.uk/ reprinted by kind permission of Natural England; p223: Sustainable food item reprinted from http://www.sustainweb.org/; p223: 2004 DEFA report reprinted from statistics.defra.gov.uk/esg/reports/foodmiles/execsumm.pdf; p225: http://www.farmersmarkets.net/findafmkt.htm reprinted by kind permission of FARMA; p228: The price of cheap beef article by kind permission of © George Monbiot, www.monbiot.com. First published in The Guardian 18 October 2005 http://guardian. co.uk; p228: http://www.choicesmagazine.org/2006-2/tilling/2006-2-12.htm reprinted by permission of Choices and the American Agricultural Economics Association; p239: Coal reserves item reprinted from http://www.worldcoal.org/pages/content/index.asp?PageID=188; p241: Cold War item quoted from The End of History? Francis Fukuyama, 1989; p242: http://www.guardian.co.uk/international/story/0,,2196422,00.html Steep decline in oil production by Ashley Seager, 22 October 2007. Reprinted by permission of Guardian News & Media Ltd © 2007; p242: http://www.guardian.co.uk/environment/2007/jul/11/climatechange.climatechange Canada flexes its muscles in scramble for the Arctic by Ed Pilkington, 11 July 2007. Reprinted by permission of Guardian News & Media Ltd © 2007; pp252–253: CoRWM item reprinted from http:// www.corwm.org.uk/pdf/FullReport.pdf pp119-124; p255: Solar photovoltaic cells item reprinted from http://www.simplyrenewable.com/c_solar_pv.htm; p258: Insulation item reprinted from http://www.energybulletin.net/35876.html; pp259–260: http://www.woking.gov.uk/environment/climate/Greeninitiatives/climatechangestrategy/ climatechange.pdf by kind permission of Woking Borough Council; p261: http://www.who.int/en/ reproduced by kind permission of the World Health Organisation; p264: http://www.unaids.org/en/KnowledgeCentre/Resources/QandA/default.asp.(UNAIDS Q and As August 2004) reproduced by kind permission of UNAIDSwww.unaids.org; p269: UA 2010 item reprinted from http://www.ua2010.org/index.php/en/g8_aids/g8_summit_broken_promises_what_happened; pp273–274: http://www.bat.com/group/ sites/uk__3mnfen.nsf/vwPagesWebLive/DO52APTT?opendocument&SKN=1&TMP=1reprinted by permission of British-American Tobacco (Holdings) Limited; p275: http://www.guardian.co.uk/business/2006/sep/26/smoking.britishamericantobaccobusiness Tobacco firms to face US class action over 'light' cigarettes by Simon Bowers, 26 September 2006. Reprinted by permission of Guardian News & Media Ltd © 2006; p281:http://health-e.org.za/news/article.php?uid=20031406 reprinted under Crown Copyright PSI License C2008000256; p282: http://www.dfid.gov.uk/news/files/ihp/default.asp and http://www.dfid.gov.uk/news/files/pressreleases/ihp.asp reprinted under Crown Copyright PSI License C2008000256.

Maps reproduced by permission of Ordnance Survey on behalf of HMSO. © Crown copyright (2008). All rights reserved. Ordnance Survey Licence number 100017284: 29 (Landranger 85), 57 (Landranger 90), 119 (Explorer 116), 124 (Explorer 184), 191, 193 and 195 (Explorer 316), 197 (Explorer 325)

All other photographs were supplied by the authors.

AQA AS Geography 978 0 7487 8258 1

Errata

The publishers wish to draw your attention to the following errors and inaccuracies in this book. We apologise for any inconvenience and disappointment that these may cause to teachers and their students, and give assurance that the errors listed will be rectified in future printings.

Page 6: Figure 1.6/Question 1 To answer this question with reference to Figure 1.6 students will need to know that peak rainfall in Carlisle was at approximately 10pm on 7 January 2005. A less precise answer may be deduced by referring to Figure 1.7. *peak Rainfall 10:00*

Page 8: Examiner's tip This should refer the student to **Question 5**, and not to Activity 12.

Page 10: Key term – Attrition This should read ' ...by repeated collision with each other and the banks and bed of the river.'

Page 13: Key terms Both definitions incorrectly refer to coastal processes. Both terms are correctly defined in the text on the same page.

Page 26: Figure 1.38 The caption to this figure is inaccurate. The three causes included on the left-hand side of the diagram are not human causes of flooding: 'natural streams meander ...', 'woodlands intercept rain ...' and 'natural grasslands ...'.

Page 54: Figure 2.10 Label '6a' on the diagram should read 'a pivot point for rotational movement'.

Page 89: Hydrolysis This should read 'The H^+ and OH^- ions in water combine with ions in the minerals found in rocks. This results in minerals like feldspar ...'.

Page 95: Figure 3.16 The reference to Figure 6.7 is included in error.

Page 111: Case study on Hurricane Katrina This incorrectly gives the date as 2004; it should be 2005.

Page 136: Wind processes/Transportation by the wind The reference to Figure 1.21 in the first line of the text is incorrect, and should be to Figure 1.19.

Page 164: Figure 5.8/Activity 12 The date of the population pyramid in Figure 5.8 is 2001. Part (a) of Activity 12 should read:

On a copy of Figure 5.8 label:

– those aged 50–54: the post-war baby boom
– those in their 40s: low fertility in the 1950s
– those in their 30s: the baby boom of the 1960s
– those aged 0–10: falling fertility in the 1990s.

Page 183: Activity 24 Part (a) of Activity 24 should read 'The y-axis needs to show separate scales for population and population density.'

Page 197: The figure number for the OS map of Longhorsley (Figure 5.60) is incorrect, and should be Figure 5.44.

Page 239: Figure 7.19 In the key, the legend for the blue arrow should read 'LPG' and not 'LNG'.

Page 249: Line 2 of second paragraph. The reference to Figure 7.24 is incorrect, and should be to Figure 7.26.

Page 257: Figure 7.36 In the key, the legend for the orange squares should read 'round 2 sites at planning stage'.

Page 284: The reference to Table 8.4 (line 4) is incorrect, and should be to Table 8.3.

Page 293: Examination-style question for Chapter 3. Section (b) should read 'Study Figure 3.12 on page 93'.

Contents

AQA introduction

Nelson Thornes and AQA

Nelson Thornes has worked in collaboration with AQA to ensure that this book offers you the best support for your AS or A Level course and helps you to prepare for your exams. The partnership means that you can be confident that the range of learning, teaching and assessment practice materials has been checked by the senior examining team at AQA before formal approval, and is closely matched to the requirements of your specification.

Blended learning

Printed and electronic resources are blended: this means that links between topics and activities between the book and the electronic resources help you to work in the way that best suits you, and enable extra support to be provided online. For example, you can test yourself online and feedback from the test will direct you back to the relevant parts of the book.

Electronic resources are available in a simple-to-use online platform called Nelson Thornes learning space. If your school or college has a licence to use the service, you will be given a password through which you can access the materials through any internet connection.

Icons in this book indicate where there is material online related to that topic. The following icons are used:

💡 Learning activity

These resources include a variety of interactive and non-interactive activities to support your learning.

✔️ Progress tracking

These resources include a variety of tests that you can use to check your knowledge on particular topics (Test yourself) and a range of resources that enable you to analyse and understand examination questions (On your marks…).

🔧 Research support

These resources include WebQuests, in which you are assigned a task and provided with a range of web links to use as source material for research.

When you see an icon, go to Nelson Thornes learning space at www.nelsonthornes.com/aqagce, enter your access details and select your course. The materials are arranged in the same order as the topics in the book, so you can easily find the resources you need.

How to use this book

This book covers the specification for your course and is arranged in a sequence approved by AQA.

The book content is divided into eight chapters matched to the eight topics of the AQA geography AS specification: Rivers, floods and management; Cold environments; Coastal environments; Hot desert environments and their margins; Population change; Food supply issues; Energy issues and Health issues. The eight chapters in this book cover all the material required for Unit 1 of the specification. On page viii is a skills matrix that enables you to navigate to the relevant parts of the book, where you will find examples of the use of a variety of geographical skills which you will be examined on in Unit 2 of the specification, the geographical skills paper.

The features in this book include:

Learning objectives

At the beginning of each chapter you will find a list of learning objectives that contain targets linked to the requirements of the specification.

Key terms

Terms that you will need to be able to define and understand.

Link

These highlight any key areas where topics are related to one another, as well as any useful further resources to investigate on the internet.

▪ Case study

Relevant case studies of the themes and issues specified in AS geography.

▪ Activities

Activities to help you develop the skills required in the study of AS geography.

▪ Did you know?

Facts and points of interest relating to the text which highlight the relevance of the topic.

▪ Skills

Descriptions of geographical skills needed for that area of the topic.

Hints from AQA examiners to help you with your study and to prepare for your examination.

Chapter summary

A bulleted list at the end of each chapter summarises the content in an easy-to-follow way.

AQA Examination-style questions

These are questions in the style that you can expect in your examination.

AQA examination questions are reproduced by permission of the Assessment and Qualifications Alliance.

Examination-style questions for each chapter can be found on pages 292–95.

▪ Web links in the book

Because Nelson Thornes is not responsible for third party content online, there may be some changes to this material that are beyond our control. In order for us to ensure that the links referred to in the book are as up to date and stable as possible, the websites provided are usually homepages with supporting instructions on how to reach the relevant pages if necessary.

Please let us know at webadmin@nelsonthornes.com if you find a link that doesn't work and we will do our best to correct this at reprint, or to list an alternative site.

Studying AS Geography

Introduction for students

Geography is about places and the people who live in those places. It is about how those places affect and are affected by the people who live there. It is about the relationships between places at a variety of scales, from local to national and regional, and right up to global.

However, geographers must understand that the relationships between people and places are never straightforward. They are part of a complex web of interrelationships and the people within that web have to make decisions about matters that can range from the trivial to the fundamentally important. As geographers, we can only understand the outcomes of this decision-making process if we can understand how they are made and how different factors inform the decision makers.

Not only do we have to be aware of our own roles as decision makers and influencers of events, we also have to understand the attitudes and values of other people and groups and factors that influence their decisions. One of the great strengths of geography is that it tries to understand how the different influences combine to produce the geography of the places that we study.

We learn to see the similarities among places, often called 'seeing patterns'. We also try to classify places. However, we have to be aware of the differences between places that may appear similar at first glance. We celebrate the uniqueness of places.

Issues in geography

Our emphasis on place, people, interactions and decision-making geography leads naturally to an interest in and concern for our environment at all scales, ranging from local to global.

We look at local issues such as:

- How can the management of a river basin be improved to reduce the risk of flooding?
- Are there equal opportunities for all income groups in the town to have access to health care?
- Is the short-term protection of coastline in one area sustainable in the light of long-term coastal retreat in some parts of the UK?
- Should a new wind farm be built on that hill, close to a settlement?
- Would the gains from building a new supermarket in the town outweigh the losses for the community?

We also look at global issues, including:

- the issues involved in migration, which can bring advantages and disadvantages to both the source area from which the migrants move and the destination in which they hope to settle
- the consequences for the global economy and the global geopolitical system if peak oil production has already been passed
- the interactions between melting ice caps, sea level around the world and the rates of erosion of coastlines and low-lying, densely populated delta areas
- the possible threats to the environment of Antarctica, where international agreements do not allow economic development at present but resources of great economic potential probably exist
- the pressure put on world food resources by the growth of world population.

Geographical understanding

As a geographer, you will develop a multidisciplinary approach to your studies, calling on a wide range of skills to make sense of complex issues.

Geography looks into the interrelated causes of many issues. It looks at the physical and human reasons why they arise. For many geographers, it is the links to both the physical and the human aspects of an issue that provide the key to our way of looking them. It allows geographers to offer a special, fully rounded understanding of the complex causes of the issues that affect our modern world. Having developed an understanding of the causes of the issues, we can go on to consider how these issues might be better managed for the long-term good of all involved.

For example, the issue of the increasing flood risk that is threatening many areas of the UK can only be understood if many aspects of geography can be brought together to study the problem. Heavy rainfall leads to flooding and something must be done to protect housing from floods, but we can look into far more complex causes. For instance:

- Is the problem of heavy rainfall linked to changing climate patterns or just a 'normal' fluctuation?
- If it is linked to climate change, is that change natural or does it have human causes?
- Have changes in land use upstream of the flood helped to cause increased runoff after the storm?

- How has the management of the river itself, its course and its banks, affected the speed with which water flows through the system and arrives at the flood point?
- Why are houses built on the floodplain to begin with?
- How has the building of houses, roads, car parking areas, etc. contributed to any flood risk?
- If the area that flooded this time is better protected, how will that influence the area further downstream the next time there is a potential flood?
- How can the authorities balance the cost of preventing or reducing the flood risk with all the other demands on their resources?

To help us understand these underlying causes, we can call on two important aspects of geography: the set of ideas, models and theories that make up an important part of the subject; and the series of case studies of other areas with similar problems and solutions that might be applicable to new cases.

In addition, we have our own ways of gathering data about the area we study, including fieldwork techniques, geographical information systems (GIS) and interrogating other data sources such as data and maps provided by the Meteorological Office, Environment Agency, census office and many other sources.

We can then use a whole range of skills (descriptive, graphic, cartographic and statistical) to present and analyse the data collected. We can combine primary and secondary data with our general theories, models and case studies to give us a holistic view of the issue and suggest realistic improvements.

Taking the examination

During the AS course you will lay the groundwork for becoming a geographer and think about issues in a geographical way.

For Unit 1 you will have to study two aspects of physical geography and two aspects of human geography, although you will be encouraged to look at the interrelationships between different aspects of the subject. You will be questioned on your understanding and knowledge of these topics and you will also start to analyse contemporary issues linked to them.

For Unit 2 you will be tested on a range of skills, including fieldwork skills. Here you will start to apply your skills to the analysis of issues.

If you finish your study of geography at the end of AS, you will have developed important ways of looking at and understanding the world around you. However, if you continue to A2 you will develop your skills and

understanding to an even greater extent. You will be in a position to make well-considered judgements on a wide variety of issues and to make well-founded suggestions as to how those issues might be better managed.

■ Introduction for teachers

The revised specification

The team that produced the new specification worked within certain constraints but also took advantage of certain opportunities. The team that produced this book then had to work within the specification but could also take the chance to develop those new opportunities as far as possible.

The specification development team made a conscious attempt to build on the strengths of the old AQA specification and to take account of the needs that were expressed by teachers. The new specification contains much that was previously popular and well taught but the content has been reduced and updated overall.

A much greater degree of choice has been allowed within the new specification, which provides the opportunity to bring in new or unfamiliar topics alongside popular old ones including, at AS, the study of arid and semi-arid environments and the geography of health issues. Moreover, throughout the new specification, there is a concentration on developing an understanding of contemporary issues.

However, the understanding of those issues is strongly based on an understanding of basic geographical themes. The subject has evolved through this development process; it has not been changed beyond recognition.

In some people's view, the new specification cannot include any opportunity for assessed coursework. However, there is still a strong emphasis in the examination on the assessment of the enquiry process. It is hoped that many teachers will take advantage of these changes to update their fieldwork and enquiry activities and engage in more issue analysis. The authors of this book and the A2 book have tried to point out ways in which enquiry can take place throughout the course, using primary and secondary sources of information to develop good practice in enquiry and issue evaluation.

About this book

This book and the supporting resources have been written by a team of authors consisting of experienced teachers, writers, examiners and advisers. The team has had access to advice and guidance from the examining team at AQA. It is endorsed by AQA.

Skills matrix

This matrix will help you to navigate to the relevant parts of this book where you will find examples of the use of a variety of geographical skills. Although certain skills have been highlighted as a skills feature in this book, skills are integral to the content of this book and this matrix helps you to find them.

Skills	1 Rivers, floods and management	2 Cold environments	3 Coastal environments	4 Hot desert environments and their margins	5 Population change	6 Food supply issues	7 Energy issues	8 Health issues
Investigative skills								
Identification of geographical questions and issues, and effective approaches to enquiry	Y	Y	Y	Y	Y	Y	Y	Y
Identification, selection and collection of quantitative and qualitative evidence from primary sources (including fieldwork) and secondary sources	11, 18, 25	78	100	147	176, 199	203, 205	235, 237	263, 264, 287
Processing, presentation, analysis and interpretation of evidence	39	78	105, 122	132,147, 150	176, 199	203, 205	235, 237	263, 264, 287
Drawing conclusions and showing an awareness of the validity of conclusions	39	78	105, 122	132, 147, 150	176, 199	203, 205	235, 237	263, 264, 287
Evaluation	39	78	105	147	199	205	235	263, 264, 287
Risk assessment and identification of strategies for minimising health and safety risks in undertaking fieldwork								
Cartographic skills								
Atlas maps		78			158, 177	201	236, 245	
Base maps								
Sketch maps		63	92, 97, 104, 120					
OS maps	29	57	119, 124		191, 197	201		
Maps with located proportional symbols					184		236, 249, 253	
Maps showing movement – flow lines, desire lines, trip lines							237, 244	
Town-centre plans								
Choropleth, isoline and dot maps	292							266, 267
Weather maps			110					
Graphical skills								
Line graphs – simple, comparative, compound and divergent	6, 15, 26	49, 50, 71		132	156, 171	215	233, 237	266

Skills	1 Rivers, floods and management	2 Cold environments	3 Coastal environments	4 Hot desert environments and their margins	5 Population change	6 Food supply issues	7 Energy issues	8 Health issues
Bar graphs – simple, comparative, compound and divergent	16, 26, 42	74		132	164, 170, 175	202	254	274, 287
Scatter graphs and best fit line	21		109		156			
Pie charts and proportional divided circles						202, 224	232	
Triangular graphs								
Kite and radial diagrams			57, 58					
Logarithmic scales					167			
Dispersion diagrams								
ICT skills								
Remotely sensed data – photographs, digital images	1, 28, 42	57, 71	112	147				
Databases, e.g. census data, EA data, Met Office data	6	49	110, 123		165, 184, 189	201	233	263, 285, 289, 290
GIS		58, 73				201, 203		287
Presentation of text and graphical/cartographic images using ICT								
Statistical skills								
Measures of central tendency – mean, median, mode								
Measures of dispersion – interquartile range and standard deviation								
Spearman's rank correlation test								
Application of significance tests								
Chi-squared test								
Mann Whitney test								

1 Rivers, floods and management

The drainage basin hydrological cycle: the water balance

Key terms

Discharge: the volume of water flowing in a river per second, measured in cumecs (m³/s).

Activity

1. Study Figure 1.1. What evidence is there that this part of the Mississippi drainage basin has physical features that support settlement, business, transportation and farming?

Whether you are reading this at home or in a classroom, the land you are on is in a drainage basin. In some areas this may be obvious, as streams, rivers and valley slopes indicate clearly how water may pass through your landscape. In other places it is less clear, but even in urban areas the land that towns are built on is part of a drainage basin system, albeit modified by human influences.

Figure 1.1 is an infrared image where vegetation appears in red. The flooded areas of New Orleans can be seen as dark areas, with lighter lines indicating the roofs of properties. It shows part of New Orleans on the delta of the Mississippi-Missouri in the USA. Where this river, which drains over 3,225,000 km² of the North American continent, meets the Gulf of Mexico, huge forces are at work. With a **discharge** of 12,743 m³/s of water carrying a daily load of 396,000 tonnes of sediment into the delta, the river has the power to constantly shift location, creating and eroding land.

Floods caused by heavy rainfall, high tides and storm surges are perhaps the most dramatic aspect of a drainage basin that directly provides water for over 18 million people and helps agribusiness supply an estimated 92 per cent of all agricultural exports in the USA. The populations supported by such basins depend on them for the changing requirements of business, domestic and leisure activities and modify them to suit human need, sometimes with disastrous consequences.

Fig. 1.1 *Flooding by the Mississippi River in New Orleans caused by Hurricane Katrina*

■ Key terms

Precipitation: all forms of moisture that reach the Earth's surface (including rain, snow and dew).

Evaporation: the transformation of water droplets into water vapour by heating.

Evapotranspiration: the loss of water from a drainage basin into the atmosphere from the leaves of plants.

Surface storage: the total volume of water held on the Earth's surface in lakes, ponds and puddles.

Groundwater storage: the storage of water underground in permeable rock strata.

Infiltration: the downward movement of water into the soil surface.

Percolation: the gravity flow of water within soil.

Overland flow: the movement of water over the surface of the land, usually when the ground is saturated or frozen or when precipitation is too intense for infiltration to occur.

Throughflow: the movement of water downslope within the soil layer.

Groundwater flow: the deeper movement of water through underlying rock strata.

Dynamic equilibrium: rivers are constantly changing over time to reach a state of balance with the processes that determine their form. As the flows of energy and materials passing through a river system vary, the river changes to move towards this equilibrium.

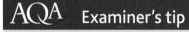

Examiner's tip

Examiners expect you to use appropriate terms in written answers. Using the correct technical vocabulary helps you describe processes like the hydrological cycle clearly. But remembering the words is only part of the skill. You need to understand the terms to be able to use them effectively.

A drainage basin is an area of land (catchment area) drained by a river and its tributaries. Drainage basins are separated from each other by ridges of higher land called watersheds. Any **precipitation** falling beyond the watershed will eventually drain into the neighbouring basin. The drainage basin hydrological cycle may be defined as a single river basin bounded by its own watershed and the sea. It may be viewed as an open system with:

■ **inputs** – precipitation (including rain and snow), solar energy for **evaporation**

■ **outputs** – evaporation and transpiration from plants (**evapotranspiration**), runoff into the sea, percolation of water to underlying rock strata

■ **stores** – puddles, rivers, lakes (**surface storage**), soil storage and **groundwater storage** as well as water stored on vegetation following precipitation

■ **transfers or flows** – **infiltration, percolation, overland flow, throughflow** and **groundwater flow**.

■ Systems theory

Geographers use an aspect of systems theory as a way of explaining how natural phenomena such as the hydrological cycle or ecosystems function. It helps us to analyse relationships between the components of the unit being considered. They are often classified into three types:

■ **Isolated** – there is no input or output of energy or matter (the universe is probably the only example of this).

■ **Closed** – there is input, transfer and output of energy but not of matter or mass (some might consider the planet an example of this).

■ **Open** – there are inputs and outputs of both energy and matter; most environmental systems are thought to be examples of this kind of system.

When inputs and outputs are balanced, the system is said to be in a state of **dynamic equilibrium**. In reality most if not all systems are rarely in balance but are changing continuously to approach this state. For example, additional prolonged rainfall will increase discharge and **velocity**, which in turn will cause more **erosion**.

Feedback loops are where deviations in inputs and outputs move systems away from their balanced state; some geographers believe one of two major situations may prevail. **Negative feedback loops** exist where changes are eventually met with responses that redress the imbalance and lead the system back towards the original state. **Positive feedback loops** are thought to exist where one change away from the original state triggers another change which leads even further away and the system appears unable to find redress.

Represented as a flow diagram, the drainage basin's open system is more easily seen as a combination of inputs, stores, flows and outputs.

Water falling on a largely natural or a heavily developed drainage basin will not necessarily pass through all the components of the cycle shown in Figure 1.2. For example, in warm climates water falling as precipitation may be lost back to the atmosphere by evapotranspiration before reaching a river system. In contrast to this relatively short cycle, in a cooler climate cycling times may be much longer, for example when precipitation falling as snow is incorporated into a glacier store.

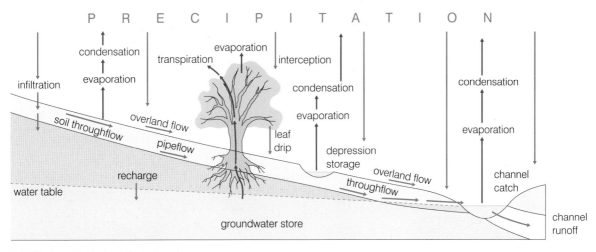

Fig. 1.2 *Drainage basin hydrological cycle*

Activities

2 Choose five of the key terms on pages 2 and 3 that you think you understand quite well. For each term write down three words that you might normally use in your explanation (e.g. precipitation – *surface* or *rain*). Now write down or explain to a partner how the process works, *without* using any of those three words. See if they can guess which words you left out. Ask them to try their key terms out on you and spot their missing words.

3 Choose 10 of the key terms to help you describe all or part of the drainage basin hydrological cycle, using the key terms in an order that makes sense to you. Ask a partner to listen to your description and try to identify any extra terms they could add. Repeat the activity with your partner choosing their 10 terms, including some not already used.

Key term

Velocity: the speed and the direction at which a body of water moves.

Erosion: the wearing away of the surface of the land. It includes the breakdown of rock and its removal by wind, water or ice.

Interception: the prevention of rain from reaching the Earth's surface by trees and plants.

Condensation: the process by which water vapour is converted into water.

Channel flow: the movement of water within the river channel.

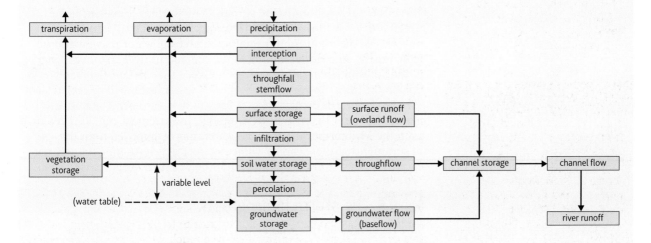

Fig. 1.3 *Drainage basin flow diagram*

Activities

4 Make a copy of Figure 1.3 on page 3. On your diagram shade in the stages: inputs (blue), stores (green), flows (yellow) and outputs (red).

5 Describe at least two different paths that water could follow from an input to an output stage.

6 Explain how different paths might exist depending on whether the environmental conditions were:

a   extremely hot and dry

b   very cold.

The balance between water inputs and outputs of a drainage basin may be shown as a water budget graph – that is, the drainage basin operates as an open physical system.

Water budget $P = Q + E$ +/– change in storage

where:

P = precipitation

Q = runoff

E = evapotranspiration

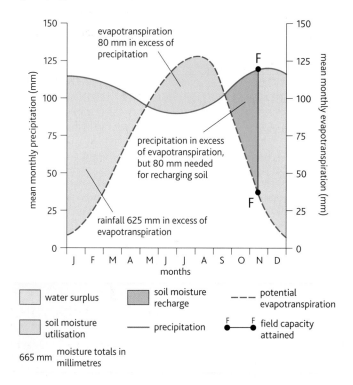

Fig. 1.4 *Model of the water budget in a drainage basin*

In a temperate climate such as that experienced in the UK, precipitation usually exceeds evapotranspiration so that over a year there is a positive water budget (or water balance). During the winter when precipitation is relatively high and evapotranspiration (as well as temperatures) are lower, there is a **soil moisture** surplus. This surplus is evident in surface runoff and a rise in river levels. In summer, rates of evapotranspiration may exceed the input from precipitation and soil water may be utilised, reducing the amount remaining in the soil and in river channels. Later in the autumn when rains once again exceed the amount that can be evaporated (as temperatures fall), the soil water levels will be replenished. This recharging of the soil takes it back to field capacity (the normal amount of water that can be held by soil). In extremely arid climates such as in the Mediterranean, so much water may be removed from the soil in summer that there can be a soil moisture deficit; that is, there is not enough water left in the soil to match the potential evapotranspiration.

The storm hydrograph

The water flowing in a river channel is referred to as its discharge. This represents the total volume of water in a river channel passing any given point every second. It is usually measured in cumecs (cubic metres = *volume*, per second = *velocity*). Measurements may be taken continuously at weirs to measure how discharge changes from hour to hour. Fluctuations in channel discharge are recorded on a **hydrograph**. An annual hydrograph indicates the yearly pattern of flow. For example, the River Caldew (near Carlisle in Cumbria) ranges between summer lows of around 7 m³/s to winter highs of about 225 m³/s. Storm (or **flood**) hydrographs (see Figure 1.5) can reveal how rivers respond to a single rainfall event. In January 2005, the discharge levels in the River Eden, which also runs through Carlisle, increased from 121 m³/s on 6 January to 1090 m³/s on 8 January, causing the river level to rise about 6 m above its normal channel flow and flooding large areas of the city.

Figure 1.5, showing the main features of a storm hydrograph, allows us to examine the relationship between a rainfall event and discharge. The diagram shows the discharge before the storm event (antecendent flow rate). The water in the channel before the precipatation event may be the result of previous rainfall gradually feeding into the stream from tributaries, throughflow and **baseflow** – in temperate regions a river is rarely dry just because it has not rained for several weeks. The peak of the storm event shown by the bar graph does not result in a sudden rise in discharge as little rain can fall directly into a river channel. Most rain falls onto the basin catchment and takes time to make its way to the channel.

Key terms

Soil moisture: the total amount of water, including the water vapour, in an unsaturated soil.

Hydrograph: a graph showing for a given point on a stream the discharge, stage (depth), velocity, or other property of water with respect to time; a graphical representation of stream discharge (volume/time) during a storm or flood event.

Flood: a temporary excess of water which spills over onto land.

Baseflow: water that reaches the channel largely through slow throughflow and from permeable rock below the water table.

Storm flow: water that reaches the channel largely through runoff. This may be a combination of overland flow and rapid throughflow.

Activity

7 Try to place the following statements (letters) on a large copy of Figure 1.5 (the blue hydrograph line and axes only) and explain why you believe that is the most appropriate position on the graph. Quote figures from the graph to support your answer.

a Most of the discharge at this point is from baseflow.

b This represents the lag time between the peak in rainfall and the peak in discharge.

c The discharge takes longer to fall as water is being released relatively slowly from the channel.

d Here the rapid rise in discharge reflects significant throughflow from the soil.

e Beyond this point water will spill onto the floodplain.

f This part of the curve is often the result of rapid overland flow.

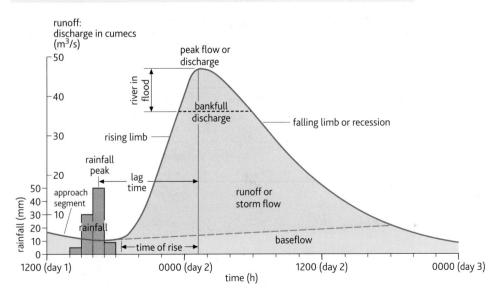

Fig. 1.5 *A storm hydrograph*

Case study

River Eden, Carlisle, Cumbria

The hydrograph for the River Eden (see Figure 1.6) shows how quickly a river can respond to a major rainfall event. The rapid rise in discharge was the result of many different factors interacting to produce flood conditions that killed three people and left thousands homeless. The hydrograph for this event shows how the discharge in the channel reacted to precipitation, but the extent to which physical or human causes were responsible for this flood event is debatable. The main possible causes of the flood event are shown in Figure 1.12. Some factors relate to the physical nature of the drainage basin and the weather, while others reflect the way people use the land and how this responds to heavy rainfall.

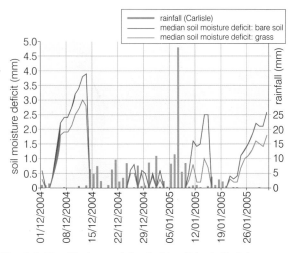

Fig. 1.6 *Flood hydrograph for the River Eden in Carlisle, December 2004 to January 2005. Peak rainfall occurred at just before midnight on 07/01/05.*

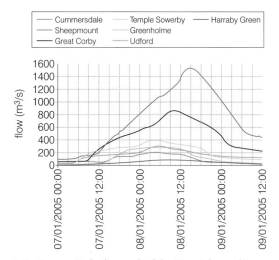

Fig. 1.7 *Composite hydrograph of the River Eden and its tributaries*

Question

1 Calculate the approximate lag time for the River Eden at Carlisle shown in Figure 1.6.

Fig. 1.8 *The Carlisle floods, 2005*

Table 1.1 *Rainfall and runoff volumes in the River Eden catchment*

Location	Volume of rainfall (m³)	Volume of runoff (m³)	Runoff (%)
River Eden at Sheepmount	201,286,000	147,205,000	73
River Derwent at Camerton	109,805,000	70,591,000	64

Table 1.2 *Some possible causes of the Carlisle floods in 2005*

Rainfall	Intense rainfall (201,286,000 m³) leading to 147,205,000 m³ of runoff (flow) = 73% runoff in River Eden at Carlisle
Vegetation	Mixed arable and grassland in valleys and rough hill pasture on uplands
Geology	Includes impermeable slate and volcanic rocks in the Skiddaw area and sandstone and limestone in the Vale of Eden
Soils	Thin soils on much of the upland area, deeper soils and alluvium in valleys
Relief	Significant areas of upland with steep slopes characterise much of the upper basin area. Much lower gradients around Carlisle
Urbanisation	Limited in upland regions, increasing spread of towns and villages in valley areas
Basin shape and size	About 2290 km² and elongated toward the south-east. The rivers Caldew, Petteril and Irthing have a confluence with the Eden just before or in Carlisle itself
History	Significant flooding over the last 100 years and three major floods over four years (including January 2005)

Question

2 To what extent do you think the factors affecting flooding shown in Table 1.2 are entirely physical or human in nature?

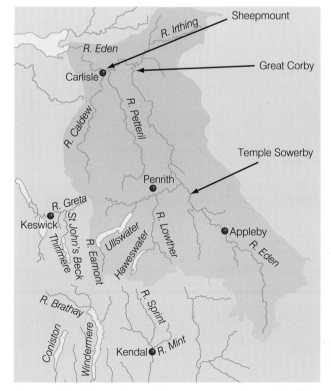

Fig. 1.9 *The drainage basin of the rivers running through Carlisle*

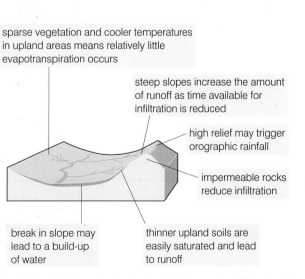

sparse vegetation and cooler temperatures in upland areas means relatively little evapotranspiration occurs

steep slopes increase the amount of runoff as time available for infiltration is reduced

high relief may trigger orographic rainfall

impermeable rocks reduce infiltration

break in slope may lead to a build-up of water

thinner upland soils are easily saturated and lead to runoff

Fig. 1.10 *A drainage basin showing the factors that affect flooding*

Questions

3 Why is a high-intensity rainfall event likely to lead to flooding?

4 How might the location of Carlisle and the physical nature of the drainage basin have made a flood more likely?

5 Discuss the extent to which you believe the Carlisle floods of January 2005 were a result of intense rainfall rather than the physical characteristics of the drainage basin.

6 Explain how the short lag time would make it difficult for the authorities to:

   a predict the flood event

   b take precautions to prepare for the flood

   c attempt to prevent the flood.

AQA Examiner's tip

Activity 12 asks you to decide whether you think the floods were mainly a result of precipitation, basin characteristics or a combination. It is important to maintain structure and balance in your response.

Structure – your answer requires a beginning (introduction), a middle (argument) and an end (conclusion).

Balance – look at more than one view or interpretation. It is important that you show the examiner that you have evaluated (weighed up) the available evidence and considered how it might support or contradict any argument you are making.

Introduction – this should not repeat the question (you don't have time) but may well use a topic sentence to frame your response ('There are many reasons why ...', 'In considering the relative importance of ...') or perhaps define some of the key terms identified in the title or question. It might provide a brief statement of the idea or concept you will develop in your main answer.

Argument – a series of paragraphs developing one point each and clearly related to the question. They should follow on logically from each other with connectives to join up the flow of your argument. Each point you make should be supported by specific evidence and explained. A commonly used technique is PEE (Point, Example/evidence and Explanation). Real, located examples with facts and figures support your arguments more effectively.

Conclusion – synthesise, don't summarise! Show how the points you made and the support and examples you used were not random, but fit together. A good conclusion:

- refers back to the title/question
- gives the essay a sense of completeness
- leaves a final impression on the reader.

Don't simply repeat things that were in your answer – it will not gain any more marks.

💡 ⓘ Changing channel characteristics

River processes may be subdivided into three main groups:

■ erosion

■ transportation

■ deposition.

All three are dependent on the amount of energy the river possesses. Energy is a function of the mass of water, the height of the river above sea level and the gradient of the channel. Gravity acting on the mass of water above sea level pulls it downwards. The altitude of the river determines how far it has to fall, thus giving it potential energy. The steepness of the gradient of the channel in which the river flows determines how much kinetic energy the water possesses. Not all of this energy is available to erode or transport sediment. Much is lost through internal friction because of turbulence within the flow of the river or via frictional contact with the bed and banks. Generally the faster the flow of the river (velocity), the greater the turbulence that is generated. Water with more turbulent flow can pick up and carry more sediment load.

Velocity is influenced by three main factors:

■ channel shape in cross-section

■ roughness of the channel's bed and banks

■ channel slope.

The channel shape is best described by its **hydraulic radius**; that is, the ratio between the cross-sectional area and the length of the **wetted perimeter**, as shown in Figure 1.11.

$$\text{Hydraulic radius} = \frac{\text{Cross-sectional area}}{\text{Wetted perimeter}} \quad \text{e.g.} \quad \frac{50 \text{ m}^2}{20 \text{ m}} = 2.5 \text{ m}$$

The **cross-sectional area** is measured by calculating the width and the mean depth of the channel. The wetted perimeter is the total length of the bed and bank sides that are in contact with the water in the channel.

■ Key terms

Hydraulic radius: the ratio of the cross-sectional area of the channel and the length of its wetted perimeter.

Wetted perimeter: that portion of the perimeter of a stream channel cross-section that is in contact with the water.

Cross-sectional area: the total length of the bed and the bank sides in contact with the water in the channel.

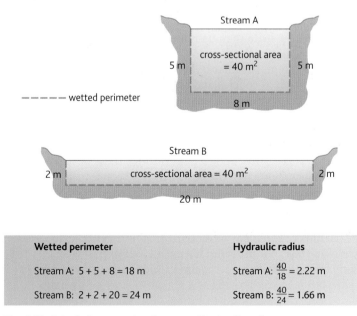

Wetted perimeter	Hydraulic radius
Stream A: $5 + 5 + 8 = 18$ m	Stream A: $\frac{40}{18} = 2.22$ m
Stream B: $2 + 2 + 20 = 24$ m	Stream B: $\frac{40}{24} = 1.66$ m

Fig. 1.11 *Calculating wetted perimeter and hydraulic radius*

As you can see in Figure 1.11, two channels may have the same cross-sectional area but because they have different shapes they have different wetted perimeters and hydraulic radii. Stream A has a larger hydraulic radius with less water in contact with the bed or banks, so it has less frictional drag and more of the water can move at a higher velocity. Stream B has a smaller hydraulic radius and has more of the total volume of water in frictional contact with the wetted perimeter. It has a less efficient flow than Stream A and a lower velocity.

In reality, few channels are perfectly symmetrical and Figure 1.12 shows how an asymmetrical channel carries faster-moving water towards the outside of a bend. This may lead to greater erosion on the outside and higher levels of deposition by slower-moving water on the inside. Figure 1.13 shows how variations in flow may produce different hydraulic radii in the same channel at different times of the year. At low flow levels (X–X) the water experiences greater frictional drag whereas at high flow (Y–Y) more of the water is free from direct frictional contact with the wetted perimeter and may flow at higher velocity. At bankfull stage (usually in winter) a river has far more energy than when experiencing low flow (in summer).

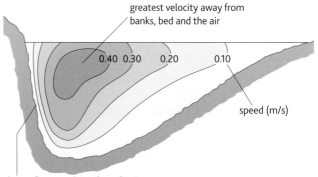

greatest velocity away from banks, bed and the air

0.40 0.30 0.20 0.10

speed (m/s)

slower flow resulting from friction

Fig. 1.12 *Changes in velocity in an asymmetrical channel*

Channel morphology is more often a reflection of the highly erosive capabilities of a river in spate than its more common, gentler, lower levels of flow. Channel roughness also has a significant impact on the efficiency of flow. A channel with an irregular bed and banks and/or containing large-calibre debris such as cobbles and boulders, will experience significant loss of energy through frictional contact and turbulent flow. In upland streams in regions where soils are thin, the channel may contain larger-calibre sediment (e.g. boulders and cobbles) which has been relatively little eroded. A higher proportion of stream energy is used up in inefficient flow as the water finds a path through these obstructions. In lowland rivers where much of the sediment has been transported and, by **attrition**, is diminished in size to finer-calibre load (e.g. sands, silts and clays), the river is often in contact with a smoother channel and more of the water experiences an efficient flow regime. This helps to explain the paradox of turbulent mountain streams on steep gradients seemingly moving fast, but in reality having a lower overall velocity than an apparently smooth-flowing river approaching the sea, which looks relatively slow but is in fact moving at a higher velocity as a whole.

■ Key terms

Attrition: the reduction and rounding of particles of sediment carried in water by repeated collision with each other and the shore.

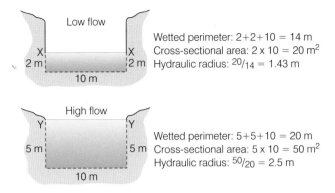

Fig. 1.13 *Changes in hydraulic radius at low flow and high flow*

Activities

8 Calculate the hydraulic radii of Streams C, D and E in the diagram below.

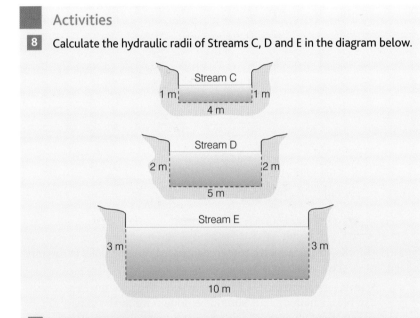

9 Explain how the efficiency of each channel section is affected by its hydraulic radius.

10 Assuming that Stream C came from near the source of the river, Stream D from the middle section and Stream E from near the mouth, select from the following the statement that you most agree with and explain why you believe it is likely to be true.

  a River velocity is likely to remain the same along the whole course of a river.

  b Rivers tend to be slower in their upper course but increase in velocity lower down.

  c A river that is much wider than it is deep will have a higher velocity than a river that is deeper than it is wide.

Skills

Measuring rivers

A number of river features can be easily measured by A Level students. For reasons of safety, relatively small streams are most suitable to gather data from. Ideally, a stream around 50 cm deep and around 3 m wide should be selected for analysis. A number of channel characteristics may be analysed:

- changes in depth and width measurements (compare upstream and downstream)
- the nature, roughness and calibre of the bedload
- comparing channel and flow characteristics at normal and bankfull conditions
- comparing channel profiles across a meander and a straight section, or a riffle and a pool
- stream gradient over a longer section of river.

Measuring the depth, width and velocity of a stream is illustrated in Figure 1.14.

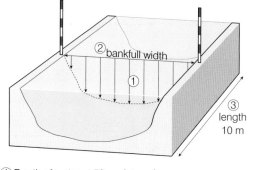

① Depth of water at 50 cm intervals
   (current level and bankfull)
② Bankfull width
③ Velocity recorded over a 10 m stretch
   (a sample of at least six readings should be taken)

Fig. 1.14 *How to measure a river*

- **Depth** – using a metre rule or calibrated ranging pole, the depth of the stream should be measured at least every 50 cm.
- **Width** – by stretching a 20 m tape across the channel the width can be calculated. This should be done once at the height the river is flowing at on the day you are measuring but also from the top of the channel to help estimate bankfull volume.
- **Velocity** – this may be measured most accurately by a flowmeter but can also be measured relatively easily by recording the time taken by a floating object (e.g. orange, cork or table tennis ball) over a known distance (e.g. 10 m). As stream flow varies according to distance from the bank, turbulence and obstructions, at least six readings should be taken and an average figure calculated. The surface water will tend to flow faster than water in contact with bed and banks, so readings are typically corrected by 0.8 to reflect the slightly slower speed of the stream overall.
- **Discharge** – as discharge represents the amount of water that passes a given point in a given amount of time, it is calculated by multiplying the cross-sectional area by the velocity, giving a reading in cubic metres per second (cumecs) or m^3/s.
- **Sediment calibre and roundness** – by sampling 30 to 50 randomly selected pieces of bedload taken from across the stream cross-section, an estimate of the nature of the stream sediment may be derived. Samples can be measured for length (long axis) and shape (degree of roundness) (see Figure 1.17). Changes in the nature of sediment deposited across meanders as opposed to straighter sections might be an interesting

a Sediment roundness

1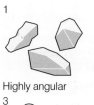

Highly angular

2

Slight evidence of roundness at jagged points

3

No very sharp edges

4

Still rather irregular in shape but all edges are rounded

5

Smooth-edged, hardly any 'edges', nearly sperical

6

As smooth as is ever likely

b Measuring the long axis

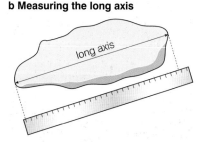

long axis

Fig. 1.15 *Sediment roundness and how to measure the long axis*

comparison. As we might expect bedload to become smaller and more rounded downstream as a result of attrition, sampling bedload at a number of predetermined points (e.g. every 2 km) down the long profile may help us to test this theory.

■ **Long profile** – this is more difficult to measure owing to the irregularity of the channel floor. One method is to use the stream surface as an approximate equivalent, by driving two measuring rods into the channel floor until the level of the water is the same on both poles. The angle of inclination between the two poles can then be read. An alternative method is to measure the change in gradient along the bank, but this may not accurately reflect the actual gradient of the channel bed.

Erosion

There are four main processes of erosion.

■ **Hydraulic action** is the movement of sediment by the frictional drag of the moving water. Turbulent flow lifts loose sediment as the velocity of the river increases. Where velocity is high, such as on the outer bend of a meander, hydraulic action can remove material from the banks, which may lead to undercutting and eventually collapse. In locations such as at waterfalls and rapids, it may be strong enough to work on lines of weakness such as joints and bedding planes until they are eroded.

■ **Abrasion** (**corrasion**) is the rubbing or scouring of the bed and banks by the sedimentary material carried along by the river. This load ranges from finer particles readily kept in suspension by turbulent flow to heavier boulders rolled along at times of bankfull flow (traction load). Where depressions exist in the channel floor, the turbulent flow of the river can cause pebbles to swirl around and enlarge the hollows into potholes.

■ **Attrition** refers to the reduction in size of the sediment particles as they collide with each other, the bed and banks. Pieces of sediment become smaller and more rounded as they move downstream, so it is more common to find rounder, smaller fragments downstream and coarser, more angular fragments upstream.

■ **Corrosion** occurs where rocks dissolve into the water and are carried away. This process is most common where carbonate rocks such as limestone and chalk are exposed in the channel.

Rivers may erode vertically and horizontally, often at the same time to varying degrees. Vertical erosion is characteristic of faster-flowing rivers where sufficient energy to downcut, coupled with larger, more angular bedloads, can produce relatively rapid lowering of the channel floor and generate steep-sided valleys. Where a river has a sizeable floodplain it may meander across the valley and lateral erosion may dominate. This is particularly evident where the floodplain is composed of fine alluvial sediments as hydraulic action may attack the outside of the meander bend, leading to undercutting and eventual collapse of river banks.

Transportation

Energy that remains after frictional drag has been overcome is available to do another kind of work – transportation. Sedimentary material that has been loosened by erosion or washed into the river from the valley sides may be carried along by the river in three main ways:

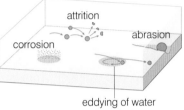

Fig. 1.16 *Four main types of erosion in a river, and how potholes form*

■ **Key terms**

Abrasion/corrasion: the wearing away of the shoreline by sediment carried by the waves.

Corrosion: includes the dissolving of carbonate rocks (e.g. limestone) in sea water and the evaporation of salt crystals which expand on formation and help the rock to disintegrate.

Fig. 1.17 *Stones in a pothole*

- **Bedload** – larger materials such as boulders and cobbles that are too heavy to be picked up by the current may roll or slide along the channel floor (traction). Material ranging from pebbles to sand grains may be temporarily lifted and bounced along the floor in a hopping motion (saltation).

- **Suspended load** – this usually forms the bulk of sediment transported by rivers and comprises fine muds and clays up to grains of sand. Faster-flowing, more turbulent rivers can carry more suspended sediment and this accounts for the muddy colour of river water approaching bankfull stage and towards the river mouth where higher velocities and finer sediment calibres are more common.

- **Dissolved/solution load** – most common where rivers run through areas of carbonate rocks (e.g. limestone/chalk). Weak acids (e.g. carbonic acid from precipitation) may act on more soluble rocks and gradually remove material in solution.

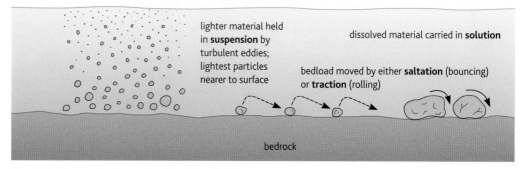

Fig. 1.18 *Three main types of sediment load in a river*

Competence

In discussing transportation of sediment load it is useful to distinguish between river competence and capacity. Competence is the maximum size (calibre) of load a river is capable of transporting whereas capacity refers to the total volume of sediment a river can transport. It is important to note the influence of river velocity. At low velocity only fine particles may be transported (clays, silt and fine sands). Larger-calibre material can be moved when velocity increases. Because the maximum particle mass that can be moved increases with the sixth power of velocity, when discharge levels are high, for example during a flood, much larger boulders can be moved.

The **Hjulström curve** illustrates the relationship between velocity and competence. It shows the velocities at which sediment will normally be eroded, transported or deposited. The mean or critical erosion velocity (sometimes called the entrainment velocity) shows the velocity required to pick up and transport sediments of varying calibre. The mean fall or settling velocity curve indicates the velocity at which each calibre of sediment is deposited because the energy level is too low to keep it in suspension. Two key points may be made:

- Very fine particles (see A on Figure 1.19) may require higher velocities before they are eroded than sand (see B on Figure 1.19) because of the cohesive properties of the fine clays and silts.

- The velocity required to keep fine particles in suspension is less than the velocity required to erode them. Therefore fine, platy-clay particles can stay in suspension even when water is almost still (see C on Figure 1.19) whereas only a small drop in velocity can mean that sediment of sand to boulder calibre will be deposited (see D on Figure 1.19).

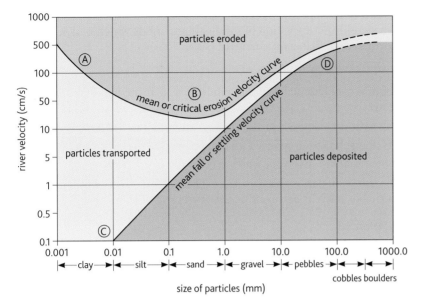

Fig. 1.19 *The Hjulström curve*

Activities

11 **a** Make a simple copy of the Hjulström curve. Your task is to consider the statements below and to suggest where you would locate the statement on this 'living graph'. Note there may be more than one possible location for each statement. You will need to justify your choice using the velocity and calibre information on the axes.

   i Cobbles can only be picked up at this velocity.

   ii The water still may not be fast enough to lift clays from the bank.

   iii Sand in suspension will proably fall out here.

   iv It would take this kind of velocity to lift a boulder.

   v As soon as the water slowed, the boulders would fall out here.

   vi Fine silt might still be in suspension at this low velocity.

   vii Sand particles would start to be lifted around this velocity.

   b For each of the statements, explain why you located it where you did on the graph, using velocity and particle size information to support your answers.

   c Why might high velocities be required to erode both the finest and the coarsest calibre of materials?

Deposition

A river deposits when it is no longer competent or has the capacity to carry all of its load. Any reduction in river velocity will reduce competence and material will begin to be deposited, starting with the coarsest sediment first as this requires a lot or energy to remain in suspension. For this reason mountain streams are often filled with large boulders whereas in the lower reaches of the river, as it approaches the sea, finer sediments dominate. Very fine material and the dissolved load may not be deposited in the river channel at all but may be carried out to sea via the estuary. The sudden reduction in velocity as the river (travelling in one specific direction) meets the sea (no distinct direction) causes significant deposition of sand, silt and muds which may lead to the formation of deltas on emergent coasts.

Deposition frequently occurs when:

- there is a sudden reduction in gradient, e.g. at the foot of a mountain range
- the river enters a lake or the sea
- discharge has been reduced following a period of low rainfall
- where there is shallower water, e.g. on the inside bend of a meander
- there is a sudden increase in the calibre or volume of sediment available, such as at a confluence or where a landslide has occurred.

Long profile

The balance between erosion, transportation and deposition changes throughout the course of the river. Figure 1.20 shows a typical long profile representing the height of the channel floor from source to mouth (thalweg). It is an idealised profile but shows how vertical erosion dominates in the initial stages of the river's course as the downcutting tendency is as yet relatively unaffected by lateral erosion owing to the limited volume of water available. As more water joins the channel from surface flow, throughflow, groundwater flow and tributaries, the river has greater volume and increased velocity, giving it more power to erode laterally. The gradient flattens out to complete the characteristic concave long profile.

This profile may vary from the idealised model as a result of many factors, including variations in rock structure and the effects of glaciation and rejuvenation.

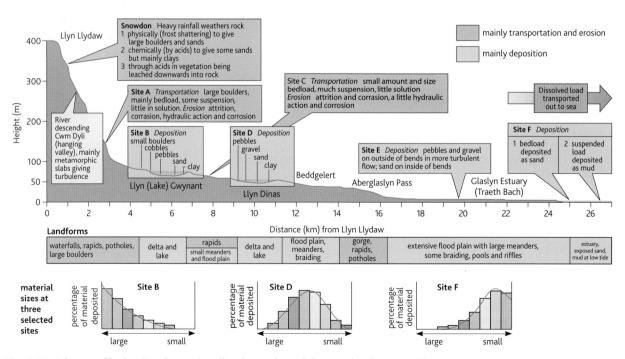

Fig. 1.20 *A long profile showing changes in valley shape, channel shape and sediment calibre*

Fluvial landforms: erosional

V-shaped valleys and interlocking spurs

In the upper course of rivers the characteristically large-calibre sediment load is usually only transported when the discharge has risen as a result of heavy rain or snowmelt. At such times the bouncing and rolling of boulders and cobbles may cause intensive vertical erosion, which in turn produces a relatively steep-sided V-shaped valley profile. The exact shape depends on three factors:

- **Climate** – sufficient water is required for the high discharge levels needed to instigate vertical erosion in the channel and to aid mass movement on the valley sides above the eroding channel.
- **Geology** – the type of rock and its structure may tend towards very steep sides (e.g. Carboniferous limestone) or gently sloping valley sides (e.g. clays and shales).
- **Vegetation** – more vegetated slopes tend to bind the soil better and may lead to more stable valley sides.

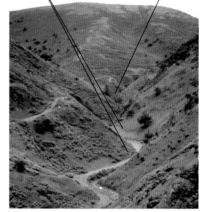

Fig. 1.21 *V-shaped upland valley showing interlocking spurs*

Interlocking spurs are also characteristic of the upper courses of rivers. These form when the river winds around protrusions, hills or ridges of land (spurs) which appear to interlock when viewed looking up or down valley. A wider valley may develop in the middle course with a near flat floodplain where lateral erosion has widened the valley floor. The edge of the floodplain may be marked by prominent slopes known as river bluffs. The lower course of the river may be characterised by a very wide, flat floodplain. The edges of the valley are often not easily discernible as reduced river competence results in large-scale deposition.

Rapids

Rapids are found where there is a sudden increase in the slope of the channel or where the river flows over a series of gently dipping harder bands of rock. As the water becomes more turbulent its erosive power increases.

Fig. 1.22 *Rapids on the River Nevis, Scotland*

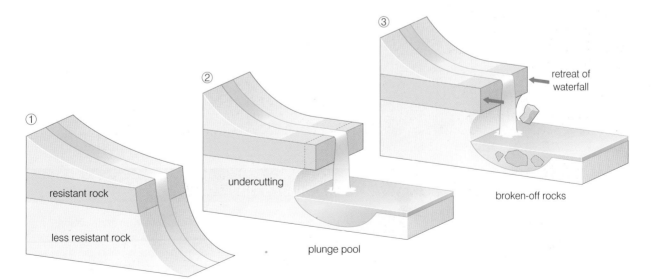

Fig. 1.23 *The process of waterfall retreat*

Fig. 1.24 *Thornton Force waterfall, North Yorkshire*

Waterfalls

A waterfall is a sudden fall of water that occurs where there are rapid changes in gradient in the river's course. They are most commonly found where there are marked changes of geology in the river valley. Where resistant rocks are underlain by less resistant beds, the plunge pool at the foot of the falls experiences the force of the swirling water around the rocks, leading to more rapid erosion. This undercuts the beds above, leaving them overhanging and prone to collapse. It is by this method that the waterfall retreats upstream, sometimes leaving a gorge behind it.

■ Skills

Sketching from a photograph

A sketch is a simplification of a complex picture. It selects only the most important features the artist wants to highlight and, when well annotated, conveys a clear message in a way that a photograph may not.

1 Draw in simple lines to depict the frame of the picture, e.g. the horizon and ground lines (see sketch 2 below).
2 Add main buildings, roads or features that are essential to help you make sense of your sketch.
3 For the main feature only draw what you need to – only what will help clarify the message.
4 Label key features that are relevant to help you describe the main components of the sketch and annotate to explain important processes and relationships and to make connections to your written argument (see sketch 3 below).

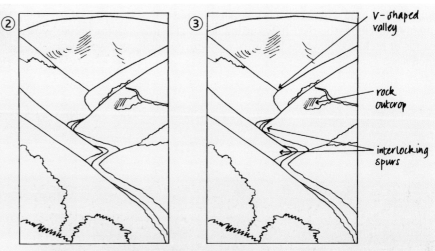

Fig. 1.25 *Sketching a V-shaped valley*

AQA **Examiner's tip**

Written answers are the most common form of response in an examination. Where there is room to add more information, a simple sketch diagram to show location, the relationship between features or how a process works can show your understanding far better than just writing more. Examiners often say that they wish a small sketch, map or diagram had been included to make it clear that the candidate did understand the locational, process and relationship factors affecting a case study.

Fluvial landforms: depositional

■ **Floodplains** – when rivers are at bankfull stage they may spill over onto relatively flat adjacent land known as floodplains. Floodwaters are shallow with extensive wetted perimeters which result in more frictional contact and lower velocities than water in the main channel. These factors combine to deposit fine sediment over the floodplain, increasing fertility and height as successive floods add to the alluvium. As rivers migrate across the floodplain over time, they may leave pointbars on the inside of meander bends, adding to the extent of the floodplain.

■ **Levées** – on some rivers the dropping of coarser material closer to the river channel during a flood has led to the development of levées. These parallel banks of sediment are formed as the heavier sediment carried by floodwater settles first, close to the channel, while the finer material travels further over the floodplain. Levées have been artificially strengthened and heightened along rivers such as the Rhine in the Netherlands and the Mississippi in the USA to act as flood defences.

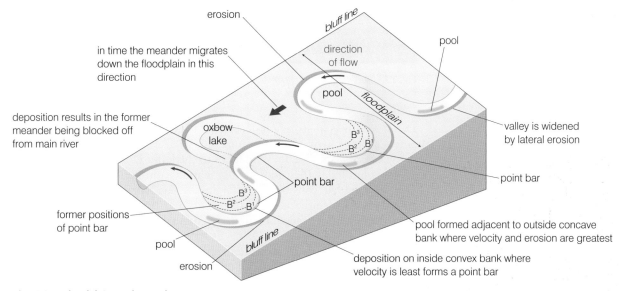

Fig. 1.26 *Floodplains and meanders*

Fig. 1.27 *Levées on the River Rhine*

Topography: the arrangement of the natural and artificial physical features of an area.

■ **Braiding** – in places where climate, geology and **topography** combine to generate periodic high sediment loads, braiding may occur. As water levels fall and energy decreases, the rapid deposition of the coarsest load begins to block the main channel. As the main river channel is no longer competent to move the material blocking its path, it may subdivide into a series of smaller diverging and converging channels that seek to find the easiest route past the obstructing sediment.

Fig. 1.28 *Braiding at Loch Etive, Scotland*

Deltas

Deltas are areas of sediment deposited at the mouth of a river when it enters a slow-moving body of water such as a sea or lake. Their name derives from a supposed resemblance to the letter D in the Greek alphabet but today their morphology is more commonly described as arcuate (rounded, convex outer margin, e.g. the Nile), cuspate (material spread evenly on either side of the estuary, e.g. the Tiber) or bird's foot (many sediment-bounded distributary channels extending out in a fan shape, e.g. the Mississippi). Deltas provide fertile land and are associated with good fishing grounds offshore, and with oil and gas deposits beneath the surface (e.g. Mississippi/Gulf of Mexico). However, they are by their nature highly changeable landforms as they are composed of unstable, unconsolidated sediments and are subject to channel migration as well as to subsidence and incursion by the sea.

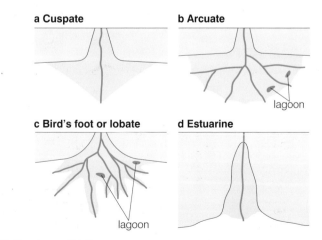

Fig. 1.29 *Four types of delta*

Meanders

To understand why and how rivers meander it is useful to remember that all rivers are heading downslope towards the sea and will take the path of least resistance open to them. With variations in geology and topography, that rarely means a straight path. Even a channel that is initially straight will at times deposit sediment in alternating bars (riffles) when experiencing low flow conditions. At such times of low flow the hydraulic radius of that part of the channel is reduced and this reduction of stream competence is what probably triggers deposition. Once created, the riffle serves to reduce the hydraulic radius for that area and water is seen to flow inefficiently over it. Water needs to find a way around these areas of higher frictional contact, so it flows, preferentially around them. Between these shallow riffle areas deeper sections are eroded (pools), especially at times of high discharge, and so a series of pools and riffles develop over time. At times of higher flow the water swinging around one side of a riffle will be propelled by centripetal force towards one of the banks, eroding it by undercutting. An outer concave bank is created while slower flow on the inside bend leads to deposition on the inside bend and a convex bank. Meanders are perpetuated by a surface flow of water to the outer bend and a corresponding subsurface return flow to the inside bend. This helicoidal flow allows material eroded from the outer bank to be deposited in part on the inner bank of the next meander bend and may become part of the floodplain. Even where meanders are well developed, riffles may occur in the relatively straighter sections of the channel between the meanders. Because the water in the meander

Activity

14 Study Figure 1.32.

a Describe the trends shown in each of the three graphs.

b Suggest reasons to explain why the relationships between the variables shown in the graphs change as they do.

c Can any of the relationships seen in the graphs be related to each other?

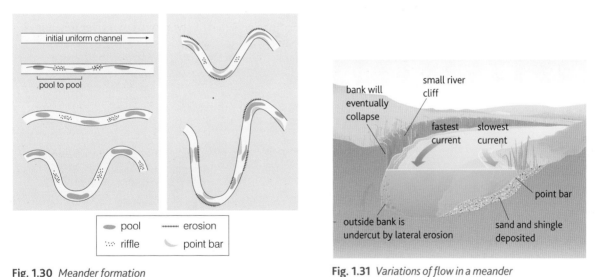

Fig. 1.30 *Meander formation*

Fig. 1.31 *Variations of flow in a meander*

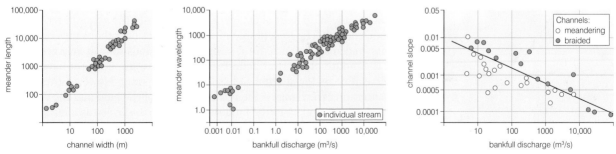

Fig. 1.32 *Meander length vs channel width, meander wavelength vs discharge, and discharge, slope and channel habit*

bend is travelling at a higher velocity (as a result of the deeper water and higher hydraulic radius), it erodes more effectively and carries the eroded sediment with it. On exiting the meander, the water enters a shallower section of the channel with a lower hydraulic radius, so it slows down and deposits some of the material which helps to maintain the riffle form.

Oxbow lakes

As meanders develop, the erosion of the outside bend tends to move them slowly downstream and downslope. The **sinuosity** of the meander may become more pronounced, with the erosion of the outer bank and deposition on the inner bank producing an increasingly narrow neck of land between the start and end of the meander. At times of flood this neck can be eroded away, giving the river channel a straighter, shorter route downstream. Initially the truncated meander loop forms a curved lake like the horns of an ox (hence 'oxbow lake'), cut off from the main channel by deposition. Over time the still waters may infill with sediment and vegetation and the lake may only be visible as a shallow depression or detected by variations in vegetation.

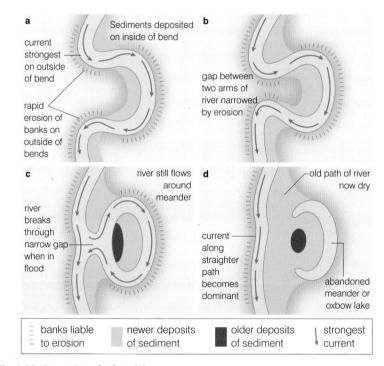

Fig. 1.33 *Formation of oxbow lakes*

Rejuvenation

The work rivers do is governed by the energy they possess. In terms of erosive power, this is related to the height the water has to fall downhill to reach sea level (potential energy) and the mass of the water in motion (kinetic energy). The long profile of a river evolves over thousands of years and its graded appearance, from steep in the uplands to relatively gentle near the mouth of the river, reflects the fact that water does not have as far to fall as it nears the sea and so has less erosive power. However, over time this situation can change if the relative heights of the land and the sea alter. **Isostatic** change refers to the land rising relative to the sea as a result of crustal movements. For example, in Scotland the land has 'bounced back' after the weight of the ice cap was removed at the end of the last ice age around 10,000 years ago.

Key terms

Sinuosity: the curving nature of a meander, described as:

$$\frac{\text{Actual channel length}}{\text{Straight-line distance}}$$

Isostatic: changes in sea level resulting from the rise and fall of land masses.

Eustatic: changes in sea level induced by variations in the amount of water in the oceans.

Change in the relative height of the land and the sea may also result from a rise or fall in sea level – this is called **eustatic** change. Sea level fall may result from many causes, one of the most common being the growth of ice caps during a glaciation. As water is locked up in the ice, less is available to be released into the oceans. The effect of a relative rise of the land means that water has further to fall and thus has more erosive power. Therefore, existing valley floors may be cut into as the river attempts to regrade itself in keeping with the new energy levels exhibited by the river. This begins in the channel nearest to the sea and then migrates back upstream, the current limit of the regrading being marked with a knickpoint, often marked by a sudden break of slope or waterfall. In the case of the lower Wye valley, downcutting into the valley floor has produced incised meanders. In the Thames valley at London, successive phases of downcutting have resulted in remnants of earlier floodplains being left as terraces running parallel to the lower current floodplain.

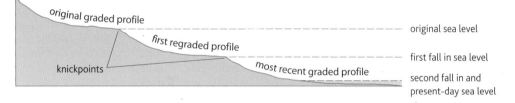

Fig. 1.34 *Rejuvenation and incised meanders*

Fig. 1.35 *Incised meanders in the Wye valley*

Flooding and flood management

Activities

15 How does the extract from T. S. Eliot's poem raise issues about the physical and human causes of flooding?

16 Type your postcode into the Environment Agency flood mapping service to find out if your area is at risk from floods.

Link

The Environment Agency flood mapping service can be found at:

www.environment-agency.gov.uk.

I do not know much about gods; but I think that the river
Is a strong brown god – sullen, untamed and intractable,
Patient to some degree, at first recognised as a frontier;
Useful, untrustworthy, as a conveyor of commerce;
Then only a problem confronting the builder of bridges.
The problem once solved, the brown god is almost forgotten
By the dwellers in cities – ever, however, implacable,
Keeping his seasons and rages, destroyer, reminder
Of what men choose to forget. Unhonoured, unpropitiated
By worshippers of the machine, but waiting, watching and waiting.

T. S. Eliot, from 'Dry Salvages' in Four Quartets

Rivers flood naturally and because people live near rivers, floods are a natural hazard. It is estimated that many rivers in the UK flood every two to three years. A combination of physical and human factors makes some places more prone to flooding than others. As humans alter natural landscapes and in particular as more people settle beside rivers, there is a need to manage the risk of flooding. Natural rivers shift position over time via erosion and deposition. Increasingly, urbanised rivers are required to flow within fixed parameters to allow roads, bridges and residential land to remain unaffected by fluctuations in discharge. Thus human activity not only prevents rivers from spreading in order to respond to natural changes in state, but by changes in land use and increases in runoff it actually increases the risk of flooding.

Floods occur when large volumes of water enter a river system quickly. Discharge increases to the point where the discharge cannot be contained in the channel and water spills out onto the floodplain.

Fig. 1.36 *Flooding at Tewkesbury, 2007*

Calculating flood frequency

The size of the largest flood for every year is placed in rank order, with 1 being the largest for all available records for any given river.

The following calculation is applied to calculate the time interval between floods of the same size:

$$T = \frac{n+1}{m}$$

where:

    T = the recurrence interval

    n = the number of years of observation

    m = the rank order

The calculated **recurrence interval** indicates the number of years within which a flood of this size can be expected. However, it is a probability based on historic evidence and does not mean floods will not occur more (or less) frequently. The Environment Agency once recommended that flood defences should be built to withstand a 1 in 50 year flood but now builds defences to withstand a minimum of 1 in 100 year flood events.

■ **Did you know?**

The Environment Agency has calculated that around 5 million people living in 2 million homes in the UK are at risk of flooding.

■ Key terms

Recurrence interval: the interval at which particular levels of flooding will occur.

Natural causes of river flooding may be classified as follows:

- Primary causes are usually the result of climatic factors (e.g. heavy autumn and winter rains in the UK in summer 2007 resulting from the passage of low-pressure weather systems, or monsoon-related rainfall in Pakistan in summer 2007).

- Secondary causes tend to be drainage-basin specific (e.g. dependent on geology, soil, topography and vegetation).

In addition to the natural causes, human influences on the drainage basin increase the risk of flooding as development of once natural landscapes for residential, industrial and agricultural purposes tends to reduce infiltration and increase runoff. Modifications of natural drainage systems can put them out of balance with the forces that originally

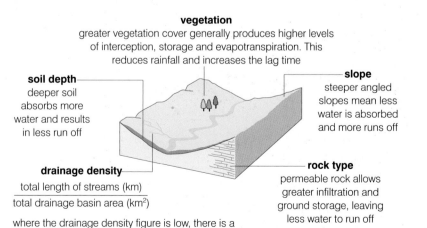

vegetation
greater vegetation cover generally produces higher levels of interception, storage and evapotranspiration. This reduces rainfall and increases the lag time

soil depth
deeper soil absorbs more water and results in less run off

slope
steeper angled slopes mean less water is absorbed and more runs off

drainage density

$$\frac{\text{total length of streams (km)}}{\text{total drainage basin area (km}^2)}$$

where the drainage density figure is low, there is a longer lag time and a reduced risk of flooding

rock type
permeable rock allows greater infiltration and ground storage, leaving less water to run off

Fig. 1.37 *Natural causes of floods*

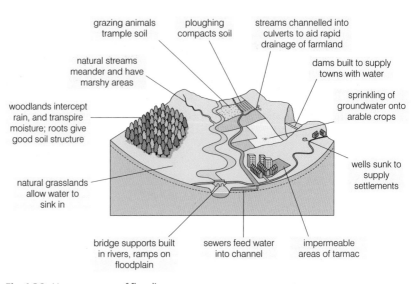

grazing animals trample soil

ploughing compacts soil

streams channelled into culverts to aid rapid drainage of farmland

natural streams meander and have marshy areas

dams built to supply towns with water

woodlands intercept rain, and transpire moisture; roots give good soil structure

sprinkling of groundwater onto arable crops

wells sunk to supply settlements

natural grasslands allow water to sink in

bridge supports built in rivers, ramps on floodplain

sewers feed water into channel

impermeable areas of tarmac

Fig. 1.38 *Human causes of flooding*

Key terms

Urbanisation: an increase in the proportion of a country's population living in urban areas. It is sometimes used to mean the process of moving from rural to urban areas.

Frequency: how often floods occur.

Magnitude: the size of the flood.

shaped them. **Urbanisation** helps to increase the **frequency** and **magnitude** of flooding in several ways, by:

- creating impermeable surfaces, e.g. roofs, car parks, roads and pavements
- speeding up the drainage of water in built-up areas via artificial conduits, e.g. drains and sewers
- impeding channel flow by building alongside or in the river, e.g. bridge supports
- straightening of channels to increase speed of flow which results in flooding downstream
- changing land use associated with development, e.g. deforestation, ploughing and overgrazing, which results in increased risk of flooding through increased runoff and increased levels of sediment washed into streams blocking channels.

The fact that urbanisation often occurs on the lower-lying land in drainage basins (and in particular on floodplains) means that the natural and human factors that result in an enhanced risk of flooding frequently coincide.

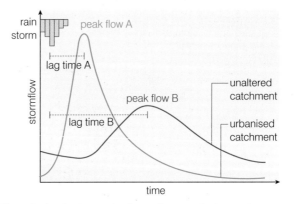

Fig. 1.39 *Effect of urbanisation on the shape of a storm hydrograph*

Flood risk rises as gardens disappear

London mayor urged to halt paving-over by homeowners

John Vidal, environment editor
Sunday 3 September 2005

The London front garden, mostly set back from the road behind a low brick wall, was known for its neatly clipped privet hedge, its row of pansies and its patch of lawn. Today it is more likely to be covered in concrete, be sprouting Mondeos, Volvos and Golfs and causing flash floods.

The London Assembly has calculated that the city's love affair with the car has led to the paving over of roughly two-thirds of its 1.9m front gardens – an area roughly 22 times the size of Hyde Park. This, it suggests, has increased the local temperature, led to a dirtier environment, greatly reduced the amount of greenery in the city and encouraged more car noise and pollution.

But, above all, says the assembly's environment committee, the loss of gardens has put immense extra pressure on drains.

'The more the ground is covered by hard surfaces, the less rainfall will soak into the ground. The drains then overflow and the contents are discharged into rivers, putting extra pressure on our already creaking Victorian sewerage and drainage systems.'

Last year more than 1 m tonnes of raw sewage overflowed twice into the Thames during flash floods. 'The huge scale on which London's front gardens are being paved over is contributing ... to the overflow of the drainage and sewerage systems during heavy rainfall,' says the report.

The study says two-thirds of front gardens are now completely or partially covered by paving, bricks or concrete. Together, these new parking bays cover 12 square miles, the size of several boroughs.

'If anyone suggested building a car park the size of the London boroughs of Islington and Hammersmith, or 22 times the size of Hyde Park, Londoners would rightly be up in arms,' says the report.

'But because this phenomenon is happening gradually and locally, it has not been taken seriously.'

The committee found that different areas of London treated applications to convert front gardens into driveways differently. Whereas Havering approved 97% of all applications, Islington only approved 76% and Merton 70%.

Yesterday, Darren Johnson, chairman of the cross-party committee, said people paved over gardens mainly to create off-street parking. 'But convenience and a desire to create minimalist gardens, fuelled by TV makeover shows, have also played a role,' he said.

The committee argued that central government should change planning laws to give boroughs more power to turn down conversions. It called on the London mayor to promote and protect the gardens.

From the Guardian

Activity

17 Draw and annotate a concept map (like the one started below) to explain how human influences may combine to increase the risk and extent of flooding in the extract above.

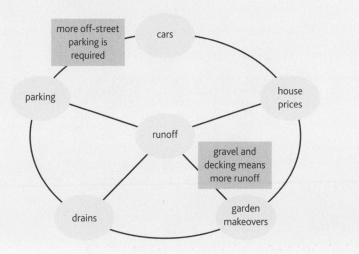

■ Impact of flooding

The following UK and Bangadesh case studies compare and contrast the impact of flooding in countries at different stages of development.

💡 Case study

Question

1 Suggest how the following might have been affected by the flood. For each example you cite give grid references and an explantion of why you think the flooding may have caused problems for these land use functions:

a communications

b residential areas

c business

d leisure activities.

Carlisle floods, January 2005

The floods that hit Carlisle on 9 January 2005 had significant short-term and long-term effects. The flood map and 1 : 50,000 OS extract (see Figures 1.40 and 1.41) illustrate the area of the town affected by the flood.

Short-term impacts

The immediate impact, which resulted from 175 mm of rainfall in just 36 hours in January 2005, was most evident in the deaths of 3 people and 120 flood-related injuries. As the waters spread over the floodplain, communications were affected. Roads became impassable, so people and their vehicles were left stranded. Around 1865 properties were flooded, most of which were residential. Businesses suffered as 300 premises were flooded and were unable to open for business because their stock was damaged. Schools, hospitals and the police station were cut off and subsequently closed in some cases.

Longer-term impacts

Some of the damage occurred during the flood event but other impacts were only evident in the days, weeks and months after the floodwaters had receded. These longer-term effects added considerably to the final estimated repair bill which approached £250 million. Houses inundated with filthy floodwaters had to be substantially rebuilt on the ground floors, which meant a lengthy drying-out period prior to replastering and redecoration. Some families were not insured, while others found their homes were now effectively uninsurable and worth considerably less. In July 2007

Flooded area

Fig. 1.40 *Carlisle flood map*

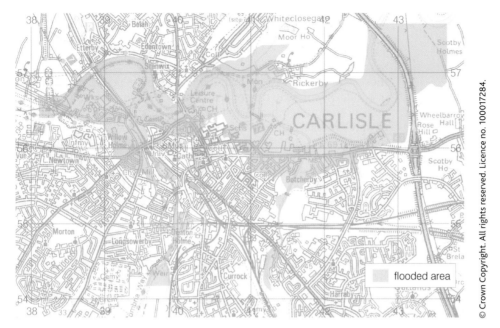

Fig. 1.41 *1:50,000 OS map extract of the Carlisle flood area, adapted from map sheet 85*

some families were still waiting to move back into their damaged homes. Businesses lost trade during the flood as well as future business because many were unable to complete orders. Some firms had to pay to redecorate and relocate. It was estimated that of the 300 firms flooded, half had to relocate or shut down. Additional impacts that were more difficult to quantify were the damage the floods did to public perception of Carlisle as a reliable place to work in or to visit, and the emotional impacts on those involved in the floods.

Table 1.3 *Flood damage costs for Carlisle*

Organisation	Damages		Details of damages incurred
	Direct	Indirect	
Civic Centre (Carlisle City Council	£4,000,000	£2,000,000	Indirect damages include costs of having to move temporary offices and distruption to staff
Cumbria County Council	£1,100,000	£3,000	Insurance claim, including emergency response (£140,000), disposal of flood (£120,000) and work on highways (£890,000). Additional teaching cover £3,000
Fire station	£72,000+	£20,000	Loss of ICT, telecommunications, 3 vehicles, 1 ATV, furniture/lockers at Carlisle fire station. Additional £20,000 includes damage to vehicles and equipment during emergency calls
Network Rail	£2,500,000	Damages not broken down	
Stagecoach	£3,000,000	£150,000	Write-off 85 vehicles, including clean-up/repair/loss of stock costs of £470,000 and £220,000 for replacement of plant, equipment and phones. Relocation to Kingmoor Park: £85,000. Two days' lost (loss of £30,000 to £40,000). Long-term effects saw reduction of 10% in takings, now reduced to 2% – may be linked to loss of 24 accessible buses for the elderly/disabled
Businesses	£14,400,000	£4,400,000	Indirect costs include loss of trade
Utilities	£8,000,000	Damages not broken down	Damages to electricity (£5,000,000), waste water (£2,000,000) and water (£1,000,000)

Intangible impacts

Although it is difficult to quantify the way people are affected both emotionally and psychologically following flooding events, these more intangible effects are significant nonetheless. Aside from those suffering bereavement and injury, many reported a sense of loss following destruction of possessions with sentimental value, anxiety stemming from the concern that it will happen again or powerlessness resulting from being able to do very little to prevent the floodwaters entering their property. The problems reported to the Communities Reunited support organisation included sleeplessness, nervousness, irritability, tiredness, loss of motivation and self-worth, loss of confidence, crying/easily upset, anxiety, feeling low, panic attacks, no energy, inability to focus or make decisions, inability to relax.

■ Flood management strategies

Flood management (or flood alleviation) strategies seek to reduce the effects of flooding on the human environment. Approaches to this problem vary from enormous engineering projects such as modifying river channels on the Mississippi, to protecting buildings from flood damage in York on the River Ouse. The main strategies can be conveniently grouped as follows:

- structural methods – offering protection through engineering
- river basin management – seeking to reduce the likelihood of flooding by managing land use
- modifying the burden of loss – by insurance schemes
- bearing the cost of flood damage – a 'do nothing' approach that only deals with the issues when they arise.

The combination of methods used to combat the threat from flooding varies from country to country. Thus developing countries may avoid expensive engineering solutions for economic reasons and rely on bearing the loss when it occurs. In more developed countries a more preventative attitude may prevail, because dealing with floods only when they occur is unlikely to gain support. This was evident in the public outcry over flood damage in July 2007 in the Midlands. Finally, attitudes to flood alleviation have evolved over time. The realisation that structural interventions may store up future problems has led to a call for more 'naturalistic' or soft engineering combined with better basin management. Preventing floods is increasingly seen as impossible and river management concentrates more on reducing losses due to flooding.

Structural methods

Flood walls, embankments and levées

Flood walls are designed to increase the height of the channel to stop water spilling out onto the floodplain. Most commonly used in towns, they restrict access to the riverside and offer little in the way of floodwater storage capacity. Embankments are often made of earth with rubble fill and are more common outside the town centre where there is more room. If set back from the channel, they can provide storage for excess floodwaters while inhabited areas remain unaffected. Levées may be artificially enhanced or introduced to raise the level of the river banks. All of these methods may reduce flooding at the expense of speeding water downstream to create problems elsewhere.

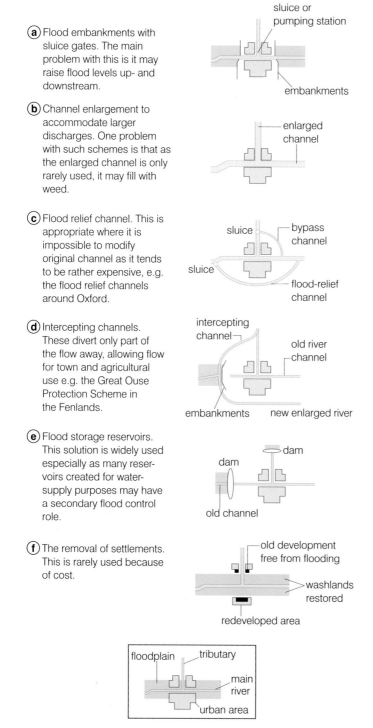

(a) Flood embankments with sluice gates. The main problem with this is it may raise flood levels up- and downstream.

(b) Channel enlargement to accommodate larger discharges. One problem with such schemes is that as the enlarged channel is only rarely used, it may fill with weed.

(c) Flood relief channel. This is appropriate where it is impossible to modify original channel as it tends to be rather expensive, e.g. the flood relief channels around Oxford.

(d) Intercepting channels. These divert only part of the flow away, allowing flow for town and agricultural use e.g. the Great Ouse Protection Scheme in the Fenlands.

(e) Flood storage reservoirs. This solution is widely used especially as many reservoirs created for water-supply purposes may have a secondary flood control role.

(f) The removal of settlements. This is rarely used because of cost.

Fig. 1.42 *Six approaches to flood defences*

Channel improvements

These methods attempt to restrict floods either by creating a smoother channel for faster flow to get the water out of the area as quickly as possible or by deepening/widening the channel. The former is often achieved by lining the channel with concrete and the latter by dredging to increase the capacity. Both schemes may increase the risk of flooding downstream and both require maintenance as the channel reverts back to a more natural state by a combination of deposition and erosion.

Relief channels

Relief channels are constructed to redirect excess water upstream of a settlement via an alternative route. Water is able to re-enter the main channel further downstream, thereby reducing the flood risk. By creating a bypass that can only be accessed at high discharge levels, the peak flow in the main channel is reduced. The relief channel may remain dry until activated by floodwaters.

Flood storage reservoirs

These aim to store excess water in the upper reaches of the catchment but are very expensive to construct as well as requiring a large amount of land. They are easier to construct in areas of high land with low-value land use – of which there is relatively little in the UK. In the UK, reservoirs are built to enhance water supply rather than just to control flooding.

Flood interception schemes

These may include re-routing a river to effect a bypass, using new channels to store excess water and flood embankments to contain flooding well away from settlements under threat. They may also include flood retention basins, washland areas and polders. These are areas of land that are deliberately flooded upstream of towns and cities. They are areas of low-value land which provide temporary storage for floodwaters, thus reducing the amount of water in the main channel and reducing flood risk. They may have amenity and/or wildlife value during the periods when they are not used for flood management.

River basin management

Even with advanced structural flood alleviation schemes, floods will occur and basin management seeks to reduce the harm done by flooding when it does occur.

Flood abatement

Abatement measures aim to reduce the possibility of flooding by managing land use upstream. This includes a variety of methods, from afforestation to farming practices like contour ploughing and reducing the amount of bare earth to avoid excessive runoff problems. Afforestation requires substantial areas in the catchment to be planted with trees.

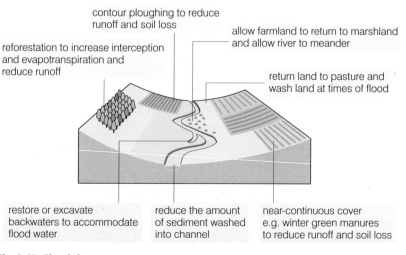

Fig. 1.43 *Flood abatement measures*

These increase **interception storage** and evapotranspiration and help to reduce runoff as well as holding the soil together to reduce silting up of river channels. However, trees take many years to mature and initial soil disturbance during planting generates more runoff at first.

Flood proofing

Flood proofing may be temporary or permanent. New buildings can be constructed with flood-proof ground floor walls or have temporary flood gates ready to be installed at times of high risk. By keeping important or vulnerable facilities at higher levels or designed so that only low-value land uses like car parks occupy ground-level sites, the potential damage from floods can be reduced.

Key terms

Interception storage: the total volume of water held on the surface of vegetation.

a

flood wall

flood proofing new buildings means they stay dry when water overflows the flood walls

sandbags to raise the height of the flood wall

new buildings with low value ground use like car parking

b

c setting flood bank back from the channel allows the floodplain to act as a storage area for floodwaters

development behind the floodplain is protected from floodwaters

Fig. 1.44 *York: flood-proofing methods*

Floodplain zoning

Records for historic flood events can help to predict the extent of future flood events. Return periods for floods of different magnitude can be linked to the areas of the floodplain that are likely to be affected and thus zones of relative risk can be mapped:

■ **Zone A: Prohibitive zones** – these are areas nearer to the channel with a relatively high risk of flooding. Essential waterfont developments may be permitted but future development is unlikely to be allowed here.

■ **Zone B: Restrictive zones** – little development is allowed and what is permitted should be flood-proofed. They are best suited to low-intensity or low-value land uses such as pasture, playing fields and car parking.

■ **Zone C: Warning zones** – areas further away and situated on higher land may be used for a wider range of developments, from residential to public buildings. Inhabitants are made aware of imminent flood danger and are instructed how to react when floods occur.

All these planning aims must be seen in the light of future developments, as many historic riverside settlements cannot be resited.

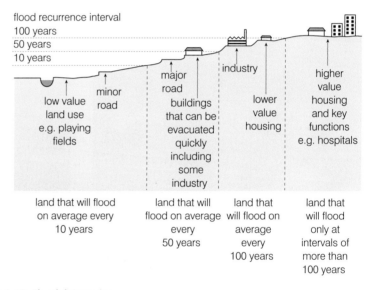

Fig. 1.45 *Floodplain zoning*

Flood prediction and warning

In the UK, rivers are constantly monitored by the Environment Agency. Records of river discharge and flooding are kept to help predict future flood events. The main methods of collecting data to aid flood forecasting are weather radar and the information from automatic rainfall and river gauges. Weather radar identifies likely and actual rainfall in weather systems approaching or moving across the UK. This alone is not always a sufficiently reliable indicator of flood risk as the evidence on the ground is also required. This comes from a network of automatic rain gauges throughout each catchment, which measure the amount of rain that actually has fallen, and river gauges, which record the rising level of the rivers at different locations along their length. The data is measured automatically and sent electronically to a central computer where a flood warning duty officer interprets the information. Flood prediction software helps to model likely outcomes, and warnings may be issued in terms of the potential severity of the flood risk and the areas that could be affected.

The Environment Agency's England and Wales flood mapping system is based on the National Flood Risk Assessment (NaFRA), which uses a method called Risk Assessment for Strategic Planning (RASP). This is a risk-based probabilistic approach which factors the location, type, condition and performance of flood defences into the risk assessment. It works by calculating the actual likelihood of flooding to areas of land within the floodplain of an extreme flood (0.1 per cent or a 1 in 1000 chance in any year). The method divides the floodplain into 100 m squares (called impact zones), or smaller areas where an impact zone is intersected by a river or coastline. It then calculates the likelihood that the centre of each 100 m square will start to flood. These results are then placed into three risk categories:

■ **low** – the chance of flooding each year is 0.5 per cent (1 in 200) or less

■ **moderate** – the chance of flooding in any year is 1.3 per cent (1 in 75) or less but greater than 0.5 per cent (1 in 200)

■ **significant** – the chance of flooding in any year is greater than 1.3 per cent (1 in 75).

Anyone concerned about their home or neighbourhood flooding can call Floodline free on 0845 988 1188 and receive a service called Flood Warnings Direct, which provides automatic telephone warnings. In areas of high risk such as York, automatic phone warnings are issued to alert inhabitants in potential flooding zones, and visits by flood wardens ensure that temporary defences are in place and/or evacuations are carried out when necessary.

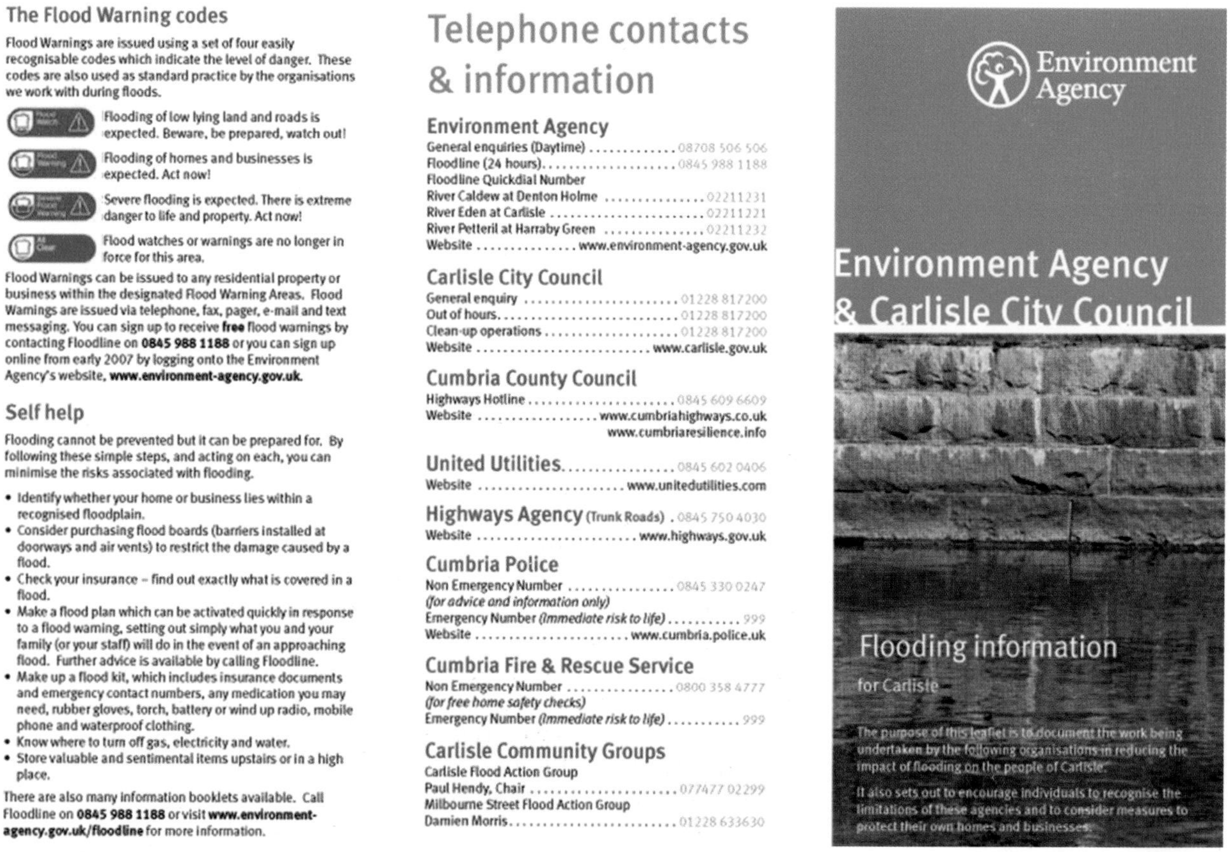

The Flood Warning codes

Flood Warnings are issued using a set of four easily recognisable codes which indicate the level of danger. These codes are also used as standard practice by the organisations we work with during floods.

Flooding of low lying land and roads is expected. Beware, be prepared, watch out!

Flooding of homes and businesses is expected. Act now!

Severe flooding is expected. There is extreme danger to life and property. Act now!

Flood watches or warnings are no longer in force for this area.

Flood Warnings can be issued to any residential property or business within the designated Flood Warning Areas. Flood Warnings are issued via telephone, fax, pager, e-mail and text messaging. You can sign up to receive **free** flood warnings by contacting Floodline on **0845 988 1188** or you can sign up online from early 2007 by logging onto the Environment Agency's website, **www.environment-agency.gov.uk**.

Self help

Flooding cannot be prevented but it can be prepared for. By following these simple steps, and acting on each, you can minimise the risks associated with flooding.

- Identify whether your home or business lies within a recognised floodplain.
- Consider purchasing flood boards (barriers installed at doorways and air vents) to restrict the damage caused by a flood.
- Check your insurance – find out exactly what is covered in a flood.
- Make a flood plan which can be activated quickly in response to a flood warning, setting out simply what you and your family (or your staff) will do in the event of an approaching flood. Further advice is available by calling Floodline.
- Make up a flood kit, which includes insurance documents and emergency contact numbers, any medication you may need, rubber gloves, torch, battery or wind up radio, mobile phone and waterproof clothing.
- Know where to turn off gas, electricity and water.
- Store valuable and sentimental items upstairs or in a high place.

There are also many information booklets available. Call Floodline on **0845 988 1188** or visit **www.environment-agency.gov.uk/floodline** for more information.

Telephone contacts & information

Environment Agency
General enquiries (Daytime) 08708 506 506
Floodline (24 hours) 0845 988 1188
Floodline Quickdial Number
River Caldew at Denton Holme 02211231
River Eden at Carlisle 02211221
River Petteril at Harraby Green 02211232
Website . . . . www.environment-agency.gov.uk

Carlisle City Council
General enquiry 01228 817200
Out of hours 01228 817200
Clean-up operations 01228 817200
Website . . . . www.carlisle.gov.uk

Cumbria County Council
Highways Hotline 0845 609 6609
Website . . . . www.cumbriahighways.co.uk
www.cumbriaresilience.info

United Utilities 0845 602 0406
Website . . . . www.unitedutilities.com

Highways Agency (Trunk Roads) . 0845 750 4030
Website . . . . www.highways.gov.uk

Cumbria Police
Non Emergency Number 0845 330 0247
(for advice and information only)
Emergency Number *(immediate risk to life)* 999
Website . . . . www.cumbria.police.uk

Cumbria Fire & Rescue Service
Non Emergency Number 0800 358 4777
(for free home safety checks)
Emergency Number *(immediate risk to life)* 999

Carlisle Community Groups
Carlisle Flood Action Group
Paul Hendy, Chair 077477 02299
Milbourne Street Flood Action Group
Damien Morris 01228 633630

Environment Agency

Environment Agency & Carlisle City Council

Flooding information
for Carlisle

The purpose of this leaflet is to document the work being undertaken by the following organisations in reducing the impact of flooding on the people of Carlisle.

It also sets out to encourage individuals to recognise the limitations of these agencies and to consider measures to protect their own homes and businesses.

Fig. 1.46 *Carlisle flood warning information leaflet*

Channelisation or naturalisation

Channelisation is an attempt to alter the natural geometry of a watercourse. It can help to prevent flooding by increasing channel capacity and preventing bank erosion, both of which reduce the chance of a river breaking out of its channel at high flow periods. Straighter, deeper channels can also help to drain wetlands and provide more manageable rivers, which allows for the extension of farmland and development. The dual benefits of flood prevention and land extension mean that this hard engineering solution to flood risk became very popular, particularly over the last century.

Resectioning a river involves widening and deepening a channel to improve its hydraulic efficiency. This increases capacity and moves water more quickly out of an area that is at risk of flooding. Dredging has been practised for centuries to remove surplus sediment from the river bed. **Realignment** (straightening) involves shortening the river course by removing meanders. The increase in gradient moves floodwaters away more quickly while improving navigation. **Revetments** made of concrete blocks, steel or gabions (wire mesh cubes filled with boulders) are used to strengthen banks, and **wing dykes** or training walls which jut out from the sides of the channel may be employed to focus the main river current in the centre of the channel and away from the banks. In urban rivers the entire channel may be lined with concrete to reduce friction and increase flow velocity. In cities, rivers may be covered over and confined to concrete **culverts** to reduce the inconvenience to development and to help remove the increased amount of runoff from impermeable surfaces.

All of these measures are expensive and offer relatively short-term advantages with high maintenance costs. In the longer term their disadvantages include the effects on upstream river sections (more downcutting) and downstream river sections (increased deposition) which may lead to more catastrophic flooding in the future. Increasingly they are seen as being opposed to a more sustainable view of basin management. This suggests that stopping rivers from their natural meander paths and regular small-scale flooding mistakenly treats the symptoms and not the causes of increased flood risk, and is ultimately doomed to failure. A more holistic approach is to look at the whole basin and to encourage more naturalistic ways of reducing flooding. These often include less intensive land use and restrictions on development.

Wetland and river bank conservation and river restoration

Naturalisation of rivers involves restoring them to a state closer to their original course by removing hard engineering and other restrictive structures. It assumes that land that is allowed to flood naturally acts like a sponge and soaks up much of the excess water before it reaches the main channel and causes flooding. There are few examples of this policy being put into practice across entire drainage basins but some aspects are increasingly evident in strategic flood alleviation schemes.

River restoration can include a variety of strategies to reclaim rivers, for example re-routing the river from its straightened course into new meandering channels. On the River Cole in Oxfordshire, remnants of the old river course were incorporated into the overall restoration, as backwaters at three locations and as a bay at another location. The sections of the old channel were only partially backfilled to allow for marsh conditions to develop. This allows the river to absorb a larger amount of additional water without undue flooding. Other schemes involve controlled access to river banks for cattle. Trampling of river banks leads to excessive erosion, but with simple wooden rail systems and improved surfaces, the cattle can reach the water without causing excessive damage. Careful bank edge planting and the use of willow hurdles to add additonal support to banks prone to erosion are seen as cheaper and more sustainable approaches than adding steel piles or concrete revetments.

Wetlands are areas that are deliberately allowed to flood at times of high discharge. They are also valuable as wildlife habitats. For example, the Nene washes are upstream from Peterborough and act as overspill for the River Nene at times of high flow. In January 2008, following four days of heavy rain, the Lincoln Washlands Flood Alleviation Scheme had its sluices opened by the Environment Agency and approximately 225,000 m^3 of water poured from the River Till onto land near Saxilby, north-west of Lincoln. This land has a total capacity of almost 10 million m^3 of water, which can be diverted onto the low-lying farmland to take the pressure off bulging rivers during extreme rainfall.

Many experts now feel that restoration of peat bogs in northern uplands would slow water reaching lowland streams and rivers, reducing the threat to towns and cities such as Ripon, Hull and Sheffield – all of which have experienced severe flooding in recent years.

Studies of the River Cherwell in Oxfordshire demonstrate how floodplains can contribute to the sustainable management of water within river basins. Computer modelling shows the impacts on floods of changes to river channel geometry and construction/removal of embankments that prevent water spreading onto the floodplain at high flows. Using embankments as a form of flood control increases the peak flows downstream by up to 150 per cent. Restoring the river channel through the floodplain to pre-engineered dimensions reduces peak flow downstream from the newly restored floodplain by around 10 to 15 per cent by increasing peak water levels on the floodplain by 0.5 to 1.6 m. These results suggest that floodplain restoration, in terms of embankment removal or reducing channel dimensions to pre-engineered dimensions, can be part of a catchment's flood management strategy.

Restoring rivers to their natural courses is clearly problematic and carries significant costs. Much of the land that will be affected by such schemes is already under profitable cultivation or developed, with existing residential, commercial and transport land uses. Such developments are made with the expectation of existing flood protection measures being maintained and/or extended. Democratic governments are answerable to the electorate, who may not view the benefits of long-term gain for all as adequate compensation for their shorter-term personal losses resulting from unregulated floods.

On a larger scale the frequent flooding of the River Rhine, culminating in the 1995 floods, led to a rethink on how to manage the problems of flooding. After centuries of attempted engineering solutions a more sustainable policy evolved which reflects a new philosophy that humans should adapt to the shape of river basins that naturally result from flooding histories. This 'Room for the River' programme is currently being translated into land-use change and relocation of inhabitants on floodplains. Arable land is being converted to forest, marsh or wet grazing meadows. Inhabitants are being relocated, with compensation, to higher elevations, and the entire floodplain cross-section can accommodate a much larger volume of water.

Measures taken include:

- an increase in 'water meadows' which can be allowed to flood when necessary
- a reduction in the use of tarmac or concrete in vulnerable areas to slow water runoff into the rivers
- increased ground coverage of vegetation with woodlands and grasslands
- restrictions on the use of soil fertilisers which affect the soil structure, reducing its ability to retain water
- metres of silt accumulated over many years have been stripped and deep trenches constructed to allow more storage space for water in the event of flooding, and more room for trees which stabilise the soil, improve the ecological balance and help to evapotranspirate moisture away from saturated soils.

Setting the levées back from the river already allows for expansion over the floodplain, creating additional storage. The addition of excavated retention basins in the form of trenches provides additional capacity and further reduces the level of the floodwaters.

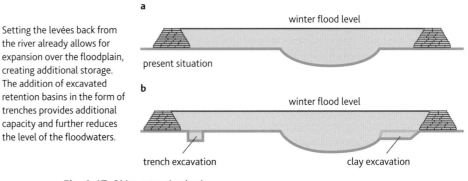

Fig. 1.47 *Rhine retention basins*

Case study

Carlisle's flood defences

With the town's flood defences breached, the council sought to establish why the existing defences had been inadequate and what needed to be done to limit damage in future. The Lower Eden Strategic and Planning Appraisal Report (SPAR) was prepared to provide an overview of flood management within the wider catchment. As part of the strategic and planning appraisal, however, a number of generic options for flood management were investigated and discounted for environmental and economic reasons.

1 **Do minimum** – this option comprises only maintenance work to ensure no further deterioration in existing structures, thereby sustaining the present level of flood defence. This low-cost approach assumes that, over the long term, increased flooding would have significant adverse impacts on human beings, the economy, heritage sites and all types of land use on the floodplain.

2 **Upstream storage** – this option would involve the creation of large-scale upstream storage reservoirs, for example through the construction of a large dam across the River Eden and excavation at the M6. A dam at the M6 would require the existing motorway embankment to be rebuilt as a dam structure, requiring temporary diversion of the motorway during its construction. The resulting reservoir would effectively double

the extent of the existing 100-year flood outline upstream of the M6, inundating areas like Low Crosby, Warwick Bridge and, potentially, Hadrian's Wall. Estimated construction costs would be likely to exceed £300 million. There would also be impacts on the SSSI.

3 **Upstream managed realignment** – this option would involve moving the existing line of flood defence back from the river to provide a larger area of natural floodplain storage. Hydraulic modelling demonstrated that the floodplains in the lower catchment are currently almost fully utilised during flood events, even during low return period flood events; and in high return period events, given the volume of water that passes down the Eden, the benefits would be few.

Question

18 You are employed by Carlisle City Council and have been asked to produce a brief illustrated report that will indicate the preferred option for alleviating flood risk. You should consider all of the evidence supplied in the text so far.

The report should include:

- statement assessing the nature of the flood problem in Carlisle
- a table showing the different options for flood alleviation and the benefits and problems associated with each
- a simple, annotated sketch map of the Carlisle area (see Figure 1.41) showing the types and location of defences you would employ
- reasons for your choices (weighing up the balance between social, economic and environmental benefits)
- a conclusion.

a

the new flood embankment set back from the River Eden to allow for floodwater storage

b

flood walls and gate to protect housing

Fig. 1.48 *New flood defences in Carlisle*

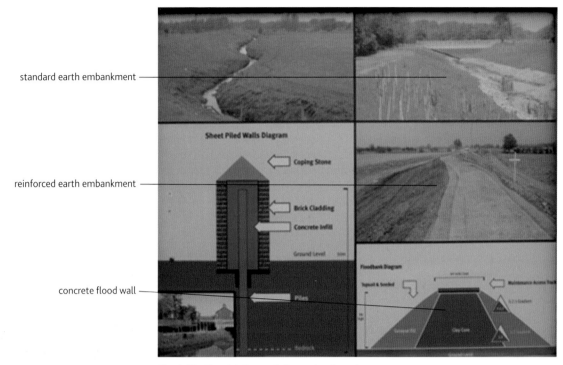

standard earth embankment

reinforced earth embankment

concrete flood wall

Fig. 1.49 *Flood defences information board*

The decision

The council had to balance the need for effective flood defences with considerations of cost and social and environmental impacts. The final appraisal determined that the do nothing/minimal approach was not acceptable owing to the risk to property and lives. The ambitious upstream storage option was ultimately rejected as it involved unsupportable economic and environmental costs without necessarily dealing with immediate flood risks to the town. A decision was made to raise existing flood defences while at the same time effecting local realignment. This meant the setting back of existing defences on the River Petteril upstream of Botcherby Bridge to create a larger storage area on the floodplain. These measures were identified as environmentally acceptable, with the latter option providing more opportunity for environmental enhancement. This was also the view of key consultees. Therefore, the combined option was identified as the preferred option for the Eden and Petteril flood risk area and would provide flood protection to an estimated 1 in 200-year standard.

Additional financial measures

In July 2005 the council agreed to allocate the £1.5 million government grant as follows:

- a survey of flood-affected homes
- £325,000 for uninsured vulnerable properties to make good any flood damage
- £325,000 for insured homes to bring them up to 'decent homes' standard, for example by improving amenities such as central heating
- £50,000 of energy efficiency grants, for example for vulnerable properties
- £15,000 for private security patrols of flood-affected areas

■ £130,000 'spring cleaning' of flood-affected areas, for example street sweeping, weed removal, footway and gully repairs.

A 25 per cent council tax discount was also agreed for flood-affected residents who were living within properties where the ground floor living accommodation was uninhabitable. Unoccupied flood-affected properties currently receive a 50 per cent council tax discount.

In July 2007 it was noted that 11 families had still to move back into their homes – 30 months after the floods.

■ Case study

Flooding in Bangladesh

DHAKA, September 11, 2007 – As there has been little respite in rain and the onrush of water from upstream, the flood situation was aggravated further in the south-central part of Bangladesh on Tuesday, taking the death toll from the monsoon flooding to 959.

At least 10.5 million people have been displaced or marooned by the floods.

The country's flood centre said two major Himalayan rivers that empty into the Bay of Bengal through Bangladesh – the Brahamputra and the Ganges – had risen alarmingly in tandem.

Fed by heavy seasonal monsoon rains upstream and melting glaciers in the Himalayas, the Brahmaputa, known as the Jamuna in Bangladesh, was now flowing well above danger level, the centre said.

Sources at the Health Department said the number of deaths caused by diarrhoea, drowning, landslides, snakebites and respiratory diseases has climbed up to 959 across the country since the flood onslaught began on July 30.

The information ministry said seven more districts were flooded afresh, raising the number of affected districts to 46 out of the country's 64 districts, where 110,000 people remained marooned.

According to the Flood Forecasting and Warning Center (FFWC), the flood situation in the south-central part of the country continued to deteriorate.

'It's a grim scenario. Major rivers have been rising alarmingly. The country is now in the grip of a second spell of flood,' said Saiful Hossain, head of the centre. 'Some 7000 people have already taken shelter at government relief centres. It's just weeks since many of them returned home. They have planted

paddy [rice] afresh in the land only to see flood water submerging them again.'

'And this time it will have devastating impact because the farmers will not have time recover their losses,' he said.

Muslim-majority Bangladesh, which has a population of 140 million, has sought an initial $150 million in help from donor agencies, with $60 million already pledged as immediate food and medical assistance.

Saudi Arabia alone promised $50 million plus a shipment of five planes of food and medicine.

The agriculture ministry estimated that $290 million worth of crops had been damaged in the initial flooding. The cost to infrastructure and housing has yet to be determined.

Major flooding occurs in Bangladesh frequently, regularly inundating between 20 and 30 per cent of the country and leading to enormous loss of life. The floods seen in the photograph above began in June 2007. Figure 1.50 shows their extent in part of the Ganges valley in India, at three dates in August. By September the floods had moved downstream into Bangladesh and had claimed over 900 lives. But they pale into insignificance compared with the 1998 floods, when nearly 70 per cent of the country was covered in water and millions were displaced. The magnitude of flooding in Bangladesh is clearly greater than in the UK but the impact of flooding on a country at a different stage of development is greater still.

■ Link

It is useful to look back at the physical and human causes of the flooding discussed in the case study on the River Eden, Carlisle, Cumbria, pages 28–30.

Question

1 As you read through this section, consider the factors that led to flooding in Bangladesh, as you did earlier on a smaller scale in the Carlisle example. Do you think the factors affecting flooding are entirely physical or human in nature? As you work through the following information it may help you to organise your thoughts by using a full-page Venn diagram.

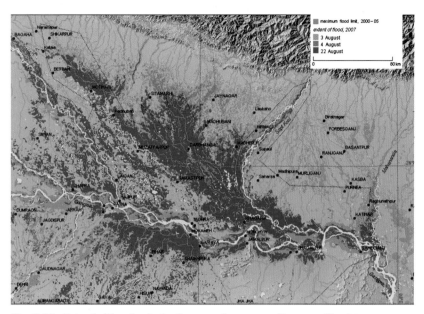

Fig. 1.50 *Extend of flooding in the Ganges valley, mapped from satellite data*

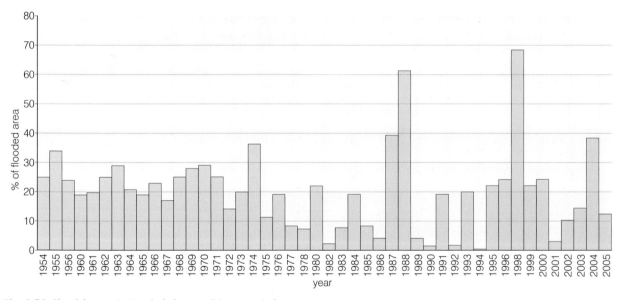

Fig. 1.51 *Flood damage in Bangladesh over a 50-year period*

The figures in this case study show how the discharge reacted to precipitation, but the extent to which physical or human causes were responsible for this flood event is debatable. Some factors clearly relate to the physical nature of the drainage basin and the weather, while others reflect the way people use the land and how this responds to heavy rainfall.

The causes of flooding in the UK and Bangladesh are similar in some ways but with significant differences. The main types of flooding are as follows:

- **Flash flooding** – extremely heavy rainfall occurs on surrounding upland areas. Not all the rainfall can be infiltrated into the soil and excess water forms runoff which can lead to rapid filling of river channels. Where this spills over onto the floodplain, enormous amounts of sediment can be deposited, damaging crops.

- **River floods** – mainly caused by meltwaters from the Himalayan mountains and heavy monsoon rains. Where the Brahmaputra and Ganges meet, high levels of discharge combine to breach embankments and flooding often ensues. This is particularly common along the Brahmaputra and Meghna rivers in early June and from mid-August along all rivers. Widespread flooding can threaten settlements and heavy silt deposits frequently bury crops.

- **Rainwater floods** – to heavy prolonged rainfall within Bangladesh causes runoff to accumulate in surface depressions, trapped by rising river levels. This may occur in April to May prior to the monsoon, and the water table rises above the level of the land. Topsoil may be washed off farmland into adjoining depressions.

- **Storm surges** – these mainly affect the southern coastal fringe of the country, where cyclones moving up the Bay of Bengal create storm surges which inundate the low-lying coastal strip. They may last for only a few hours but floodwaters can be trapped by embankments or roads with widespread damage to farmland and significant loss of life.

Did you know?

It is widely assumed that flood-waters depositing silt on the land must improve the fertility of the land and improve crop yield for farmers. In fact, a large amount of new alluvium deposited on the land may take several years to release its nutrients. Increases in rice production following flooding are more likely to be the result of nitrogen-fixing by blue-green algae which feed off the decomposing waterlogged plants.

Table 1.4 *Impacts of the 1988 and 1998 Bangladesh floods*

	1988	1998
Duration of floods	21 days	65 days
Percentage of country affected	60%	75%
Percentage of capital city covered by flooding	67%	50%
Area flooded	2,282,000 km²	Over 1 million km²
People affected	45 million	31 million
Houses totally or partially damaged	7.2 million	980,000
Human lives lost	2379	1050
Livestock lost – cattle and goats	172,000	26,500
Rice production lost	2 million tonnes	2.2 million tonnes
Trunk roads damaged	3000 km	15,900 km
Flood embankments damaged	1990 km	4528 km
Industrial units flooded	Over 1000	Over 5000
Schools flooded	19,000	14,000
Rural hand tubewells (for irrigation) flooded	240,000	300,000

Flood defences

After the 1988 floods, which affected 45 million people and claimed over 2000 lives, a Flood Action Plan (FAP) was devised (see Figure 1.52). The overarching aim of the plan, which comprises 26 projects, is to create flood protection for the country.

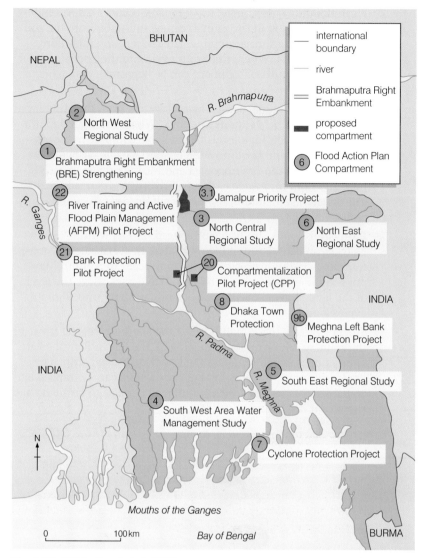

Fig. 1.52 *FAP for Bangladesh, 2007*

A key part of the plan is to construct new flood embankments alongside the Brahmaputra and Ganges in Bangladesh, initially starting with the upstream sections of these rivers and spreading downstream, allowing the river to adjust gradually to changing flow conditions. Behind thcsc embankments compartments of land are created by building internal walls to link up to the riverside embankments. The aim is not to completely stop flooding but to keep it within levels that the local farmers find manageable. A flood forecasting system is planned to alert local inhabitants of impending floods. Preparation to deal with the consequences of flooding will include the provision of boats so that people can escape to shelters on higher land.

The Jamalpur Priority Project Study illustrates some of the issues surrounding the potential impacts of embankment construction. Four options were discussed and local councils were asked to decide on the optimum solution:

A flood proofing and drainage improvement

B controlled flooding of the entire area with some compartmentalisation

C controlled flooding of about half the area

D all areas compartmentalised – all river flooding excluded.

The economic and social impacts of options C and D meant they were rejected early on. Option A was seen to be of potential benefit to the fishing, non-farming and landless population. Option B appeared to offer more benefits to the land-owning and farming households, with the promise of greater economic growth for the area as a whole. The disagreement on which option was best meant that delay was inevitable and threats of sabotage to any embankments ('public cuts') built under the option B scheme indicate the difficulty in reaching a compromise decision. There was also concern that areas outside of this scheme that did not have the same degree of flood prevention would suffer worse floods as a consequence.

Embankment issues

Positioning

Many people in Bangladesh want the embankments located close to the channels to protect as many people and as much farming land as possible. However, building close to the river increases river depth and speed at times of high flow in channels that are already unstable, braided and meandering. Studies have shown that there is a far greater risk of erosion and collapse when embankments are built close to the river banks. By building further away (up to 5 km), the risk of a breach is lower and the areas permitted to flood between the distant embankment and the river banks serve as floodwater storage areas. The more distant alternative embankment scheme was estimated to cost half as much as the bankside schemes (which require additional groynes to support them) and the embankments were thought cheaper to maintain – but an additional 5 million people would find themselves in the flood zone.

Longer-term impacts

Studies from elsewhere, including the Mississippi (USA) and the Maas (Netherlands), suggest that most attempts to restrain rivers within relatively narrow confines by engineering higher embankments tend to eventually raise the level of the channel floor by deposition, which in turn requires higher embankments. If these start to gradually raise the channel above the level of the surrounding land, any eventual breaches can be catastrophic.

Faster and deeper flow regimes in upstream channel sections controlled by embankments inevitably lead to increased erosion, producing greater sedimentation downstream as the river slows down. This may result in channel obstruction and an increased likelihood of flooding.

Although compartmentalisation controls floodwaters when they occur, the retention of large amounts of river water in smaller areas has implications for human health, crop production and fishing. In some instances, deprived of the natural bounty of floodwater fishing, public cuts have been made to release the floodwaters out onto a wider area of land. This may also allow farmland to regenerate faster and reduce the risk of waterborne disease.

Question

2 In a piece of extended writing, compare and contrast the ways in which flood risk is managed in countries at different stages of development.

✔ 𝒊 💡 *In this chapter you have learnt:*

- that rivers change in their course from source to mouth – they are dynamic and are constantly changing over time

- that rivers erode more vertically in their upper reaches and more laterally in their lower reaches

- that rivers alter their velocity according to channel shape and size, and this gives rise to characteristic valley landforms for different stages of their course

- how hydrologists use models such as hydrographs and the basin hydrological cycle to help us understand how water moves within basins – they are a framework with which we can compare and contrast our own observations

- that floods occur naturally in all rivers and it is the proximity of human development that makes them hazardous

- that floods occur when water enters the river so quickly that the channel cannot contain it all

- that people contribute to flooding by land-use practices that exacerbate the amount of runoff and restrict the natural flow of rivers

- that most floods are caused by a combination of natural and human causes

- how a variety of strategies can alleviate the effects of flooding, and how flood frequency analysis tells us that no river basin can be permanently protected from flooding

- that different groups in society hold conflicting views on how flood risk should be best managed, and that flood alleviation schemes seek to choose the optimium solution with imperfect knowledge.

2 Cold environments

The global distribution of cold environments

In this section you will learn:

- how the Earth has been affected by glaciations over time

- to consider glaciers as systems with inputs, processes and outputs that make up their glacial budgets

- how ice moves through the glacier system.

Fig. 2.1 *Striding Edge, Helvellyn, in the Lake District*

Activity

1 Study Figure 2.1.

   a How typical is the scene of the average UK climate, landscape or experience?

   b Do the landforms tell us most about the processes acting on the landscape today or are they a relict of the past?

   c Two walkers died in snowy conditions on Helvellyn over the winter of 2007/08. Low temperatures caused an estimated additional 25,000 people to die during the winter of 2005/06 in Britain – more than in Siberia. Why is very cold weather a potential problem?

Avalanche warning as snow hits Lake District
Saturday 5 January 2008

An avalanche warning was issued for one of England's highest peaks yesterday as the freezing weather brought chaos. The Lake District National Park Authority warned walkers not to scale Helvellyn, England's third highest mountain, because of treacherous conditions.

At the end of the last ice age 10,000 years ago, the last glaciers retreated from Britain and Ireland. Today we can recognise the extent of the ice masses from erosional and depositional features they left behind. The polar climate experienced by Britain and Ireland was gradually replaced by the temperate climate we enjoy today but, over a wider time frame, the thousands of years of relative warmth are a minor blip and most glaciologists believe that we are heading towards another ice age.

The study of glaciations is made difficult by the vast amounts of time involved and the complexity of climatic cycles themselves. This is exacerbated by recent evidence of global warming. Are glaciers in retreat, or are they advancing? The evidence is not wholly conclusive. Today many glaciers in the world are retreating (e.g. the Robert Scott glacier in Antarctica), but in other places (e.g. the Svaritsen glacier in Norway) there have been significant advances. In the longer term, we are most probably heading for another glacial phase but the timing and nature of the event are too far distant to be determined with real accuracy.

■ Key terms

Quaternary period: the latest period in geological time spanning the last 2 million years. It is sub-divided into the Pleistocene epoch (the most recent ice age) and the Holocene epoch (the post-glacial period of the last 10,000 years).

Glacial: a period of time when masses of ice develop and advance into lower altitudes due to a sustained decline in temperature. Extensive continental ice sheets form during such periods.

Interglacial: a period of time, such as the present day, when ice still covers part of the Earth's surface but has retreated to the polar regions.

Accumulation: the net gain in an ice mass. The sources of accumulation are direct snowfall and avalanching from higher slopes.

Sublimation: a transition from the solid state (ice) to gas (water vapour) with no intermediate liquid stage (water).

Ablation: the process of wastage of snow or ice, especially by melting.

■ Link

To get an impression of what glaciers are like today, take a virtual walk up to a Swiss glacier:

www.swisseduc.ch/glaciers.

Select 'Unteraargletscher' under 'Glaciers of the Alps', then select the virtual excursion.

However, regions of the planet characterised by polar climates today are significant enough to allow us to study the effects of glacial and periglacial processes. The geological record also shows the impact of ancient glaciations dating back to the Precambrian period (see Figure 2.3).

Ice ages

Ice ages begin as a result of global climatic changes. Every 200 to 250 million years during the Earth's history there appear to have been major periods of glacial activity. During the **Quaternary period**, which began just over 2 million years ago, the ice began to spread from the polar ice caps, particularly into North America and northern Europe. In fact, sediments extracted from ocean floor cores suggest that the advance was more complex than previously thought, with up to 20 **glacials** (cold periods) and **interglacials** (warmer periods). The fluctuation in global temperatures during these times was no more than 6°C. At its greatest extent the ice covered nearly a third of the Earth's surface and only 18,000 years ago, at the peak of the last advance, ice covered the UK from the Bristol Channel across to Norfolk.

Climatic influences

Reasons for the climatic fluctuations are thought to include:

■ changes in the Earth's position in space, its orbit and tilt

■ variations in sunspot activity changing the amount of solar radiation received by the Earth

■ changes in the amount of volcanic dust affecting the amount of radiation trapped by the atmosphere

■ trapping of carbon dioxide by the oceans reducing the total amount in the atmosphere and thus cooling the planet

■ variations in ocean currents.

Glaciers as systems

Glaciers are masses of ice (and debris) which are continually changing and may be seen as an open system with inputs (e.g. snow and avalanches) which add to the mass, and outputs (e.g. evaporation and meltwater) which decrease the mass. Near the source of a glacier, inputs generally exceed outputs and this is known as the zone of **accumulation**. There are several interrelated factors that combine to help develop glaciers. At higher altitudes there is more precipitation (the orographic effect), mainly in the form of snow. New snow is highly reflective, absorbing less heat and therefore melting more slowly. Stronger winds at high altitudes cause snow to be blown into hollows and basins so that snow accumulates. As temperatures are low, **sublimation** (the change in state from solid to vapour) and other losses are low, and meltwater is likely to refreeze.

The zone of **ablation** is found at lower altitudes towards the snout of the glacier, and is where outputs exceed inputs. Here there is less snowfall and temperatures are higher, resulting in outputs in the form of melting (surface, basal and within the glacier), sublimation, evaporation and calving.

The dividing line between the two zones is called the firn (or equilibrium) line. Gravity moves ice continually down to the equilibrium line, replacing that lost at the snout by ablation.

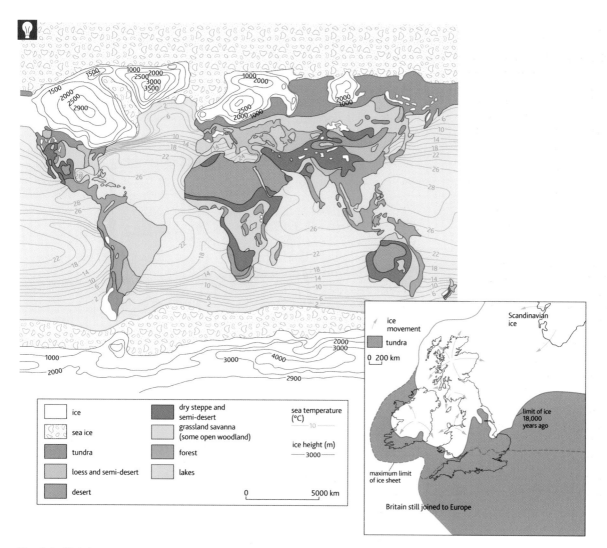

Fig. 2.2 *Global temperatures 18,000 years ago, showing polar, periglacial, arctic and alpine regions*

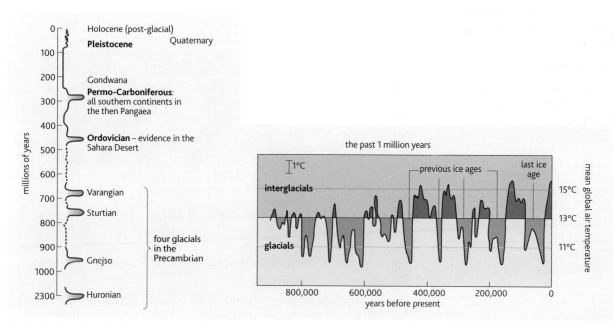

Fig. 2.3 *Glaciation timeline showing the glacials and interstadial episodes*

The difference between the total accumulation and total ablation for the whole of the glacier over one year is called the **glacial budget** or **net balance**. This is calculated for the balance year which runs from autumn to autumn, when summer ablation will have reduced the total ice mass to a minimum. There is a positive winter balance and a negative summer balance; for example, a typical Alpine glacier may lose ice at over 10 m a year through melting and is normally replenished by ice flowing from above.

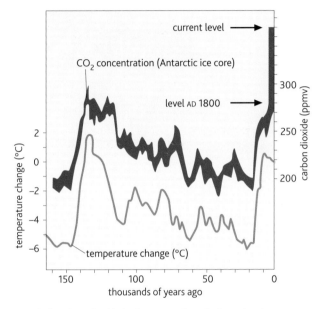

Fig. 2.4 *Record of carbon dioxide in the atmosphere in Greenland*

Key terms

Steady state: when the amounts of accumulation and ablation are equal over the course of a year. As a result, the snout of the glacier will remain stationary.

Surge: a short-lived phase of accelerated glacier flow.

When the amounts of accumulation and ablation are equal, the glacier is said to be in a **steady state**. The snout may not move but the mass of ice is passing through it like a conveyor belt.

Glacial surges

Glaciers may take many years to react to changes in accumulation or ablation but where snowfall is exceptionally heavy the glacier may react quickly and **surge** forward.

Fig. 2.5 *Athabasca glacier, showing valley glacial features*

a The glacier system: it is in equilibrium if the accumulation wedge balances the ablation wedge

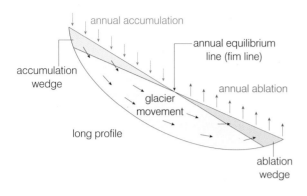

b The glacier balance year: there is a zero net balance if the positive balance and the negative balance are equal

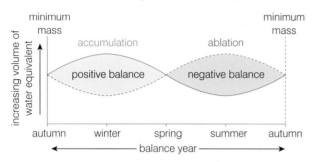

Fig. 2.6 *The glacial budget*

Rates of movement of flowing glaciers are extremely variable, with the fastest parts flowing at anything between 50 m and 400 m a year (even faster if they end in the sea). Flow rates of 1000 m a year or more are seen in large ice streams in Antarctica and outlet glaciers in Greenland.

Glacier size and shape

Ice mass classifications can vary in detail. Here is a standard list, from smallest to the largest:

- **Niche glaciers** are small patches of glacier ice found on upland slopes. They are most prevalent on north-facing slopes in the northern hemisphere. They have relatively little effect on topography.
- **Cirque (corrie) glaciers** are small ice masses on mountain slopes which gradually erode armchair-shaped hollows. If they develop to be too large for the hollow, they spill over the lip to feed a valley glacier.
- **Valley glaciers** are larger masses of ice that flow from icefields or a cirque and usually follow preglacial river valleys, developing steep sides as they erode their course.
- **Piedmont glaciers** are large lobes of ice formed when glaciers spread out. They may merge on reaching lowland areas and escape the confines of their valleys.
- **Ice caps** are huge, flattened, dome-shaped masses of ice that develop on high plateaus. They are similar to an ice sheet, but are less than 50,000 km² in area. Above 50,000 km² they are known as **ice sheets**. The Antarctic ice sheet attains a thickness of over 4000 m.
- **Ice shelves** are extensions of ice sheets that reach out over the sea. These shelves of floating ice can be up to 1000 m thick but diminish to around 500 m on average at the edge where icebergs calve.

Fig. 2.7 *An ice sheet and calving icebergs*

Link

A good range of glacier types can be seen at:

www.swisseduc.ch/glaciers.

Select 'Glaciers of the world', then the glacier family.

Warm- and cold-based glaciers

Cold-based (polar) glaciers occur in polar latitudes where the temperature of the snowfall is far below freezing and the glacier remains at well below freezing point. Ice remains frozen to the bedrock and as a result there is very little ice movement and thus limited erosion.

Warm-based (temperate) glaciers include most glaciers outside of Antarctica and the northern Greenland ice caps. Water is present throughout the ice mass and acts as a lubricant. This allows for movement of between 20 and 200 m per year (and, on occasion, up to 1000 m), which greatly increases the capacity of the glacier to erode the bedrock.

Ice movement

How glaciers move

A key factor in determining the rate of ice movement is the temperature of the ice. Some ice is warmer than other ice and this depends on the **pressure melting point (PMP)**, the temperature at which ice is on the verge of melting. Although PMP is normally 0°C at the surface of the glacier, it is lower within the glacier because the ice is under pressure. In short, ice melts more easily when it is under pressure, and all ice is under some pressure, especially towards the base of the glacier.

The movement of ice has two main components: internal flow and basal slippage (see Figure 2.8).

Internal flow or internal deformation – this is movement within the glacier ice resulting from the stresses applied by the force of gravity. Where ice crystals orientate themselves in the direction of the glacier's overall movement, they may slide past each other. Such movements often result in the formation of crevasses within and at the surface of the ice.

Basal slippage – this is the sliding effect of a glacier over the bedrock by either regelation slip or creep. Regelation slip operates most effectively with smaller obstacles while creep is the process that mainly overcomes larger protuberances. On the upglacier side of an obstacle, the increasing pressure in the lower ice causes pressure melting locally. The meltwater permits slippage of the ice over the obstacle but then refreezes in the lower-pressure conditions on the downglacier side of the obstacle. The

Key terms

Pressure melting point (PMP): the temperature at which ice under pressure will melt.

Extensional flow: also known as extending flow, this is the extension and related thinning of glacier ice in those zones where velocity increases.

Compressional flow: also known as compressing flow, this is the type of glacier flow whereby a reduction in velocity leads to an increase in thickness of a glacier.

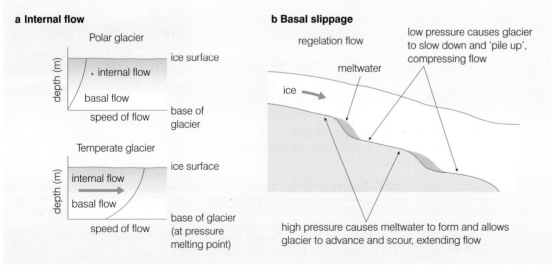

Fig. 2.8 *Internal flow and basal slippage*

thin layer of ice where this happens is called the regelation layer. Creep may occur where there is little or no regelation slip. It refers to the plastic deformation that occurs within the ice when its course is impeded by larger obstacles. Larger obstacles greatly increase the stress in the ice and cause it to become more plastic in behaviour so that it creeps or flows around the obstacle.

Extensional flow and **compressional flow** – velocity increases steadily in the accumulation zone as the firn line approaches, as downvalley ice is consistently pulling away from upvalley ice. Such a condition is called extensional flow. Below the firn line, velocities fall as ice from the upper valley is continually pushing against downvalley ice. This is compressional flow. In reality, this theoretical model is complicated by the irregularities found in the preglacial valley. Generally, where the slope steepens, velocity increases and extensional flow operates. Conversely, where the gradient is less, velocity falls and compressional flow occurs. Sudden breaks in gradient such as at icefalls give rise to extreme extending flow and large transverse and longitudinal crevasses are generated, creating a landscape of sharp-crested angular blocks called **seracs**.

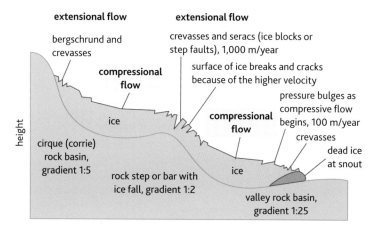

Fig. 2.9 *Extensional and compressional flow*

Rotational flow – this movement is characteristic of cirques where the ice slides down into an armchair-shaped hollow about a central point of rotation (see glacial erosion, pages 54–59).

Influences on the rate of movement

■ Snow and ice masses do not generally move downslope until the thickness exceeds 60 m.

■ Steep glaciers flow faster than gently graded ones and thus are usually thinner.

■ Movement is faster over an impermeable surface compared with a permeable surface in temperate zones as basal meltwater is retained, which aids slippage.

■ The amount of precipitation and ablation are significant factors.

■ The greatest velocity is usually at the firn line, as velocity is directly related to thickness.

■ The centre of the glacier, where the ice is thickest, moves more rapidly than the margins, where friction plays a considerable role in reducing speed.

Link

Look at:

www.swisseduc.ch/glaciers.

Select 'Glaciers of the world' then 'Living ice' and also 'Nature's conveyor belt'.

Glacial processes and landscape development

In this section you will learn:

- about glacial erosion and deposition and how they create characteristic landforms

- geographical skills to analyse glacial landforms

- to investigate the periglacial processes and landforms.

Glacial weathering and erosion

It is important to distinguish clearly between the processes of erosion and those of **weathering** and ice movement. Physical weathering processes dominate, e.g. frost shattering (freeze–thaw). Relatively little chemical or biological weathering is evident in glacial environments as both these processes work most effectively at higher temperatures. Frost shattering produces much loose material which may fall from the valley sides onto the edges of the glacier to form lateral moraine, or plunge down crevasses to be transported as englacial debris.

Processes of glacial erosion

Abrasion – angular material is embedded in the glacier as it rubs against the valley sides and floor, gradually wearing it away. The scratching

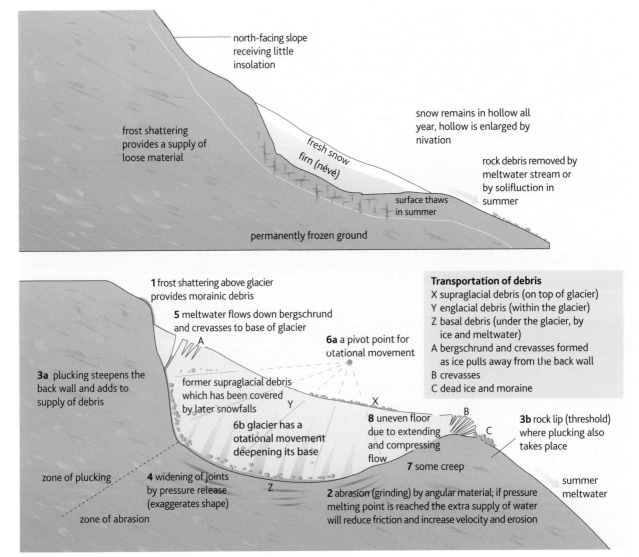

Fig. 2.10 *Glacial erosion processes: early stages (above) and advanced stages (below)*

and scraping action may leave striations (elongated grooves) as well as generally smooth, gently sloping landforms.

Plucking – this occurs where the glacier freezes onto rock outcrops, after which ice movement pulls away masses of rock. The pressure of overlying ice and/or heat generated by frictional contact may cause partial melting of ice on the upstream side of obstructions, and the removal of some of the pressure on the downstream side may cause regelation (refreezing) on the downstream side. Once the material is attached to the main ice flow, it can be more easily removed. It is likely that mainly previously loosened material is removed. Plucking generally creates a jagged-featured landscape.

Rotational movement – as with rotational slumping in landslides, this is a downhill movement of ice pivoting around a central point of rotation. Cirques are largely created by this rotational scouring of depressions on mountains. The process is most effective where temperatures fluctuate around 0°C (allowing frequent freeze–thaw to operate), particularly in areas of jointed rocks where weaknesses may be exploited. It is also evident where tributary glaciers join or in glacial valleys that steepen or narrow, producing increased depth of ice and thus downward pressure.

Landforms produced by glacial erosion

Cirques – known as corries in Scotland and cwms in Wales, they are depressions shaped like the hollow of a cupped hand, with a steep back wall and a rock basin. In the UK most cirques are located on slopes facing between north-west and east/south-east, where ablation is lowest and snow accumulation is highest because this aspect experiences least insolation. Wind direction may also have affected cirque distribution: south-westerly winds deposited snow on south-west facing slopes, which then drifted over to accumulate on north-east facing slopes, where it was colder. Therefore, the snow remained for longer. The hollow is deepened initially by nivation (essentially the combined effects of repeated freeze–thaw and removal by melting snow). As ice accumulates in the hollow and begins to rotate because of overlying pressure, abrasion and plucking deepen the hollow further and help to develop the steep back wall. In addition, water trickling down the bergschrund (see Figure 2.11) encourages more freeze–thaw action, which helps the cirque to grow larger. At the front of the cirque, where pressure and thus erosion are reduced, there is a rock lip. This may be added to later by moraine deposition and in some cirques it helps retain a small lake or tarn, e.g. Red Tarn in the Lake District. It is likely that cirques in the UK were formed following a series of glaciations and periglacial phases.

■ Link

Look at:

www.swisseduc.ch/glaciers.

Select 'Glaciers of the world' then 'Shaping the landscape'.

■ Key terms

Weathering: the breakdown of rocks in situ (in their original location, without them being moved away). This produces finer particles that can then be moved by agents of erosion such as wind and running water.

a Early stage of glaciation

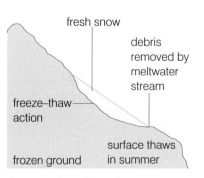

b During glaciation

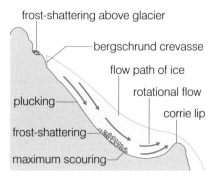

c Post-glacial

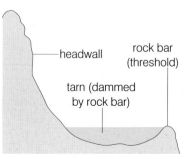

Fig. 2.11 *Cirque formation*

Arêtes – when two or more cirques erode back towards each other from opposing sides, they produce a knife edged ridge between them called an arête, e.g. Striding Edge above Red Tarn, Lake District.

Pyramidal peaks – where three or more cirques erode back towards each other, a pyramidal peak may form, e.g. the Matterhorn (see Figure 2.13).

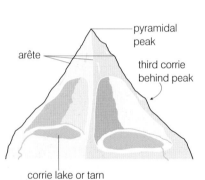

Fig. 2.12 *Pyramidal peak*

Fig. 2.13 *Pyramidal peak: the Matterhorn*

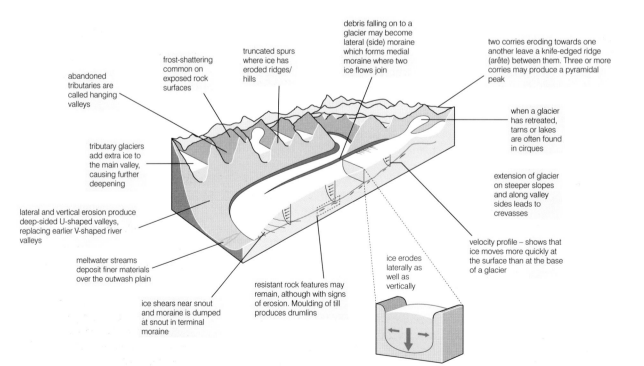

Fig. 2.14 *Glacial landforms*

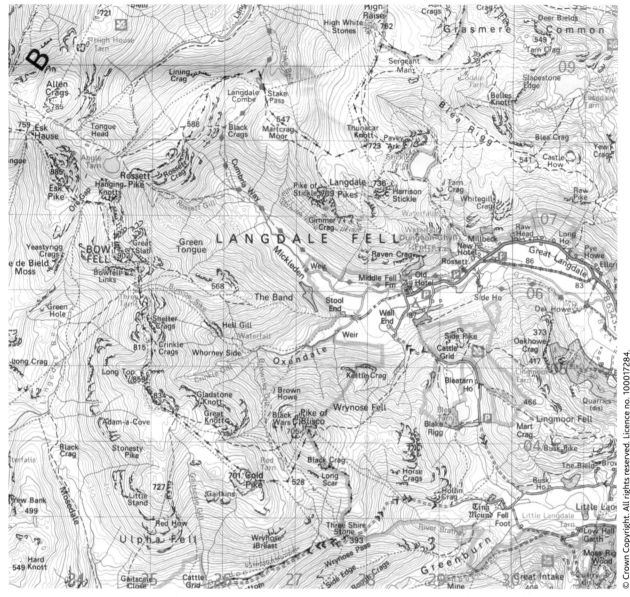

Fig. 2.15 *OS 1:50,000 map extract of the Langdales, part of map sheet 90*

Rock steps, truncated spurs and hanging valleys – valley glaciers alter the preglacial valleys they travel down. They straighten, widen and deepen them, changing the original V-shaped, river-formed feature into the characteristic U-shape typical of glacial erosion, e.g. Wastwater in the Lake District. This is because, unlike river erosion, which in upland areas is often dominated by vertical channel erosion allied to mass movement on the valley sides, glaciers erode horizontally as well as vertically. As a result they are better able to erode obstructions that streams and rivers would meander around. Glaciers typically produce steep-sided, flat-floored valleys which are known as glacial troughs. The flatness of the valley floor may be accentuated by later post-glacial deposition of glacial and fluvioglacial debris. The overdeepening of the valleys is also partly the result of extending and compressing flow, and these extra-deep sections may be occupied by long, narrow ribbon lakes in post-glacial times. Wastwater in the Lake District is a good example of a lake

■ Link

Look at:

www.swisseduc.ch/glaciers.

Select 'Glaciers of the Alps' then 'Grosser Aletschgletscher' then 'Comparison 1'.

Here you can see evidence of glacial retreat in how a tributary glacier (Mittelaletschgletscher) now fails to feed the main valley glacier (Grosser Aletschgletscher).

Link

For a virtual tour of one glacier that shows how many of the features mentioned so far are being created today, visit:

www.swisseduc.ch/glaciers.

Select 'Vadret da Morteratsch – QTVR panoramas'. The panoramic shots require Quicktime.

formed in a glacial trough. Extension flow may leave less eroded, more resistant rock steps. Where the deepening of the trough continued below the former sea level, rises in sea level may cause the valley to become submerged to form a **fjord**.

Glacial erosion along the valley sides may remove the tips of preglacial interlocking spurs leaving cliff-like truncated spurs. Hanging valleys result from differential erosion between a deeper main glacier and smaller tributary glaciers. Where the tributaries joined a main glacier, the floor of the tributary was higher than the floor of the main glacier valley, and it is left hanging in a post-glacial era. Sometimes a small misfit stream or waterfall indicates where the old tributary glacier would once have joined, e.g. where Blea Water hangs above Langdale in the Lake District.

Smaller erosion features, such as those described below, may be found within the larger features already described, e.g. roche moutonnées within a glacial trough. Along with the orientation of valley forms, they may help to indicate the direction of ice movement.

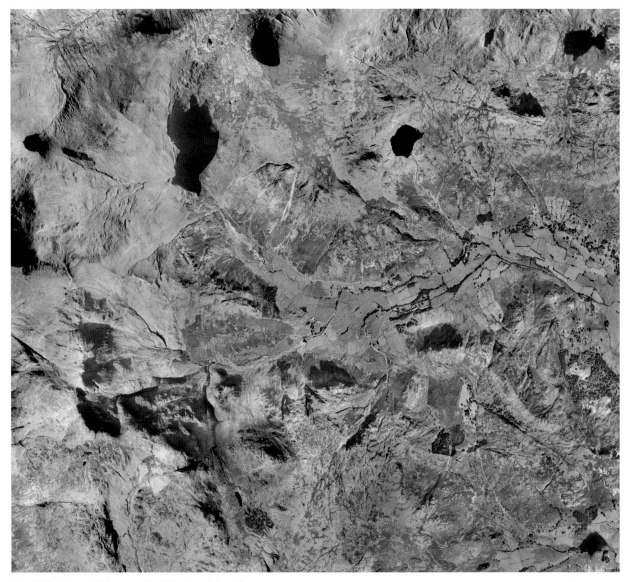

Fig. 2.16 *An aerial photograph of the Langdale valley*

Activity

2 Study Figures 2.15 and 2.16.

a   i   Identify the following features on Figure 2.15: cirque, arête, hanging valley, tarn, truncated spur, U-shaped valley.

   ii   For each feature you have identified, give a grid reference and describe the feature using map information that helps to characterise each landform. For example: 'The tarn at GR_____ is about ___ m in height. It is shown as a body of water about ___ m across and is surrounded by steep slopes on three sides forming a horseshoe shape cut into the hillside.'

b   Suggest how the formation of at least three of the features may be linked.

c   Suggest a possible direction of ice flow when the area was glaciated and cite at least two pieces of evidence to support your decision.

d   What evidence is there on the map that people can settle and make economic use of post-glacial landscapes? Describe the distribution of land use and suggest reasons for the patterns you see.

Roche moutonnées – these are masses of more resistant rock that have smooth, rounded upvalley (stoss) slopes formed by abrasion. The lee or downvalley sides are steep and jagged, which reflects the plucking action that formed them. Abrasion on the upvalley side may have left striations as pieces of rock debris within the ice were dragged across the surface under great pressure.

Rock drumlins – these are more streamlined bedrock and lack the jagged lee slope.

Crag and tail – this consists of a larger mass of resistant rock or crag and a gently sloping tail of less resistant rock and/or sediment on one side. At Edinburgh, the castle sits on a hard volcanic plug of basaltic rock (the crag), while the Royal Mile runs down softer sedimentary rocks that were protected on the lee side from erosion (see Figure 2.18).

Striations – when glaciers move across exposures of rock, angular debris embedded within the ice may leave parallel scratches and grooves called striations.

Glacial deposition

Glacial deposits, often referred to as drift deposits to distinguish them from in situ rocks of the underlying geology, include boulders, gravels, sands and clays. They are conveniently subdivided into:

■ **till** – all material deposited directly by the ice, largely unsorted in nature

■ **fluvioglacial material** – sediments deposited by meltwater streams. These usually have been sorted with coarser material nearer to the original glacier snout and finer particles carried further away by meltwaters.

The occurrence, distribution, orientation and temporal order of these features may tell us much about how far, from where and when the ice advanced across the landscape.

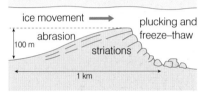

Fig. 2.17 *Roche moutonnée formation and striations*

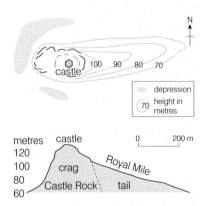

Fig. 2.18 *Crag and tail: Edinburgh Castle*

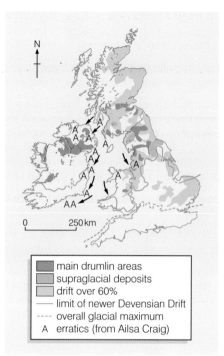

Fig. 2.19 *Extent of glaciation across the British Isles*

Till

Till, formerly known as boulder clay, is an unsorted mixture of rocks, clays and sands. Once carried as supraglacial (on the surface of the ice) debris and later deposited to form moraines, it was deposited during periods of ice movement or during glacial retreat. Owing to the nature of transportation in ice, little rounding of debris tends to occur and stones are subangular in form as opposed to the rounded boulders of a river. The composition of till depends on the nature of the rocks over which the ice has passed; for example, some deposits on the north Norfolk coast originated in southern Norway.

■ **Skills**

Till fabric analysis

Plotting the orientation of glacial till material on a rose diagram can help to reveal the flow direction of the ice that deposited it. Because debris beneath the glacier is often under immense pressure, the pebbles and fragments of rock within the till tend to align their long axes to the orientation that offers the least resistance. When the ice has gone, the pebbles retain the orientation, so a sample of pebbles can be extracted from the till and their orientations recorded using a compass. In Figure 2.20 the orientation of 50 pebbles from the Endon Valley till in Staffordshire have been plotted on a radial graph at 15° intervals (note that only the large gradations are shown on the graph). Each concentric circle moving out from the centre represents four pebbles, so the length of the line from the centre represents the number of pebbles that fall into that orientation group. A pebble with an orientation of 225° at one end has an orientation of 45° at the other – both are plotted and joined to give a symmetrical effect. The graph cannot show you where the ice came from or where it was going to, only the axis along which the ice was

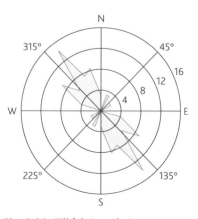

Fig. 2.20 *Till fabric analysis*

moving. Additional information, such as the shape of the body of till, or the orienatation of other features in the area, is required to make a decision on direction of origin.

Activities

3 Plot the following data on a rose diagram or use a radar plot in Excel.

Clasts	Degrees
0	0–14/180–194
1	15–29/195–209
11	30–44/210–224
13	45–59/225–239
8	60–74/240–254
3	75–89/255–269
1	90–104/270–284
1	105–119/285–299
2	120–134/300–314
2	135–149/315–329
1	150–164/330–344
1	165–179/345–359

a Does the orientation of the pebbles suggest a glacial origin?

b Suggest the direction of ice movement in the area.

4 a What other sources of information might help determine the direction of ice movement in this area?

b How might one of these feature reveal the direction of ice travel?

Erratics

As a huge stone is sometimes seen to lie
Couched on the bald top of an eminence;
Wonder to all who do the same espy,
By what means it could thither come, and whence;
So that it seems a thing endued with sense:
Like a sea-beast crawled forth, that on a shelf
Of rock or sand reposeth, there to sun itself.

William Wordsworth, from 'Resolution and Independence'

Erratics are fragments of glacial debris which range in size from pebbles to large boulders. They have been carried by glacier ice before being deposited, e.g. Big Rock (16,500 tonnes) in Alberta, Canada. They are said to be ex situ (not in their correct place) rather than in situ (in the place where they belong – usually still connected to the underlying geology) and may travel hundreds of kilometres. For example, some volcanic rocks from Ailsa Craig in the Firth of Clyde are found in the till in Lancashire some 250 km to the south, and Shap granite erratics are often found in the Holderness area on the East Yorkshire coast 180 km east-south-east of their Cumbrian origins. Erratics are usually distinguishable from local strata by their lithology – that is, they are likely to be of a different rock type from the underlying rock, and by their attitude – they do not lie in the same manner as the local strata.

Moraines

Moraines are landforms that develop when material carried by a glacier is deposited. The main types of moraine are the following:

Lateral moraine – formed from debris fallen from the sides of the valley and transported along the edges of the glacier. After glaciation it appears as elongated embankments of debris at the sides of the valley.

Medial moraine – where two glaciers meet, the lateral moraines may combine to form a medial moraine towards the middle of the main glacier. This may eventually form a depositional feature once the glacier has retracted. However, the location of a medial moraine towards the centre of the valley may be destroyed by subsequent fluvioglacial action.

Terminal or end moraine – this is often a high mound or series of mounds of debris that extend across a valley; it marks the furthest extent of the glacier/ice sheet.

Activity

5 Select any three features of glacial deposition shown in Figure 2.21 and describe their formation.

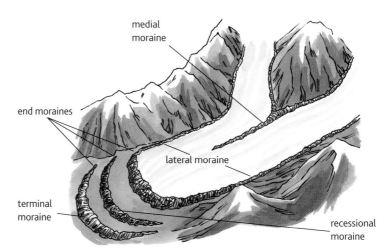

Fig. 2.21 *Different types of moraine*

Fig. 2.22 *Moraine dumps, Haweswater*

Recessional moraines – often parallel to terminal moraines, these mounds of debris mark the retreat of the glacier. Each recessional moraine reflects a stage when glacier retreat was halted long enough for deposition to concentrate in one area.

Push moraines – these form where a deterioration in climate triggers glacier re-advance and allows earlier moraines to be pushed forward into a new landform. Internally the orientation of stones may reveal the secondary disturbance they have undergone.

Drumlins

These asymmetrical elongated mounds of till can reach 50 m in height, more than 1 km in length and up to 0.5 km in width. Their characteristically smooth shape reflects the way the subglacial debris was fashioned by the pressure of ice, probably when the glacier began to deposit debris it could no longer carry. Drumlins often appear in groups known as **swarms** and are always longer than they are wide, with a long axis parallel to the direction of ice movement. They typically have a steeper stoss end facing the direction the ice came from and the gentler lee slope tailing off in the direction the ice travelled.

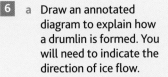

Activity

6 a Draw an annotated diagram to explain how a drumlin is formed. You will need to indicate the direction of ice flow.

  b Study Figure 2.24. What can you determine about the direction of ice flow that deposited the drumlins and its likely ultimate destination? (Hint: look back at Figure 2.19.)

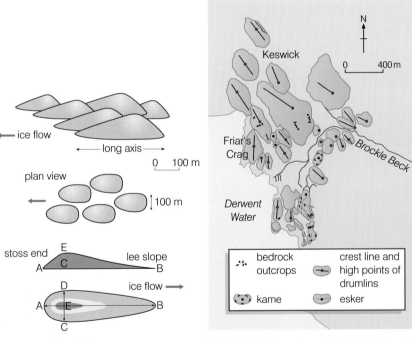

Fig. 2.23 *Drumlin formation*

Fig. 2.24 *Orientation of Lake District drumlins*

■ Fluvioglacial processes and landforms

Fluvioglacial landforms are created by the meltwater from glaciers, largely through deposition but also by erosion. Glaciers in temperate zones in particular lose a great deal of water to ablation throughout the summer months. Discharge occurs through supraglacial and subglacial streams (at the base of the glacier), often under great pressure in the latter case. This water has the power to erode subglacial valleys deeper than 15 m and their turbulent flow picks up more sediment than a comparably sized surface river.

Outwash plains (sandur)

Comprising gravels, sands and clays, these sediments are deposited by meltwater streams that emanate from the front of the glacier during the summer or when the glacier retreats. The material may be glacial in origin and redeposited by the meltwater streams. Sometimes it forms a final deposit on top of till when the glacier is in its final retreat phase. These plains tend to sort the sediment so that the coarser material, like sand, is closer to the snout, and finer clay furthest away. Outwash material may also be deposited on top of till following the retreat of the ice.

Varves

These are glacio-lacustrine sediments deposited annually in lakes at the glacial margins. Varved clays exhibit alternating layers of darker-coloured silt on top of layers of lighter-coloured sand. The larger-calibre materials are deposited during late spring when meltwater streams experience peak discharge and maximum load. In the cooler autumn, when volumes of meltwater decrease, streams experience lower discharge and can only carry finer-calibre sediments, so finer, darker-coloured silt is deposited. Each year new bands of light and dark materials are deposited and by counting the number of varves it is possible to obtain the age of the sediments. Thicker or thinner varves may indicate warmer periods (more meltwater) and colder periods (less meltwater).

Braided streams

Seasonal variation in the discharge of meltwater streams leads to fluctuations in the sediment load being carried across the outwash plains in front of glaciers. Deposition of excess sediment during times of lower discharge may obstruct flow, leading to braiding of the channels as the water seeks to find a more efficient way through, e.g. the River Eyra in Iceland.

Eskers

These sinuous ridges mark the course of streams that once transported subglacial meltwater beneath the glacier. They are composed of sorted coarse sands and gravel that filled the ice-restricted channels and were revealed when the ice retreated.

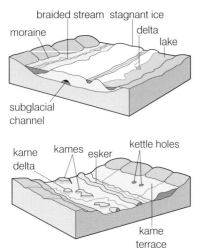

Fig. 2.25 *Fluvioglacial features*

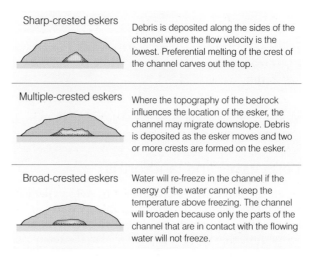

Sharp-crested eskers	Debris is deposited along the sides of the channel where the flow velocity is the lowest. Preferential melting of the crest of the channel carves out the top.
Multiple-crested eskers	Where the topography of the bedrock influences the location of the esker, the channel may migrate downslope. Debris is deposited as the esker moves and two or more crests are formed on the esker.
Broad-crested eskers	Water will re-freeze in the channel if the energy of the water cannot keep the temperature above freezing. The channel will broaden because only the parts of the channel that are in contact with the flowing water will not freeze.

Fig. 2.26 *Esker formation*

Kames and kame terraces

Kames are deposits of sand and gravel left by meltwater along the front of a melting ice sheet. These irregular undulating mounds are often ill-sorted as they collapse when the supporting ice melts. Better-sorted deposits are found as kame terraces, which are formed by meltwater streams flowing along the edge of the glacier where it meets the valley wall.

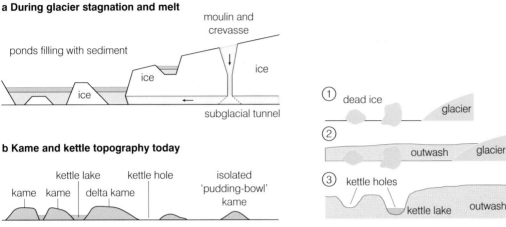

a During glacier stagnation and melt

ponds filling with sediment

moulin and crevasse

ice

ice

ice

subglacial tunnel

b Kame and kettle topography today

kettle lake   kettle hole

kame   kame   delta kame

isolated 'pudding-bowl' kame

Fig. 2.27 *Formation of kames*

① dead ice   glacier

② outwash   glacier

③ kettle holes

kettle lake   outwash

Fig. 2.28 *Kettle hole formation*

Kettles or kettle holes

Blocks of ice are left behind as the glacier retreats. Partially buried by fluvioglacial deposits (kames), they leave enclosed depressions when the ice melts. The depressions often fill with water (kettle hole lakes) and help to create distinctive kame and kettle topography.

Proglacial lakes

Where bodies of water develop next to glaciers and ice sheets as a result of the accumulation of meltwater, they are known as proglacial lakes. There are good examples of the deposits and landforms left by these meltwater lakes in several regions of the UK:

- In Shropshire, the preglacial River Severn was blocked on its path northward to where the Dee estuary is today, by Irish Sea ice. The build-up of meltwater created Lake Lapworth which eventually overflowed southwards towards the position it holds today, and cut the Ironbridge Gorge in the process.

- A similar event in the Warwickshire area saw the preglacial River Avon blocked on its way north-east and it was forced to flow south-west towards the Bristol Channel, on the course it follows today.

- On the North York Moors, Lake Pickering was created when meltwater from the surrounding ice sheets prevented water from flowing away. To the north, the River Esk had its exit to the North Sea blocked by ice, so it developed a meltwater lake known as Lake Eskdale. When this overflowed south-westwards, it cut the flat-bottomed Newtondale valley and Lake Pickering developed. The sediments that built up created the flat, fertile plain that is seen around Pickering today. Lake Pickering also formed an overflow valley when it cut Kirkham Gorge and created the path for the current River Derwent.

■ Periglacial processes

Periglacial areas are those that experience a cold climate, with intense frost action and the development of **permafrost**. Today up to 25 per cent of the Earth's surface may be described as periglacial, from mountainous areas in temperate zones to the vast areas of North America and Russia that lie above the Arctic Circle. They experience conditions that are physically close to glacial (they are near an ice sheet, e.g. Greenland), or temporally close (they could be glacial or they have been glacial, e.g. Highland Scotland). These places experience, or have experienced, an extremely cold climate and generate their own distinctive landforms. In the past, many of these areas would have been classified as periglacial, although today they may exhibit temperate climates.

Permafrost

Permafrost is permanently frozen ground. Subsoil temperatures must remain below zero for two years or more for permafrost to develop. The extent, depth and continuity of the permafrost layer varies through time according to fluctuations in climate. During the summer, when air temperatures rise above freezing, the surface layer thaws to form an **active layer** up to 4 m deep.

There are three main types of permafrost:

Continuous permafrost – this is found in the coldest regions such as the Arctic, where there is little thawing even in summer. It affects the soil and rock to a depth of up to 700 m in parts of Canada and over twice that depth in some regions of Siberia.

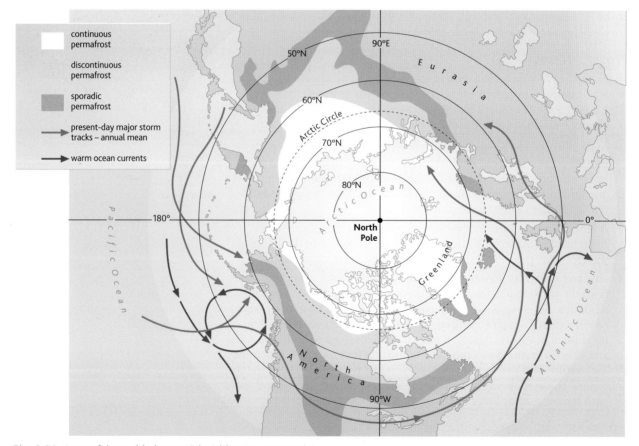

Fig. 2.29 *Areas of the world where periglacial features occur today*

Discontinuous permafrost – this is found in slightly warmer regions where freezing conditions do not penetrate to such great depths (average 20 to 30 m). It is called discontinuous because there are breaks in the permafrost around rivers, lakes and the sea.

Sporadic permafrost – here mean annual temperatures are around or just below freezing point and permafrost occurs only in isolated spots.

Frost heave

This process results from the direct formation of ice crystals or lenses in the soil. On freezing, fine-grained soils expand unevenly upwards to form small domes. As stones cool down faster than the surrounding soil, small amounts of moisture in the soil beneath the stones freeze and turn to ice, expanding by 9 per cent as they do so. By repeatedly freezing and thawing over time, these ice crystals and lenses heave stones upwards in the soil profile. In areas where temperatures fluctuate between 0°C and –4°C, the frost heaving and subsequent thawing is able to sort material to form **patterned ground**. The larger stones move outwards down the very low slopes of smaller domes because of their weight. On gentler slopes **stone polygons** are created, but where the ground is steeper (greater than 6°) the stones are dragged downhill by gravity into more linear arrangements known as **stone stripes**.

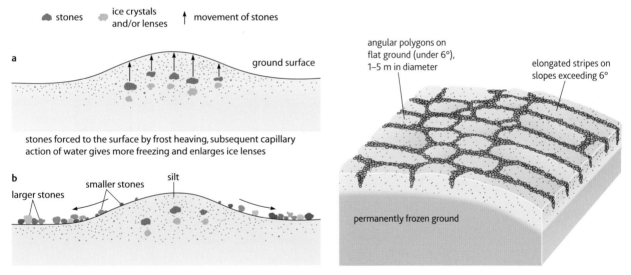

Fig. 2.30 *Frost heave*

Groundwater freezing

Freezing of water in the upper layer of soil where permafrost is thin or discontinuous leads to the expansion of ice within the soil. This causes the overlying sediments to heave upwards into a dome-shaped feature known as a **pingo** (less than 50 m in height). These dome-shaped hills may be 0.5 km across and are found mainly in sandier soils. This type of pingo is referred to as an open-system or East Greenland type.

Closed-system pingos or Mackenzie-type pingos are more typical of low-lying areas with continuous permafrost. On the site of small lakes, groundwater can be trapped by freezing from above and by the permafrost beneath as it moves inwards from the lakeside. Subsequent freezing and expansion of the trapped water pushes the overlying sediments into a pingo form. If the centre collapses it may infill with water to form a small lake. Over a thousand of these pingos have been recorded in the Mackenzie delta (Canada).

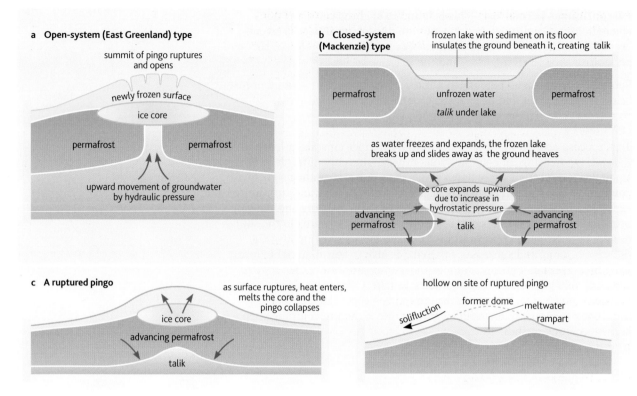

Fig. 2.31 *Pingo formation*

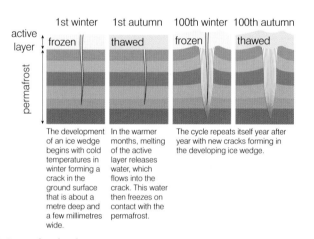

Fig. 2.32 *Ice wedge development*

Ground contraction

Refreezing of the active layer during winter causes the soil to contract and cracks open up on the surface. During melting the following summer, the cracks open again and fill with meltwater and its associated fine sediment, which helps to partially fill the crack. Repetition of the process over many years widens and deepens the crack to form an **ice wedge** up to 1 m wide and 3 m deep. A near polygonal pattern is produced on the surface, similar in form to the polygons produced by frost heaving. They are therefore known as **ice-wedge polygons**.

Nivation

Nivation occurs mainly between north- and east-facing slopes beneath patches of snow in hollows of bare rock. It is essentially frost action affecting the land beneath a blanket of snow and may involve freeze–thaw weathering as well as solifluction and meltwater. Freeze–thaw action causes the underlying rock to disintegrate. During the spring thaw, the weathered particles are moved downslope by the meltwater and by solifluction. Over a period of time, this leads to the formation of nivation hollows which may be a step in the formation of cirque development in some areas (see page 55).

Solifluction

The effect of the summer thaw on the active layer is to release a great deal of meltwater. As this water is unable to percolate downwards (because the ground below is still frozen), it saturates the soil, reducing the internal friction between particles, thus making it highly mobile. The lack of substantial vegetation to fix to the saturated soil means the soil begins to flow even on slopes of only a few degrees. This process is known as **solifluction** and the deposits it leaves behind are characterised by rounded, tongue-like features often forming terraces on the sides of valleys. These solifluction lobes are stepped features that may be formed beneath a turf of vegetation which is pushed forwards and rolled under like a caterpillar truck. Where vegetation is sparse, stones heaved to the surface are pushed to the front of the advancing lobe and form a small stone bank at the front of the lobe. Many parts of southern Britain experienced these conditions during the Quaternary ice age and these deposits are locally known as **head** in the UK.

What has the tundra to do with me?

The threat to permafrost in tundra areas today is increasing as global warming accelerates. In some areas the active layer is deepening and widening in the thaw. The actual temperature at the surface of the permafrost table has risen by up to 1.5°C in some regions of Alaska. This may have significant impacts on the global climate for a range of reasons. There may well be an increase in the thermokarst – the hummocky land where sediments are over 70 per cent ice by volume and where the seasonal thaw is deep enough to reach beyond ice wedges. One key concern is that, in areas such as Siberia, the permafrost helps to retain enormous amounts of carbon dioxide in the frozen state. Recent research has shown that as the summer melt lasts longer each year and the permafrost is shrinking, carbon-rich peat deposits are beginning to release their organic carbon and methane reserves. This organic material – the remains of rotted plants and long-dead animals that fell to the bottom of Siberian lakes and bogs in preglacial times – has decomposed to form methane.

Eventually, during a thaw, this methane bubbles to the surface. Between 1974 and 2000, a period that matches figures for local warming, the spread of thaw lakes caused methane emissions in Siberia to rise by up to 58 per cent. This could generate a positive feedback loop as it releases the billions of tonnes of stored methane locked in the ground and under frozen lakes in Canada and Siberia. It is potentially a vicious circle: global warming warms up the permafrost, which releases trapped methane, and the methane adds to the greenhouse effect. Volume for volume, methane is 21 times more effective at trapping solar heat than carbon dioxide. Scientists say that methane accounts for a fifth of the manmade greenhouse effect of the past 200 years. The addition of methane released from the turndra will only accelerate the process.

Exploitation and development of cold environments

In this section you will learn:

- about ways in which humans use and are in conflict with cold environments

- about some sustainable ways in which arctic environments may be managed.

Case study

Tundra: Old Crow Flats

Old Crow Flats lies in the north of Yukon in Canada, just a short distance from the Alaska border. It is an area of low relief, approximately 300 m above sea level, made up mostly of polygonal peat bogs. To the north, the land is mountainous with rolling hills and pediment slopes. The hills are covered with stands of spruce woodland separated by dwarf birch, willow, cotton grass and lichens which form a ground cover. Tussock tundra vegetation covers the more gentle slopes on the pediment.

Here we look at how people have developed a traditional way of life and learned to survive in a fragile environment, despite the harshness of the physical conditions. They depend on the existence of other life forms in the region that are equally precisely fitted to the fragile environment – but all are now under threat from modern, global developments.

Old Crow climate statistics

The January mean daily temperature is –35°C

The July mean daily temperature is 15°C

The annual mean total precipitation is 200 mm.

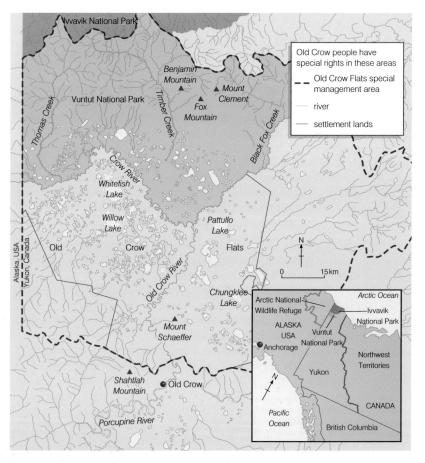

Fig. 2.33 *Old Crow Flats*

During the last ice age this area was not glaciated. It was part of an area, known as Beringia, that was never covered by the ice sheet even at its farthest extent. Instead, Old Crow Flats was covered by an enormous lake caused by impeded drainage. There are about 7 m of lacustrine (lake bed) deposits across the area overlain by post-glacial peat. The peat formed in the periglacial conditions when vegetation could grow during the short summer but the remains could not decay because the boggy conditions meant there was no oxygen to allow decomposition. Figure 2.34 shows how the soil at 50 cm depth never thaws, so it remains impermeable.

The polygonal shapes of the lakes are a result of the freezing and thawing of the surface layers in a process similar to the formation of stone polygons.

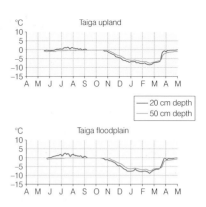

Fig. 2.34 *Soil temperature, Old Crow*

The Vuntut Gwitchin

The temperature, low precipitation, delicately balanced soil structures, isolation and long hours of winter darkness all mean that this is a very fragile environment. Survival here is difficult for both wildlife and humans. One community that can survive here are the Vuntut Gwitchin.

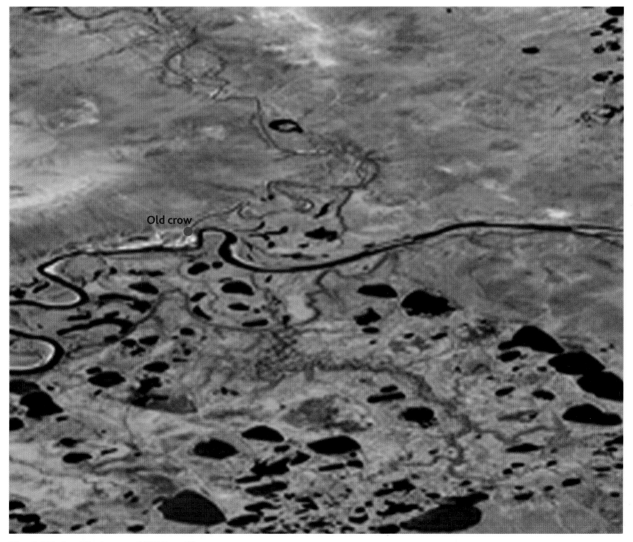

Fig. 2.35 *Satellite image of Old Crow Flats*

■ Link

Look at:

www.taiga.net/caribou.

Go to 'Caribou and Climate, a slide show'. A slide show illustrates the caribou migration and shows some of the factors affecting the size of the herd.

Then, to see an interactive predictive model suggesting how the herd size might vary in future, given changing climate conditions, go to 'Caribou population model'.

The local government has a Caribou Coordination Department. Its web page is at:

www.vgfn.ca/caribou.php.

To see the Vuntut Gwichin view of the caribou go to:

www.vgfn.ca.

Select 'Caribou coordination'.

There are details of a 'cultural technology' camp at the site of one of the old caribou fences at:

www.oldcrow.ca/diniizhoo.

The panorama gives a good view of a tundra landscape; the last photo in the gallery shows the remains of a caribou fence.

For full details of life at a trapping camp go to:

www.oldcrow.ca/cf1.htm.

The village of Old Crow is home to about 300 people from the Vuntut Gwitchin community. Their name means 'People of the Lakes'. There are 19 Gwitchin villages spread across the north of Canada and their 7500 people make up the Gwitchin nation. They originally lived an entirely nomadic life, hunting, trapping and collecting fruit and berries. They are now settled but the Vuntut Gwitchin still follow many aspects of their traditional culture, which is largely based on the seasonal migration of the caribou herds across the tundra, with further seasonal migration by some families to trap muskrat.

The Porcupine caribou herd

The Porcupine caribou herd is so named because the animals cross the Porcupine River during their spring and autumn migrations (see Figure 2.38). In spring they migrate north to the coastal plains of Yukon and north-east Alaska to calve and to graze on the rich pasture and shrubs that are exposed when the snow cover melts. This area is favoured by the caribou because it is flat and featureless so they can easily spot any predators. Also, there is a sea breeze that provides some relief from the aggravations of the mosquitoes that are present throughout the summer.

On the Canadian side of the border these calving grounds form part of the Ivvavik National Park and so are very well protected from development. On the Alaskan side they are part of the Arctic National Wildlife Refuge which offers a much lower level of protection from development. The issues that this raises are discussed in more detail below.

In winter the herd migrates south. The animals spread out to forage for food, mainly mosses and lichens, beneath the snow. Inland from the coast, the snow cover is less deep and so the animals have to spend less time scraping to reach their food.

The Vuntut Gwitchin people have always relied on the caribou to provide them with meat and hides for their clothing and tents. The bones and antlers can also be used for making soups or for tools such as needles and spears. There is still evidence of the traditional hunting methods, for example the remains of caribou fences made from wood and designed to trap the herd after they had passed through a gap in the forest or a ford across a stream. As the herd was funnelled into the U-shaped trap, they were easy prey for the huntsmen, who could kill enough caribou to feed the tribe for up to six months until the return migration.

Nowadays the people still hunt the caribou during their migrations, still eating the meat and drying some by traditional methods to last through the following months. However, they are no longer nomadic, having established homes in Old Crow, just by the crossing point on the Porcupine River, which was always an important strategic point in the migration of the caribou. In addition they now use snowmobiles to travel rather than the old dog sledges, and they use rifles rather than spears and arrows.

Are these modern methods leading to overhunting?

Surveys have shown that the size of the caribou herd has changed since 1971, in particular it fell during the 1990s (see Figure 2.36). However, a survey carried out by local ecologists concluded that hunting only killed 4 per cent of the adults in the herd in any one

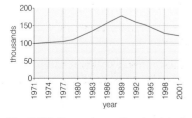

Fig. 2.36 *Porcupine caribou herd size*

year and that the annual birth rate of calves was more than enough to compensate for this. They concluded that the fluctuation in numbers was due to climatic changes. Have a look at these quotations:

> Biologists believe that the recent declining trend in the 1990s is probably related to weather conditions (high snow accumulations on the wintering grounds and short summers in the early 1990s). The body condition of adult female caribou in March has also been declining over the same period. This supports the idea that environmental stresses on adult caribou are limiting current growth of the herd.

www.taiga.net

> We as Gwitchin people truly RESPECT the VUTZUI [caribou] and take only what we need. This is our way of conserving. We are dependent on the caribou in many ways. We are grateful that the caribou come back our way, close to Old Crow every year. Sometimes they are delayed; however, we still wait patiently because the caribou have never let us down yet. Our prayers have been answered when the hunter sees the caribou on Crow Mountain and calls out 'Vutsui!' When they do this, everyone gets excited. Our stomachs will be full again and we will continue to survive and be a proud and strong nation. For this, we say 'Massi cho!' [Thank you!].

Mary Jane Moses, Old Crow, Yukon

Other aspects of life in Old Crow

Some seasonal work in hunting and fishing also provides income. In particular, some groups of Vuntut Gwitchin go up to the lakes on Old Crow Flats just before the thaw starts to trap muskrat – small animals that live in shelters they build on the ice, using mud and sticks, a bit like beavers building their lodges. The animals provide meat, which helps the people over the period before the caribou migrate, but the main product from the muskrat is fur. This can provide winter clothing for the families but it is mainly used for trade and is one of the main sources of income for the Old Crow community.

> A very limited market-based economy in Old Crow supplements traditional activities. Government services provide a significant share of total employment in the market, or money, economy. More than half of measurable employment falls into this category. Government services in Old Crow include the First Nation government and administration of services for First Nation members, as well as services like policing.
>
> Since the Vuntut Gwitchin Council is responsible for providing most services in Old Crow, First Nation government employment includes such things as construction, building maintenance, water and fuel delivery and similar services. First Nation government activities also involve social services and support for the elderly. Other First Nation employees find seasonal work in projects run by the First Nation or in seasonal federal and territorial jobs.
>
> Education and health care also provide some employment. The Northern Store employs several people from the community. Other industry sectors either offer no employment in Old Crow or in numbers too small to measure.

www.yukoncommunities.yk.ca

Question

1 Using the text and the websites in the Link boxes, describe how the way of life and the hunting of the Vuntut Gwitchin has:

a stayed the same

b changed from its traditional patterns.

Link

The description of other work in Old Crow is taken from the Yukon Community Profiles produced by the Canadian government. The Old Crow section can be seen in full at:

www.yukoncommunities.yk.ca.

Look up 'Communities' then 'Old Crow'.

A description of life and work in Old Crow from the local government site can be seen at:

www.vgfn.ca.

One particular aspect of government-sponsored development in the area which brings jobs to people and money into the community is the gravel quarry that was started in 2003. The gravel is needed for many purposes, including developments in the village like shoring up river banks against erosion, and for building and improving roads in the wider area. There is still no road link that connects Old Crow to the outside world. All contact has to be by boat or air. However, local roads are needed if any development is to take place, and local resources have to be used to build such roads; it would be far too expensive to bring them in.

The quarry was built on the side of Crow Mountain, 6 km from the village. A crushing plant to produce the gravel was also built. Constructing the quarry and its road provided two years' work for 12 men. Operating the quarry also provides some local employment.

Figure 2.37 shows that Old Crow's population of around 300 has a disproportionately large number of young people and old people when compared with the rest of Yukon. This is because quite a lot of people of working age migrate away from the area to seek paid work elsewhere. However, most return permanently and many return during the seasons when caribou hunting takes place.

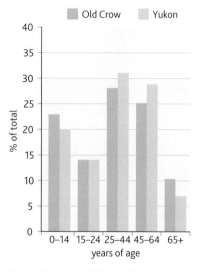

Fig. 2.37 *Age profile for Old Crow*

Question

2 Study the text and the websites for this case study.

a Describe the attractions of life in Old Crow for people from the Vuntut Gwitchin Community.

b Describe the pressures on people from the community to move away.

c How well is the community protecting itself from these pressures?

The threat to the caribou from oil exploration

The Arctic National Wildlife Refuge is a habitat for over 250 animal species, including wolves, grizzly bears, caribou and millions of migrating birds. It contains areas of world-class wilderness boreal forests, dramatic peaks and tundra. It features a complete range of

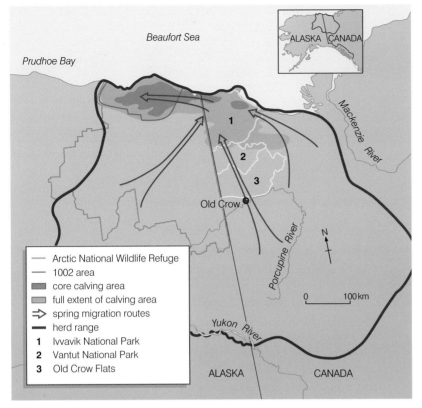

Fig. 2.38 *Caribou migrations*

arctic and subarctic ecosystems. At 8 million hectares, this north-east Alaskan refuge is the largest in the USA. It was first established in 1960 to preserve this unique part of Alaska bordering the Arctic Ocean west of the Canadian border in northern Yukon.

The northernmost part of the Arctic Refuge is a 6070 km^2 area known as the 1002 lands (named after Clause 1002 of the Alaska National Interest Lands Conservation Act). This area of the coastal plain between the Brooks Range and the Beaufort Sea is the only portion of the Arctic Refuge that does not have protected wilderness designation. The 1002 lands constitute about 75 per cent of the total coastal plain of the Arctic Refuge and could hold large petroleum deposits. It is also the core calving ground for the Porcupine caribou herd.

In January 2008 a proposal was presented to the United States Congress to open the 1002 lands of the Arctic Refuge for petroleum exploration and development.

Many groups are in favour of this development. They include:

- the oil industry
- the three Alaska representatives in Congress
- many of the people of Alaska who, each year, receive money from the Alaska Permanent Fund (set up in 1970 as a savings account for state revenues from taxation of the oil industry; in 2007 every eligible citizen received $1654)
- those who argue that the USA's national security depends on producing its own oil as far as possible, to avoid relying on imports from other countries.

Link

Look at:

www.wilderness.org.

Select 'Our Issues' and 'Arctic National Wildlife Refuge' and you will find some superb descriptions of the area and its wildlife, along with pictures.

■ Question

3 **a** If the caribou herds were to be damaged by the search for and the exploitation of oil and gas in the 1002 lands, how might this affect the community at Old Crow?

b Suggest how the development of the 1002 lands could damage the caribou herds.

c Suggest how the oil industry could develop the area without damaging the herds.

d Discuss whether exploration of the 1002 lands should be allowed to go ahead.

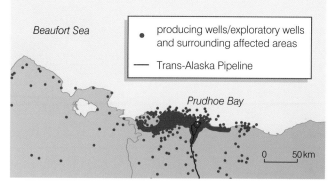

Fig. 2.39 *Oil developments on Alaska North Slope*

Groups against the development include:

■ Native Alaskans and First Nation Canadians who rely on the caribou herds for their way of life and much of their food and income

■ the small, but growing, Yukon and Alaska tourist industries

■ wildlife and wilderness conservationists in Alaska, Canada, mainland USA and the rest of the world – in a recent US poll, 70 per cent of Americans called for permanent protection of the Arctic Refuge's coastal plain.

Apart from the obvious arguments about conservation, these opponents to development say that:

■ there is only a 50/50 chance of discovering oil in the 1002 lands

■ even oil industry estimates suggest that production from this area would only produce enough oil and gas to meet total US demand for 90 days

■ the strategic argument is flawed because legislation has recently been passed, supported by Alaska's representatives in Congress, to allow Alaska oil to be exported to Asia.

■ Oil and gas exploitation in Alaska

The case study on the Vuntut Gwitchin people looked at certain issues from the point of view of those people. They have very strong views on the future of the 1002 lands in north-east Alaska. However, there are alternative views to those. In this section you may change your views on the 1002 lands or at least come to understand and appreciate another point of view. A study of the living graph in Figure 2.40 should help you to see why some people are in favour of the development of the area.

Alaska North Slope gas pipeline project

The oil companies, including BP, that have developed the gas fields on the north coast of Alaska have sent their gas out in pressurised tankers through the Bering Straits up until now. However, there have been several big new gas discoveries in the last few years, so now they are proposing to build a pipeline to carry the gas to mainland USA. Figure 2.42 shows some aspects of the plans to develop the pipeline.

The plan is to take the pipe to Alberta, which is already at the centre of the Canadian oil and gas industry, and to distribute it from there to different parts of the USA.

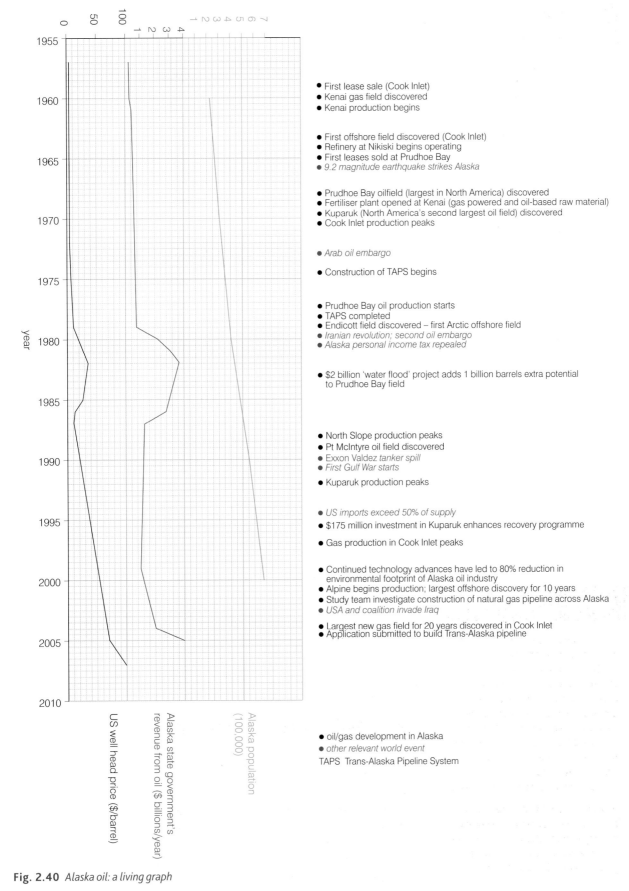

year

US well head price ($/barrel)

Alaska state government's revenue from oil ($ billions/year)

Alaska population (100 000)

● First lease sale (Cook Inlet)
● Kenai gas field discovered
● Kenai production begins

● First offshore field discovered (Cook Inlet)
● Refinery at Nikiski begins operating
● First leases sold at Prudhoe Bay
● *9.2 magnitude earthquake strikes Alaska*

● Prudhoe Bay oilfield (largest in North America) discovered
● Fertiliser plant opened at Kenai (gas powered and oil-based raw material)
● Kuparuk (North America's second largest oil field) discovered
● Cook Inlet production peaks

● *Arab oil embargo*

● Construction of TAPS begins

● Prudhoe Bay oil production starts
● TAPS completed
● Endicott field discovered – first Arctic offshore field
● *Iranian revolution; second oil embargo*
● *Alaska personal income tax repealed*

● $2 billion 'water flood' project adds 1 billion barrels extra potential to Prudhoe Bay field

● North Slope production peaks
● Pt McIntyre oil field discovered
● *Exxon Valdez tanker spill*
● *First Gulf War starts*

● Kuparuk production peaks

● *US imports exceed 50% of supply*
● $175 million investment in Kuparuk enhances recovery programme

● Gas production in Cook Inlet peaks

● Continued technology advances have led to 80% reduction in environmental footprint of Alaska oil industry
● Alpine begins production; largest offshore discovery for 10 years
● Study team investigate construction of natural gas pipeline across Alaska
● *USA and coalition invade Iraq*

● Largest new gas field for 20 years discovered in Cook Inlet
● Application submitted to build Trans-Alaska pipeline

● oil/gas development in Alaska
● *other relevant world event*
TAPS Trans-Alaska Pipeline System

Fig. 2.40 *Alaska oil: a living graph*

Link

Look at:

www.bp.com.

Select 'USA' from the location choices and then 'Alaska'.

Activities

7 Study Figures 2.40 to 2.42 and the BP website in the Link box.

a What connections can you see between the three lines on the graph showing the price of oil, Alaska's oil revenue and the population of Alaska?

b Suggest explanations for the links that you have seen.

c What does the evidence suggest about the future potential for oil and gas production in Alaska?

d About how long does it take for a major new oil field to go from discovery to production?

8 a Taking the role of an Alaska state representative to Congress, outline a case for allowing oil exploration on the 1002 lands.

b Discuss the advantages and disadvantages of building a gas pipeline along the lines proposed.

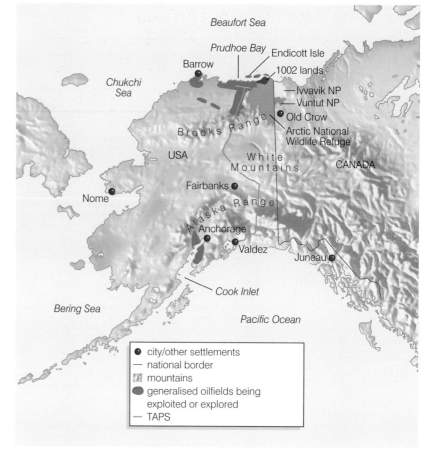

Fig. 2.41 *Alaska oil industry*

Legend:
- ● city/other settlements
- — national border
- mountains
- ● generalised oilfields being exploited or explored
- — TAPS

Gas treatment plant
- ● ~4.5 billion cubic feet per day
- ● remove CO_2, other impurities
- ● chilling
- ● initial compression

The resource
- ● Prudhoe bay
- ● Point Thomson
- ● other known fields
- ● exploration

Total investment: $20 billion

Alaska to Alberta pipeline system
- ● buried, high pressure, chilled pipeline
- ● large diameter, 2500 psi
- ● intermediate compression
- ● refrigeration (northern stations)

NGL extraction facility
- ● process gas to delivery spec.

Arctic and project management experience is critical

Alberta to Market pipeline system
- ● ~4 billion cubic feet per day
- ● large diameter, buried pipe
  and/or

Existing pipeline systems
- ● excess capacity
- ● expansions

The Alaska Natural Gas Pipeline Project will provide huge benefits to Alaskans
- ● Enormous job opportunities
- ● Billions of dollars in state revenues
- ● State control over shipping and marketing its gas. The state can sell to whomever it wants, in state or out of state
- ● A state ownership share of the pipeline, providing a steady, stable revenue stream and a greater level of decision-making ability than would be available to non-owners

Fig. 2.42 *Proposals for an Alaska gas distribution network*

AQA Examiner's tip

On page 76 you were told that this section would consider the development of Alaskan oil from a positive point of view. Do remember the context of what you read and write, particularly when you do activities like Activity 8.

Antarctica and the Southern Ocean

Antarctica is a continental land mass that is approximately centred on the South Pole. This is unlike the Arctic, which is a sea that is partly covered with a floating ice cap. The continent is almost completely covered by ice fields that are thousands of metres thick in places. It is surrounded by ice shelves, layers of ice floating on the sea water that are fed by the flow of ice off the continent.

The Antarctic covers an area somewhat larger than Europe but it has no permanent residents. A number of governments maintain permanent research stations throughout the continent. The number of people conducting and supporting scientific research and other work on the continent and its nearby islands varies from about 4000 in summer to about 1000 in winter.

The main economic activity in the area today is fishing. Antarctic fisheries in 2000–01 reported landing 112,934 tonnes.

Small-scale 'expedition tourism' has existed since 1957, regulated by the International Association of Antarctica Tour Operators (IAATO). Travel is largely by small or medium ships, focusing on scenic locations with accessible concentrations of iconic wildlife. A total of 37,506 tourists visited during the 2006–07 summer. The number is predicted to increase to over 80,000 by 2010. There is concern that this might damage the very environment and ecosystems that attract the tourists. A call for stricter regulations for ships and a tourism quota have been made by some environmentalists and scientists. Now 'site use guidelines' set landing limits at the more frequently visited sites.

Fishing and whaling in the Southern Ocean

The first semi-permanent inhabitants of regions near Antarctica were British and American sealers who used to spend a year or more on South Georgia, from 1786 onwards. During the whaling era, which lasted until 1966, the population of that island varied from over 1000 in summer (over 2000 in some years) to some 200 in winter.

The hunt for whales and seals was the reason for the initial exploration of Antarctica and the Southern Ocean that surrounds it. Reports of abundant stocks drew the adventurous from the early 19th century onwards. Before long there were major crashes in the populations of some wildlife. The Antarctic fur seal, for example, was almost totally wiped out at many locations by 1830, leading to a decline in the sealing industry, although it continued on a smaller scale well into the 20th century. Seals were hunted for meat and skins.

No commercial sealing has been carried out in the Southern Ocean since the 1950s. Seals were killed in order to provide food for dog teams that were stationed in Antarctica up to the point where the dog teams were finally removed due to worries that the disease of canine distemper might spread to seals.

Whales

The story of Antarctic whaling has often been a story of the 'mining' of a resource. Once the most profitable species had been hunted to a point of great scarcity, the next species was hunted until it too was very rare, then the next, and so on. The story of the blue whale – the largest animal that has ever lived on Earth – is typical. Before it began to be hunted in the 19th century, there are thought to have been 275,000 blue whales in the world's oceans, many of them in the Southern Ocean. They were

Did you know?

Antarctica has no government and belongs to no country. Since 1959, all claims to sovereignty in Antarctica have been suspended and the continent is considered politically neutral. Its status is regulated by the 1959 Antarctic Treaty which was signed by the 12 countries with the greatest interests in the area. It set aside Antarctica as a scientific preserve, established freedom of scientific investigation and environmental protection, and banned military activity there.

A further agreement, the Madrid Protocol, came into force in 1998. It bans all mining activities in Antarctica, designating the continent as a 'natural reserve devoted to peace and science'. The protocol will be reviewed in 2048. Although coal, hydrocarbons, iron ore, gold and other mineral deposits have been found, they are currently not considered large enough to exploit.

■ Link

The Japanese Whaling Association has its home page at:

www.whaling.jp/english/index.html.

Cool Antarctica is a brilliant site with lots of information on whaling:

www.coolantarctica.com.

Click on 'Whales' and 'Whaling Antartica 1'.

Look up the Greenpeace website at:

www.greenpeace.org/international.

Select 'What we do', 'Defending our Oceans' then 'Whaling'.

hunted without any thought for conservation and by the 1930s there are estimated to have been fewer than 40,000 left and by 1964 numbers were between 1000 and 2000. In the 1960s a ban on whaling was introduced and numbers have recovered to some extent. Now there are thought to be over 5000 individual blue whales. Other species are recovering too.

The early whalers in Antarctica operated in a very difficult and dangerous environment. Ships hunted the whales and then launched rowing boats that could approach much closer to them. Then a harpooner hurled a harpoon (a barbed spear) into the whale and the boat's crew hung on to the attached rope fighting the whale and trying to harpoon it several more times until the whale was dead. Finally the carcass was cut up into pieces and hauled aboard the ship. It was taken back to the base – usually on South Georgia – and processed, mainly to extract the oil which was the most prized part of the whale.

In 1868 the exploding harpoon was invented. It used an explosive charge, which made it safer for the sailors and a more humane and quicker way of killing the whale.

In 1925 factory ships were introduced. These were bigger than the hunting ships and served a fleet of the smaller ships. They had slipways at the rear and whole whales could be dragged on board and then processed on the ship. This meant that the whalers did not have to keep returning to land and so could hunt much more efficiently. It was that efficiency which led to the catastrophic decline in whale numbers and eventually to the treaties limiting commercial whaling

Some countries, notably Japan, Iceland and Norway, are now seeking to overturn the ban on whaling. In January 2008, Japan sent a whaling fleet to Antarctica to hunt whales for what it called scientific research. Such research is allowed by the conventions against commercial whaling. No doubt research is carried out but people have to kill the whales before they can do the research and the dead whales are used for meat, etc. A whale carcass can be worth $1 million by the time it reaches the restaurant table.

The Southern Ocean food chain

More than anything else, krill are the engine that powers the Antarctic ecosystem. They are a small semi-transparent crustacean like a shrimp, about 4–5 cm in length when fully grown. They feed on microscopic phytoplankton which are fed by upwellings of water where currents meet. These upwellings bring huge quantities of dissolved nutrients towards the surface. During the 24-hour daylight period of summer, the nutrients and sunlight combine to produce this superabundance.

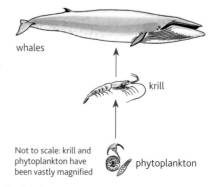

Not to scale: krill and phytoplankton have been vastly magnified

Fig. 2.43 *Antarctic food web*

Krill drift around in huge swarms. Observed swarms have been estimated at 2 million tonnes of krill spreading over more than 450 km². This means that many large animals such as seals, penguins and whales are able to tap the food chain close to the production of the phytoplankton before energy is lost, so the Antarctic supports a large population of these large animals.

In the 1970s attempts were made to fish for krill using fleets of boats with factory ships. Fortunately for the ecosystem, the krill do not store well and such attempts have been largely abandoned. However, krill numbers are thought to be declining, probably because of changes brought about by climate change.

▪ Link

You can find far more about krill and the food chain at:

www.coolantarctica.com.

Click on 'Site Map' and then select 'Krill' from 'Antarctica Animal Life'.

☑ 🗲 💡 *In this chapter you have learnt:*

- glaciations have affected the planet for billions of years

- over 20 major phases of glaciation have been identified, which appear to occur every 200 million to 250 million years

- the last glacial to affect Britain ended 10,000 years ago and the warmer interglacial we are currently experiencing will give way in time to a new glacial period

- glaciated regions are affected by ice which shapes pre-existing landscapes through the processes of erosion and deposition

- warm-based glaciers move by flow and sliding and are the most erosive; cold-based glaciers move by flow and because they are stuck to the rock floor they are relatively less erosive

- ice erodes because the rock debris that has been quarried from one part of the valley floor is trapped within the ice and abrades the valley lower downslope

- landforms of glacial deposition range from moraines deposited by the glacier and glacial till trapped beneath moving ice sheets, to outwash plains created by finer debris that has been distributed by meltwater

- periglacial regions experience very cold climates with a mean annual air temperature around 0°C and are characterised by permanently frozen ground

- cold environments are fragile and human interference may bring irreversible changes to these important habitats

- careful, sustainable development of Antarctic regions is necessary if the wilderness areas, with unique habitats and endangered communities, are to survive.

3 Coastal environments

The coastal system

In this section you will learn:

- how waves and tides interact with geology to create coastal landforms
- that weathering and mass movement combine with marine processes to transform coastal landforms
- to consider the relationship between people and changing coastal environments.

Activity

1 Study Figure 3.1.

   a Describe which areas are most likely to experience the greatest coastal changes in the future.

   b Speculate on how life may be affected. Draw a spidergram to help you consider the different ways in which life in Britain might change.

Key terms

Wavelength: the distance between two successive crests.

💡 We all recognise the shape of the UK. Over 13,000 km of shoreline define the edge of the country seen on countless maps. However, in geological terms, the familiar image is a relatively recent creation. Only 5000 years ago, as the sea level rose following the last ice age, the shape of Britain was very different. Animals and humans travelled by land bridge to the continent of Europe. As the sea rose, the coastline shifted as the land mass of Britain shrank. In 5000 years' time, with sea level rising at accelerated rates as a result of global warming, the location and extent of the coast will be very different again.

With some 25 million Britons living within 10 km of the coast, the rate at which the coastline changes is of real interest to the inhabitants of this country. In countries like Bangladesh, where more than 40 per cent of the land area is within 10 m of sea level, the changing nature of the coast is a matter of life or death. It is estimated that globally over 600 million people – one-tenth of the planet's entire population – live in coastal areas that lie within just 10 m of sea level.

The coast is a narrow zone where the land and the sea overlap. Coasts are perhaps the most varied and rapidly changing of landforms as this is the zone that witnesses the interaction of terrestrial, atmospheric and marine processes. In addition, human intervention on the coast has an increasing impact on the nature of our coastlines.

Waves

Waves are created by the action of wind on the surface of the sea. At any time, coasts may experience a combination of waves derived from local winds (sea), and those created by distant storms (swell) which may travel thousands of miles. Both types are created by the frictional drag of wind but locally generated waves are typified by steeper, shorter-period and higher-energy waveforms. Swell tends to exhibit less steep, longer-period and lower-energy waves.

The energy waves possess is determined by:

- **wind velocity** (wind speed)
- **duration** (period of time during which the wind blew)
- **fetch** (distance over which the wind blew).

The south-western peninsula of England is often exposed to westerly waves that may have originated thousands of kilometres away across the Atlantic Ocean. The south-eastern shore of England around Essex may be exposed to waves of very limited fetch given the smaller size of the North Sea and the proximity of mainland Europe.

Wave motion is confined to a depth of one **wavelength** in the open sea. Particles within the wave follow a circular orbit but do not actually change their position greatly; it is the energy in the shape of the

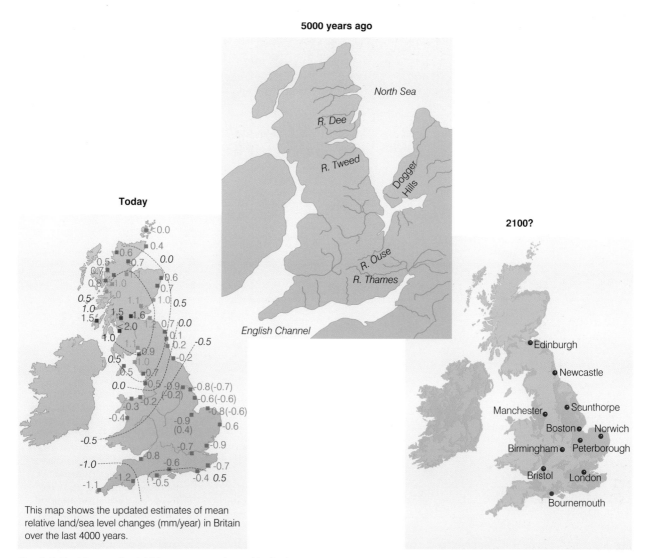

5000 years ago

Today

This map shows the updated estimates of mean relative land/sea level changes (mm/year) in Britain over the last 4000 years.

2100?

Fig. 3.1 *The UK coastline 5000 years ago, today and in the future*

waveform that moves. This is illustrated by the circular movement of the object in Figure 3.2. This orbital movement is affected by the shallowing of water and the relative rising of the sea floor as a wave approaches the coast. This causes wave height to increase and wave length to shorten as the coast nears, until the upper portion of the wave plunges or spills forward. The breaking wave is a translation of energy up the beach in the form of **swash**, a mass of foaming water. The return of this water back down the beach as a result of gravitational pull is known as **backwash**.

Breaking waves may be usefully divided into two types. **Constructive waves** are associated with swell and are characterised by longer wavelengths and lower height and **wave frequency**. The swash on these waves is greater than the backwash, as the spilling water has time to percolate into the beach. This results in sediment being added to the beach which the backwash cannot entirely remove, producing a gentle build-up of beach material. **Destructive waves** are more often associated with storm conditions and have a steeper, shorter wavelength with more frequent waves. As these waves plunge from the near vertical, they produce a strong backwash which is capable of moving sediment downslope and impeding incoming waves. The sediment that has been dragged off the beach will be deposited as a longshore or breakpoint bar.

Key terms

Wave frequency: the number of waves per minute.

Wave crest: the highest point of a wave.

Wave trough: the lowest point of a wave.

Wave steepness: the ratio of the wave height to the wave length (note that this cannot be steeper than 1:7 as this is when the wave breaks).

Wave period: the time taken for a wave to travel between one wave length.

Wave energy: $E \propto$ (is proportional to) LH^2 where L is wavelength and H is wave height. A small increase in wave height will result in a large increase in energy.

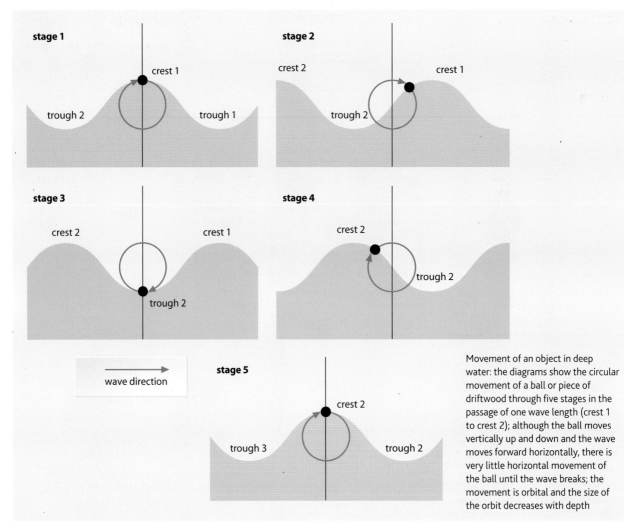

Movement of an object in deep water: the diagrams show the circular movement of a ball or piece of driftwood through five stages in the passage of one wave length (crest 1 to crest 2); although the ball moves vertically up and down and the wave moves forward horizontally, there is very little horizontal movement of the ball until the wave breaks; the movement is orbital and the size of the orbit decreases with depth

Fig. 3.2 *Circular movement of an object (e.g. a ball or piece of driftwood) through five stages in the passage of one wavelength (crest 1 to crest 2)*

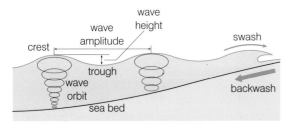

Fig. 3.3 *Swash and backwash*

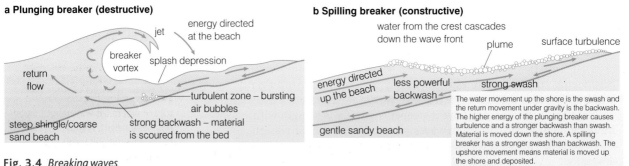

a Plunging breaker (destructive)

energy directed at the beach

jet

breaker vortex

splash depression

return flow

turbulent zone – bursting air bubbles

strong backwash – material is scoured from the bed

steep shingle/coarse sand beach

b Spilling breaker (constructive)

water from the crest cascades down the wave front

plume

surface turbulence

energy directed up the beach

less powerful backwash

strong swash

gentle sandy beach

The water movement up the shore is the swash and the return movement under gravity is the backwash. The higher energy of the plunging breaker causes turbulence and a stronger backwash than swash. Material is moved down the shore. A spilling breaker has a stronger swash than backwash. The upshore movement means material is moved up the shore and deposited.

Fig. 3.4 *Breaking waves*

Wave refraction

As waves approach the coastline, they leave deep water and are increasingly affected by frictional drag resulting from contact with the seabed. This causes them to gradually realign to become more parallel to the line of the coast. Where the coastline is irregular (see Figure 3.5), some parts of the wave will be slowed down by frictional contact (shallower water) and some will remain largely unimpeded (deeper water) and may move faster. Thus there is a concentration of **wave energy** on the headlands and dissipation of energy in the bays. The orthogonals (lines drawn at right angles to the crest) converge on the headlands and represent higher-energy waves but diverge in the bays and represent lower-energy waves.

Activity

2 Draw two annotated diagrams to show the relationships between the following terms for waves:

a wave crest, wave trough, wave steepness, wavelength and wave period

b swash and backwash, constructive and destructive waves.

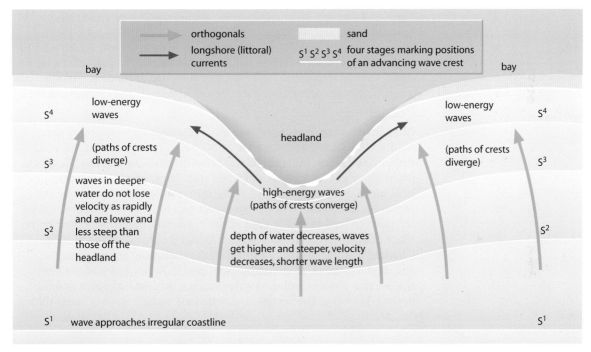

Fig. 3.5 *Wave refraction*

Sediment sources and cells

The coastal sediment or littoral cell system is a simplified model that examines coastal processes and patterns in a given area. Sources of sediment at the coast include coastal erosion, the sediment transported by rivers and the wind, the biogenic input (e.g. shells) and marine deposits transported either along the coast by longshore drift or onshore by tide and currents from offshore deposits (e.g. those left on the sea floor after the last ice age). Sediments may be lost to the coastal system if they are blown inland, transported offshore or removed by human action.

We may look at sediment cells at a variety of scales. There are 11 on the England and Wales coastline running around Britain from St Abb's Head on the north-east Scottish border to the Solway Firth in the west. A sediment cell is defined as a length of coastline that is relatively self-contained as far as the movement of sand or shingle is concerned, and where interruption to such movement should not have a significant effect on adjacent sediment cells. Each major littoral cell is divided into a number of sub-cells.

Did you know?

The Holderness coastline is part of a sediment cell that stretches from Flamborough Head to the Wash in East Anglia. The sediment movement is largely north–south to Spurn Head but elsewhere sub-cells may show local variations.

c Tides

Tides are regular rising and falling movements of the surface of the sea. They are caused by the effects of the gravitational pull of the moon and sun on the oceans. The moon has the greatest influence; although its gravitational pull is less than that of the sun, it is much closer. This pull creates an outward bulge in the oceans closest to the moon, and another on the other side of the Earth away from the moon. This creates the effect of high tide, whereas the draining of water from the intervening areas between these bulges manifests itself as low tides.

As the moon orbits the Earth every 29 days, the high tides follow the moon around the Earth. The tide cycle (the gap between the two peaks of high tide) is 12 hours and 25 minutes so there are approximately two high tides and two low tides per day. When the moon is between the Earth and the sun, their combined gravitional pull creates the biggest bulge of water and the highest tide or spring tide. At this time the high tides are at their highest and the low tides at their lowest, so the tidal range is at its greatest. When the Earth, moon and the sun form a right angle, their gravitational pulls interfere with one another and this is when neap tides occur, giving the lowest high tides and the highest low tides (smallest tidal range).

In reality this regular pattern of tides is significantly modified by the nature of the ocean bed, the proximity of land masses and the effect of the **Coriolis force**. Most significantly for the tides around the UK, places where there is a narrow neck of water usually experience the greatest local tidal range. For example, when water from the Atlantic Ocean and the North Sea are confined in the narrowest sections of the English Channel, the tide can be 6 m higher than in the open seas. In narrow estuaries the effect can be even more pronounced. When the tide rises in the Bristol Channel it is increasingly confined in the narrowing Severn estuary and a tidal range of 13 m can be experienced. At key times of the year this sudden rise and influx of water sends a tidal wall of water rushing upriver, known as the Severn bore, when a 1 m high wave of water moves

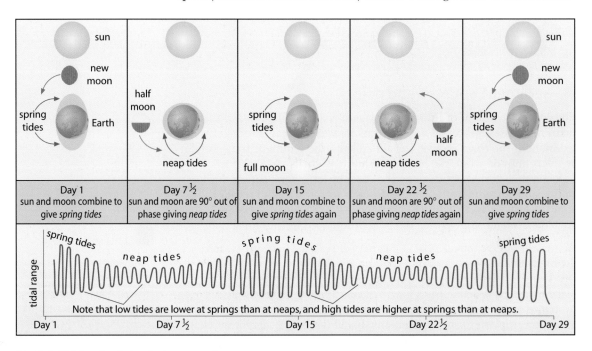

Fig. 3.6 *Tidal cycles during the lunar month*

upstream at 30 km per hour. Conversely, in almost landlocked seas such as the Mediterranean, the tidal range can be as little as 0.01 m as the Straits of Gibraltar are too narrow and shallow to allow for significant exchange between the Mediterranean Sea and the Atlantic Ocean.

The tidal range determines the vertical range of erosion and deposition and the length of time the littoral zone is exposed to subaerial weathering. The speed of the incoming and outgoing tides can also significantly affect scouring. Tidal ranges can be classified as:

- macrotidal = more than 4 m
- mesotidal = 2 to 4 m
- microtidal = less than 2 m.

The combined effect of high tides and the storm surges that may accompany intense low-pressure systems can result in enhanced erosion. The great storm of 1953 saw an intense low-pressure system produce a storm surge of between 2 m and 2.5 m on the east coast of the UK, and 3 m in the Netherlands. With waves added to this surge, sea defences were breached on either side of the southern part of the North Sea, leading to 264 deaths in south-east England and 1835 in the Netherlands (see the case study on pages 109–11).

 Activities

3 Define the terms spring tides, neap tides, tidal range and tidal bore.

4 Explain why tides are important in some areas of the coast.

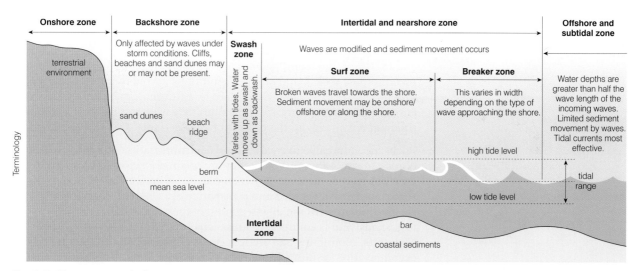

Fig. 3.7 *Shore zone terminology*

Coastal processes

Coastal zones are among the fastest-changing areas on the planet. The diverse nature of the UK coastline is in part explained by the varying geology and structure of the rocks exposed in the narrow coastal strip that surrounds Britain. The presence of harder and softer rock helps to explain why some areas are characterised by towering cliffs while others present gently sloping bays. Sedimentation adds to this picture, creating landforms such as beaches, mudflats and dunes where deposition rather than erosion appears to shape the coastline. In reality the processes that shape our coasts are complex and interrelated. The landforms we see are the result of the interaction of these processes with the geology over time. These processes do not act equally on all parts of the coast at any given time and their influences change over time.

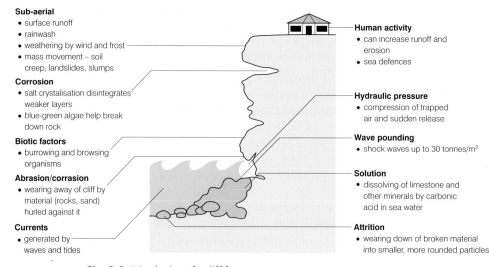

Sub-aerial
- surface runoff
- rainwash
- weathering by wind and frost
- mass movement – soil creep, landslides, slumps

Corrosion
- salt crystalisation disintegrates weaker layers
- blue-green algae help break down rock

Biotic factors
- burrowing and browsing organisms

Abrasion/corrasion
- wearing away of cliff by material (rocks, sand) hurled against it

Currents
- generated by waves and tides

Human activity
- can increase runoff and erosion
- sea defences

Hydraulic pressure
- compression of trapped air and sudden release

Wave pounding
- shock waves up to 30 tonnes/m^2

Solution
- dissolving of limestone and other minerals by carbonic acid in sea water

Attrition
- wearing down of broken material into smaller, more rounded particles

Fig. 3.8 *Weathering of a cliff face*

Subaerial weathering

All slopes are subject to constant change whether they are near the coast or not. Some movements are slow (like soil creep) whereas others are rapid (rockfall). For these mass movements to occur, the underlying rocks must be weakened by the processes of subaerial weathering. Most rocks are formed at great depth at high temperatures (e.g. igneous and metamorphic rocks) and/or great pressure (igneous and some metamorphic rocks), and often in conditions devoid of water or oxygen. When they are exposed at the surface by earth movements, they are in entirely different conditions to the ones they were formed in. They look solid but are already in the process of change – they are breaking down.

Rocks are vulnerable to weathering, the disintegration and decomposition of rock in situ – that is, where they are originally exposed. Weathering does not require movement of material, but it does create material that is more easily eroded and transported elsewhere. Physical weathering involves the disintegration of rock into smaller particles (e.g. sands) and is common in areas largely free from vegetation, such as deserts, mountains and arctic regions. Chemical weathering involves decomposition resulting from chemical change. Typically, rock-forming minerals break down releasing elements to produce new minerals that are more stable in the new conditions at the Earth's surface. Some are soluble whereas others form clays which are weaker minerals than the ones they replace. Chemical processes dominate in warmer, moist climates associated with good vegetation cover and they tend to operate to a greater depth than physical weathering processes.

Freeze–thaw is the process whereby water repeatedly freezes and melts within joints/cracks in rocks in areas where the **diurnal range** hovers around 0°C, e.g. in the Scottish Highlands. As water expands by about 9 per cent in volume on turning into ice, pressure is exerted on the surrounding rock then is subsequently released when the ice thaws. With repeated fluctuations in pressure, fragments of rock may break off (**frost shattering**) and produces and scree or talus slopes beneath exposed rock faces.

Pressure release occurs when jointed rocks have the pressure of any overburden removed and expansion can further open up joints/cracks to weathering. This can be seen in the granite tors of south-west England, and sea cliffs where rocks are exposed and do not have support from surrounding rocks.

Key terms

Diurnal range: the difference between the lowest temperature and the highest temperature in a 24-hour period.

Solution: the dissolving action of water on rocks, particularly carbonate rocks such as limestone.

Acid rain: a broad term used to describe several ways that acids fall out of the atmosphere. A more precise term is acid deposition, which has two parts: wet and dry.

Biological weathering refers to weathering resulting from organic agents. These may be tree roots growing into and physically widening joints, or animals burrowing. For example, rabbits have burrowed into weaker periglacial head deposits off Start Point in Devon. The secretions of molluscs, sponges and sea urchins can also weather exposed rocks in the tidal zone, particularly in low-energy coastal environments.

Chemical weathering tends to occur where there is alternate wetting and drying and/or towards the bottom of slopes where material and moisture often accumulate.

- **Oxidation** – where rocks are exposed to oxygen in the air or water, e.g. where ferrous iron is changed by the addition of oxygen into the ferric state and appears a rusty colour.
- **Hydration** – where rocks that may include salts absorb water and swell, making them more susceptible to decomposition. This is most effective where there are alternating phases of wetting and drying such as may be found in intertidal zones.
- **Hydrolysis** – a common form of weathering leading to decomposition. The H^+ and OH^- ions in water combine with ions in the mineral and result in minerals like feldspar (found in granite) breaking down and producing a weaker clay such as kaolinite (china clay).
- **Carbonation** – carbon dioxide in solution found in rainwater produces carbonic acid (H_2CO_3). This attacks the calcium carbonate found in limestones and many other rocks, with the the soluble product being washed away. As limestone is often a well-jointed and well-bedded rock, the prolonged exposure of the joints and cracks to weak carbonic acid results in distinctive landforms.
- **Solution** – the dissolving action of water on rocks.
- **Organic weathering** – humic acids derived from plant decay contain important elements such as calcium, magnesium and iron which are released by a process known as chelation.
- **Acid rain** – human activities have released large amounts of carbon dioxide, sulphur dioxide and nitrous oxide into the atmosphere, which may form acids in solution in rainwater. Limestones and sandstones containing calcium-rich cements are vulnerable to accelerated weathering from these acids.

Link

For more on acid rain, see Chapter 7.

Mass movement

Weathered rocks exposed in coastal zones are susceptible to mass movements.

Soil creep is the slowest form of mass movement (less than 1 cm per year) and is propagated by three main mechanisms. Raindrop impact in intense storms may cause a splash of soil particles. Those particles that fall on the downslope side fall further, resulting in net downslope movement. Wet periods add additional moisture to soil particles which swell upon wetting, expand and fall slightly downhill under gravity when the soil dries. Freeze–thaw affects soil during colder times when the expansion of water in the soil by 9 per cent on freezing heaves particles up at right angles to the slope. On thawing, the particles fall down under gravity and thus move slowly downhill.

Solifluction occurs mainly in tundra areas where soils are often frozen for around nine months of the year and where vegetation is sparse. When the topsoils thaw in the brief summer months, the additional water (frozen soils at depth preclude percolation) and lack of vegetation to hold the saturated soil together leads to a flowing active layer.

saturated material at foot may flow and form a lobate structure but this will be removed by waves in coastal areas

curved rupture surface

Fig. 3.9 *Rotational slumping on the Holderness coast*

Earthflows and mudflows

These are faster movements (5 to 15 km per year) than soil creep and occur on steeper slopes (5° to 15°) which have become saturated. They produce bulging lobes of soil. Mudflows are faster than earthflows and are most likely to be found on unconsolidated material after very heavy rainfall.

Slides and slumps

Whereas flows are characterised by a chaotic internal structure, slides largely retain their internal structure and move as a large mass. Slumps occur where the movement appears to have a rotational element to it and may produce a curved rupture surface (see Figure 3.9). Cliffs formed of relatively weak and/or impermeable rocks such as clays are susceptible to rotational slumping after prolonged rainfall as the raising of the water table underground reduces the internal friction of particles and facilitates failure. Although slumped masses may have some internal cohesion, the highly saturated toe or frontal lobe of the slump may flow as it approaches the foot of the slope or cliff.

Rockfall

Rockfalls are rapid though relatively rare movements and are found where slopes exceed 40°. They may result from extremes of physical or chemical weathering and they produce debris slopes beneath the cliff as the material from the rockfall disintegrates at the cliff foot.

All these mass movements are exacerbated by the agents of marine erosion, which may increase the instability of slopes by undermining them.

Runoff

Runoff has the ability to move fine material downslope, particularly where overland flow occurs as a thin continuous layer (sheet flow) and washes silt and clay-sized particles. This is best seen in areas where there is little vegetation to anchor soil particles or impede the flow of runoff. Some material will also be removed in solution.

Marine erosion

In addition to the subaerial processes that affect the coast, the shoreline is exposed to agents of marine erosion.

Rates of coastal erosion are determined in part by the processes of marine erosion acting on the coast, the geology and structure of the rocks exposed at the coast, and the amount and nature of the beach sediment.

Waves and beaches

Waves that break at the foot of the cliff are likely to cause most erosion, whereas those that break earlier dissipate a lot of energy before they reach the cliff. Steeper, high-energy waves are more powerful and are often linked to a longer fetch which allows for a greater build-up of energy. Steeply shelving beaches give way to deeper water offshore, which allows waves to approach the cliff foot unimpeded, generating higher, steeper waves. Beaches act as buffers between the waves and the land and are in dynamic equilibrium, reflecting the balance between the supply of sediment from eroded material (both local and transported from elsewhere) and the removal of sediment along the coast or offshore. The composition of the beach also has a significant effect. Sandy beaches tend to exhibit lower gradients than shingle beaches. The coarser particle size of the shingle permits higher rates of infiltration, thereby reducing backwash, which over time results in more sediment being moved up the beach than is dragged back down. Finer sands permit less infiltration of backwash and over time more sediment is carried down the beach.

Geology

Generally, marine erosion occurs more rapidly where the sea is in contact with weaker rocks (e.g. at Holderness glacial tills have eroded by 120 m in 100 years) rather than hard rocks (e.g. granite at Land's End, 0.1 m in 100 years). However, the structure and dip of the rocks must also be taken into account. Where strata lie horizontally or are almost vertical in attitude, steep cliffs tend to develop. Where beds dip towards the sea, undercutting by waves acting on the base of the cliff may cause slippage of strata so that the eventual angle of the cliff is closely related to the dip of the beds.

Human activity

The development of coastlines by people, including the building of houses, reclamation of marginal land and extraction of sediments, disturbs the dynamic equilibrium of coastal systems. This occurs most obviously when human activity impedes natural erosion or obstructs the supply of sediment to the coast. The natural protection of the coast at the fishing village of Hallsands in Devon was unintentionally reduced when a shingle beach was lowered by 5 m in 1913 to supply 670,000 tonnes of material for the construction of a new naval dockyard at Devonport, near Plymouth. Severe storms in 1917 meant that huge waves were able to cross the reduced shingle bar unimpeded. They attacked the cliff on which the village of Hallsands stood. The resulting collapse of the cliff left only half of the village intact and it was later abandoned. The cliff retreated by 6 m over 50 years.

Sea walls and coastal defences – it is increasingly thought that such structures may exacerbate erosion in nearby unprotected areas. Wave energy that might have been dissipated by eroding cliffs and transporting material is reflected by such structures, leaving more energy available to attack the coast elsewhere.

Land reclamation – for centuries, land that was once sea has been drained and/or infilled to create new land for farming and construction. Dutch engineers helped to drain the East Anglian fens to create rich farming land, but the land is only protected from the sea by extensive drainage systems and sea walls.

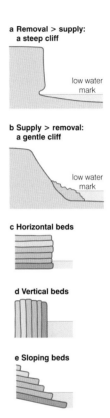

a Removal > supply: a steep cliff

low water mark

b Supply > removal: a gentle cliff

low water mark

c Horizontal beds

d Vertical beds

e Sloping beds

Fig. 3.10 *The effect of geology on coastal erosion*

Activity

5 Using what you have read so far, draw and annotate a concept map to explain how natural and human influences contribute to the likelihood of coastal erosion.

Development – development of cliff tops in particular affects the natural drainage of the land. New housing increases runoff, and there are often issues regarding saturation and subsequent instability of soil and weaker rocks which can lead to cliff failure. For example, at Charmouth on the Dorset coast, bungalows built in the 1960s required a local stream to be culverted and directed to a soakaway. This saturated the solifluction (head) deposits, which then slid over the silty clay strata beneath and led to rates of cliff retreat of up to 5 m per year until the land was stabilised.

Landforms of erosion

Although any rocks being eroded by the sea may produce headlands and bays to some degree, it is where rocks of varying degrees of resistance are found that preferential erosion of the softer beds leads to the creation of **headlands** (where the more resistant rocks are located) and **bays** (indicating the presence of weaker beds). These inherent differences are subsequently moderated by the action of the waves. Once created, headlands are more vulnerable to wave erosion as refraction concentrates wave action here and erosion dominates over deposition. In the bays, however, dissipation of wave energy occurs as the wave crests are extended over a wider area leading to more deposition than erosion.

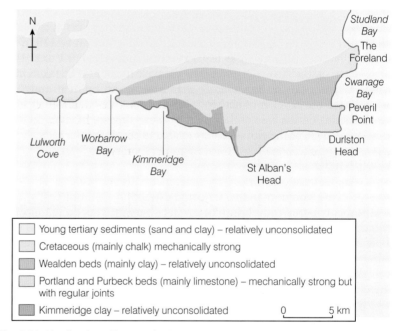

Fig. **3.11** *Headlands and bays on the Dorset coast*

Geos, caves, blow holes, arches and stacks

The action of marine erosion on jointed and bedded rocks such as limestone and chalk tends to enlarge any zones of weakness like joints and faults. Where erosion excavates enough material along a joint or plane of weakness, a steep-sided inlet may form called a **geo**. If this inlet continues to extend into the cliff, a **cave** will form. If this develops further, there may be collapse of overlying rocks and a **blow hole** can develop as the cave is opened up to the sky. Where the erosion continues at right angles to a headland, caves and arches can cut through the headland and eventually **stacks** may form.

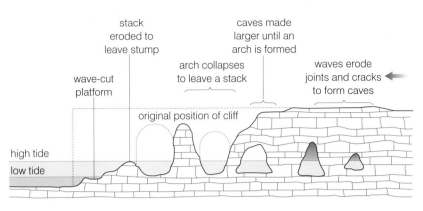

Fig. 3.12 *The formation of caves, arches, stacks and stumps at a headland*

Wave-cut platforms

The retreat of cliff lines occurs when breaking waves at the foot of
a cliff produce a wave-cut notch. As it develops, the overlying beds
are undermined and eventually collapse. The base of the notch thus
migrates inland, leaving a remnant of the cliff as a wave-cut platform
with a low slope of less than 4°, which is often only fully exposed at low
tide. Although these platforms rarely extend more than a few hundred
metres, they do have a significant effect on the ability of waves to erode
the cliff base, because as the platform grows the waves have further to
travel in very shallow water. This means they tend to break earlier and
dissipate their energy before they can do great damage to the cliff, thereby
reducing rate of erosion of the headland and limiting the further growth
of the platform. There is some debate as to the origin of some wave-cut
platforms because the theory of their formation assumes that the sea level
remains constant for a considerable period of time. Some have suggested
that they are relict features formed many thousands of years ago, before
the last ice age, and merely modified by contemporary sea levels.

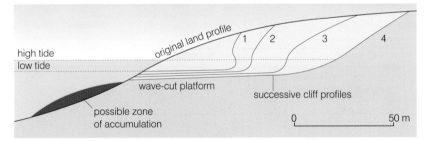

Fig. 3.13 *How a wave-cut platform is created*

Transportation

The swash and backwash on beaches is mainly responsible for the
movement of material up and down the beach profile, although in some
regions this is assisted by the power of the wind, particularly on dry sand.

Longshore drift (littoral drift)

Although refraction ensures that waves approaching a beach tend
towards a course aligned to the shore, a completely parallel approach is
rare. This is because the seabed influences the direction of wave travel
only in the last few hundred metres before the shore. In addition, the
variable nature of a coast with headlands and bays means that most
wave crests will be seen to strike the beach at an angle. The resultant

current is known as **longshore drift** or **littoral drift**, which is responsible for moving large amounts of sediment along the coast, usually in one direction. For example, the prevailing south-westerly winds and wave direction along the south coast of England mean that longshore drift is mainly from west to east. On the beach itself, an easily observed manifestation of the effect of waves breaking obliquely along the beach is the zigzag movement of material along the shore. The swash from waves breaking at an angle impels material up the beach at that oblique angle, but the greater influence on the backwash is gravity, which simply pulls material back down the beach at right angles to the shore. The net effect of these two movements is a lateral shift of material over time. Where removal along the coast by longshore drift exceeds supply of new sediment, beach erosion may occur. Because beaches are valued for many reasons, including protection for seafront towns and their amenity value, groynes have traditionally been built at right angles to the waterline. These wooden fence-like constructions help to slow down the effects of longshore drift, but by trapping additional sediment in one section of the shoreline they may starve another section further down the coast.

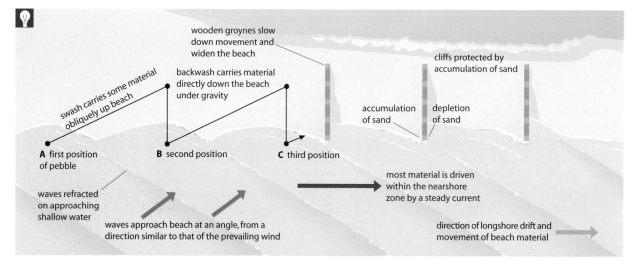

Fig. 3.14 *Longshore drift*

Fig. 3.15 *The cliffs at Flamborough Head*

■ Landforms of deposition

Landforms of deposition are most developed where sand and shingle accumulate faster than they are removed, particularly where lower-energy waves predominate or where coastal erosion provides an abundant supply of material to feed the beach-building processes.

Beaches

Beaches are a constantly changing buffer between the coast and the sea. They range from wide and flat to narrow and steep. They usually have three main components. Starting from offshore, these components are the nearshore (where the sea bed begins to affect the waves), the foreshore (intertidal or surf zone) and the backshore (usually above the waves). The backshore often represents the accumulation of material deposited by storm waves. The strong backwash on many sandy beaches leads to the development of **ridges** and **runnels** in the sand running parallel to the shoreline at the low-water mark. The runnels are disrupted by channels that help to drain the water down the beach.

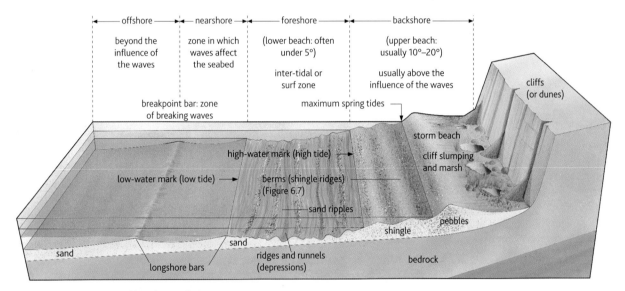

Fig. 3.16 *Wave zones and beach morphology*

The storm beach built up by strong swash during spring high tides consists of the largest-calibre material thrown up by the largest waves. They remain largely unmoved because subsequent tides cannot reach them. Beneath the storm ridge may be a series of ridges known as **berms**, which mark the successively lower high tides as the cycle goes from spring tide to neap tide. On beaches where there is a junction of the shingle and sand, cusps may form. These are semicircular depressions which form when waves break directly onto the beach and swash and backwash are strong. Once the curving shape is created, swash is concentrated in the small bay in the centre of the cusp, which produces a stronger backwash that removes material back down the beach. The cuspate form is further developed by the preferential deposition of rather coarser/heavier material on the horns of the cusps, perpetuating and enhancing the crescent shape. Ripples, developed on the sand by wave action and/or tidal currents, characterise the beach below this level.

Spits and bars

A spit is a long, narrow piece of sand or shingle that has one end joined to the mainland and projects out into the sea or part of the way across an estuary. Some spits are composite in nature, beginning with shingle and extending in sand. As shown in Figure 3.17, they all begin when there is a sudden change in the orientation of the coastline, because of an embayment or an estuary, for example. The prevailing winds may have generated a particular direction of longshore drift, e.g. west to east, but the change in orientation of the coast takes the beach sediment away from the land. As this material begins to project eastwards, storms build up more material, making the feature more substantial. Finer material is then carried further eastward, extending the feature into the deeper water of the estuary. However, the river channel runs deep through the middle of the estuary and this is an obstacle to further development of most spits. As its eastward progress stalls, the spit begins to curve round as wave refraction carries material round into the more sheltered water. Also, the second most dominant wind and wave direction may help to push the spit material back towards the shore. Several recurved ends may develop, reflecting the main secondary direction of the waves, but the eastward progress overall is maintained by the more frequent waves coming from the west. In the sheltered waters behind the spit, finer sediments can settle and begin to infill this area, which may herald the eventual development of a **saltmarsh** as the area is colonised. Where strong winds can lift sediment off the beach and spit and propel them inland, **dunes** may form, particularly where the additional stabilising influences of pioneer plants such as marram grass help to anchor the sand in place.

A bar or barrier island may form where there are changes in coastal direction but no estuary to break the sequence of sedimentation along the spit. If the spit develops to close off an embayment it may create a lagoon, in which case it is termed a **bar**. Where ridges of sand and shingle link the coast to an island they are called **tombolos** (e.g. Llandudno, north Wales). Where beach material is exposed to longshore drift in opposing directions, **cuspate forelands** may be generated, as at Dungeness in Sussex. In some parts of the eastern seaboard of the USA, barrier beaches have formed at various points between the Gulf of St Lawrence and Miami. These may have formed initially as offshore bars and been rolled inland by rising sea levels. Alternatively they may have

Link

For more on saltmarshes, see pages 98–99 and 124–125.

Activities

7   Distinguish between spits, bars and tombolos.

8   Suggest why barrier islands are uncommon around the UK.

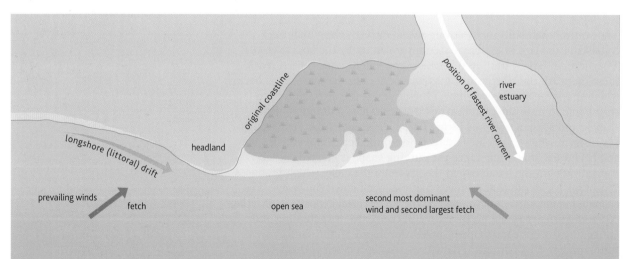

Fig. 3.17 *Formation of a spit*

begun as beach ridges or dunes that became separated from the mainland by rising sea levels. Despite being vulnerable to Atlantic storms, they are widely used by people for desirable residential developments.

Sand dunes

Dunes are concentrations of mound-like landforms composed of sand that has been blown off the beach by onshore winds. Where sufficient sand is deposited in the intertidal zone it may, on drying out, be blown up the beach by **saltation** (bounced along the surface). This is most likely where there is a large tidal range and a gently sloping sandy beach. The sequence of sand dune development is as follows:

▓ Initially sand may become trapped by debris towards the back of the beach, for example on a high berm or storm beach. The sand has a high pH (carbonate from seashells) and is not moisture retentive, so only very hardy pioneer plants such as lyme grass can colonise at this stage.

▓ The first dunes to develop are known as **embryo** dunes. Grasses such as sea couch, lyme and marram survive here because they grow upwards through accumulating wind-blown sand, stabilising the surface. These robust species have advantages such as the ability to spread underground via rhizomes (marram), succulent leaves to store water (sea couch) and deep tap roots to reach down for water. All these plants add organic matter to the dunes, aiding water retention and making the environment more hospitable for later plants.

Table 3.1 *Dune system data*

	Ⓐ Embryo	Ⓑ Foredunes or yellow dunes	Ⓒ Grey dunes and dune ridges	Ⓓ Wasting dunes with blowouts
Dune height (m)	1	5	8 to 10	6 to 8
Percentage of exposed sand	80	20	less than 10	over 40 on dunes
Humus and moisture content	very little, mixed salt and fresh water	some humus, very little moisture, fresh water	humus increases inland, water content still low, fresh water	high humus, brackish water in slacks
pH	over 8	slightly alkaline	increasingly acid inland: pH 6.5 to 7	acid: pH 5 to 6
Plant types	sand couch, lyme grass	marram, xerophytic species	creeping fescue, sea spurge, some marram, cotton grass and heather	heather, gorse on dunes, *Juncus* in slacks

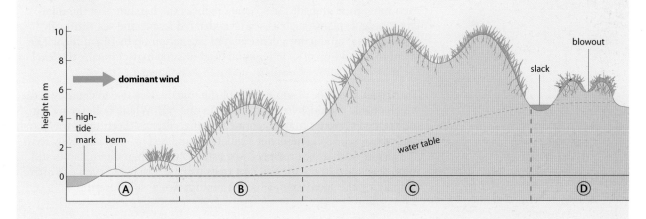

Fig. 3.18 *Cross-section of a dune system*

■ As the embyo dunes grow they develop into bigger foredunes (yellow dunes), which are initially yellow (sand colour) but darken to grey as decaying plants add humus to the soil over time.

■ Further colonisation by new species allows the dunes inland (grey dunes and dune ridges) to become more fixed. As the soil receives more organic material, the nutrient supply and water retention improve and the microclimate is more congenial to plants that could not tolerate the early dune conditions. For example, lichens, mosses and flowering plants begin to appear along with red fescue grass, creeping willow and dewberry.

■ Depressions between the dune ridges may develop into **dune slacks**, which are damper areas where the water table is closest to the surface. Here mosses, reeds, rushes and willows will thrive if there is enough moisture.

■ Behind the yellow and grey dunes, very little new sand is added from the beach, so these wasting dunes and dune heath exhibit smaller dune features. Plants such as heather, gorse, broom and buckthorn can thrive here as the soil is more acidic, humus-rich and water retentive. In time the rear of the dune system may be colonised by pine, birch and oak, which are the first steps to the development of the type of woodland that in time could reflect the climatic climax vegetation for the British Isles. Where a succession of stages of plant growth develops, from colonisation of bare sand to climax vegetation, it is called a **psammosere**. If specific trees are planted or if sheep/cattle graze the area then it will not follow all the stages of development to a true climatic climax for the area, but will be at a substage (stalled by human interference) called a **plagioclimax**. Where wind is funnelled through areas and removes the sand, blowouts may be found which, if they are not stabilised, can mean that significant volumes of sand are lost.

Saltmarshes

Saltmarshes may occur in sheltered river estuaries or behind spits. In these areas of intertidal mudflats, vegetation will develop and in time begin to colonise the silts and muds. Initially the mudflats are colonised by eelgrass, for example, which serves to slow water down and trap more sediment. Pioneer plants that can tolerate these conditions in this salty environment, which is submerged at high tide (**halophytes**) include glasswort, sea blite and spartina. Spartina was introduced to Britain and has become the dominant vegetation on tidal flats as it grows all year round. It has a root system that secures the plant at the surface and anchors it in up to 2 m of sediment, at the same time further slowing the tidal flow and trapping even more mud and silt. As spartina reduces the harshness of the tidal environment, plants such as sea lavender, red fescue and sea thrift can also colonise, producing a dense mat of vegetation up to 15 cm high. The additional build-up of sediment and dead organic matter means the level of the marsh can grow upwards at up to 25 mm per year.

The irregular profile of some areas of the marsh gives rise to creek systems which enable the tidal waters to come in and out. Where hollows are cut off, trapped seawater may evaporate, leaving saltpans. Eventually the marsh rises above sea level and is not regularly inundated by seawater. Now reeds and rushes such as sea rush become established. When the marsh is still more developed, moisture-tolerant trees like alder, ash and even oak arrive, completing the succession, which is now known as a **halosere**.

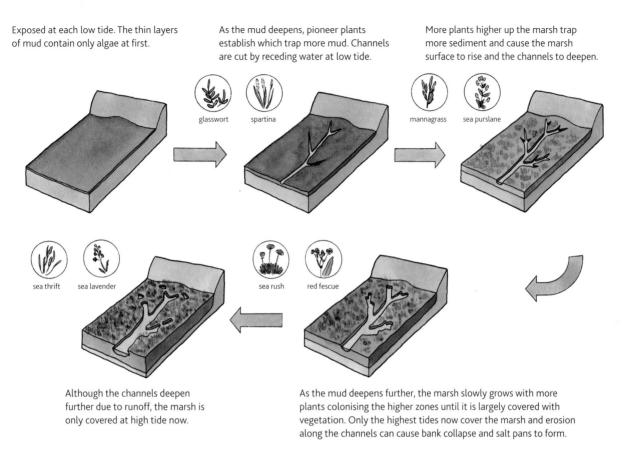

Exposed at each low tide. The thin layers of mud contain only algae at first.

As the mud deepens, pioneer plants establish which trap more mud. Channels are cut by receding water at low tide.

More plants higher up the marsh trap more sediment and cause the marsh surface to rise and the channels to deepen.

glasswort   spartina

mannagrass   sea purslane

sea thrift   sea lavender

sea rush   red fescue

Although the channels deepen further due to runoff, the marsh is only covered at high tide now.

As the mud deepens further, the marsh slowly grows with more plants colonising the higher zones until it is largely covered with vegetation. Only the highest tides now cover the marsh and erosion along the channels can cause bank collapse and salt pans to form.

Fig. 3.19 *The sequence of saltmarsh development*

Skills

Sampling techniques

Dune systems offer many opportunities for fieldwork as they can generate reliable 'hard' data. It is important to consider the purpose of your data collection before you begin. Think about:

- what data you need for your study
- how you are going to record the information you collect
- which method of sampling you will use (random, systematic or stratified).

Random sampling

This is the most accurate method as it shows no bias. A sample is chosen using random numbers known as number tables. There are three ways of using random numbers: point, line and area (see Figure 3.20). In random point sampling, a grid is placed over the area of the map, and points are identified and plotted on the grid. In random line sampling, numbers are used to obtain two ends of a line. In random area sampling, areas of constant size are obtained using random numbers.

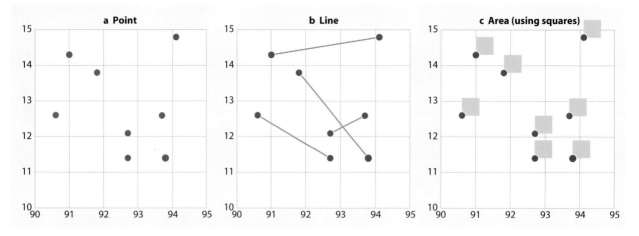

Fig. 3.20 *Random sampling using point, line and area techniques*

Systematic sampling

This involves selecting values in a regular way, e.g. in a 500 m transect you might sample at 50 m intervals. Like random sampling, it can be carried out by using points, lines or areas (see Figure 3.21). Although this method is quick and easy to use, some bias or selection is involved, which might result in features being missed.

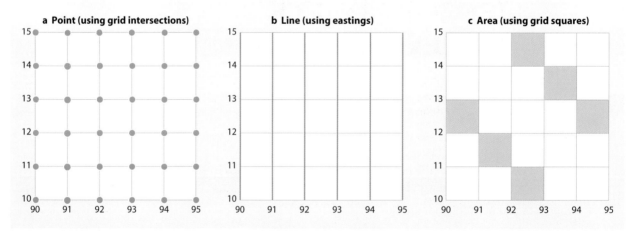

Fig. 3.21 *Systematic sampling using point, line and area techniques*

Stratified sampling

Stratified sampling is more complex and involves dividing the sample into categories (strata) and sampling within each using random or systematic point, line or area techniques. Figure 3.22 shows the distribution of a particular plant species on two contrasting soil types. Sandy soil occupies 60 per cent of the total area and humus-rich 40 per cent. To find out whether the proportion of the plant species cover varies with soil type, the sampling must be in proportion to their relative extents. Thus if a sample size of 30 points is obtained using random numbers, 18 are needed within the sandy area (18 is 60 per cent of 30) and 12 within the humus-rich area (12 is 40 per cent of 30). This method of sampling is useful as it can be carried out randomly or systematically, but take care to select appropriate strata.

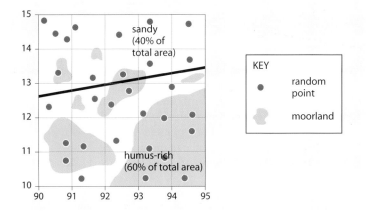

Fig. 3.22 *A random point sample, stratified by area*

■ Case study

Coastal erosion at Holderness

Hull and East Riding Mail

CLIFF-TOP COUPLE LIVING ON THE EDGE

For one couple, the new year offers little hope for a lifeline. Colin and Josephine Arnold have spent the past year demolishing their beloved coastal farmhouse in Ulrome, near Skipsea, as the tide continues to eat away the cliff on which it stands. Unable to afford the cost of paying East Riding Council to demolish the 150-year-old Cliff Farm, the Arnolds have been demolishing the property by hand.

Mr Arnold, 62, said the coastal erosion had slowed down in recent months, but the couple were still facing a bleak future. He said: 'We need to find somewhere else to go, but we just haven't got any real options. That's the sum of the problem. At the moment we have no choice but to stay put and see what happens.'

The couple bought the seaside property 20 years ago for £10,000. When they moved into Cliff Farm there was 70ft of land between the house and the edge of the cliff. Now there is less than 10ft.

All that is left of the once proud farmhouse is a few back rooms and a static caravan nearby, where the Arnolds now live. Having spent a year demolishing their home, the couple have called a temporary halt on the back-breaking work.

'We've lost about two metres of land in the past six months, but the weather's been kind this winter so not too much more has gone recently,' said Mr Arnold. 'We've demolished as much of the house as we can at the moment, and are just holding out for as long as we can. It's just exhausting work.'

The couple's one hope is that steps may be taken by the council and the Government towards a compensation package for victims of coastal erosion. While money would not save their home, financial aid would help the couple relocate and start a new chapter in their lives. But for now, the Arnolds are once again bracing themselves for an uncertain future. 'It's a long slog,' said Mr Arnold. 'We are always having to look over our shoulders.'

Hull and East Riding Mail, *28 December 2007*

Link

For a film of the Easington coast, go to:

www.hull.ac.uk/coastalobs/easington.

The Holderness coast is one of the fastest-eroding areas in Britain. From the resistant chalk headland of Flamborough in the north of the region to the vulnerable spit of Spurn Head in the south, the evidence of erosion is clear.

The landforms that remained following the retreat of the ice sheets 10,000 years ago initially determined the nature of the Holderness coastline. To the north around Flamborough Head the chalk with rare flint beds creates a promontory deeply indented in parts by erosion along faultlines and bedding planes. As can be seen in Figure 3.24, the spectacular evidence of erosion here belies the fact that this is one of the more resistant parts of the Holderness coastline. The article on page 101 refers to the unstable nature of the unconsolidated till deposits that lie above the chalk and which may slide when saturated. However, the debris from the chalk cliffs is chalk and highly soluble. Surprisingly little of it travels very far south to protect the more southerly parts of the Holderness coast.

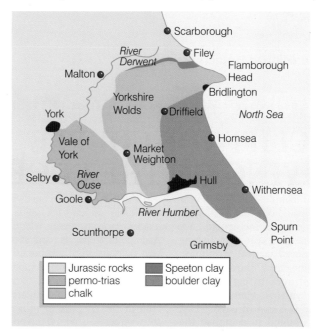

Fig. 3.23 *Geology of the East Yorkshire coast*

The majority of this coastline is made of glacial till. These structurally weak clays were laid down underneath the ice and today are prone to saturation and failure, typically rotational slumping. Historical records suggest the cliffs are eroding at a rate of 1.5 to 2 m per year on average.

Despite the loss of at least 30 villages since Roman times, cliff-top development has continued until the present time, creating the need for regular maintenance of coastal defences, mainly around settlements. The East Yorkshire coastline is undergoing a north–south drift of sediment as tides in the southern North Sea flow southwards and storms from the north-east tend to be the most powerful. Where a beach exists that is sufficient to absorb the wave energy without affecting any exposed clay surfaces, relatively little damage is done. Long-term change occurs where the beach is worn away and the underlying clay substrate is removed. Once this has happened, the clay cannot be replaced and change is more permanent. The long-term result is that the whole coast is gradually

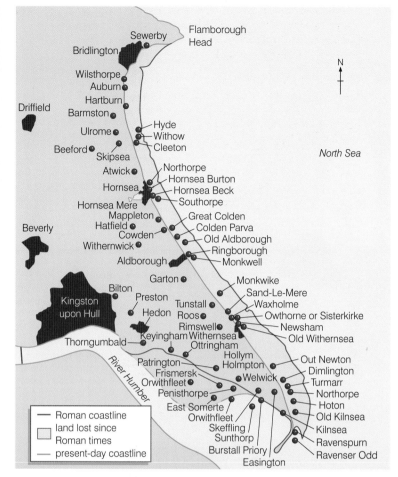

Fig. 3.24 *The lost villages of East Yorkshire*

attempting to develop a shape that lies at right angles to the predominant north-easterly wave direction.

Initially the relatively resistant chalk cliffs of Flamborough formed the only such hard point to protect the coast from the forces of the sea but they have since been supplemented by various manmade defensive frontages. These have concentrated on existing settlements, e.g. Hornsea (pop. 8300) and Withernsea (pop. 6000) and key communications or amenities, e.g. the gas terminals at Easington.

Although rising sea levels and the relatively weak nature of the cliff materials largely explain the physical reason behind the rapid erosion, there may also be some human contributions. A contentious issue in relation to sediment flow and coastal erosion is the dredging of aggregates offshore. During 2000, 3,811,044 tonnes of material were removed under seven licences and, although any links between dredging and coastal erosion are arguable given the distances offshore where the dredging takes place, there are some concerns that there may be unlicensed dredging going on closer to the shore.

As the adjacent undefended coastlines recede, the fixed 'defensive' points (see Figure 3.25) gradually project further seawards. The ever-increasing obstacles to the free flow of sediment help to retain sand on beaches to the north and, as beaches reorient themselves parallel to incoming waves, a wide bay shape is created. It is thought

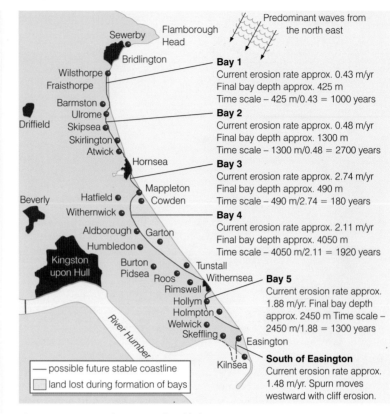

Fig. 3.25 *Managed retreat and stable bays*

that these 'stable' beaches will reduce the rates of future erosion. However, these bays may take 500 to 1000 years to develop and they involve considerable modification of the coastline. Defended villages and towns may lead to the formation of such stabilised bays, suggesting a means by which future erosion can ultimately be controlled, but they may in turn become headlands upon which wave energy will concentrate. The cost of maintaining them may then become unsustainable.

The socio-economic impacts of coastal erosion on settlements are significant and far-reaching. Properties at threat from erosion lose their value long before they may fall into the sea, leaving owners with negative equity – that is, their houses are worth considerably less than the amount of money they paid for them or still owe on their mortgages. Many of these settlements rely heavily on tourism and, should they be left undefended, their trade would diminish as facilities close down. With little or no new investment to sustain local communities, they would not be able to maintain viable populations to warrant schools and shops. The loss of jobs makes the drift of younger people away from these towns and villages more likely.

Spurn Point

The balance between physical and human influences on coastal development is well illustrated by Spurn Point. Development of the first peninsula at Spurn began following the retreat of the last ice age. The subsequent flooding of the North Sea basin about 6000 years ago exposed the newly created glacial tills to the sea and the cliffs soon began to erode. The longshore drift of sediment eroded from further up the coast built the spit out across what is now the Humber estuary. The tip of Spurn is protected by hard glacial

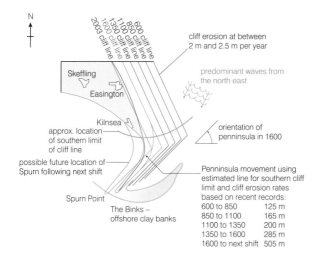

cliff erosion at between
2 m and 2.5 m per year

predominant waves from
the north east

orientation of
penninsula in 1600

approx. location
of southern limit
of cliff line

possible future location of
Spurn following next shift

Spurn Point

The Binks –
offshore clay banks

Penninsula movement using
estimated line for southern cliff
limit and cliff erosion rates
based on recent records:

600 to 850	125 m
850 to 1100	165 m
1100 to 1350	200 m
1350 to 1600	285 m
1600 to next shift	505 m

Fig. 3.26 *The realignment of Spurn Point*

deposits and, inside this protective rim, sand dunes have created an island. This island is connected to the mainland by a beach. The island was originally connected to the mainland by a shingle beach, creating a moving causeway. The shingle was removed in the 18th and 19th centuries to be used as ballast for whaling ships. The removal of shingle caused the ridge to erode more rapidly and it subsequently had to be protected by groynes and sea walls. However, the fixing of the spit at key points has only served to accentuate the attack elsewhere and the ridge has now been eroded into a narrow strip that is out of line with both the mainland and the island. It is likely that the crumbling defences and ever-narrowing neck – as little as 10 m wide in places – will soon fail. Breaches will then become common as erosion continues to lower foreshore levels, allowing the area to flood at each high tide. Ultimately, the spit will be no more and Spurn will be left as an island.

It has been suggested, following study of historical records, that this destruction and rebirth follows a 250-year cycle; the last cycle ended in the mid-1800s. The defences built then and subsequently have prolonged the life of a landform that today is home to a small community based around the lifeboat station. This is the only permanently manned station the RLNI has in the UK, which reflects its importance as a base from which the Humber pilots guide ships through the busiest estuaries in Britain. The only link to the mainland is a narrow road under constant threat from the sea. In 1961 the decision was taken, following escalating maintenance costs, to abandon the defences and allow natural processes to take control once again.

Question

1 You work for the Environment Agency and have been given the responsibility of writing to the people of the village of Atwick on the Holderness coast to explain to them that under the 'roll back plan' their village will in future not be defended. At the current time the retreating sea cliffs are less than 2 km away. Use any of the information in this case study to write a letter of no more than 300 words persuading them that there are strong geographical reasons to withdraw the option of coastal defences.

Link

Some good images of Spurn Point can be seen at:

www.spurnpoint.com.

Select 'Photograph album'.

See the section on 'Sediment sources and cells' on page 85.

AQA Examiner's tip

To achieve higher grades in extended answers, you often need to demonstrate the ability to consider a different point of view. You will spend a lot of time trying to explain the most likely answer as concisely as possible. But when command words such as *discuss*, *evaluate* or *justify* are used in the question, they often signal the need for more extended writing. You must show that you have considered other viewpoints as well as deriving your own. Explore the pros and cons of various options and the way different interested parties may see the same solutions or outcomes differently. What is sometimes required is a form of persuasive writing that uses evidence to support arguments, considers how contributing factors are linked and explains why the conclusion reached or the option chosen is not only valid but addresses the concerns of interested parties.

Sea level change

World sea level changes over time as a result of two major influences. The global water balance is fixed because the Earth is in effect a closed system. However, at different times the amount of water available to the world's oceans has fluctuated because of the amount of water locked into ice caps, and tectonic changes affecting the rise and fall of land masses. In geologically recent times, the world's sea level was lowest around 18,000 years ago during the last major ice age. The extent of ice was at its maximum and less water was able to reach the seas. This was an example of a **eustatic** fall in sea level. Around 10,000 years ago, as ice caps melted, there was eustatic rise in sea level. This was accompanied by a slower **isostatic** uplift as the mass of ice was lifted quite quickly from the Earth's surface and many land masses rose up as a result. This process is still operative in parts of the world today. A simple sequence of sea level changes may be summarised as follows:

1 Formation of glaciers and ice sheets produces a eustatic fall in sea level and a lowering of the world sea level.

2 Continued growth of ice sheets depresses the land surface under the ice and produces a relative isostatic rise in sea level which may moderate the eustatic fall in some areas.

3 As ice sheets begin to melt, a rapid eustatic rise in sea level occurs, with a positive change in base level.

4 As the ice sheets and glaciers continue to retreat, there is a buoyancy effect and the land springs back upwards in some areas. This isostatic uplift (isostatic readjustment) of the land formerly under ice sheets results in a local negative change in base level. For example, Scandinavia and Scotland are still rising by 4 to 20 mm a year. In addition to these isostatic rises, places like north-western Britain are rising at the same time as south-eastern England is sinking, owing to differences in their geological structure. Such local tilting (epeirogeny) has significant implications for coastal flooding in such areas.

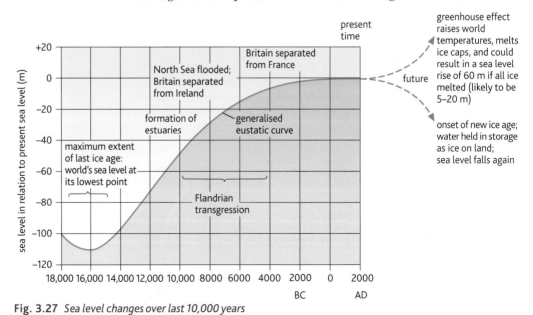

Fig. 3.27 *Sea level changes over last 10,000 years*

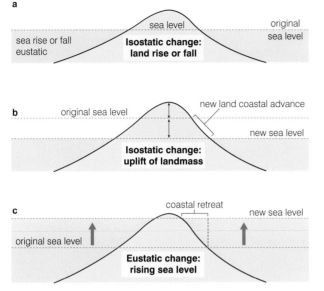

Fig. 3.28 *How isostatic and eustatic changes can create sea level changes*

Submergent features

The rise of sea level allows the sea to inundate land masses most easily in areas of low-lying land such as existing river valleys. Drowned river valleys, resulting from post-glacial rises in sea level, include most estuaries to some extent. **Rias** are formed when valleys in a dissected upland are submerged. They can be significant features and are characterised by deep water near the mouth and shallower water inland, for example the Dart estuary in Devon. **Dalmatian coasts** are a variation of rias which occur where local drainage patterns typically have rivers flowing almost parallel to the coast rather than at right angles to it. Such a coastline can be found in Croatia.

Fjords are formed by the drowning of glacial troughs and as a result are very deep, steep-sided inlets of the sea that typically maintain significant depth for a considerable way inland. Sometimes a glacial rock basin offers the deepest water where a glacier once overdeepened the valley. Fjords may be shallower at the mouth where a threshold marks where the glacier once exited the valley. These are evident in Scotland but are perhaps better exemplified in Norway, New Zealand and Chile, where flooded U-shaped glacial valleys produce extensive fjords with cliff-like valley sides. Glaciated lowland areas, for example Strangford Lough in Northern Ireland, may be inundated by water in a similar way to fjords but the effect is a wider, more gentle-sided feature called a **fjard**.

Emergent features

In areas where isostatic readjustment, especially following the removal of ice, results in the land rising relative to the sea, landforms of marine deposition or erosion may be lifted above the influence of the waves that originally created them. **Raised beaches** are former wave-cut beaches and their associated beaches which are now raised up above current sea level. On the west coast of Scotland, for example Arran, where these relict beaches are not uncommon, remains of the eroded cliff line may be found behind the raised beach, still displaying recognisable features of marine erosion, such as wave-cut notches and caves. Subaerial weathering and the lack of marine erosion means that weathered debris collects at the cliff foot and produces gentler slopes over time. On the Isle of Arran,

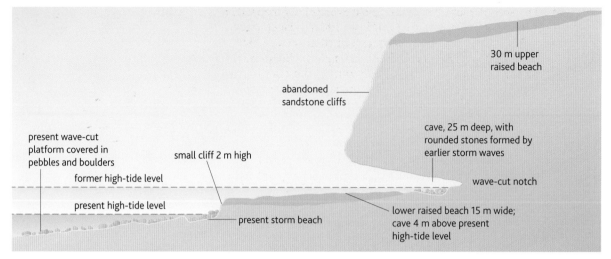

Fig. 3.29 *Raised beaches, Arran*

Activities

9 Explain the terms eustatic and isostatic when used with reference to sea level change.

10 How could an ice age or tectonic movement lead to sea level change?

11 For one landform associated with significant sea level rise and one landform associated with significant sea level fall, describe its characteristics and how it was formed.

three distinct raised beaches can be seen, called the 8 m, 15 m and 30 m beaches, although their actual height above sea level varies laterally. These beaches appear to represent distinct changes in relative sea level and are now more correctly referred to by the approximate age of their creation – that is, the late glacial raised beach is the 30 m level. On the Isle of Portland in Dorset, a 15 to 16 m raised beach is found with periglacial head deposited on top, resulting from eustatic change. This beach relates to the high sea levels experienced around 125,000 years ago, while the head would have been deposited during a colder phase when sea levels were much lower, during the last glaciation.

Coastal flooding

Although over 600 million people live in coastal areas that lie within just 10 m of sea level, according to some experts global warming and sea level rise could affect up to 1 billion people. Half the world's population live within 200 km of a coastline. The average population density in coastal

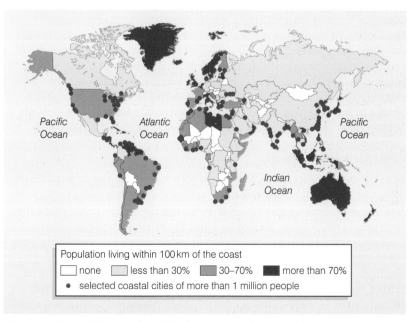

Fig. 3.30 *The world's coastal populations*

areas is about 80 persons per km² (twice the global average). Of the world's 17 largest cities, 14 are located along coasts and two-fifths of cities with populations of 1 million to 10 million people are located near coastlines. The UK has around 20 per cent of its population living near the coast. Unfortunately, the most vulnerable areas include some of the most highly populated, along the south-east coast and around major estuaries such as the Thames – areas that are tilting down into the rising sea.

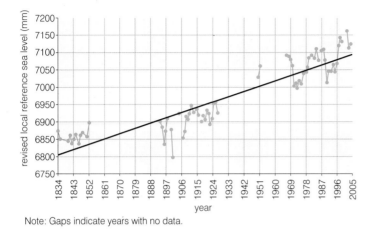

Note: Gaps indicate years with no data.

Fig. 3.31 *Sea level change at Sheerness, Kent*

Case study

The storm surge of 1953

Three of the key factors contributing to the likelihood of coastal flooding are:

- the height of the land above sea level
- the tidal range
- the incidence of storm surges.

These factors all played an important role in the storm surge of February 1953 which tracked down the North Sea towards the low-lying land of East Anglia in Britain and the Dutch lowlands. A deep depression moved from the Shetland area down towards the Netherlands. The low-pressure air allowed the sea to rise overall by 0.5 m and, as strong winds were drawn into the centre, waves over 6 m high were generated on top. Coincidentally this was all happening during the spring high tides when all the rivers were already discharging into the North Sea at flood levels. As the storm surge funnelled water down towards the narrower sections of the southern North Sea, the tides reached 2 to 3 m above normal in East Anglia, the Thames Estuary and the Netherlands, leading to widespread flooding. Over 260 people lost their lives in England and 1835 died in the Netherlands.

The storm surge was an undeniable natural phenomenon but the role of people in the disaster was less immediately obvious. The Netherlands has a long history of reclaiming land from the sea and it was engineering skills from that country that were imported to drain large parts of marshland in East Anglia. The rich agricultural lands that were the reward of reclamation encouraged the spread of population. East Anglian coastal settlements had significant advantages, with busy trade links by sea to the rest of the UK and the

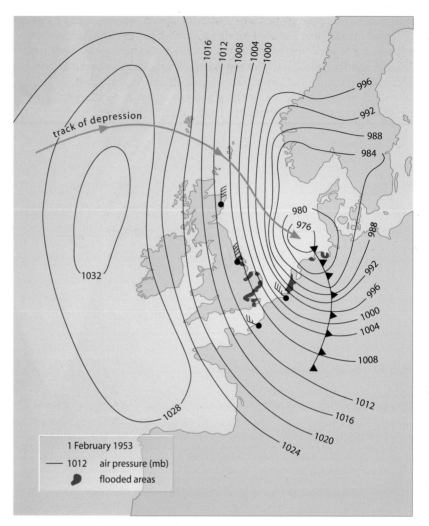

Fig. 3.32 *The depression that caused the 1953 storm surge*

continent. As maritime trade has diminished, the attraction of coastal locations for property development has been clear. The desire for a holiday or permanent home near the sea has helped to fuel an increase in coastal populations in the UK. This trend has accelerated in recent years, despite the gradual acceptance that global warming induced by human activity poses an increasing threat to those living by the sea. Although sea defences have increasingly struggled to hold back the tides, recent history has shown that it is difficult to justify public money for expensive defence schemes. Despite warnings, the coastal defence schemes of 1953 were inadequate. The events of 1953 and the sight of water lapping at the parapet walls of central London served as a wake-up call. A year after the disaster, the government claimed '12 years' work had been completed in 12 months' to shore up Britain's coastal defences, the *Manchester Guardian* reported. A total of £20 million had been spent on reinforcing 'thousands of miles of sea and tidal river defences', the newspaper said. Soon after, it was recommended that a Thames Barrier should be built to protect London from floods. However, although the Netherlands had completed many improvements to its flood defences by November 1970, and despite warnings that 300,000 people could perish in any future floods, the Thames Barrier did not become operational until 1982. The East Anglian defences and the Thames barrier have not been significantly compromised since then, but with sea levels rising and more extreme storms predicted over the next 25 years by the Met Office, there is no room for complacency. The Thames Barrier may not be able to cope with flood levels after 2030. The Environment Agency is currently budgeting £200 million over 12 years to be spent on extra defences and, according to the 'Future Flooding' report in 2004, predicted investment in flood defences and coastal erosion will rise by up to £30 million a year. This might limit the average annual damage of flooding to £2 billion a year by 2080 – it is already £1 billion a year. In July 2006 the Environment Agency warned that 4 million homes in Britain were at risk from flooding and protecting London and the south-east in the next century will cost at least £4 billion.

■ Link

Images of the Thames Barrier can be seen at:

http://photoguide.to/london/thamesbarrier.html.

Case study

Hurricane Katrina, 2004

The countries surrounding the Gulf of Mexico do not exhibit high tidal ranges but they do have a lot of very low-lying land in one of the most hurricane-prone areas of the world. The city of New Orleans (pop. 485,000), situated on the Mississippi delta, exemplifies the problems presented by high population densities in low-lying coastal areas. It is estimated that 51 per cent of New Orleans is at or below sea level, with the more densely populated areas generally on higher ground. The mean (average) elevation of the city is 0.5 m below sea level, with some areas as low as 3 m below sea level. The city is protected from the sea by artificially heightened levées. When Hurricane Katrina (Category 4 to 5 on the Saffir-Simpson hurricane scale) made landfall along the US coast, winds of well over 100 km per hour were recorded in New Orleans and the coast experienced a storm surge greater than historical maximums. The combination of a storm surge of up to 10 m, wave action and high winds resulted in widespread destruction. The failure of earthen levées and flood walls left parts of New Orleans under 6 m of water after the storm had passed. The total number of lives lost is conservatively estimated at over 1800 and the value of property damaged at between $60 billion and $125 billion.

The physical causes of the coastal flooding are clearly related to the proximity of low-lying land in the path of a massive storm surge that was caused by a hurricane. However, the significant human cost and financial losses meant that searching questions are being asked about the impact of the flooding, particularly in terms of the number of poorer people of largely black origin who appear to have suffered disproportionately. They tended to inhabit the poorer, lowest-lying and therefore most vulnerable areas. Criticisms of government agencies, ranging from allegations of inadequate sea defences and delayed implementation of rescue plans to implications of racial bias, appear to have stimulated new thinking on the way vulnerable coastlines can be protected from flooding.

Pledges to rebuild affected cities have been made by the government but a new strategy appears to be evolving that may indicate how to manage coastal flooding in other countries. The USA is working on a multibillion-dollar plan to depopulate vast swathes of coastline along the Gulf of Mexico, in the hope of re-establishing a natural barrier

Fig. 3.33 *Aerial photograph showing coastal flooding caused by Hurricane Katrina*

against catastrophic flooding. The federal government seems to favour a retreat from the coastline rather than rebuilding, while the Army Corps of Engineers has a radical plan to re-establish the wetlands that have been disappearing at an increasing rate in recent years.

The overall plan includes $40 billion to be spent on the Mississippi coastal region. Part of this would be for a voluntary buyout of 17,000 houses in the region, particularly in Bay St Louis, east of New Orleans, but probably to be extended to New Orleans and Louisiana.

Environmentalists argue that the wetlands provided a natural barrier against flooding and their erosion has left areas vulnerable to hurricanes. The loss of the wetlands is partly the result of human activity: regular inputs of silt from the Mississippi helped build up these wetlands but they have been prevented from reaching the Gulf by flood protection levées built to contain the river.

According to Susan Rees, director of the Army Corps project, 'The whole concept of trying to remove people and properties from the coast is very, very challenging. The desire to live by the water is strong.' The emotional and financial links people have with their coastal locations must be balanced by physical realities: the coast is eroding, sea levels are rising and there is growing concern that hurricanes will become stronger in the future.

Activity

12　**a**　Read the two case studies of coastal flooding and consider how natural, economic, social and political factors may have contributed to the occurrence and impact of coastal flooding in each case. For each case study, write down as briefly as you can the 10 most important factors that you think led to the flood event being so significant; number them NS1 to NS10 for the North Sea and HK1 to HK10 for Hurricane Katrina.

　　b　Make a large copy of the diagram below. Place the numbers of the key facts for each case study on the diagram, taking into account whether you think they are mostly to do with natural, economic, social or political factors. Here is an example:

　　HK1 = Katrina was a category 5 hurricane

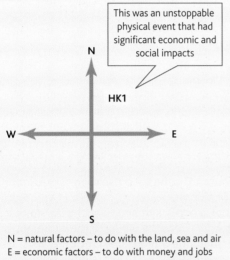

N = natural factors – to do with the land, sea and air
E = economic factors – to do with money and jobs
S = social – to do with people, including quality of life
W = who decides? Who is responsible? Politics and power

　　c　When you have plotted both sets of factors, answer this question:

　　To what extent were these coastal flooding events similar and how did they differ?

▪ Coastal protection and management

With a coastline of over 13,000 km and surrounded by the Atlantic Ocean and the North Sea, both capable of producing significant waves, the UK offers a good example of the erosion problems facing countries all over the world. As a natural process, marine erosion is inevitable but in a country of over 60 million people, of whom 25 per cent live within 25 km of the coast, it is likely to be of great concern. Some areas may erode more slowly as they are made of resistant rocks, on emergent coasts, sheltered from the direct onslaught of the Atlantic Ocean and the North Sea. But where softer rocks dominate, where the land is tilting down into the sea or where the coast is unprotected from the power of the sea, erosion rates of up to 4 m per year may occur. In locations where there are few settlements, industries or communications, erosion is rarely newsworthy. However, Britain's coastline, like many around the world, is highly developed and supports significant populations, businesses and commercial concerns – all land uses which tend to assume that land is fixed rather than a constantly shifting entity.

In striving to manage the coast to serve the needs of people, a range of methods are employed, from costly hard engineering to softer engineering that allows for more managed retreat. There may be conflicts of interest where the demands of threatened communities clash with the realisation that coastal defence systems are not only an expense that the taxpayer may not be willing to afford but that the schemes may not be sustainable and in some instances may actually lead to greater problems in the future.

Hard engineering approaches

The hard engineering approach has traditionally been used to deflect the power of the waves in areas where settlements have been threatened. There are various types of these sea defences.

Sea walls – these aim to protect the coast from wave energy by shielding it with a facade of stone, steel and concrete. Some are recurved structures with a lip at the top to throw waves backwards. Sea walls must have a continuous facing and drain outlets so that water does not accumulate behind them. They are often criticised for the way they cause waves to rebound so that their energy is still available for erosion elsewhere down the coast. Fulfilling a similar function, **revetments** are concrete or wooden structures placed across the beach to take the full force of wave energy.

Coastal barrages – in some bays and estuaries such as at Cardiff Bay in Wales, large coastal barrages have been constructed. These multipurpose structures involve building a partly submerged wall with sluice gates to control the flow of river water from the land and the variations in tidal flow from the sea. They maintain a more constant water level which at Cardiff was deemed essential for effective economic regeneration of surrounding land. Barrages can be used to control flooding (by using sluice gates to control the impact of high tides), generate hydroelectric power using tidal flows (e.g. La Rance in Brittany, France) and improve navigation. However, their environmental impacts are considerable

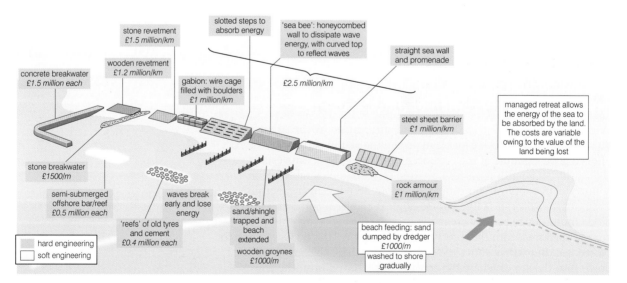

Fig. 3.34 *Different types of coastal defence*

because they affect river and tidal flows, causing large changes in sedimentation patterns. In particular, they remove the intertidal habitats of wading birds.

Rock armour or rip-rap – this consists of large boulders dumped in front of a cliff or sea wall to take the full force of the waves. Rock armour presents an irregular surface to the waves and, although not fully fixed to the earth, it is believed to absorb more of the wave energy while offering a lower-cost but nevertheless resilient protection. Gabions work in a similar way to rip-rap but the smaller boulders are contained in a cage of steel mesh, which maintains stability to a degree. They are not as long-lasting as sea walls.

Groynes – the Victorians recognised the benefits of retaining beach material as a buffer between the waves and the cliff line; they constructed groynes along many beaches. These are wooden or steel breakwaters built nearly at right angles to waves and are meant to slow down longshore drift by trapping sediment. They are still used today, especially with sea walls, as they also break up the waves. However, halting the longshore drift in one area may have serious effects further down the coast as a reduction of the supply of beach material can accelerate erosion.

Cliff fixing – this is often done by driving iron bars into the cliff face to stabilise it and to absorb some wave power. Metal mesh netting may also be added between the bars to try to stop loose rock falling too easily and thus making any cliff-foot pathways unsafe for pedestrians.

Offshore reefs – these encourage the waves to break offshore, which reduces their impact on the base of cliffs. They may have a secondary use in some areas as they can be used to generate surfing waves in tourist areas.

Hard engineering offers visible, reassuring protection for communities threatened by coastal erosion but it has several disadvantages:

- Structures can be expensive to build and to maintain (to repair a sea wall can cost up to £15,000 per metre).
- Defence in one place can have serious consequences for another.
- Defence structures may need to be continually enhanced as rising sea levels render existing structures inadequate.
- Structures are sometimes visually unappealing, spoiling the landscape, which is a significant economic issue in coastal towns that depend on tourism.

Soft engineering approaches

Soft engineering uses beaches, dunes and saltmarshes to absorb wave and tide energy. These natural systems for coastal defence can adjust with time, especially if they are manipulated and maintained by people, for example by adding sand, shingle and vegetation. One example is beach feeding, whereby additional material is added to the beach by dredging from another part of the beach or from elsewhere, such as offshore sediment traps.

Advantages of these methods include:

- relatively lower cost
- retention of the original form and fundamental structures of the landforms
- a more natural appearance with limited visual intrusion
- little reduction of amenity value.

Disadvantages include:

- the need for very regular maintenance
- the shifting nature of the defences
- less likely to be effective against extreme storm events.

■ Case study

Seaford, East Sussex

In October and February each year, the Environment Agency moves around 60,000 m³ of shingle from the eastern and western ends of the beach at Seaford back to the centre of the beach. The shingle is loaded by excavator into lorries which then transport it to where it is needed. Bulldozers then use the material to build up the beach. This recycling of shingle helps reduce the risk of coastal flooding in low-lying parts of the town where over 300 residential and 50 commercial properties would eventually be left with an unacceptable risk of flooding.

Shingle recycling at Seaford ensures that the 4 km long shingle beach that acts as part of the sea defences continues to take the energy and force out of the waves so that they do not damage or break over the sea wall, while still allowing the natural coastal processes to continue.

According to Andrew Gilham, Environment Agency flood risk manager for Sussex, 'In December 2006 and January 2007, Seaford's shingle beach performed well when faced with high waves and gale-force winds. Although there was minor flooding of the road causing some inconvenience, no properties were flooded. Had the shingle beach not been in place it is likely that we would have seen significant property flooding.'

Managed retreat

✍ Managed retreat involves abandoning the current line of sea defences and then developing the exposed land in some way, perhaps with saltmarshes, to reduce wave power. In this way the scale and extent of hard sea defences can be reduced. To allow for managed retreat in the future, some regions are effectively banning new developments on the coast.

Advantages:

- newly flooded areas are effective at absorbing wave power and tidal energy
- limited maintenance
- creation of attractive and still rare wetland habitats.

Disadvantages:

- loss of agricultural and residential land
- interruption of communications, need for new road and pipelines to be laid in some instances.

Other coastal management policies

With the Environment Agency responsible for around 1400 km of over 13,000 km of Britain's coastline, it is clear that not all of it can be protected. Some areas require very little attention but tens of millions of pounds are spent annually on coastal protection already and the demand is always for more. A realistic approach in the eyes of many people is to do nothing, particularly where land is of little economic value, and pay compensation to those who are affected. The suggestion that large tracts of land should be surrendered to the sea is not surprisingly unpopular among coastal communities. However, as local councils or regional powers do not have the financial capability to protect their coastlines, the expectation is that the national government is ultimately responsible. If, as predicted, sea levels continue to rise and areas of the UK continue to sink, the use of public money to defend the undefendable is also unsustainable. In reality, a do-nothing approach exists in many areas as it is the only affordable solution. Coastal erosion experts confirm that reflecting wave power and locally starving the sea of sediment by covering the coast in concrete only worsens erosion elsewhere, so the more sustainable approach of generally allowing retreat but protecting key developments and communications where possible, remains the most likely course. We know from geological records that in the long term the coast will shift. In the short term we want our settlements to be permanent and demand protection from the sea. The increasing threat from rising sea levels may finally trigger a shift in where we choose to live.

Current policies may be summed up as follows:

Do nothing – there is no further active intervention. Without intervention the defences would eventually fail and areas currently protected from flooding would no longer be protected.

Hold the line – this involves maintaining the existing flood defences and control structures in their present positions and increasing the standard of protection against flooding in some areas.

Managed realignment – place new flood defences landward of the existing flood defences or realign existing defences to higher ground. This is achieved through the partial or complete removal of the existing flood defences or through regulated tidal exchange. This method uses sluice gates to permit flooding when required but retains the option of presenting a barrier to flooding at other times.

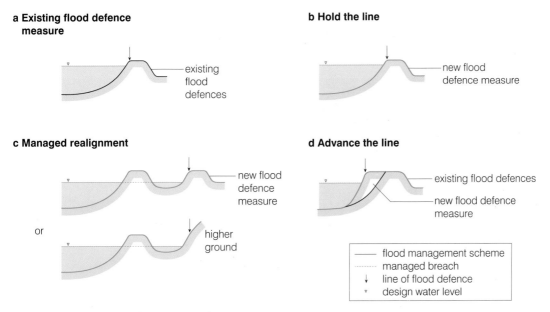

a Existing flood defence measure
existing flood defences

b Hold the line
new flood defence measure

c Managed realignment
new flood defence measure

or higher ground

d Advance the line
existing flood defences
new flood defence measure

flood management scheme
managed breach
↓ line of flood defence
▽ design water level

Fig. 3.35 *Different coastal protection policies*

Advance the line – this policy involves the construction of a new flood management scheme in front of existing flood defences.

Land use/activity management – in areas under significant threat from coastal erosion, the local government may seek to restrict the nature of land use. Where policies of managed retreat or 'roll back' are implemented, long-established patterns of land use are disturbed. Farmland, roads and homes are lost and commercial and amenity value is reduced as coastal land is rendered unsafe for businesses and visitors. Difficult decisions have to be made with regard to what is sufficiently important to be saved and which land uses and activities are not important or possible to defend. In Holderness, where coastal retreat is among the most rapid in the UK, coastal development is guided by the following key principles:

■ To ensure that development in the coastal zone is of an appropriate nature, scale and siting, e.g. residential development in the open countryside will not normally be permitted except where it is essential for the purposes of agriculture or forestry.

■ To enable the relocation of infrastructure and property at risk from erosion, where appropriate.

■ To ensure that the landscape qualities of the coastal zone are protected, particularly with regard to the heritage coasts and the undeveloped coastal area.

■ Case study

Lyme Regis, Dorset

Lyme Regis has had to defend itself from the ravages of the sea since the 11th century. Situated in a natural bay between crumbling cliffs to the west and east, the town of 4400 people has always owed its living to the sea, initially as a fishing port and now as a tourist town. It is at the centre of the Heritage Jurassic Coast and its summer population is boosted by 14,000 visitors enjoying a range of activities from fossil hunting to sailing and watersports. Lyme Regis is exposed to the south-westerly waves from the Atlantic and the stormy conditions of the English Channel. By the 1990s the repeatedly patched-up sea walls were on the verge of collapse as winter storms had removed beach material, allowing waves to undermine the base of the walls. Too much was invested in the

Questions

1. Study Figures 3.36 and 3.37. Try to identify as much evidence as you can that:

   a   Lyme Regis attracts many visitors

   b   the town might be subject to marine erosion.

2. Make a simple sketch plan of the area. Annotate your plan with evidence of tourist activity, and give reasons why you think the area is subject to erosion.

Fig. 3.36 *A storm batters Lyme Regis*

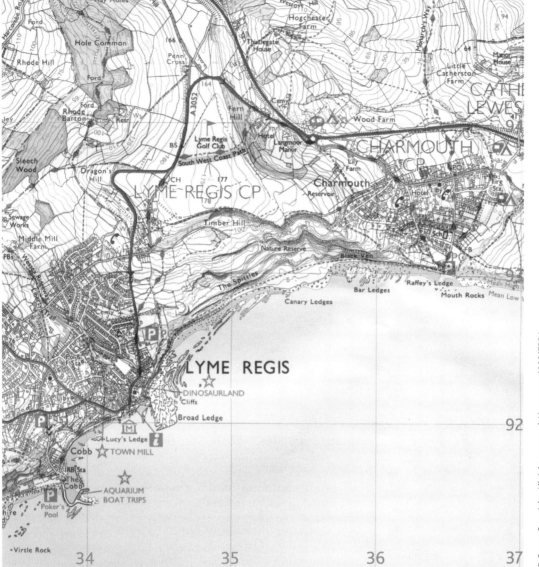

Fig. 3.37 *OS 1:25,000 map of Lyme Regis, part of map sheet 116*

town to allow this to continue. Lyme Regis was not going to be abandoned to the sea. Something had to be done and the solution had to be effective, affordable and environmentally sustainable.

The beach that was once continuous along the front of the whole of Lyme Regis is now in long-term decline. There is no longer any natural supply of beach-forming shingle. The seabed geomorphology is closely related to the underlying geology, with the more rugged rocky parts of the seabed corresponding to the outcrop of Blue Lias, and the more subdued and sediment-covered areas corresponding to the outcrop of rock known as Shales-with-Beef. The seabed and shore platform in front of the sea walls have undergone considerable erosion and lowering over the last two centuries, and as a result the sea walls' exposure to wave attack has increased. The natural west to east longshore drift was interrupted by the connection of the Cobb (the ancient harbour wall) to the mainland in the 1750s and this has resulted in the substantial build-up of Monmouth Beach on the west side of the Cobb.

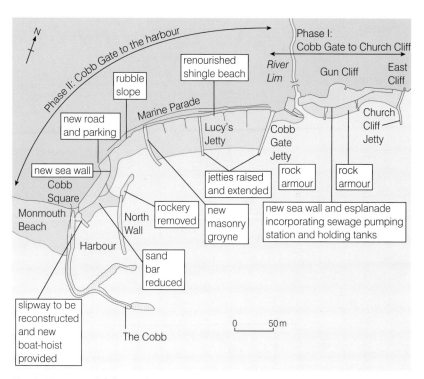

Fig. 3.38 *Coastal defence phases at Lyme Regis*

Link

To explore the area more thoroughly
you may wish to use a GIS site such
as:

http://maps.live.com or http://earth.
google.com.

The weak rocks in these parts have not only led to problems of
seafront erosion but have also helped to trigger landslides. The
shales that the town is largely built on are relatively weak and
particularly unstable if they become saturated.

A plan for coastal defence

The final scheme for the town has to balance the need to protect
existing land uses with preserving the attractive character of the
harbour area. The immediate impact of hard engineering solutions
may outweigh the apparent advantages of soft engineering options.
The final scheme was proposed by Costain Engineering and
accepted by West Dorset County Council. It involves several stages:

■ phase I: Cobb Gate to Church Cliff (scheme completed)
■ phase II: Cobb Gate to the harbour (scheme completed)
■ phase III: Monmouth Beach and Ware Cliffs (incorporated into
phase II)
■ phase IV: East Cliff
■ phase V: the Cobb.

Phase I (completed in 1995) provided the eastern part of the town
with sea defences while also improving Lyme's sewerage system.
In the past, raw sewage had poured into the sea close to the
beaches where thousands of summer visitors relaxed and swam.
Costain Engineering built a combined sewage pumping station
and stormwater storage tank inside the new sea wall, which was
protected by 21,400 tonnes of rock armour. Originally the plan
involved the siting of three offshore breakwaters (reefs or bars) to
reduce the impact of waves on the beach, but these were dropped
because local opposition said they ruined the area's appearance. The
environmental improvements scheme is the second stage of a long-
term plan to offer security for homes and businesses in the town.

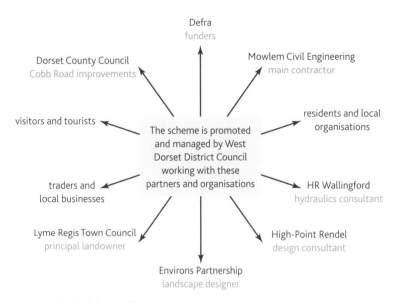

Fig. 3.39 *The decision-making process*

Phase I was awarded the Secretary of State's special commendation for environmental excellence at the British Construction Industry awards. The works also won a 1997 Civic Trust award for outstanding contribution to the quality and appearance of the environment and helped the district council gain beacon status in 2004. The council also successfully completed £1.4 million of stabilisation works at East Cliff, Church Cliff and land behind the harbour during the winter of 2003–04.

Phase II (2005–07) aims to protect the foreshore along the main frontage from the sea and to stabilise the land behind. The initial cost of this section of the scheme was estimated at £17 million. This has used a combination of hard and soft engineering to defend the town in a way that will not unduly detract from its environmental and tourist appeal. The scheme required the following materials:

- rock armour 36,000 tonnes
- beach shingle 71,000 tonnes
- beach sand 41,000 tonnes
- drainage material 7500 tonnes
- masonry 400 tonnes
- piles 1150
- drainage 2300 m
- jetties 110 m
- new sea wall 250 m
- planting 7500 m².

The sea wall has a recurved top to reflect the energy of the waves back and away from the promenade. There is a rock armour apron in front of the wall in some places to prevent excessive scouring. Piling is used to support slopes elsewhere and this is aided by improved drainage to prevent saturation of slopes (which fail more easily) and additional planting to increase soil stability and disguise remedial work. Sand and shingle have been imported to offer a greater buffer to the power of the waves and serve the threefold purpose of protecting the sea wall from all but the most severe storms, offering greater amenity value to tourists who wish to have a beach holiday, and softening the visual impact of some of the hard engineering solutions. As surveys have indicated that there are no real sand and shingle supplies offshore to feed the longshore drift that might replenish the beaches naturally, it is anticipated that these additional sediments will need to be added at intervals to top up the material that is removed by erosion and transportation.

Question

3 Study the plans for phase II of the Lyme Regis scheme in Figure 3.38. You are going to complete an environmental impact assessment (EIA) for the scheme. This must be done for all major new developments to try to predict the impact in terms of environmental and socio-economic factors.

a You should give each criterion in the table below a score of –3 to +3 and mark the relevant box with a cross or circle.

	Criteria	–3	–2	–1	0	1	2	3
Physical factors	Erosion							
	Sedimentation							
	Pollution							
	Wildlife							
	Visual impact							
Socio-economic factors	Safety							
	Property values							
	Business							
	Amenity value							
	Traffic							

b When you have finished using all the criteria, you can connect the points with a coloured line to produce a profile.

c Do you think the profile would have looked any different if you had been completing the EIA from the point of view of:

■ the local chamber of trade

■ an environmentalist

■ a holidaymaker?

Cost–benefit analysis

The total cost of implementing all the proposed schemes was estimated at £33 million. The amount of funding required had to be justified before permission could be given for construction. The cost–benefit analysis in Table 3.2 is part of that justification. It had to demonstrate sufficient economic benefit in implementing the schemes to confirm the viability of the coastal protection strategy. Without it, the scheme could not get government grant aid funding.

The value of properties at current market values was estimated independently. Planners had to calculate present value benefits. This is a calculation which looks at the likelihood of properties and amenities being lost to erosion over time and the estimated monetary benefit of saving them from destruction. By comparing these potential benefits with the actual cost of the new defences, cost–benefit ratios can be calculated. Analysis indicates that there would be considerable economic benefits in implementing coast protection works with benefit/cost ratios of more than five. These relatively high benefit/cost ratios not only show that the schemes are viable but that 'serious sea wall failures or coastal instability would have a devastating effect on the town and, in the do nothing scenario, would threaten its very viability as a commercial town in its present form'.

Benefits

In addition to the cost–benefit analysis, the scheme has other benefits, including:

- more sand and shingle on the beach
- new promenade
- increased shelter around the harbour
- improved ramp access to the gardens and Holmbush car park
- relandscaped public gardens with more walks
- improvements to Cobb Road
- access along the beach, even at high tide.

To the west of Lyme Regis and further towards the east, near Charmouth, the cliffs are unstable and frequently fail, giving rise to landslides. However, these locations are sparsely populated and they are being allowed to retreat naturally. This is partly because the cliffs are not particularly valuable land and partly because the erosion supplies sediment which longshore drift distributes along the shore. These cliffs to the east of Lyme Regis also form part of the Heritage Coastline and sea defences would not be allowed here. The policy at Lyme Regis of defending the most valuable areas with a mixture of hard and soft engineering, providing more limited protection for neighbouring areas, and no protection for the cliffs away from inhabited areas, appears to offer a sustainable scheme for the moment, but sea level rises may unravel even these carefully laid plans.

Question

4 Write a brief report outlining why you do or do not think that the coastal defence scheme for Lyme Regis is likely to remain successful in 50 years' time.

Table 3.2 *Lyme Regis scheme: summary of estimated costs, benefits and benefit/cost ratios*

Scheme	Number of properties	Non-discounted value				Total (£m)	Present value (PV) benefits				Total (£m)
		Property	Services and infrastructure	Amenity	Harbour		Property	Services and infrastructure	Amenity	Harbour	
		£m					£m				
Phase II: Cobb Gate to the harbour	297	53.08	4.90			57.98	37.98	4.02	63.00		105.0
Phase IV: East Cliff	172	34.31	4.00			38.31	24.79	3.08	41.80		69.67
Phase V: the Cobb	63	7.06	1.00		7.84	15.90	2.51	0.36	10.09	3.86	16.82
Total	532	94.44	9.90		7.84	112.18	65.28	7.46	114.90	3.86	191.49
% of total		84	9		7	100	34	4	60	2	100

Scheme	Design properties		Construction contract		Maintenance per annum		Total PV cost (£m)	Benefit/cost ratio
	Cost	PV cost	Cost	PV cost	Cost	PV cost		
	£m		£m		£m			
Phase II: Cobb Gate to the harbour	1.35	1.32	16.70	15.20	0.01	0.24	16.76	6.27
Phase IV: East Cliff	0.95	0.88	13.00	11.04	0.01	0.22	12.14	5.74
Phase V: the Cobb	0.20	0.17	3.30	2.61	0.002	0.04	2.82	5.96
Total	2.50	2.37	33.00	28.85	0.02	0.50	31.72	6.04

Link

Go to the Essex Wildlife Trust website to find out more about the Abbots Hall Farm project:

http://essexwt.org.uk/main/welcome.htm.

Enter 'Abbots Hall Farm' into the search box at the top right of the screen.

Case study

Essex marshes coastal realignment

A new approach to coastal management is being trialled on the Essex coast. As policy makers begin to question more carefully our ability to pay for defences for every threatened part of the coast and the desirability of protecting land in the short term from inevitable loss in the long term, it becomes clear that difficult decisions have to be made. Coastal realignment allows for managed retreat and surrenders part of the coast in the belief that this will act as a more natural buffer to the advancing sea. In areas where, for centuries, regularly maintained sea walls have allowed farmers to benefit from the land, the concept of giving land back to the sea is, not surprisingly, controversial. A limited trial of a new sustainable approach to coastal management is being carried out along along the Blackwater estuary, one of the largest estuaries in East Anglia. It covers almost 4400 ha and is threatened by 'coastal squeeze' due to sea level rise. Along the Essex coast, sea level is rising by around 6 mm per year as a result of global warming and the settling of the land mass in the south-east due isostatic readjustment. Coastal squeeze is the result of the sea rising over the saltmarshes and then being pinned against the sea wall, leading to deeper water which causes erosion. It is estimated that up to 40 per cent of Essex saltmarsh has been lost in this way over the last 25 years.

At Abbotts Hall Farm the sea wall was deliberately breached in October 2002. The scheme works by allowing salt water back onto

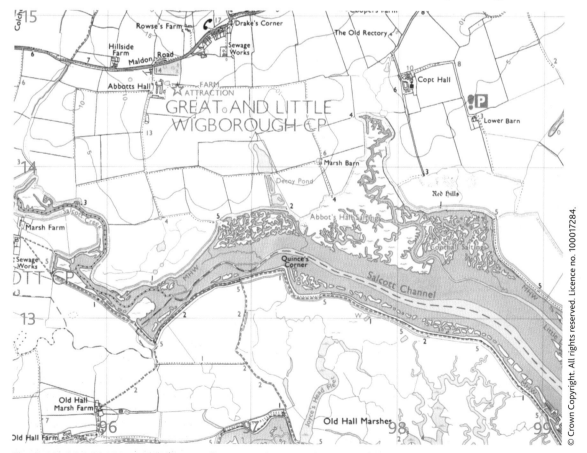

Fig. 3.40 *OS 1:25,000 map of Abbotts Hall Farm marshes, part of map sheet 184*

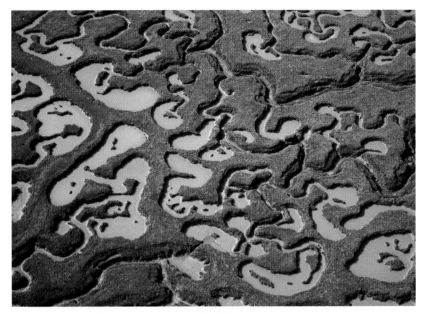

Fig. 3.41 *An aerial view of saltmarsh at the Blackwater estuary*

Abbotts Hall Farm realignment will allow for the development of saltmarsh inland of the breached sea wall. This will act as a buffer against rising sea levels.

land originally reclaimed by the construction of the sea wall over 300 years ago. Two counter walls have been constructed at either end of the site to protect neighbouring land. Elsewhere the land rises gently away from the sea wall and serves as a natural check to the incoming tide without manmade sea defences. The breaching of the sea wall was timed to precede spring tides, allowing each tide to float in seeds from the existing marsh outside the breached sea wall. By midsummer, thousands of new saltmarsh seedlings were covering the fields. The development of 81 ha of mudflat, pioneer saltmarsh and coastal grassland had begun. The changes to the ecosystem are very welcome as saltmarsh is rare in Europe. Even more welcome is the fact that these coastal floodings seem to have reduced the pressure on sea walls elsewhere along the estuary. In addition, nearby oyster farms have not recorded undue levels of silting up in the oyster beds, which need clear water to be productive. The Abbotts Hall Farm initiative, which won the RSPB/CIWEM Living Wetlands Award, has saved £500,000 in sea defences, as well as boosting habitats for a range of birds, fish and plants.

Extending the scheme

The Abbott's Hall Farm project is the centrepiece in a conservation jigsaw that links together over 1200 ha of wildlife-rich land along a 25 km stretch of the Essex coast. The wider scheme to develop saltmarsh was begun in 1992 by the National Rivers Authority. It started an experimental project to use **polders** to encourage saltmarsh creation and has now established a total of 26 polder sites in Essex estuaries and monitored their progress. In this area a polder is a tidal area enclosed by wooden fencing that is designed to regulate tidal flow. This reduces erosion and encourages deposition of sediment. Suitable sites can see the development of beneficial saltmarsh with modest capital and maintenance costs. The materials used (willow hurdles) are low-cost and sustainable, naturally decomposing as the saltmarsh becomes established.

The sites have in most instances helped to establish a stable foreshore, especially in sheltered estuarine areas. The sites act

Did you know?

In the Netherlands a polder is an area below sea level that has been reclaimed by the construction of walls and pumping of water to create dry land. The word polder is used in rather a different way in Essex.

a With sea wall

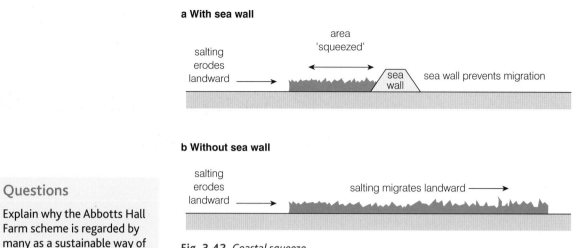

b Without sea wall

Fig. 3.42 *Coastal squeeze*

Questions

1 Explain why the Abbotts Hall Farm scheme is regarded by many as a sustainable way of dealing with sea level rise.

2 Draw a Venn diagram to compare the two different approaches used at Abbotts Hall and Lyme Regis.

3 'Coastal defences must be environmentally sustainable in the long term as well as effective against rising sea levels in the short term.' In a piece of extended writing, discuss this assertion and refer to examples you have studied.

as a natural flood defence by dissipating wave energy, reducing the effects of sea level rise and storms. In some cases the polder areas can be sited to protect the foot of a sea wall, thereby saving on maintenance of the wall. They also reduce the environmental impact of sea defence works, and the project has promoted the wider sustainable use of natural resources in flood risk management. The coppiced willow used is a native English species and comes from the neighbouring area. Prior to polder construction all of the sites were eroding but now the vast majority are stabilising as vegetation traps more sediment. In addition, the saltmarsh habitats provide feeding and breeding grounds for important species of birds such as redshank and fish such as herring.

✔ 💡 *In this chapter you have learnt:*

- that coastal zones are complex areas shaped by many interdependent natural processes which interact with geology to create landforms of deposition, erosion or both

- how natural and human processes interact in coastal regions and how changes can result from that interaction

- that careful management is necessary in managing the coast, as many different groups use or are responsible for coastal areas in the UK, which can cause conflict

- how the management of coastlines is achieved through a variety of strategies and according to the local nature of the coast

- that in choosing the correct management strategy, short-term and long-term views must be considered

- how coasts in the UK are managed and how action at one part of the coastline may have significant positive or negative impacts on another

- that sustainable management schemes are based on the idea that coastal erosion and deposition are natural processes and that, although people can influence them, they cannot control them.

Hot desert environments and their margins

The physical geography of arid and semi-arid lands

In this section you will learn:

- where to find hot deserts and what they are

- how the location of the hot deserts affects their climate

- how their climate affects their vegetation

- how climate and vegetation affect desert landforms

- the relative importance of water and wind in forming desert landforms.

💡 Desert environments can present extraordinary sights, quite unlike anything that we are familiar with in the temperate, moist climate of the UK.

Activity

1. a. Study Figures 4.1 and 4.2. Describe the landforms that you can see in each photograph. Make reference to:
   - the structure of the rocks
   - processes that you think might be affecting the rocks
   - the landforms that have been produced.

   b. What makes these landscapes different from landscapes in the UK? Are there any similarities?

Fig. 4.1 *Colorado, USA*

Fig. 4.2 *Southern Wadi Rum, Jordan*

What are hot deserts and where are they?

The simplest and most traditional definition of a desert is 'a place receiving less than 250 mm of rainfall a year'. However, this is too simple because it would also include tundra regions as desert.

Most definitions are more complex and are linked to the water balance. In these definitions:

- P = total precipitation
- E = evapotranspiration
- PE = potential evapotranspiration (or the amount of water that would be evaporated if enough were available).

Using these figures, an aridity index can be calculated for any place. Figure 4.3 shows how much of the world falls into the different categories of aridity and humidity. Almost 20 per cent of the land surface is arid and 33 per cent is arid or semi-arid.

The areas that fall into the arid and semi-arid categories are marked on Figure 4.4. However, it should be noted that the Gobi Desert is not actually classified as a hot desert. Its great altitude means that its winters are very cold and therefore many of the processes and landforms there are rather different from those in the true hot deserts. So too are the human adaptations needed to survive there.

What causes hot deserts?

There are three main, interlinked causes of hot deserts:

- the formation of the subtropical high-pressure cell
- the rain shadow effect in the belt of easterly trade winds
- the effect of the cold currents off the west coast of the continents at these latitudes.

The subtropical high pressure cell

It is well known that the sun's rays are most concentrated at or close to the equator and that this leads to the heating of the air lying above the ground surface. The hot air contains large amounts of water vapour, evaporated from the ground or transpired from the vegetation. This heated air rises in the form of convection currents and then cools, causing thick clouds to form and torrential rainstorms to fall (see Figure 4.5). What then happens?

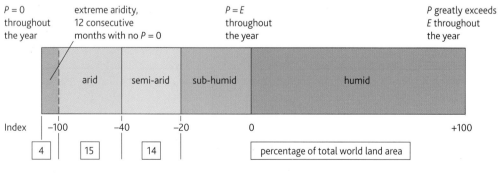

Fig. 4.3 *Aridity index*

Fig. 4.4 *Arid areas of the world*

Legend:

- extreme aridity
- arid
- semi-arid

H high pressure
R rain shadow
M mid-continent
U upwelling of cold water

1 Australia (e.g. Simpson, Great Sandy) **HRM**
2 Gobi **M**
3 Thar **H**
4 Iran **HM**
5 Turkestan **M**
6 Arabia **H**
7 Somalia **H**
8 Kalahari **HM**
9 Namib **HU**
10 Sahara **H** (**U** in west, **M** in centre)
11 Patagonia **R**
12 Monte **H**
13 Atacama **HRU**
14 Sonora **H**
15 Mojave **HR** (**U** on coasts)
16 Great Basins **R**

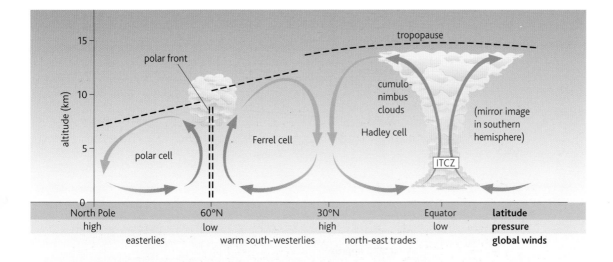

Fig. 4.5 *The tricellular model of atmospheric circulation*

The air that had risen in the convection currents stops when it reaches a layer in the atmosphere called the tropopause. It cannot continue to rise, so it is forced to flow towards the North Pole or the South Pole. As air flows away from the equator – away from its main source of heat – it cools.

The cooling makes the air more dense, and much of this denser air sinks back towards the Earth's surface at about 30° north or south of the equator. This sinking produces a high-pressure air mass with the following characteristics:

■ It is warm because it is heated by compression as it sinks.

■ It is dry because most of the water vapour it contained was dropped in the convection rainfall near the equator and it dries anyway, as it warms.

■ It is stable, with skies that are generally clear and cloudless.

■ Winds blow outwards from the area of high pressure. Some winds blow back towards the equatorial low-pressure area and some blow polewards to bring warm westerly winds to the mid-latitudes.

Figure 4.6 shows the subtropical high pressure belt in the northern hemisphere. The Sahara Desert in north Africa can be seen clearly, as can the Arabian Desert. Because the image was taken in the northern summer, the high pressure has extended northwards over the Mediterranean region. To the south is the doldrum belt of the intertropical convergence zone (ITCZ) with its convection rain clouds. To the north lies the area where the westerlies meet the polar winds to create the belt of depressions. These depressions can be seen forming over the Atlantic Ocean and moving towards Britain and western Europe. Note also the small area of cloud close to the Atlantic coast of north Africa. These clouds are explained below.

Fig. 4.6 *The subtropical high-pressure belt in the northern hemisphere*

The rain shadow effect of the easterly trade winds

Most of the deserts lie in the belts of the trade winds. These winds blow from the north-east in the northern hemisphere and from the south-east in the southern hemisphere. They tend to drop most of the moisture they are carrying on and close to the eastern edges of the land masses that they reach, so they are fairly dry by the time they reach the continental interiors. The western sides of the continents are in an even stronger rain shadow.

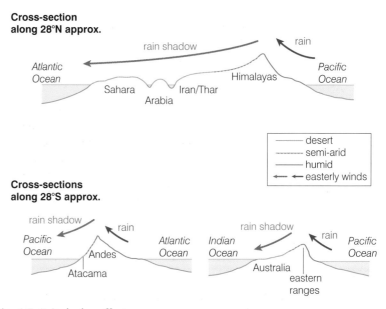

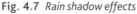

Fig. 4.7 *Rain shadow effects*

In North and South America the main mountain ranges, the Rockies and the Andes respectively, lie towards the western side of the continent. Therefore the rain shadow effect covers a fairly narrow area and the Sonora and Atacama deserts are also fairly narrow. In Australia, on the other hand, the mountain ranges lie close to the east coast and so the deserts cover a much larger proportion of the continent. However, the Sahara and Arabian deserts stretch right across their land masses, because they lie in the rain shadow of the Asian land masses.

The cold current effect

The circulation patterns of the oceans are controlled by:

- wind directions
- the rotation of the Earth
- differences in water temperature hence the density of sea water.

These factors combine to produce cold currents, moving towards the equator from a poleward direction, along the west coast of most of the continents. These areas also have an upwelling of cold water from deep in the ocean towards the surface.

When winds do blow towards the shore their lower layers are cooled by contact with the water. This causes mist or fog to form just offshore. The mist may then roll inland, but it soon evaporates again in contact with the warm surface. However, the air has lost some moisture and it becomes drier as it warms. This means that rain becomes even less likely.

Characteristics of hot deserts

The descending air of the deserts is warmed by compression. It is warmed further by insolation, which is strong in these latitudes not far from the equator. Insolation is particularly strong during the summer period, when the sun is overhead or almost overhead for several months. During summer, therefore, shade temperatures can rise as high as 50°C (58°C has been recorded in the southern Sahara). Even in winter, daytime shade temperatures of over 20°C are common.

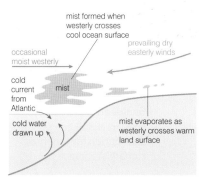

Fig. 4.8 *Formation of offshore mists off the west coast of the Sahara Desert*

However, at night the lack of cloud allows heat to radiate away very quickly and temperatures fall considerably. **Diurnal ranges** as high as 30°C are often experienced. This cooling can lead to mist and dew forming. In many desert areas dew is one of the major forms of precipitation. Rainfall in deserts is low, but it is not unknown.

Convection currents often build up because of the heating of the surface but they are rarely strong enough to overcome the downward pressure of the descending air. When they do, they can rise high enough to cause enough cooling for rain to form and this can lead to torrential storms. Average figures for rainfall in the true deserts mean little, though. Rain is so infrequent that the average monthly figures are very unreliable. Several years may pass with no rainfall and then a sudden storm can bring hundreds of millimetres in a few hours.

Around the edges of the deserts lie the semi-arid climates. Any definitions of the borders between climate regions are quite arbitrary and the borders are very indistinct.

On the equatorward margins, the desert gradually gives way to the tropical wet and dry climates. The semi-arid margins form the transition zone and a short wet season, coinciding with the period of overhead sun, starts to become noticeable.

Link

Tropical climates are covered in the A2 book.

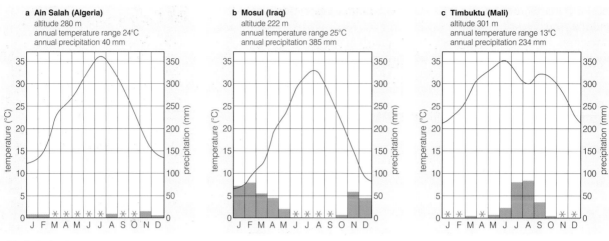

Fig. 4.9 *Climate graphs for Ain Salah, Mosul and Timbuktu*

* indicates trace

Activity

2 Study Figure 4.9.

a Use an atlas to find the locations of these three climate stations.

b Compare temperature, temperature range, total annual rainfall and rainfall distribution for the three climate stations.

c Suggest explanations for the differences that you observe.

d How is the annual range shown by these figures different from the diurnal range?

e Maximum temperatures in Ain Salah and Timbuktu are higher than the maxima in places that are on or close to the equator. Give two reasons for these differences.

Link

For more on desert soils, see also duricrust on page 134 and salination on page 143.

On the poleward side, the depressions that are characteristic of the temperate west coast climates start to affect the area more often. They bring rain in the cooler season. This cool season rain evaporates less quickly than the hot season rain that falls on the equatorward desert margins, so it is more useful for plant growth.

Winds are probably no more common in deserts than elsewhere but there are three reasons why their effect seems to be more marked:

▪ There is so little vegetation to break their force.

▪ There is little protection for the broken rock particles, sand, etc. that lie on the surface, so they are are easily picked up and carried by the wind. This makes the winds very erosive; it also makes them look more spectacular.

▪ Hot air can cause convection currents that can set off little twisters of wind that look like mini tornadoes, but which are usually short-lived and not very damaging.

Desert soils

In desert areas the climate is too dry and the vegetation too sparse for any significant chemical weathering of bedrock or for the accumulation of organic material. In the few places where the water table is close to the surface, soil moisture is likely to be drawn to the surface by evaporation and capillary action. This causes salts and bases to be deposited at or near the surface to give an alkaline soil. However, the absence of humus means that the soils generally lack horizons and are thin.

Desert soils are generally unproductive because of the lack of humus and water, but they are not particularly infertile. In areas where irrigation water can be supplied and humus added, these soils can be made productive, helped by the high base content.

Desert vegetation

With shortage of water being the main feature that defines deserts, it is quite clearly difficult for plants to survive. However, deserts are far from barren and plants have many special adaptations that allow them to survive in all except the most inhospitable parts. There is not enough rainfall to support a continuous cover of vegetation, so desert vegetation is sparse and scattered. Individual plant adaptations include the following:

- **Drought avoidance** or producing seeds that can lie dormant for long periods between rain events and which germinate, flower and produce seeds very quickly when rain does arrive. Such plants are known as **ephemerals**.

- **Drought resistance** or adapting to survive with the minimum of water. Drought-resistant plants (or **xerophytes**) have thin, tough, spiky leaves and tough bark to reduce water loss by transpiration. Many also have a covering of silvery hairs to cut wind speed, to reduce water loss and to reflect light so that the plant stays cooler.

- **Water storage** in plants, including succulents like cacti which store water in their roots and stems.

- **Water seeking** by sending out long roots to tap water deep under ground (**phreatophytes**) or to control the water supply of a wide area. The creosote bush is the most characteristic and widespread shrub in the deserts of the USA.

- **Oasis vegetation** is found where there are sources of water in the desert. The classic oasis forms where a layer of permeable rock has taken in water in an area outside the desert (see Figure 4.17, page 137). The layer then runs as an aquifer beneath the surface, carrying its water trapped between other impermeable layers of rock. Then the aquifer comes to the surface, either because of folding or because of erosion of the rocks above it. The water from the aquifer seeps out and allows plants to grow nearby. Note that most oases are now settled and cultivated. Little natural vegetation remains.

Vegetation is also thicker than normal along wadis and dry stream beds in the deserts and semi-deserts. Even though the streams that cut the valleys may appear dry there is often some moisture close to the surface in the stream beds and plants can take advantage of this.

Did you know?

Nomadic camel herders say that their camels are upset by distant thunder. They claim that the animals know the thunder means rain and that rain means vegetation growth. Therefore their natural instinct is to travel towards the source of the thunder in the hope of fresh pasture. Domestic camels are tethered and cannot follow their instincts but they are so prepared for the journey that they stop producing milk for a day or two after a storm.

Link

Find out more about the creosote bush:

http://en.wikipedia.org/wiki/Creosote_bush.

Desert bushes in south-west USA are spread quite widely because each plant has an extensive network of roots deep below the surface. The deep roots are matched by their long, spindly branches which bend easily in the wind. Leaves are practically non-existent but this is the wet season so the bush has burst into flower. Note the tussocks of grasses between the bushes. They have shorter root systems so they do not compete for water directly with the bush.

Cacti can survive in gravelly soil or even in cracks in the rock where water can seep down. Water is stored in the bodies of the plants. The needles cut down on water loss, protect the plants from being eaten and hold a layer of air close to the plants to protect them from wind.

Fig. 4.10 *A desert bush*

Fig. 4.11 *A cactus growing in rocky ground*

3 Study Figure 4.12.

a Describe the vegetation that you can see.

b Explain how climate and soil conditions in this area make it difficult for vegetation to survive.

c Suggest how this vegetation is adapted to survive here.

Fig. 4.12 *Cactus and scrub vegetation in California, USA*

Desert landforms

Weathering and erosion in deserts

Mechanical and chemical weathering

For many years it was thought that the main process involved in desert weathering was the mechanical breakdown of rocks due to the repeated intense heating followed by cooling of the rocks. The large diurnal range led to expansion of rocks close to the surface during the day and then sudden contraction at night due to the rapid cooling. This set up stresses in the rock that caused it to crack so that the outer layers peeled away. The process was known as **exfoliation** or **onion-skin weathering**.

However, closer observation proved that this explanation was not enough to fully explain the weathering of rock to produce sand. It seems that the presence of some water is probably necessary for this type of weathering to take place at all; it certainly speeds up the process in a number of ways:

Fig. 4.13 *Exfoliation on a coarse-grained rock in the Arabian Desert*

■ Sudden rain can cool the rock very quickly, speeding up the process of exfoliation.

■ The presence of moisture (often in the form of early morning dew) can combine with certain minerals (**hydration**), causing the rock to swell and the outer layer to peel off.

■ Salt can be dissolved and brought to the surface by water. When the water evaporates, salt crystals can form and force the rock apart (**salt weathering**).

■ Related to this is the formation of **duricrust**. Other minerals can be dissolved from the rock and are then brought to the surface and deposited due to evaporation. This forms hard layers or crusts at the surface but generally weakens the rocks beneath the surface and allows them to be weathered more easily once they are exposed.

Another contributory factor in the process of exfoliation could be **differential expansion**. This happens when a rock is made up of different minerals. When they are heated the different minerals expand at different rates. The differential expansion sets up extra stresses in the rock. This is even more marked when the minerals have different colours. Light-coloured minerals reflect heat whereas darker ones absorb heat more quickly and so are more likely to expand.

The rocks were weakened and are now eroded fairly easily but where the duricrust is still present it protects the rocks below from erosion, helping to create rock pillars.

Fig. 4.14 *Duricrust formed on an old rock surface*

Wind and water erosion

In the late 19th and early 20th centuries, geomorphologists working in Africa and Arabia considered that wind erosion was the most important process in the formation of desert landforms. Later in the 20th century, work in North America suggested that the actions of running water were more important in the formation of most landforms in most areas. Now it is largely accepted that both wind and water are important but that different processes are dominant in different areas and at different times.

In fact, it is now clear that desert regions experienced climate change, just like the areas closer to the poles, during the periods that we call the ice ages and the post-glacial period of the last 20,000 years. This means that places that now seem to be very dry may well have experienced much wetter climates in the geologically recent past, and vice versa.

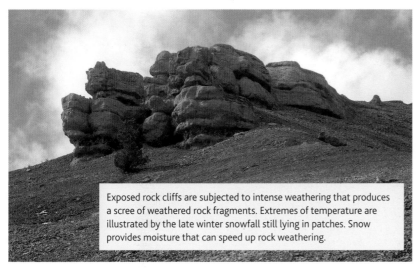

Exposed rock cliffs are subjected to intense weathering that produces a scree of weathered rock fragments. Extremes of temperature are illustrated by the late winter snowfall still lying in patches. Snow provides moisture that can speed up rock weathering.

Fig. 4.15 *Weathering and scree in Bryce Canyon, USA*

Wind processes

Transportation by the wind

Figure 1.21 on page 15 shows the model known as the Hjulström curve. It shows the speeds at which running water picks up, transports and then deposits particles of different sizes. A similar pattern is followed by the wind when it erodes the surface.

Wind moves material by three main processes, similar to those seen in a river: surface creep, saltation and suspension.

Surface creep is similar to the traction load of a river. The wind can roll heavier particles along the surface. This is speeded up considerably if there is also some movement by saltation because, as pebbles that have been lifted up land on the surface again, they may knock into particles at rest and provide the extra force that is just enough to get them moving.

Saltation occurs as the wind speed increases, as long as the particles on the surface are light enough and are lying so that the wind can get underneath them and lift them. Once a particle has been lifted, it can be blown forward and then bounce up again, or it can dislodge another particle and allow that to be blown forward. If the wind blows strongly enough and consistently in the same direction, it can produce a sandstorm in which visibility is reduced almost to zero.

Saltation usually only raises particles a few millimetres off the ground, although the worst sandstorms can lift sand particles to a metre or even more in height. This has obvious implications for the way wind-blown sand erodes the solid rock surfaces that it comes into contact with.

Suspension happens when very fine material is picked up and raised high into the air. This produces a **dust storm**. Dust storms carry material to the edges of the desert and even beyond. Occasionally these storms even carry their fine red dust over the UK, leaving thin red deposits on windows and cars. More common are the dust storms that blow sand from the Sahara out westwards over the Atlantic Ocean. From time to time they are visible on satellite images of the Atlantic weather. The dust storms on the desert margins of the American Midwest in the 1930s are still famous from books like *The Grapes of Wrath* and the songs of Woody Guthrie.

When the dust is eventually deposited it produces very fine material known as **loess**. This yellow or red soil is most common on the plains of

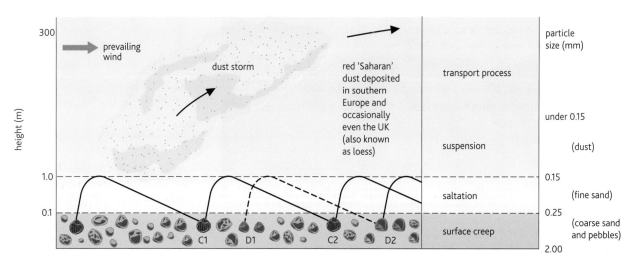

Fig. 4.16 *Wind erosion processes*

eastern China where the loess was blown from the deserts of central Asia like the Gobi Desert.

Wind erosion

Deflation is the gradual removal of fine sand particles by the wind, leaving pebble-strewn surfaces or flat rock surfaces called **desert pavements** or (in the Sahara) **reg**.

Deflation can also produce depressions or **deflation hollows**. They probably form where there is some structural downwarping of the rock surface. On cold nights the cold air sinks into these hollows and dew forms. The dew speeds up the weathering of the rock and makes particles available for removal by the wind. Progressive development of these processes can lead to depressions that are many metres deep. Some in Egypt have bases over 100 m below sea level.

It is thought that some of the oases of the Sahara were formed by deflation lowering the surface until an aquifer (a layer of water-bearing rock) is reached. The water seeps out at the surface and provides a base below which the deflation is unlikely to proceed. The water allows the presence of vegetation which binds the soil together and prevents its removal, and thus prevents further deflation.

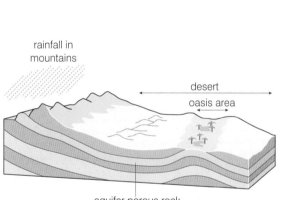

The softer parts of the rock close to the ground have been picked out and eroded by wind-borne sand. The flat area in front of the rock is a product of deflation.

Fig. 4.17 *Oasis formation*

Fig. 4.18 *Camel Rock in Wadi Rum, Jordan*

Abrasion is like the effect of sandblasting a building. It can pit the surface of a rock or it can wear it smooth. However, its most spectacular effect is to pick out the layers of soft rock close to the ground surface, leaving spectacular pillars perched on very narrow bases or carving strange shapes like those in Figure 4.18. However, wind-eroded features like Camel Rock are unusual. More common though less spectacular are features known as **yardangs** and **zeugen**.

Yardangs are formed where ridges of hard and soft rock run parallel to the direction of the prevailing wind. The wind erodes the softer rock and leaves the ridges standing up as yardangs. Gradually they are undermined and broken into discontinuous features, but the ridge pattern can still be seen in aerial photos and satellite images. Some of the most spectacular yardangs on Earth can be found in the Lut region of Iran. They show up on satellite images. The term 'yardang' is derived from a Turkish word for a steep bank.

Link

The US Geological Survey (USGS) has information on and images of yardangs at:

www.tec.army.mil.

Type 'Yardangs' into the search box.

Did you know?

Extensive yardang scenery has been found on Mars. Some features on Venus are probably yardangs.

Fig. 4.19 *Yardang formation*

① direction of prevailing wind — trough

soft rock   hard rock

wind abrasion turns the beds of soft rocks into troughs

② wind turbulence causes curved sides to yardangs — yardang

hard rocks are undercut and they stand up as narrow ridges called yardangs

Link

For more on duricrust, see page 134.

Zeugen are similar in appearance but they are formed on horizontal bedded structures rather than vertical beds. They are often formed where the surface has developed a hard duricrust. When the harder surface rock is broken in places, wind abrasion can quickly wear away the softer underlying rock to leave a series of flat-topped zeugen. The zeugen are further undercut by the wind, getting smaller and smaller, and eventually they are destroyed completely.

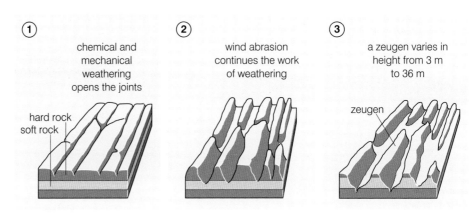

① chemical and mechanical weathering opens the joints

hard rock
soft rock

② wind abrasion continues the work of weathering

③ a zeugen varies in height from 3 m to 36 m

zeugen

Fig. 4.20 *Zeugen formation*

Wind deposition

As with a river, wind drops the material that it is carrying when it:

- is carrying too much material for the available energy
- slows down
- loses energy because of increased friction.

The heaviest particles are dropped first and the lighter ones can be carried much further. This leads to sorting of the deposited material by size and density. It also leads to the formation of distinct types of desert surface:

- **sandy desert** (called *erg* in the Sahara), which is an undulating plain of sand, moulded by the wind
- **stony desert** (called *reg* or *serir* in the Sahara), which is covered with angular pebbles and gravel that cannot be moved far by the wind

- **rocky desert** (called *hamada* in the Sahara) that has been stripped of loose material by deflation.

In the sandy deserts, the surface is often moulded into dune shapes. These shapes vary but there are many similarities between the formations of sand in sandy deserts, in coastal sand dunes, on beaches, on seabeds and on river beds, although the features are on different scales.

This suggests that the shaping allows the most efficient movement of a fluid (air or water) over an unconsolidated surface. The body of moving air or water does not flow in a perfectly straight line but it meanders and eddies. This moulds the surface into a shape that allows the easiest possible movement and reduces friction between the flowing current and the surface material.

Different dune forms seem to be linked to the strength, direction and consistency of the wind and to the amount of sand that is available. Perhaps the best-known type of desert dune (although not necessarily the most common) is the **barchan**. Barchans are crescent-shaped dunes of up to 30 m in height. They are not fixed and they migrate forward in the direction of the wind. Some textbooks suggest that they originally form

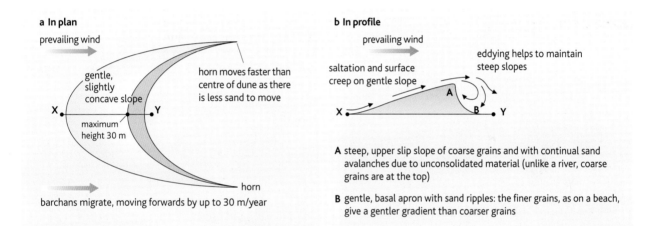

a In plan

prevailing wind

gentle, slightly concave slope

horn moves faster than centre of dune as there is less sand to move

X

Y

maximum height 30 m

horn

barchans migrate, moving forwards by up to 30 m/year

b In profile

prevailing wind

eddying helps to maintain steep slopes

saltation and surface creep on gentle slope

A

X

B

Y

A steep, upper slip slope of coarse grains and with continual sand avalanches due to unconsolidated material (unlike a river, coarse grains are at the top)

B gentle, basal apron with sand ripples: the finer grains, as on a beach, give a gentler gradient than coarser grains

Fig. 4.21 *Barchan movement*

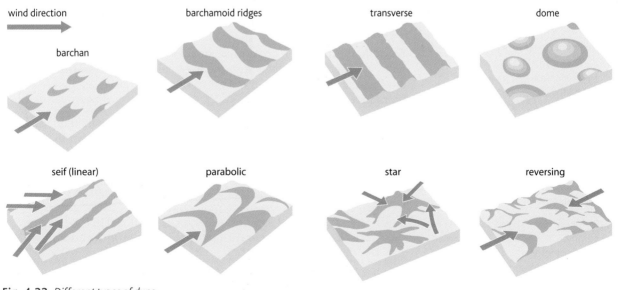

wind direction

barchan

barchamoid ridges

transverse

dome

seif (linear)

parabolic

star

reversing

Fig. 4.22 *Different types of dune*

■ Activity

4 Study Figure 4.23 and 4.24. They show part of the Wadi Rum area in Jordan, close to the border with Saudi Arabia and the Grand Canyon in Colorado, USA.

What evidence can you find of running water helping to produce the scenery in these two areas? Refer to evidence of weathering, erosion and deposition.

around an obstruction like a boulder or a shrub, but this is not always true and observations have shown that barchans can be formed purely by wind action.

Working with the help of satellite images and air photos of deserts, geomorphologists have been able to classify the worlds' dunes into a number of different groups. However, it should be noted that these groups are linked and some areas have dunes where the different types seem to merge together.

Water processes

Figures 4.23 and 4.24 show that water has clearly had a big impact on the landforms of desert areas in different parts of the world. In some cases, climate change might have reduced the impact of water, so the features that are seen today are fossilised remnants of past conditions but, as seen earlier in this chapter, there are few if any areas of desert where water does not play at least some part in the formation of landforms.

Fig. 4.23 *Wadi Rum, Jordan*

Fig. 4.24 *Grand Canyon, Colorado, USA*

■ Key terms

Exogenous: these desert rivers rise in rainy, mountain regions outside the desert and continue flowing across the desert. Two examples are the Colorado and the Nile.

Endoreic: this type of drainage occurs where rivers flow into the desert area but dry up and terminate in inland seas (like the River Jordan in the Dead Sea) or salt flats (see Figure 4.23).

Ephemeral: these streams are most common in the desert. They flow intermittently after rainstorms, or seasonally in desert margin areas.

There are three different types of rivers in deserts: **exogenous**, **endoreic** and **ephemeral**.

Exogenous streams erode just like streams in humid latitudes do. However, there is usually quite a different balance between stream erosion and mass wasting of the valley sides in desert areas than in humid areas.

In humid areas a lot of a river's energy goes to removing material that has been weathered on the valley sides and then carried down to the stream by mass wasting.

In deserts, on the other hand, weathering is slower and mass wasting is much less apparent. This means that less material is being brought down to the river for removal, so much more of the river's energy goes into downwards erosion and less into widening the valley. This gives rise to the typical canyon formation with steep sides, often with cliff formations.

The Grand Canyon (see Figure 4.24) has certain features that are unique to that valley and are due to two particular features of the geological history of the region:

- The area has flat-bedded rocks with sediments and lava flows alternating. Some strata are harder than others.
- The whole area has been uplifted by tectonic forces as the river has cut down into the surface, so the river was constantly being rejuvenated.

The nature of the rock strata has produced the alternating steep and very steep sections of the valley sides, with the harder strata standing out as cliffs and the softer rock worn back.

Uplift has led to the great depth of the valley – almost 2000 m (over a mile) deep in places. Figure 4.25 shows the Grand Canyon much nearer the river's source than in Figure 4.24. In this area the river has only cut a fairly narrow and shallow valley as yet.

Endoreic streams rise outside the desert area and then flow towards it. However, they do not flow on but run into inland lakes or dry up. They often form playas.

AQA Examiner's tip

Note that canyons are different from glaciated valleys. They both have steep sides but canyons usually still meander, with the meander pattern being incised into the surface as the river cuts down. Glacial troughs tend to be much straighter. The troughs also have broad bottoms whereas canyons have narrow bottoms with little or no floodplain.

Fig. 4.25 *Upper part of the Grand Canyon*

Ephemeral streams can rise and fall very quickly. They often have a short lag time and high peak flow because:

- rainfall in desert areas is often torrential
- there is little vegetation to absorb the rainfall or to break up the surface with root systems
- surfaces are often hard and impermeable because the high temperatures bake the surface and the duricrust that is often present inhibits infiltration.

As a result of these conditions, overland flow, with sheets of water flowing over the surface, happens after downpours in semi-arid regions and even occasionally in true desert areas.

When such sheet flow occurs, large amounts of material can be moved short distances. Then, if the water does infiltrate, the sediment is dropped as suddenly as it was picked up. The deposited material is sorted roughly by density when it is dropped. The classification of deserts into sandy, stony and rocky was given on pages 138–39. However, some geomorphologists think that water erosion and deposition might also

Fig. 4.26 *Edge of the Grand Canyon*

Fig. 4.27 *Bryce Canyon, USA*

Activity

5 Write a detailed account of the exogenous river valleys shown in Figures 4.1, 4.26 and 4.27. In each case refer to the structure of the area's rocks, the processes that have affected and are affecting the landscapes, and the features that have been produced.

have played a part in their formation – during a period when the climate was considerably wetter with more frequent floods.

When it happens, sheet flow is a very short-lived event. If the water does not infiltrate, it often collects into runnels and these join to form steep-sided ravines, known as *wadis* in Arabia or *arroyos* in Hispanic areas, including those in the south-west USA.

Pediments and playas

Pediments form at the foot of cliffs. They are gently sloping surfaces (between 7° and 2°) either cut in solid rock or covered with a thin layer of debris – sand or pebbles. The pediment is normally separated from the cliff by a scree where weathered material has accumulated after falling from the cliff, or by an alluvial fan to which the weathered material has been carried by an ephemeral stream. The material on the pediment usually gets finer with distance from the foot of the cliff.

cliff face – weathering active

scree slope – unsorted debris

pediment – material sorted by the action of runoff (flash floods) and wind causing deflation

Fig. 4.28 *Cliff, scree and pediment at foot of slope, Wadi Rum, Jordan*

Playas are often found at the foot of the pediment. They are ephemeral lakes which are fed by endoreic streams which flood occasionally and then dry up, leaving behind a bed of salt and very fine sediment (see Figure 4.23).

In fact, the formation of the salt flats that often form in playas is the result of an extreme development of a process that influences the surface in many parts of deserts – **salination**. This happens when water infiltrates into the soil or rock and is then evaporated by the heat. While the water is in the ground it dissolves salts from the rock or soil in a chemical reaction that is speeded up by the high temperature. When the water is drawn back to the surface and then evaporated, the salts are deposited at the surface. In many places this forms duricrust. If there is insufficient salt to form the duricrust, there is generally still enough to form a very saline soil. Further rainfall may carry these salts into the playa to form a salt pan – like the Bonneville salt flats in Utah (which are so flat and smooth that they were used for attempts on the world land speed record), or the salt flats around the edges of the Dead Sea on the borders of Israel and Jordan.

> ### Activity
>
> **6** Look back at the photos of desert and semi-desert landscapes in this section. Look in each one for these features, described in the section above:
> - flat or gently sloping upland
> - cliff or very steep slope that may be a valley side or may be the edge of a highland area
> - scree or debris fan lying at between about 30° and 20°
> - pediment of finer, sorted material at between 7° and 2°
> - playa formed of silt or salt at less than 2°.

■ Mesas, buttes and inselbergs

Mesas, buttes and inselbergs are different types of isolated highland which are typically surrounded by scree, pediment and/or playa. There have been many suggestions about the origins of these features but most were probably formed by a combination of wind and water action. They were probably also affected by climate change, having been at least partly formed during periods when the climate was wetter than it is at present.

A **mesa** (from the Spanish for 'table') is a fairly extensive, flat-topped, steep-sided hill that remains after the surrounding rocks have been eroded away. Mesas probably represent the remains of a former surface that has mostly been eroded away after a period of uplift.

A **butte** (from the Spanish for 'tree trunk') is a smaller version of a mesa, or a mesa that has been eroded until it has been almost completely removed, or a small, detached section of a mesa (see Figure 4.29).

An **inselberg** (from the German for 'island mountain') is a more rounded and smooth-sided version of a mesa or butte. Often inselbergs are formed in unbedded, crystalline, volcanic or metamorphic rocks, whereas mesas are formed in flat-bedded sedimentary rocks or lava flows.

One question that has puzzled geomorphologists is: Why is this striking combination of slope angles, with sharp breaks between different slope segments, so common in desert and semi-desert regions?

Fig. 4.29 *Buttes in Bryce Canyon, USA*

Part of the answer may be that they just seem striking and unusual to people who are used to more humid climates with abundant vegetation and well-developed soil. In fact, this combination of slope elements may be much more widespread than the rounded slopes that most of us are more used to. It may be that, without the soil and vegetation, similar slope segments with sharp breaks would be very widespread in the UK and other parts of western Europe. They are often found on coasts and in recently glaciated landscapes where soil and vegetation have not had time to develop.

However, the combination of angles is common in deserts. The main controlling factor may well be that there is just one main part of the landscape where active weathering is taking place, and that is on the steep, exposed slopes. These slopes are exposed to rapid changes in temperature and to any precipitation that falls. Much of the rest of the landscape is protected, either by a layer of deposited material or by duricrusts.

The steep slopes are weathered, and the debris falls to the foot. Wind and water remove, sort and reduce the size of the debris. It is then deposited as pediment, playa or dune landforms. As long as debris is being removed from the foot of the scree slope, the material that is weathered from the cliff cannot build up and cover the cliff. The height of the different slope segments is the outcome of the balance between weathering and removal.

- If weathering is more rapid than removal, the scree will build up and protect the cliff.
- If the two are more or less in balance, the cliff will remain exposed but will gradually retreat.
- If removal is more rapid than weathering, the scree will only be temporary and the cliff will be much higher.

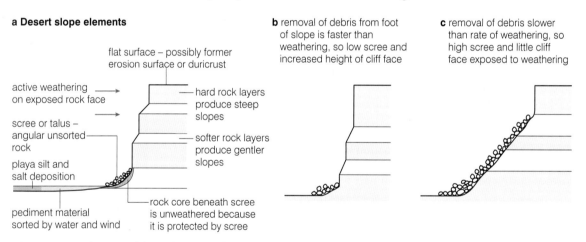

a Desert slope elements

flat surface – possibly former erosion surface or duricrust

active weathering on exposed rock face

hard rock layers produce steep slopes

scree or talus – angular unsorted rock

softer rock layers produce gentler slopes

playa silt and salt deposition

pediment material sorted by water and wind

rock core beneath scree is unweathered because it is protected by scree

b removal of debris from foot of slope is faster than weathering, so low scree and increased height of cliff face

c removal of debris slower than rate of weathering, so high scree and little cliff face exposed to weathering

Fig. 4.30 *Development of slope elements in deserts*

■ Badlands

Badlands are a type of arid terrain with clay-rich soil that has been extensively eroded by wind and water. Canyons, ravines and gullies are common in badlands. They are often 'bad lands to walk through', which is why the early settlers so named them. Badlands usually have a spectacular colour display that alternates from dark black/blue coal to bright yellow clays to red sandstones. Much of the landscape in Bryce Canyon (see Figures 4.27 and 4.29 on pages 142–3) has badland topography. The soft rocks have been deeply eroded by occasional heavy rainstorms.

Desertification

Key terms

Desertification: the making of deserts or the spreading of a desert into new areas around its margins.

ℹ️ In the second half of the 20th century, **desertification** was identified as a problem that was affecting many parts of the world and was having a particulalrly serious effect in the Sahel region of Africa. However, it was realised that this was not the first time that desertification had occurred. Many features of desertification had been seen in the creation of the dust bowl in the American Midwest in the 1930s, and the same effects had probably occurred in the north African wheat-growing areas that had fed much of the Roman Empire until the second and third centuries, and in other places at other times.

The causes of desertification

Areas around the edges of deserts can be used for the grazing of flocks and herds. In fact, the Bible has large sections devoted to descriptions of the life of nomadic herders, such as Abraham, in the desert and desert margin lands of Palestine long before the birth of Christ. Some such herders still survive in this area today and there are even settled farmers growing crops where sufficient water is available. Many of the desert nomads supplemented their incomes by trade, often based largely on camel transport, but now many of the remaining nomads supplement their income from their involvement in tourism.

However, population pressure and/or changes to the traditional way of life in such areas can lead to desertification in desert margin ares. Desertification turns productive land into non-productive desert as a result of poor land management. Desertification occurs mainly in semi-arid areas (average annual rainfall less than 600 mm) bordering on deserts. In the Sahel (the semi-arid area south of the Sahara Desert), for example, the desert moved 100 km southwards between 1950 and 1975, according to some people who studied the area.

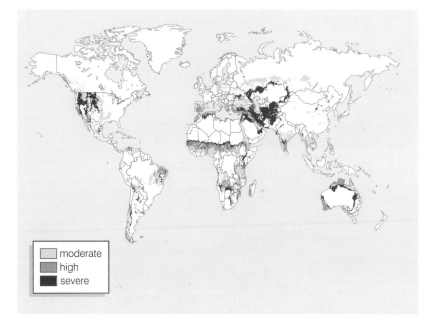

moderate
high
severe

Fig. 4.31 *Areas at risk of desertification*

■ Key terms

Carrying capacity: the largest population of people or animals that a particular area or ecosystem can support at a given level of technological development.

Salinisation: the process whereby soluble salts accumulate in the soil. It happens naturally when rainwater sinks into the soil, dissolves salts and is then evaporated, precipitating the salts near the surface. However, if irrigation water is drawn up from below ground, it can cause even more rapid salinisation. This can be toxic to many crop plants.

■ Link

The section on 'Diseases of poverty' in Chapter 8 relates to this topic.

■ Link

See the section on 'Fuelwood' in Chapter 7. Figure 7.27 shows how desertification can affect both the ecosystem and the people in these areas.

However, since that time, other studies have suggested that the move was not permanent and may have been a temporary fluctuation due to a series of particularly dry years. They suggest that the land and the way of life of the area's people can adapt to periods of drought, but that in the long term there may be a gradual reduction in the quality of the soil, the biodiversity and the **carrying capacity** of the land, and that this may also be a cause of reduction in rainfall and water availability.

Figure 4.32 shows some of the causes of desertification. However, this is an oversimplification of a complex reality and there are many complex feedback loops between the different levels of the diagram.

At the simplest level it should be obvious that there is a link between population growth and the number of animals being kept on the land. Also, growth of the population in farming areas is shown on the diagram as leading to more land being ploughed for food crops, but this land was often used previously by herdsmen and the loss of their land pushes them into more marginal areas, putting ever-greater pressure on the vegetation and soil.

At a more complex level it is possible that the decrease in vegetation cover leads to more rapid runoff after rainfall, so this moisture is not available for evapotranspiration in the area where it fell, hence the air becomes less humid, leading to reduced rainfall.

Other contributory factors to the process of desertification can include:

■ destruction of vegetation in arid regions, often for fuelwood

■ poor grazing management after accidental burning of semi-arid vegetation

■ incorrect irrigation practices in arid areas, which can cause **salinisation** (the build-up of salts in the soil) that may prevent plant growth.

■ where livestock has a social importance beyond food, people might be reluctant to reduce their stock numbers.

These feedback loops make desertification self-reinforcing; that is, once the process has started, conditions are set for continual deterioration. However, the desertification cycle can be broken or reversed, either through changes in climate or through changes brought about by improved management of the affected area.

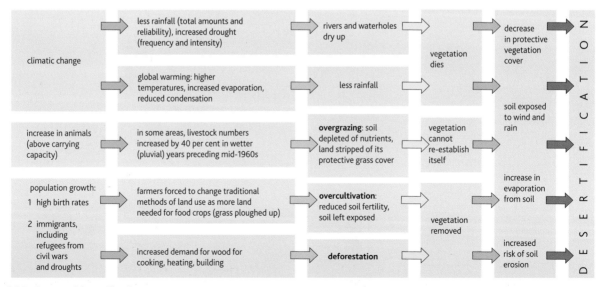

Fig. 4.32 *Causes of desertification*

During the early 1980s satellite photographs clearly showed that the Sahara Desert was expanding. This expansion coincided with a period when rainfall totals across the area were lower than average. At the same time, many people living in the area were known to be migrating away from the drier areas.

In the late 1980s all these changes seemed to be reversed. Geographers and environmentalists wanted to work out how these changes were linked. They produced the data which is shown in Figures 4.33 and 4.34. In Figure 4.34, the residual trend could be due to:

░ a deterioration in vegetation caused by human activity

░ the cumulative impact of a series of dry years.

░ Activity

7 Study Figures 4.33 and 4.34.

    a   Describe the changes in rainfall deficits in the Sahel region between 1980 and 1984 and between 1984 and 1989.

    b   Describe the changes in the extent of the Sahara in these two periods.

    c   Describe the residual extent of the changes in the area of the Sahara when the effects of rainfall variation are removed.

    d   Does this suggest that changes in the area were:

        ░ mainly due to fluctuations in rainfall

        ░ mainly due to the effects of human activity

        ░ due to a combination of these two causes?

    e   What lessons should this provide for policy makers and the inhabitants of this region?

It represents the increased area of the Sahara when the effect of a high rainfall deficit for that year is ignored.

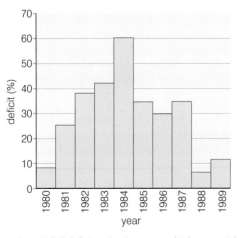

Fig. 4.33 *Rainfall deficit – the degree to which potential evapotranspiration exceeds rainfall in a year*

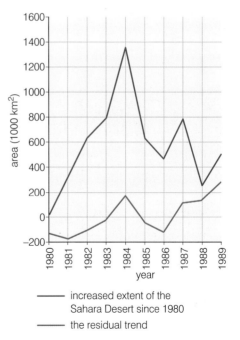

increased extent of the Sahara Desert since 1980

the residual trend

Fig. 4.34 *The increased (or decreased) extent of the Sahara Desert compared to its extent in 1980 when the known effect of rainfall changes is removed*

■ **Link**

The full article is available on the BBC website at:

http://news.bbc.co.uk.

Enter 'Sahara Desert Frontiers' into the search box.

The PAF is described in a detailed case study on the website of the United Nations Food and Agriculture Organization:

www.fao.org/docrep/X5301E/x5301e00.htm#Contents.

■ Case study

The Sahel

> Satellite pictures of northern Africa show that areas lost to the Sahara desert during decades of drought are turning green again. Analysis of images shows deserts retreating in a broad band stretching from Mauritania to Eritrea, according to research in the British magazine *New Scientist*.
>
> The driving force behind the retreat of the deserts is believed to be increased rainfall. Better farming methods have also played a critical role, according to researchers.

This is part of a 2002 story on the BBC News website. It went on to describe changes in northern Burkina Faso. It said that 20 years ago much of this area had been turned into a desert. Now, satellite surveys show, vegetation is returning to many areas. One of these areas is Yatenga Province in Burkina Faso. This was the scene of Projet Agro-Forestière (PAF), funded by Oxfam in the 1980s.

Fig. 4.35 *Burkina Faso*

Yatenga Province lies on the central plateau of Burkina Faso and had two problems:

■ high population density (70 to 100 people per km^2)
■ severely degraded land.

Over 50 per cent of the land was under cultivation and there was little or no opportunity to allow a fallow period, so the land was deteriorating further. Much of the remaining land was eroded with gullies cut into a duricrust layer, which cannot be cropped without being improved. Overgrazing added to the problem. Locally these barren expanses of land are known as *zipeela*.

To make matters worse, the rainfall had decreased significantly from the long-term average of 720 mm per year to 440 mm within the 20 years to 1989. Not only was the rainfall low, it was also very unreliable.

In the 1960s a large-scale aid project called GERES used heavy machinery to construct earth bunds over entire catchments, whether the land was used for agriculture or not. The bunds were designed to drain rainfall runoff away from the fields to protect the soil from erosion.

However, as the rainfall totals fell, this had a disastrous effect. People needed the runoff on their fields to increase the moisture for their crops. Local people had not been consulted, they had not participated in the project, and they did not bother to maintain the bunds, which quickly lost their effectiveness.

GERES failed completely. The land deteriorated further: biodiversity was reduced, agricultural productivity fell and the people were faced with a stark choice – improve the land or migrate to the cities.

When PAF began in 1979 it was, as its name suggests, an agro-forestry project. It planned to improve tree planting using micro-catchment techniques which collect rainfall runoff and concentrate it around tree seedlings. The long-term aim was to improve the vegetation and by doing so to:

- bind the soil together, slow down runoff and reduce gullying and soil erosion
- break up the duricrust with tree roots
- provide a fuelwood supply.

However, it quickly became apparent that the people were not interested in planting trees. Their most urgent need was food production. A local saying went: 'If you have a thorn in your foot and a thorn in your backside, which do you take out first? The thorn in your backside. Then you can sit down and remove the thorn in your foot!' In other words, 'First things first. Provide us with food and then maybe we can think about planting trees.' PAF was flexible enough to change direction according to people's priorities.

Traditionally, simple lines of stones had been built across fields to help reduce erosion, but this practice had largely been forgotten. Through discussions with the people, PAF saw this as the basis for improved food production. The technique was resurrected and improved by building the stone lines along the contour. Contour stone bunds became the focus of the project's attention from 1982. PAF provided the motivation and financial support and suggested ways of improving the lines, and the villagers provided the labour.

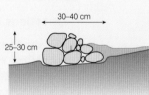

1 Eroded or abandoned land is selected for treatment.
2 Contours for the bunds are surveyed using a water tube level starting at the top of the field and working downwards.
3 Lines are marked on the ground with a hoe.
4 A shallow foundation trench is dug for each bund.
5 Construction begins with large stones in the rear of the trench (downslope side).

6 Smaller stones are used to build the rest of the bund. The stones must be packed carefully, especially at the bottom.

7 Earth from the trench is piled up in front of the bund.
8 If the land treated is an abandoned plot, the stone bunds are left for a year to catch sediment. Cultivation begins only in the second season.

9 Grasses and tree seedlings are planted alongside the bund during the rains.

Measurements:
spacing: 15–30 m apart
bund: 25–30 cm high and 30–40 cm wide at base
foundation trench: 5 cm deep, 30–40 cm wide

Fig. 4.36 *Some material developed for aid workers in Burkina Faso*

All the planning of the work is carried out by village committees, to ensure local control. PAF will only provide support and training once the village committee is set up and requests help. Then PAF will provide incentives to the villagers, but these are kept to a minimum as the philosophy of the project is that people must want to do what they are doing because it is of direct benefit to them. However, incentives do include:

- pickaxes, shovels and wheelbarrows
- donkey carts for groups who buy their own donkeys
- the loan of the project's lorry where the supply of stones is very limited and a large area has to be treated
- additional help for the poorest farmers, which comes in the form of a food loan, so they can feed the group when work is done on their fields.

The training courses consist of discussions about the need for conservation and land improvement. The main features of the courses are:

- using a model to demonstrate the effect of contour bunds (rarely needed now but in the beginning used a great deal)
- training in the use of the water-tube level for surveying contours
- construction of improved stone bunds.

In the first few years of the PAF, results showed significant yield increases: 40 to 60 per cent in the first season. There is some evidence that yields continue to increase for several seasons as fertile deposits are built up on the fields. Most importantly, even in very dry years, treated fields yield some harvest. One survey showed that treated plots yielded an average of 972 kg/ha whereas plots left untreated yielded an average of only 612 kg/ha.

Figure 4.37 shows an extract from a questionnaire developed by the FAO. It was based on the good practice seen in the PAF scheme, and in five other schemes studied. It provides guidance for development workers in areas of desertification in the Sahel region, to assess whether a project is likely to meet the needs of local people and so stand a good chance of success.

Questions to ask and things to remember

How should we go about planning a soil and water conservation project in one of the dry areas of sub-Saharan Africa? How can we be sure that the project will benefit people – and the benefits will last?

There is no easy answer, but based on the lessons drawn from the six case studies here is a summary of the most important things to remember, and some of the questions we must ask ourselves. Use this as a checklist.

First we will look at project organisation and management, and then we will consider technical points.

1. PROJECT ORGANISATION AND MANAGEMENT

	Yes	No
Participation is the key to a successful project.		
Participation		
Have we got the respect and the cooperation of the local people – the 'beneficiaries'?		
Are we answering their 'felt needs'?		
Are we involving them in all stages of planning, implementation, monitoring and evaluation?		
Training puts skills into the hands of the people.		
Training and motivation		
Are we using technology which is appropriate – such as simple surveying instruments?		
Are we taking training needs seriously?		
Work with existing groups.		
Existing institutions		
Are there traditional working groups?		
Which local institutions are the strongest? _____		
Which institutions could help with planning at the village level? _____		
Flexibility is strength.		
Flexibility		
Does the workplan allow a modification in targets or a change in direction?		
Are we ready to evaluation progress and make changes if necessary?		
Don't expect dramatic results too quickly.		
Life of the project		
Have we planned for a long enough period of project activity?		
Is there provision to extend the project if things take off slowly?		

Fig. 4.37 *Extract from the FAO questionnaire*

■ Link

The UN has published a study of 10 desertification projects at:

http://www.unccd.int/regional/africa/docs/tenAfricanExpr-eng.pdf.

Another major UN-sponsored study with references to desertification is the Millennium Ecosystem Assessment. GreenFacts has published it in a very useful interactive version at:

www.greenfacts.org/en/desertification.

■ How the world might address desertification

Following the lessons learnt from projects like PAF in Burkina Faso and the five other projects described in the FAO document quoted above, the United Nations set up the Convention to Combat Desertification in Africa. The Convention supported and studied a variety of other small and medium-scale projects to try to help reduce or reverse the spread of deserts.

The digest of the UN report on desertification contains two summary diagrams that illustrate:

■ some of the links between climate change, desertification and biodiversity loss, showing how these three processes may well be reinforcing each other (see Figure 4.38)

■ some of the human factors which increase the downward spiral of desertification and some ways to reverse the spiral (see Figure 4.39). Note that the PAF scheme and others referred to above are all examples of such initiatives.

The Millennium Ecosystem Assessment document (see the Link box) is quite complicated but try to follow it as well as you can in the time available to you. The last section reaches some very interesting conclusions about the future of the world's arid lands between 2006 and 2050, in a set of four possible scenarios (see Figure 4.40).

The two globalised scenarios consider what might happen in a world where countries work together and plan through bodies like the UN and the FAO. The two regionalised scenarios consider a world where individual countries and small groups act in their own interests without full global cooperation.

The two reactive scenarios consider what might happen if people and organisations wait for crises to arise and then respond to them as well as they can. The two proactive scenarios consider what will happen if people and organisations plan ahead, either sharing high-tech solutions on a worldwide basis or adapting traditional technologies to best fit local needs.

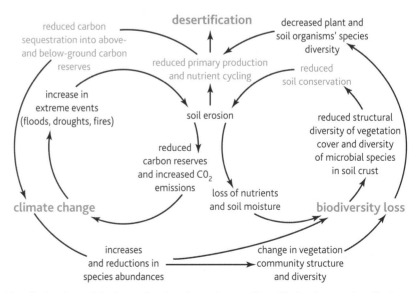

Note: The inner loops of the diagram show how climate change and loss of biodiversity cause desertification. In turn, desertification feeds back to increase climate change and biodiversity.

Fig. 4.38 *Desertification linkages, loops and development*

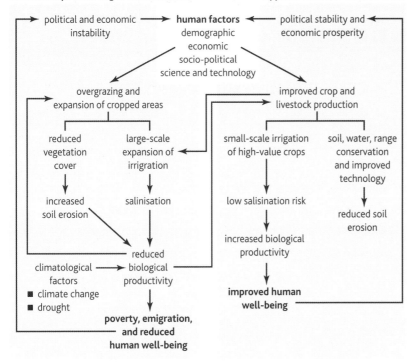

downward spiral leading to desertification   approach to avoid desertification

Fig. 4.39 *Desertification downward spiral and possible development pathways*

The scenarios are predicted to have different consequences for the spread of desertification. The document describes a best case and a worst case for each scenario. All the worst cases lead to a much greater spread of

Link

By clicking on any of the scenarios on the GreenFacts website, you can obtain a fuller explanation of the reasoning. The reasoning for the Adapting Mosaic scenario is given at:

www.greenfacts.org/en/ecosystems/toolboxes/scenarios-am.htm.

When you have finished this chapter, you could go to the following website and complete the quiz on desertification:

http://managingwholes.com/quiz.

Click the 'Desertification' radio button and then click on 'Take the quiz now!'

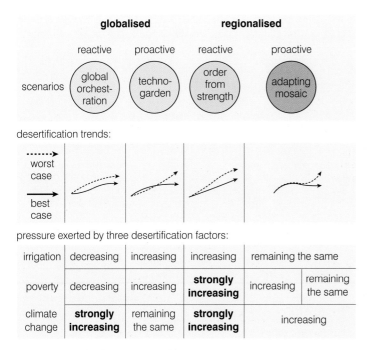

Fig. 4.40 *Key findings on desertification*

desertification whereas all the best cases predict a slowing or even a possible reversal in three of the four scenarios.

In this chapter you have learnt:

- what deserts are like
- what causes deserts to form and what might cause them to spread
- how desert and desert margin climates, vegetation and landforms are interlinked
- about the combined roles of wind and water in the formation of desert landforms
- some of the interlinked human and climatic causes of desertification
- some of the ways in which desertification can be tackled
- why some of these methods are more successful than others
- some possible long-term solutions to desertification
- how people might use the land on the edges of deserts for sustainable farming.

5 Population change

How has the rate of population growth changed over time?

In this section you will learn:

- how and why the global population is increasing
- how the rate of growth varies from place to place
- to think how the rate of growth may alter in future
- to consider what affects the rate of population growth.

Fig. 5.1 *World population clock, 14 December 2006*

Link

You can visit the Worldclocks website at:

www.tranquileye.com/clock or www.poodwaddle.com/worldclock. swf.

AQA Examiner's tip

When presented with a resource like this, you should try to:

- find out who produced it
- find out why they produced it
- evaluate its accuracy and reliability.

On 14 December 2006, at 1230 GMT, the Worldclocks website showed the following values:

World population	**6,553,497,917**
Total productive land	**8,564,267,236 hectares**

By April 2008 the figures had changed to:

World population	**6,659,341,191**
Total productive land	**8,558,624,885 hectares**

How has this been done? How did you react? Visit the website given in the Link box and check the latest figures.

Activity

1 Work out how rapidly the population is growing and how rapidly land is being lost.

There are three common reactions to these sets of data and the way that they are changing:

- Panic!
- Bury one's head in the sand!
- Think carefully, as a geographer, so that you can start to take control of your situation by knowing the complex causes, some of the possible outcomes and some of the ways of managing the outcomes better, for yourself and for the planet.

This section of the book will guide you through a geographer's way of thinking about the issues, and help you to take a rational view of population change.

Figure 5.2 on page 156 shows how the world's population increased between 1950 and 2006 and how experts predict that it will go on increasing up to 2050. The pattern shown on the graph is fairly straightforward. It is shown, more or less, by a straight line. However, careful study shows that there is a rather more complicated pattern.

Activities

2 Study Figure 5.2. How long did it take for the population to increase from:

a   3 billion to 4 billion?

b   4 billion to 5 billion?

c   5 billion to 6 billion?

According to the prediction, how long will it take to increase from:

d   6 billion to 7 billion?

e   7 billion to 8 billion?

f   8 billion to 9 billion?

3 a   How long did it take to double from 3 billion to 6 billion?

b   Can you predict how long it will take to double from 6 billion to 12 billion?

4 Discuss the class's predictions, in the answers to 3b. What might happen to upset those predictions?

5 What is happening to the rate of growth?

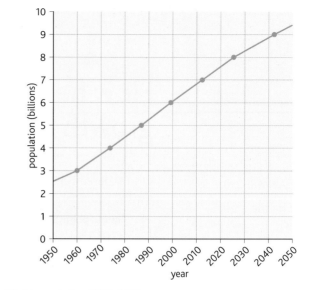

Fig. 5.2 *World population, 1950–2050*

Figure 5.2 is based on population predictions for the next 40 years derived from the trends observed over the last 60 years or so. However, Figure 5.3 looks at the issue on quite a different timescale.

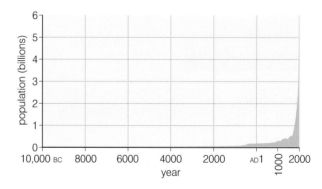

Fig. 5.3 *World population curve, 10,000 BC to the present*

Activity

6 Study Figure 5.3.

a   From this graph, can you predict what will happen to population over the next 50 or 100 years? Will simple projections of past trends into the future be possible using this graph?

b   Can this rate of growth continue?

c   Is this rate sustainable?

d   Might it be true to say that the growth of population in the 20th century was unique and can never be repeated?

The statistics for Table 5.1 were based on a series of estimates of total world population, made by a variety of historians, ecologists, archaeologists, and so on. You can study them in more precise detail in Table 5.2. These estimates are also based on a variety of sources of information.

 Activity

7 Study Figure 5.3 and Table 5.1 together. Using your general historical knowledge, try to think of explanations for some of the surges in world population and for some of the sudden falls.

Different people have interpreted their information in a variety of ways, and sometimes they have come up with different estimates. For some years a lower and an upper estimate have been given. When the estimates did not agree, only the lower estimate was used for the graph.

Many of the increases were a result of developments in technology such as:

- the development of crop growing rather than simple gathering
- the invention of metal tools
- advances in plant breeding
- inventions of machinery that could be used in agriculture
- advances in medicine and hygiene
- developments in the preservation and storage of food.

Of course, changes in the organisation of society were also needed to allow these technological developments to be used and transmitted to people across a large area. These changes often led to increased urbanisation. Administrators, traders, scientists and other groups came together in cities. The people in the cities both supported and relied on the farmers in the surrounding rural areas.

On the other hand, when the organisation in the cities broke down there was often a reduction in the population. This was particularly evident in the areas around the Mediterranean Sea after the fall of the Roman Empire. Other important falls in population came when plagues spread widely.

The biggest, most rapid and most sustained growth in world population clearly occurred in the period between about 1700 and the present. A number of factors came together and supported each other to start this remarkable rate of growth. These included:

- the industrial revolution
- the agricultural revolution, including developments in the breeding of plants and animals, the mechanisation of agriculture, scientific use of fertilisers, improved transport and marketing, etc.
- medical advances
- better understanding of hygiene and its importance in reducing the spread of disease
- improved transport and navigation, which opened up many parts of the world to trade and allowed the spread of the technologies described above.

Table 5.1 *Historical estimates of world population*

Year	Summary	
	Lower	Upper
–10000	1	10
–8000	5	
–6500	5	10
–5000	5	20
–4000	7	
–3000	14	
–2000	27	
–1000	50	
–500	100	
–400	162	
–200	150	231
1	170	400
200	190	256
400	190	206
500	190	206
600	200	206
700	207	210
800	220	224
900	226	240
1000	254	345
1100	301	320
1200	360	450
1250	400	416
1300	360	432
1340	443	
1400	350	374
1500	425	540
1600	545	579
1650	470	545
1700	600	679
1750	629	961
1800	813	1125
1850	1128	1402
1900	1550	1762
1910	1750	
1920	1860	
1930	2070	
1940	2300	
1950	2400	2557

All figures are in millions, based on a variety of estimates by archeologists

In the 1970s, as the world population passed 4 billion, the following headline appeared:

It's not that we have started breeding like rabbits, more that we have stopped dying like flies

Table 5.2 *Some countries and their population statistics*

Country	Population (millions)	0–14 (%)	15–64 (%)	>65 (%)	Growth rate (%)	Birth rate (‰)	Death rate (‰)	Migration rate (%)	Infant mortality rate (‰)	Life expectancy (LE) (years)	LE (men)	LE (women)	Fertility rate/ woman	GDP per capita ($)
Algeria	32.9	28.1	67.1	4.8	1.22	17.40	4.61	−0.35	29.87	73.26	71.68	74.92	1.89	7,700
Bangladesh	147.4	32.9	63.6	3.5	2.09	29.80	8.27	−0.68	60.83	62.46	62.47	62.45	3.11	2,200
Botswana	1.6	38.3	57.9	3.8	−0.04	23.10	29.50	6.07	53.70	33.74	33.90	33.56	2.79	11,400
Brazil	188.1	25.8	68.1	6.1	1.04	16.56	6.17	−0.03	28.60	71.97	68.02	76.12	1.91	8,600
Chad	9.9	47.9	49.3	2.7	2.93	45.73	16.38	−0.11	91.45	47.52	45.88	49.21	6.25	1,500
China	1314	20.8	71.4	7.7	0.59	13.25	6.97	−0.39	23.12	75.28	70.89	74.46	1.73	7,600
Cuba	11.3	19.1	70.3	10.6	0.31	11.89	7.22	−1.57	6.22	77.41	75.11	79.85	1.66	3,900
Ethiopia	74.7	43.7	53.6	2.7	2.31	37.98	14.86	0	93.62	49.03	47.86	50.24	5.22	1,000
France	62.7	18.3	65.3	16.4	0.35	11.99	9.14	0.66	4.21	79.93	76.10	83.54	1.84	30,100
Germany	82.4	14.1	66.4	19.4	−0.02	8.25	10.62	2.18	4.12	78.80	75.81	81.96	1.39	31,400
Ghana	22.4	38.8	57.7	3.5	2.07	30.52	9.72	−0.11	55.02	58.87	58.07	59.69	3.99	2,600
Hungary	18.0	15.6	62.2	15.2	−0.25	9.72	13.11	0.86	8.39	72.66	68.45	77.14	1.32	17,300
India	1095.4	30.8	64.3	4.9	1.38	22.01	8.18	−0.07	54.63	64.71	63.90	65.57	2.73	3,700
Japan	127.5	14.2	65.7	20.0	2.02	9.37	9.16	0	3.24	81.25	77.96	84.70	1.40	33,100
Kenya	34.7	42.6	55.1	2.3	2.57	39.72	14.02	0	59.26	48.93	49.78	48.07	4.91	1,200
Malaysia	24.4	32.6	62.6	4.7	1.78	22.86	5.05	0	17.6	72.50	69.80	75.38	3.04	12,700
Pakistan	165.8	39.0	56.9	4.1	2.09	29.74	8.23	−0.59	70.45	63.39	62.40	64.44	4.00	2,600
Singapore	4.5	15.6	76.1	8.3	1.42	9.34	4.28	9.12	2.29	81.71	79.13	84.49	1.06	30,900
South Korea	48.8	18.9	71.9	9.2	0.42	10.00	5.85	0	6.16	77.04	73.61	80.75	1.27	24,200
UK	60.6	17.5	66.8	15.8	0.28	10.71	10.13	2.18	5.08	78.54	76.09	81.13	1.66	31,400
USA	298.0	20.4	67.2	12.5	0.91	14.14	8.26	3.18	6.43	77.85	75.02	80.82	2.09	43,500

💡 ℹ️ How is population measured?

Demography is the study of **population structure** and change. Demographers need to define the main factors that contribute to population change. These are sometimes called the vital rates.

Table 5.2 gives some examples of countries and their vital population statistics. All the statistics are estimates for 2005, made by the United Nations and based on the most up-to-date census figures available for each country.

Activities

8   a   For each column in Table 5.2:
- list the three top-scoring countries
- list the three bottom-scoring countries.

     b   Discuss whether it is good, bad or neither to be top of the list.

     c   Compare the countries that do well across all the different columns. Do any patterns emerge?

     d   Compare the countries that do badly across all the different columns. Do any patterns emerge?

9   How well can the ranking of any of the population statistics be explained by comparison with the GDP of the countries?

10   Draw scatter graphs to show the relationships for a number of different sets of statistics.

Skills

Drawing a scatter graph

1   Place GDP on the *x*-axis, because it is the independent axis and we think that it may influence the other variable.

2   Place the other (dependent) variable on the *y*-axis.

3   Plot each country with a point. Do not join the points as this is not a line graph.

4   Look carefully to see if there is a trend. This might be a **positive trend** or a **negative trend**; it might be **strong** or **weak.**

5   If there is a trend, draw a **best-fit line**, or **trend line**. This is a line drawn through the centre of the distribution of points. It is usually drawn as close as possible to the majority of the points, to show the trend of the relationship.

6   You can draw the best-fit line by eye, estimating where it should go. Make sure there are equal numbers of points above and below the line.

7   You could make the best-fit line more accurate by working out the **average point** and drawing your line through this point. To do this, work out the mean of all the values on the *x*-axis and the mean of all the points on the *y*-axis; then mark this point on the graph. Use a symbol that is different from that used for marking each country's position.

8   Identify any **residuals** – points that lie well away from the best-fit line and which do not fit the general pattern shown by the rest of the points.

A graph of the relationship between GDP and fertility rate is shown in Figure 5.4.

a Plotting the graph

2 Work out a scale and complete the *y*-axis.

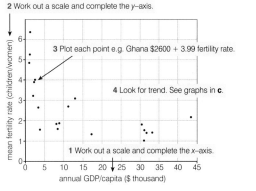

3 Plot each point e.g. Ghana $2600 + 3.99 fertility rate.

4 Look for trend. See graphs in **c**.

1 Work out a scale and complete the *x*-axis.

b Drawing the best fit line

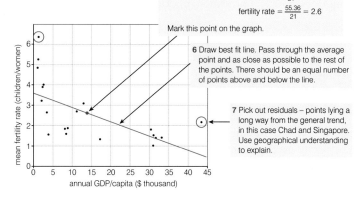

5 Calculate 'average point': GDP = $\frac{308{,}600}{21}$ = $14,700

fertility rate = $\frac{55.36}{21}$ = 2.6

Mark this point on the graph.

6 Draw best fit line. Pass through the average point and as close as possible to the rest of the points. There should be an equal number of points above and below the line.

7 Pick out residuals – points lying a long way from the general trend, in this case Chad and Singapore. Use geographical understanding to explain.

c Interpreting the graph

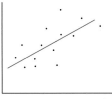
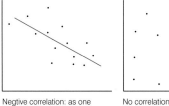
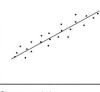
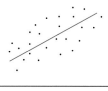

Positive correlation: as one variable goes up, so does the other

Negtive correlation: as one variable goes up, the other goes down

No correlation

Strong correlation

Weak correlation

Fig. 5.4 *Drawing a scatter graph*

Key terms

Death rate (DR): the number of deaths per thousand population per year, expressed as deaths per thousand (‰).

Birth rate (BR): the number of live births per thousand population per year, expressed as births per thousand (‰).

Infant mortality: a measure of the number of infants dying under one year of age, usually expressed as the number of deaths per thousand live births per year.

Natural increase/decrease: the difference between the numbers of births and deaths for every hundred people per year expressed as a percentage.

Link

To see how some of these rates apply to Britain today, and how they have changed over time, go to:

http://vision.edina.ac.uk/index.jsp.

What causes population change?

Activity 10 probably showed that there are strong correlations between a country's wealth and aspects of its population geography. **Death rate (DR)** and **birth rate (BR)** both seem to fall as GDP increases. But it only showed that countries with higher GDP tend to have lower BR and DR. Table 5.2 shows data for one year only and it does not show that there is a change over time.

However, Figure 5.5 shows how the UK's BR, DR and total population have altered during the last 300 years or so. Reliable estimates and census returns go back further for the UK than for any other country. Here are some of the factors that help to explain the changes in the population.

■ Death rates fluctuated up until about 1740. In years of plenty the DR fell, rising again in periods of scarcity. It also rose when epidemics of illness struck. The BR stayed high to compensate for the high DR.

■ Between 1770 and 1870 **infant mortality** fell, mainly as a result of improved nutrition.

■ From 1780 onwards, improvements in agriculture helped to provide a more reliable food supply for the population.

■ From 1800 the industrial revolution led to a move to towns. Factory owners tried to ensure that there was enough food to keep the workforce efficient.

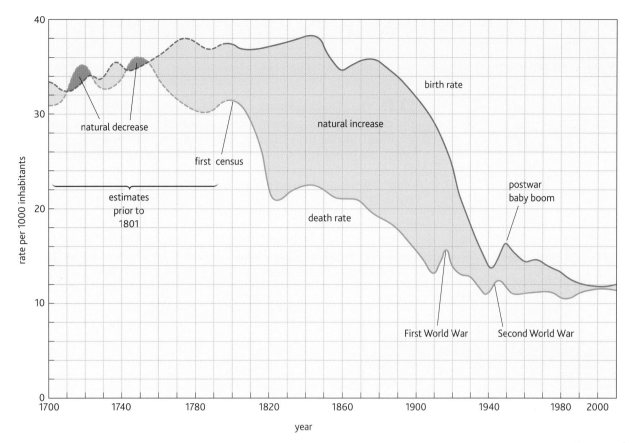

Fig. 5.5 *Changes in Britain's birth and death rates, 1700–2006*

- As the towns grew, the DR increased due to insanitary conditions in the towns.
- Public health acts in the mid and late 19th century led to improved water supply and sewage disposal systems in the towns.
- Through most of the 19th century, demand for labour in the factories and low wages for the workers meant that it was an economic advantage to have a large family to add to household income.
- Compulsory education and factory reforms after 1870 made employment of children much more difficult.
- In the 1870s Annie Besant published pamphlets advocating birth control.
- In 1906 the government took positive action to improve the health of mothers, infants and schoolchildren.
- From 1870 onwards, scientific developments steadily improved medical and surgical practice.
- The birth rate fell during the two world wars and the depression of the 1930s.
- There was a marked baby boom after the Second World War.
- The use of oral contraceptives and other contraceptives became widespread after about 1960.
- The Abortion Act 1967 legalised abortion in some circumstances.

Activity

11 Annotate a copy of Figure 5.5 with some of the words and phrases from the list of causes of population change.

The demographic transition model

The demographic transition model is based on experience of the changes that took place in Britain, and some other industrialised countries, during the 19th and 20th centuries. In several of these countries, population – in terms of birth rates, death rates and total population – was seen to have gone through a series of stages in a logical order. The original version of the model had four stages, as shown in Figure 5.6.

The model shown in Figure 5.6 was a purely descriptive model – it showed what had happened. However, the model began to be used as a predictive model. It was suggested that what had been seen to happen in some industrialised countries over a period of two centuries would happen in other countries in different circumstances (see Figure 5.7).

The demographic transition model has strengths and weaknesses. It is particularly strong as a descriptive model but less strong as a predictive model.

Strengths:

■ It is dynamic, showing change through time.

■ It describes what has happened in the UK.

■ Many other countries in Europe and North America went through similar stages as they industrialised.

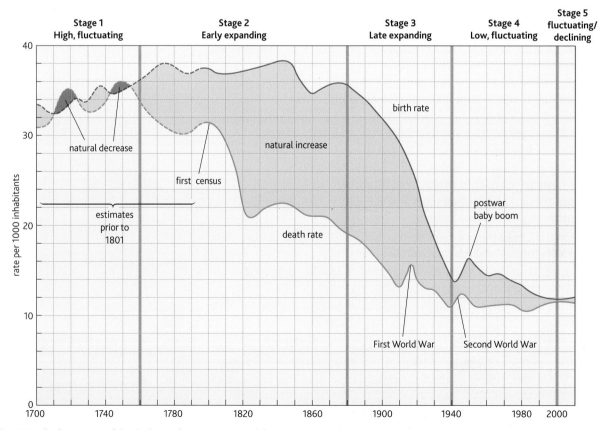

Fig. 5.6 *The five stages of the demographic transition model*

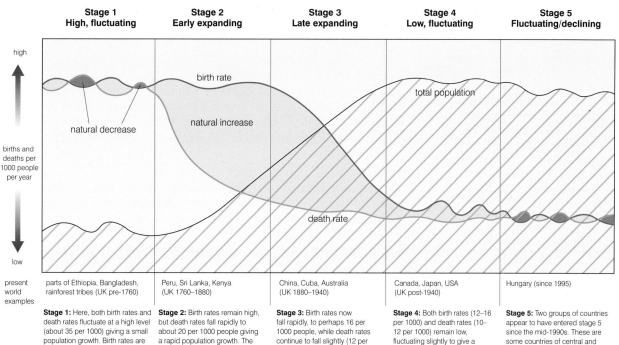

Stage 1 High, fluctuating	Stage 2 Early expanding	Stage 3 Late expanding	Stage 4 Low, fluctuating	Stage 5 Fluctuating/declining

present world examples

parts of Ethiopia, Bangladesh, rainforest tribes (UK pre-1760)	Peru, Sri Lanka, Kenya (UK 1760–1880)	China, Cuba, Australia (UK 1880–1940)	Canada, Japan, USA (UK post-1940)	Hungary (since 1995)

Stage 1: Here, both birth rates and death rates fluctuate at a high level (about 35 per 1000) giving a small population growth. Birth rates are high because:
- no birth control or family planning
- so many children die in infancy that parents tend to produce more in the hope that several will survive
- many children are needed to work on the land and support parents in old age.

High death rates, especially among children, are due to:
- disease and plague (bubonic, cholera, kwashiorkor)
- famine, uncertain food supplies, poor diet
- poor hygiene: no piped, clean water and no sewage disposal
- little medical science: few doctors, hospitals, drugs.

Stage 2: Birth rates remain high, but death rates fall rapidly to about 20 per 1000 people giving a rapid population growth. The fall in death rates result from:
- improved medical care: vaccinations, hospitals, doctors, new drugs and scientific inventions
- improved sanitation and water supply
- improvements in food production, both quality and quantity
- improved transport to move food, doctors, etc.
- a decrease in child mortality.

Stage 3: Birth rates now fall rapidly, to perhaps 16 per 1000 people, while death rates continue to fall slightly (12 per 1000 people) to give a slowly increasing population. The fall in birth rates may be due to:
- family planning: contraceptives, sterilisation, abortion and government incentives
- a lower infant mortality rate leading to less pressure to have so many children
- increased industrialisation and mechanisation meaning fewer labourers are needed
- increased desire for material possessions and less desire for large families
- emancipation of women, enabling them to follow their own careers rather than being solely child-bearers.

In countries like the UK, these changes developed slowly over many years. However, the changes were introduced quickly and suddenly into many countries of Asia, Africa and South America.

Stage 4: Both birth rates (12–16 per 1000) and death rates (10–12 per 1000) remain low, fluctuating slightly to give a steady population.

Stage 5: Two groups of countries appear to have entered stage 5 since the mid-1990s. These are some countries of central and eastern Europe where the birth rate has fallen below replacement level and some countries of southern Africa where HIV/Aids has caused a rapid rise in the death rate. However, is this second group really Stage 5 or a return to Stage 1?

Fig. 5.7 *The demographic transition model, adapted to show an expanded fifth stage*

▨ Some newly industrialised countries (NICs) such as Singapore and South Korea also seemed to go through similar stages, but faster than countries like Britain had done.

▨ The model helps to explain what has happened and why it has happened in that particular sequence.

Weaknesses:

▨ It is based on the experience of industrialising countries and is not so relevant to non-industrialising countries.

▨ The model assumed that stage 2 followed from industrialisation. In many countries this has not been the case. The factors that caused the death rate to start falling (better medical care, better sanitation, etc.) were imported from colonising countries and so arrived far more quickly than in Europe.

▨ Similarly, the model assumed that stage 3 followed several decades after stage 2 and that the death rate fell as a consequence of changes brought about by changes in the birth rate. This has often not been

HIV: human immunodeficiency virus, which attacks the immune system of people who are infected. Infection is caused when body fluids from an infected person are passed into the body of another. This can happen through unprotected sexual intercourse, blood transfusions, sharing of needles, or from mother to baby during childbirth.

Aids: acquired immune deficiency syndrome; a group of infections, including pneumonia, TB and skin cancers, that strike people whose immune system has been damaged by the HIV virus.

Dependency ratio: shows how many young people (under 16) and older people (over 64) depend on people of working age (16 to 64). The dependency ratio is worked out with this formula:

$$\frac{(\% \text{ under } 15) + (\% \text{ over } 65)}{\% \text{ between } 15 \text{ and } 64} \times 100$$

Countries that have a high dependency ratio have more people who are not of working age, and fewer who are working and paying taxes. The higher the number, the more people who need looking after.

the case. In some countries the onset of stage 3 was held back by the population's attitudes to family size, birth control, status, religion, etc. In other cases the fall was speeded up by government intervention, such as China's policy of one child per family and some of its subsequent population policies.

■ The original model has had to be adapted to include a fifth stage. This seemed to be happening in some countries of western Europe and in Japan in the late 20th century. It is now clearly seen in some countries in east and central Europe where the death rate exceeds the birth rate.

■ Countries of southern Africa (and other areas may follow), where the death rate has risen dramatically because of **HIV/Aids**, appear to have slipped back into a situation more like stage 1. The model does not help to predict the future of these countries.

Population pyramids and the demographic transition model

Birth rates and death rates affect a country's population structure. A very good way to show the structure of a country's population is by drawing a population pyramid. Figure 5.8 shows the population pyramid for the UK.

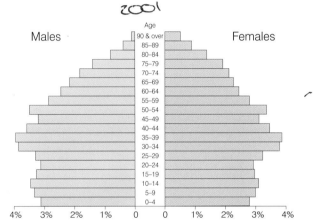

The percentages on the pyramid represent the percentage of males (to the left) and females (to the right) that are in that age/sex group.

Fig. 5.8 *Population pyramid for the UK*

■ Activities

12 a On a copy of Figure 5.8 label:
■ those in their 50s and 60s: the postwar baby boom
■ those in their 40s: the baby boom of the 1960s
■ those in their 30s: low fertility in the 1970s
■ those aged around 10: low fertility in the late 1990s.

b Also add labels to show that:
■ there has subsequently been an increase in birth rate in the early years of the 21st century
■ over the age of 70 there is an increasing majority of women over men
■ women over 90 outnumber men of the same age by more than 5 to 1.

13 Describe the overall shape of the UK pyramid.

Activities

14 Suggest what the pyramid shows about the UK's birth and death rates and about its position on the demographic transition model.

15 Use the statistics in Table 5.3 to draw your own population pyramid for Kenya. Annotate your pyramid for Kenya to show its main features.

16 Describe the main differences between the pyramid for Kenya and the pyramid for the UK.

17 Explain why the pyramid for Kenya is typical of a country in stage 2 of the demographic transition model.

Figure 5.9 shows some outline pyramids. These represent short-hand versions of the pyramids of five countries at different stages in the transition. Note that each of these pyramids has lines drawn on it to separate the age cohorts 0–15, 16–65 and over 65. These are often considered to be young dependent, working age and retired sectors of the population respectively. Of course this is a marked oversimplification of reality. In the UK and other developed countries, a decreasing proportion of people start work at 16 and many retire before 65. In many poor countries, most children start work before they are 16. However, the lines still illustrate a useful idea – the **dependency ratio**.

Table 5.3 *Kenya census, 2001*

Age range	Males	Females
85 and over	0.1	0.1
80–84	0.1	0.1
75–79	0.2	0.1
70–74	0.3	0.2
65–69	0.5	0.4
60–64	0.7	0.6
55–59	0.9	0.8
50–54	1.1	1.1
45–49	1.7	1.6
40–44	2.0	2.0
35–39	2.4	2.4
30–34	3.3	3.1
25–29	4.5	4.5
20–24	5.4	5.4
15–19	5.9	5.8
10–14	6.0	6.0
5–9	6.5	6.5
0–4	8.9	8.8

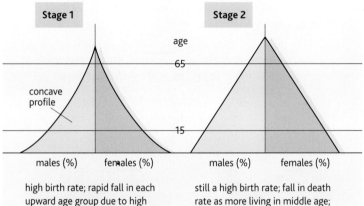

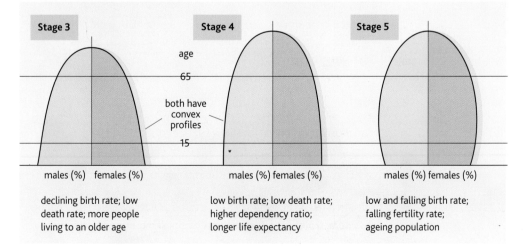

Fig. 5.9 *Outline pyramids showing different stages in the DTM*

■ **Key terms**

Life expectancy: the average age to which the population lives. It is expressed in terms of years. Male and female life expectancy figures are often given separately.

Using population pyramids for predictions

A population pyramid represents a snapshot of a country's population at any one time. However, a pyramid can be animated to show how that country's population might develop in future. Computer programs to do this are based on the knowledge of:

▓ the present population structure

▓ present birth rates and fertility rates

▓ present death rates and **life expectancy**

▓ predictable future variations in the vital rates.

These variables are used to predict how many children will be born to each cohort of the pyramid as they move through the age ranges, and then how long the members of each cohort will survive for.

■ **Link**

Follow this link to watch a pyramid progress over the years:

www.statistics.gov.uk/populationestimates/svg_pyramid/default.htm.

■ **Activity**

18 Study Figure 5.10.

a What happens to the size of the cohort that is 0–4 in 2000 on both the 2025 and 2050 pyramids? Select other age cohorts and follow them through the three graphs.

b Study the 0–4 cohort on each of the three graphs. How does its size vary?

c Describe and explain the overall changes in the shapes of the pyramids for the UK and Kenya.

d Suggest how the population structure might be changed by trends such as the in-migration of European workers, the out-migration of retired people to homes in Spain and other such movements.

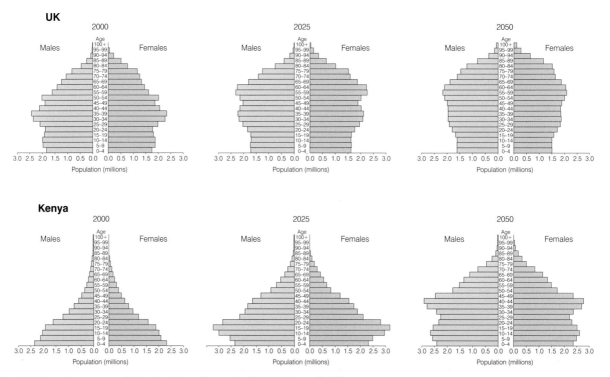

Fig. 5.10 *Population pyramids for the UK and Kenya for 2000, 2025 and 2050*

The consequences of different population structures

Look back at the information on world population on page 155. Try to work out how much the world population has increased since you started work on this chapter.

The world probably had its period of most rapid population growth between about 1960 and 2000. Although the population is still increasing, the rate of increase has slowed down and the most respected predictions suggest that the rate of increase will continue to slow down. However, the rate differs markedly from one world region to another and the predictions suggest that the differences will continue to be apparent.

The rates from 1950 to the present and the predicted rates up to 2050 are shown on Figure 5.11 (note that this is a semi-logarithmic graph).

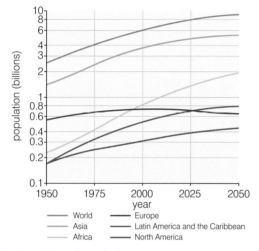

Fig. 5.11 *World and continental populations*

Skills

Reading logarithmic graphs

Logarithmic graphs are drawn on special logarithmic graph paper. There are two types of log graph paper:

- Logarithmic (or log/log) graphs have logarithmic scales on both axes.
- Semi-logarithmic graphs have a log scale on the *y*-axis but a normal scale on the *x*-axis.

Semi-log graphs are often used for presenting and interpreting data showing changes through time. They are especially useful when a value is increasing at a constant rate. For instance, Figure 5.11 shows a set of values from 1950 and 2050. On normal graph paper it would be very difficult to show such a big range of values (180 million is the lowest and 9 billion is the highest). A graph drawn on standard graph paper would be very difficult to read. A semi-log graph changes the shape of the curve and can make it far more manageable, as illustrated in Figure 5.11. In fact, the curve for total world population is transformed from a parabolic line (like the one in Figure 5.3 on page 156) to become an almost straight line.

Link

You can download log/log and semi-log graph paper at:

www.printfreegraphpaper.com.

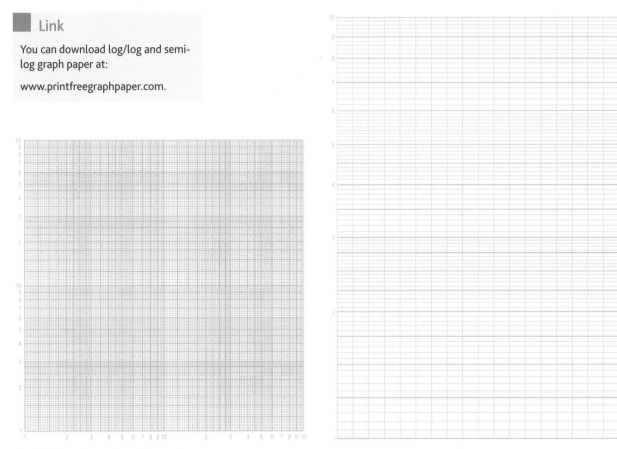

Fig. 5.12 *Log/log and semi-log graph paper*

Note that the logarithmic scale on the *y*-axis consists of a series of cycles. Each cycle is numbered from 1 to 9 and then to 1 again. Also note that the distance between the lines gradually decreases with distance from the origin in the bottom left-hand corner of the graph.

Each cycle should be numbered by adding noughts to the printed numbers. This can make a cycle represent 1 to 100, or 100 to 1000, or 1000 to 10,000, and so on. Alternatively, a cycle can go from from 0.1 to 1, from 0.01 to 0.1, and so on.

Over- and underpopulation

In order to understand whether rises or falls in population are good or bad for countries, it is useful to consider the concept of **optimum population**. Linked to this concept are the ideas of **overpopulation** and **underpopulation**.

Overpopulation is not the same as dense population, and underpopulation is not the same as sparse population. In fact, the concept is closely linked with availability of resources. A resource-rich country can hold a large population at a good standard of living, while a resource-poor country could be overpopulated even though its population appears to be low and its population density sparse.

Note that the definition of optimum population refers to the level of technological development of the society. Advances in technology could make the area more productive and could enable the exploitation of resources that had not, up to that moment, been of any value.

People must also be counted as a resource, or at least the people who are productive or potential members of the workforce. Education and training too can make people more productive and so increase the potential of the area to support more people. Refer back to Figure 5.3 and Table 5.1 on pages 156–7 to see how changes in technology led to changes in the world's population. Was necessity really the mother of invention? Was it a growing population that forced people to develop new technologies to support their growth?

One word of warning is necessary about the concept of optimum population. It was developed in the period before the idea of sustainability had become so important to geographers (and to environmentalists, economists, politicians and the general public). Nowadays, when we consider the three concepts of optimum, over- and underpopulation we need also to consider how sustainable the land and the resources are at any given level of population and technological development.

Activity

20 Discuss the advantages and disadvantages that might arise for a continent or a country from:
- a rising population
- a falling population.

Activity

21 To see how the concepts apply, discuss the following situations. Does each one describe overpopulation, underpopulation or optimum population?

- London in the first decade of the 21st century is one of the most densely populated areas in Europe, and yet it is drawing in migrants from all over the UK, Europe and the world to fill its ever-increasing need for workers.

- Rural France has been losing population throughout most of the last hundred years. People move to the cities for an improved standard of living. Many of the areas that they have left have become desirable as holiday homes for the British, seeking the peace that depopulation has brought. Has the sparse population has become a resource?

- Darfur is a sparsely populated region of Sudan. It is experiencing massive unrest, described by some people as **genocide**, as different groups compete for control of the land. Some people consider that the ethnic rivalry is a form of competition for land as climate change leads to a growing shortage of water and farmland.

- Israeli settlers have moved into several areas of the West Bank, which used to be occupied by Palestinian farmers and herdsmen. The high-tech style of Israeli farming means that the land can now support more people with a higher standard of living. However, the displaced Palestinians are now refugees in camps in Gaza and are forced to live on aid.

Optimum population does not just depend on a country's or region's total population. In present societies it is just as much dependent on the age and sex structure of the population. For instance, many European countries are concerned about the population time bomb, or the ageing population structure.

From the 1960s onwards, people have been able to take more and more control over their own individual fertility. Here are some of the consequences:

- reduced birth rate and a reduced fertility ratio because of the availability of family planning services and abortion
- later first births for women

Key terms

Optimum population: the population at which the quality of life of the people of a country or a region is the highest possible, at a given level of technological development.

Overpopulation: when any increase in population reduces the average quality of life of the population.

Underpopulation: when an increase in population could increase the average quality of life.

Genocide: the deliberate and systematic destruction or killing of an entire people who belong to one racial, political, cultural or religious group.

■ women are able to pursue their careers for longer

■ families often come to depend on the mother's income

■ house price inflation because families with two incomes are now competing for houses.

These consequences have led to a reduction in the size of the cohorts entering the labour market. As this has been accompanied by an increasing life expectancy and an aspiration towards earlier retirement, there has been a steady decrease in the size of the working population and an increase in the retired population. This has produced a decrease in the number of working taxpayers and an increase in the number of people expecting to live off their pensions.

Other structural changes in society are expected to follow in the wake of these changes. For example, as populations age there will be pressure to reduce the workforce in teaching or to keep the workforce and reduce class sizes. At the same time there will an increase in the demand for services for the old. Ultimately this will take the form of an increased need for the provision of long-term residential care for the old.

In 2007 the Office for Population Statistics announced that the early years of the 21st century had seen a marked increase in the birth rate in England and Wales. This was caused by:

■ women in their 30s starting the families they had postponed while working

■ increased birth rate among recent immigrant groups who had started families after settling in the UK.

■ Case study

Italy

The situation in Italy is particularly interesting. In many European countries there is concern about low birth rates, falling fertility ratios and ageing populations. Figure 5.13 and Table 5.4 show that Italy is one of the countries where these concerns are greatest.

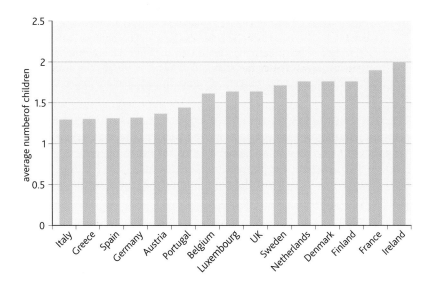

Fig. 5.13 *Children per woman in Europe*

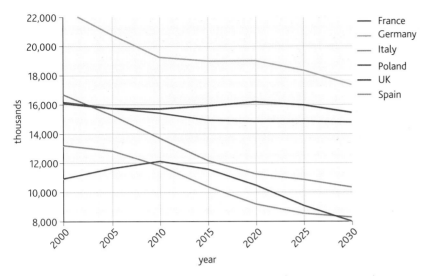

Fig. 5.14 *Population aged 20–40 in six European countries (excluding migrants)*

Table 5.4 *Italy's population: some facts*

Italy's population was 58 million in 2005. It will decline to 56 million by 2025, even with net immigration of 150,000 per year
With no net immigration it will decline to 54 million
That 4 million decline will be the net result of three changes: ▪ a 2 million decrease in the 0–19 age cohort ▪ a 5 million decrease in the 20–64 age cohort ▪ a 3 million increase in the 65+ age cohort
Total fertility in 2004: 1.33 (a slight recovery from the lowest figure of 1.19 in 1999), almost the lowest in the West (Spain slightly lower)
Italy's life expectancy of 81 is among the highest in the world
Italy's median age in 2025 is expected to be 51 years, the highest in western Europe

Given some of the stereotypes the British hold about the Italians, this seems to be an odd situation. We often think of the Italians as very family centred with large extended family units living close together. We think of them as practising Catholics who are unlikely to use artificial birth control and abortion. Why does the country have such a low fertility rate?

Perhaps it is partly a result of that very close family structure that we associate with the Italians, which has always tended to keep young Italians living at home with their parents longer than other young Europeans. This tendency has been reinforced by changing economic circumstances in the past 10 to 20 years:

▪ More Italians stay in full-time education than used to be the case, and this makes them more dependent than ever on their parents.

▪ The price of housing has increased, especially in the northern cities, making it more difficult for young adults to set up home on their own.

▪ There are fewer well-paid but low-skill jobs than before.

▪ State social security expenditure for families and children is much lower than in most other EU countries (see Table 5.5).

Table 5.5 *Social expenditure for families and children in selected European countries, 2002*

	Fraction of total social expenditure (%)	Per capita expenditure (euros)
Italy	3.8	189
Spain	3.6	107
France	12.7	867
Sweden	12.9	1148
Mean (EU 15)	10.8	736

This has had a massive effect on the age at which young Italians leave home, marry or enter into a long-term relationship and start a family (see Table 5.6).

Table 5.6 *Young Italians cohabiting with their parents, 1993 and 2003*

| | Percentage of the same age | | | |
| | Women | | Men | |
Age	1993	2003	1993	2003
20–24	78.9	83.7	90.9	92.3
25–29	36.8	51.7	60.5	70.5
30–34	12.2	21.4	24.9	37.4

Italian commentators suggest that the government needs to develop policies to deal with this impending crisis, achieve sustainable development and keep a balanced population structure of workers and dependants by:

■ empowering young people and reversing the 'postponement syndrome' through grants for education and allowances for families

■ a structured programme to manage immigration by carefully selecting new migrants to match labour force vacancies

■ allowing access to citizenship rights for migrants, to encourage them to settle and raise families.

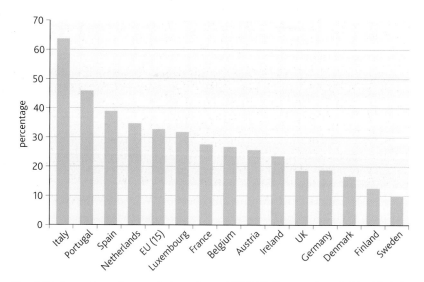

Fig. 5.15 *Percentage of unmarried people aged 20–34 in Europe who cohabit with their parents, 2003–04*

■ Case study

China's one-child policy

Nowhere in the world is population policy more important than in China. In 1950 China's population was around 0.6 billion and the state's philosophy was that every birth was a valuable addition to national resources and power.

By 1975 total population was over 0.9 billion with a birth rate of around 30 per thousand. The government now realised that such rapid growth, if it continued unchecked, would lead to **famine** and **starvation** on a massive scale. Therefore in 1981 it introduced a policy of one child per family.

At the heart of the policy was a letter from the government to the Communist Party throughout the country urging people to have just one child and encouraging local party workers to enforce the policy. In some parts of the country the policy remained as advice

Key terms

Famine: a time when there is so little food that many people starve.

Starvation: a state of extreme hunger resulting from lack of essential nutrients over a prolonged period.

Fig. 5.16 *Small families allow China to modernise and families to find wealth and happiness*

and guidance to the people; in other areas the policy was strictly enforced by local authorities. In some areas and at some times, incentives were paid to people who followed the policy; in other places and at other times, people were fined heavily for failing to follow the policy, and compulsory abortions and sterilisations were carried out.

Throughout the country, contraceptive advice was freely available and people were encouraged into late marriages. Some of the most zealous enforcers of the policy were the famous 'granny police', who were given responsibility for encouraging the young people in their district to use contraception and avoid unplanned pregnancies.

Two unforeseen consequences of the policy were the practice of female infanticide and of the abandonment of baby girls. Most reports of this came from rural areas where tradition had always

Did you know?

In May 2008 an earthquake struck Sichuan province in China. It destroyed a middle school along with many other buildings. Imagine the doubling of parents' grief when so many of the dead were only children, a further unforeseen consequence of the one-child policy.

said that sons would marry and bring their wives to live on the parents' farm to support the parents in old age. In such a society, not having a son was an economic disaster. Therefore, right from the very early stages, the policy was relaxed to a certain extent in rural areas.

After nearly 30 years of the policy, what is the present situation? In 2000 the government was willing to relax and adjust the policy but made it clear to the people that the policy was going to stay in place.

> **We cannot just be content with the current success, we must make population control a permanent policy.**
>
> As a result of all these efforts, China has had 338 million fewer births in the past 30 years.
>
> *People's Daily*, June 2000

China's population was around 1.3 billion in 2007. Without the one-child policy it would be more than 25 per cent higher.

In 2007 the birth rate was around 14 per thousand and the annual growth rate about 0.5 per cent. What is even more significant is that the population momentum had slowed. That is, the population structure now had a much smaller cohort of women of child-bearing age than would have been the case without the policy and so the tendency to grow rapidly in future has been drastically reduced. It is unlikely that China's population will ever grow at such a rapid rate in future. In fact, China is now concerned that it will face a problem of an ageing population by 2025, when the great baby-boom generation of the 1950s reaches old age.

There is, though, a good chance that the country will be able to provide a reasonable quality of life for its old people due to the economic progress that has been made in the 1990s and 2000s. It is doubtful if that progress would have been possible if those extra 338 million mouths had needed feeding.

There have, of course, been many stories in the Western media about the excesses of the one child per family policy. These will often have been based on truth but they may also have been exaggerated. These views can be balanced by the views of Chinese women themselves – or at least those living in the cities – which sound very similar to the views of UK women.

'The idea that kids are great because they will care for their elderly parents is disappearing,' said Dr Wang, a 55-year-old female doctor. 'Work pressure, women staying in school longer, and a desire for more consumer goods, as well as a wish to have a solid economic base before having kids – all of these factors influence women.'

Link

Go to the People and the Planet website at:

www.peopleandplanet.net.

Enter 'one-child policy' in the search box in the top right.

You can also search for 'one-child policy' on the BBC Radio 4 Woman's Hour website and listen to an article on the subject:

www.bbc.co.uk/radio4/womanshour.

Iran's baby boomers

Iran's population was 70,049,262 according to the 2006 census, with nearly one-quarter of its people aged 15 or younger.

DEMOGRAPHIC SNAPSHOT

The Islamic Republic of Iran is undergoing a demographic and socio-economic transition. The defining feature of its population structure is a large cohort of some 18 million 'baby boomers' – young men and women born between 1979 and 1989. This is a result of the dramatic demographic shifts over the last 30 years.

Throughout much of the 1980s, population growth accelerated rapidly. It then decreased even more quickly to about replacement level. The emergence of the baby boomers into adulthood offers the country the possibility of economic growth – if young people are provided with the skills and opportunities to become productive economic agents. It could result in a second baby boom if the success of the country's family planning efforts are not sustained.

The country's youthful population structure and long life expectancy (about 70 years on average) means that the country will eventually have to confront a large proportion of people over 65 compared with younger people. In 2002, people over the age of 65 accounted for about 5 per cent of the whole population, whereas this group will account for almost a quarter of the population by 2050. Migration of Afghan refugees to Iran, as well as the migration of large numbers of people from rural to urban areas, are other important demographic concerns.

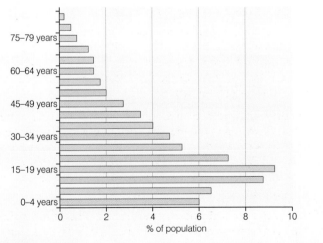

Fig. 5.17 *Iran's population*

www.unfpa.org

Link

This article on Iran is taken from this website:

www.unfpa.org/countryfocus/iran/demographic.htm.

It looks at the general challenges of population and development in the very special circumstances of a country like Iran.

Now study:

www.unfpa.org/countryfocus/iran/women.htm.

It deals with education for women and their reproductive health.

■ Case study

Changing population structures of sub-Saharan Africa

The countries of sub-Saharan Africa are undergoing a population crisis. From the time they gained independence (mostly in the 1960s) right up to the late 1980s they have been characterised by high birth rates and rapidly falling death rates. In fact they have been typical of countries at stage 2 of the demographic transition, with rapid population growth. Towards the end of that period there were signs that birth rates were starting to fall in some of the countries.

Then, in the 1990s, the HIV/Aids epidemic struck the area. It spread more rapidly here than in any other part of the world. The spread was encouraged by these and other factors:

■ poor levels of education

■ low status of women

■ a mobile population where many people migrated to seek work

■ poor levels of basic health care and health education

■ traditional societies where Aids sufferers were stigmatised

■ the slowness of governments to act to tackle the problem

■ the high cost of drugs in a poor society.

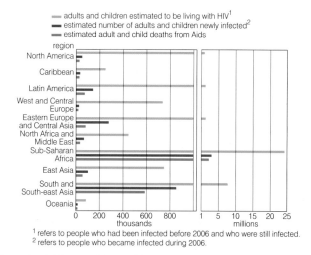

[1] refers to people who had been infected before 2006 and who were still infected.
[2] refers to people who became infected during 2006.

Fig. 5.18 *HIV/Aids around the world in 2006*

■ Questions

1 Carry out a statistical survey of a country in sub-Saharan Africa where the population structure is being affected by the HIV/Aids epidemic.

Go to www.unfpa.org/profile/compare.cfm. Here you can select statistics about population, health, level of development, etc., for up to four countries at a time.

You will be given statistics for each of your chosen countries in 1990 and in the most recent year (usually about two years ago).

Select up to three of the following countries of southern and eastern Africa:

Angola	Botswana	Kenya	Lesotho
Madagascar	Malawi	Mozambique	Namibia
South Africa	Swaziland	Tanzania	Uganda
Zambia	Zimbabwe		

You should also select a country from outside this region of Africa for comparison. Poland might be a useful example as it one of the few European countries where UNFPA collects statistics.

2 Compare the key population statistics and see what conclusions you can draw about:

- the present population structure
- factors creating that structure
- possible changes to the structure in future
- links between fertility rates, mortality rates, education, health care and the status of women.

You will need to pay particular attention to certain statistics like:

- growth rate, birth rate, death rate and urban/rural ratio
- fertility rates and contraceptive usage rates
- GDP and poverty rates
- water supply, antenatal care and female literacy rates
- reproductive health indicators, particularly those linked to HIV/Aids
- urban and rural fertility rates.

Fig. 5.19 *Political map of sub-Saharan Africa*

Population and resources

In this section you will learn:

- how to study some of the models that relate to population and resources

- to assess the strengths and weaknesses of these models on present-day issues.

Look back to the population clocks that you studied at the start of this chapter (see page 155). They are designed to show the changing balance between population and resources in the world as a whole.

The world's population has grown much faster during the last century than it has ever grown before. The growth rate is showing some signs of slowing down, but the population is still growing and it still has a momentum towards further growth.

Many geographers, economists and other academics have tried to work out just how much the world's population can grow before the planet is overwhelmed. These discussions have also been applied to regions of the world and to individual countries. The discussions come up with a variety of answers that depend on the assumptions made, the figures used and the predictions about what might happen in future. In general the resulting models of development have been classified into two groups: **optimistic models** and **pessimistic models**.

It is worth considering some of the early views of the balance between population and resources. Looking at the historical development of such ideas helps to develop an understanding of modern models. The key early models were developed by Malthus (in the late 18th century), Boserup (in the 1960s) and Simon (in the 1980s). The Club of Rome model is often described as neo-Malthusian. Although published in 1972, it is summarised here in greater detail because it is probably the most influential on modern thinking about the subject.

Malthus

Thomas Malthus was an English church minister. In 1798 he wrote his 'Essay on the Principle of Population as it Affects the Future Improvement of Society'. In it he argued that population, if unchecked, grows at a geometrical rate. Meanwhile food supply grows, at best, at an arithmetic rate:

- Population growth   1, 2, 4, 8, 16, 32, etc.
- Food supply growth   1, 2, 3, 4, 5, 6, etc.

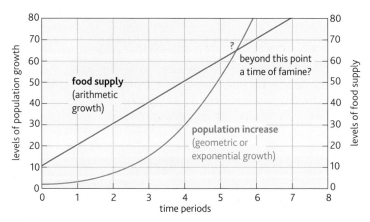

Fig. 5.20 *Relationships between population growth and food supply according to Malthus*

He said that this would inevitably lead to famine, unless mankind showed moral restraint and limited its population growth.

Malthus's predictions did not come true during the 19th century. Although population grew rapidly in Britain, food supply also grew more rapidly due to:

- the agricultural revolution
- the discovery and opening up to trade of new agricultural lands, particularly the North American prairies
- emigration from Britain and Europe to newer territories such as North America and Australia.

However, Malthus's ideas have not been forgotten. Some people, like Boserup and Simon, have presented optimistic models that contradict Malthus's views. Others, like the Club of Rome group, have presented neo-Malthusian or pessimistic models.

■ Boserup and Simon

Esther Boserup was a Danish agricultural economist. In 1965 she put forward her theory to explain why Malthus's ideas had not proved to be true. She said that increases in population act to stimulate changes in agricultural methods. She saw that necessity is the mother of invention. In primitive agricultural societies, increased population had led to reductions of fallow periods, increased use of manure and fertiliser, harvesting of more than one crop per year, irrigation, and so on. All these methods were used to increase intensity of production and to support the increased population.

Boserup saw that similar pressures were leading to the green revolution – the science-based increase in agricultural productivity that took place in many parts of the less developed world from the 1950s onwards.

Julian Simon was an American economist, writing later in the 20th century. His most influential book was *The Ultimate Resource*. In this he argued that the supply of natural resources is really infinite. As a resource appears to be running low, its price will rise and so it will be worth people investing time and thought in producing technology that will:

- find more of that resource
- extract more from what is already known to be available
- discover alternative resources that can replace the one in short supply
- produce alternative ways of organising society to manage without that resource.

In short, there is only one scarcity: human brain power. This is the ultimate resource.

Simon wrote: 'The main fuel to speed the world's progress is the stock of human knowledge. And the ultimate resource is skilled, spirited, hopeful people, exerting their wills and imaginations to provide for themselves and their families, thereby inevitably contributing to the benefit of everyone.' It then follows that population growth rates are not a problem, except possibly in the sense of being too slow.

■ The Club of Rome

The Club of Rome model is currently the most influential of the three models. It was a computer-based simulation of the future development of

■ **Link**

See the section on 'Strategies to increase food production' on page 210.

■ **Link**

Find *The Ultimate Resource* on this website:

www.juliansimon.com.

Look under 'Writings' then 'Ultimate Resource II'.

Link

The full text of *The Limits to Growth* is available at:

www.cluboframe.org.

Search under 'Archive' and then 'Reports'.

Activity

22 *The Limits to Growth* is a very important book. In order to help you to understand the extract and to remember the main arguments, you could use the following strategies.

■ Make a copy of the text.

■ Use a number of coloured pens or highlighter pens to mark key sections of the text.

Either

Underline one or two key phrases from each paragraph of the text, then write a summary of the main arguments in the text, using the highlighted phrases.

Or

Choose three or four main themes from the article. In this case they might be:

■ the basic assumptions that were used to set up the model

■ what happened when the model was run

■ what the model can teach us about our future behaviour.

Then underline points that are relevant to each of these themes. Use a different colour for each theme.

■ Write summaries under the three main headings. You could write each paragraph in the same colour that you used for your underlining. This might help to reinforce the ideas in your memory.

the world's population, based on the most up-to-date computing power available at that time. The findings were published in 1972 as *The Limits to Growth*. Here is an extract:

> Our world model was built specifically to investigate five major trends of global concern – accelerating industrialisation, rapid population growth, widespread malnutrition, depletion of non-renewable resources, and a deteriorating environment.
>
> The model we have constructed is, like every model, imperfect, oversimplified, and unfinished … none of the five factors we are examining here is independent. Each interacts constantly with all the others. We have already mentioned some of these interactions. Population cannot grow without food, food production is increased by growth of capital, more capital requires more resources, discarded resources become pollution, pollution interferes with the growth of both population and food.
>
> Furthermore, over long time periods each of these factors also feeds back to influence itself and each of the other factors.
>
> All levels in the model (population, capital, pollution, etc.) begin with 1900 values. From 1900 to 1970 the variables agree generally with their historical value to the extent that we know them. Population rises from 1.6 billion in 1900 to 3.5 billion in 1970. Although the birth rate declines gradually, the death rate falls more quickly, especially after 1940, and the rate of population growth increases. Industrial output, food and services per capita increase exponentially. The resource base in 1970 is still about 95 percent of its 1900 value, but it declines dramatically thereafter, as population and industrial output continue to grow.
>
> The behavior mode of the system is that of overshoot and collapse. In this run the collapse occurs because of nonrenewable resource depletion. The industrial capital stock grows to a level that requires an enormous input of resources. In the very process of that growth it depletes a large fraction of the resource reserves available. As resource prices rise and mines are depleted, more and more capital must be used for obtaining resources, leaving less to be invested for future growth. Finally investment cannot keep up with depreciation, and the industrial base collapses, taking with it the service and agricultural systems, which have become dependent on industrial inputs (such as fertilizers, pesticides, hospital laboratories, computers, and especially energy for mechanization). For a short time the situation is especially serious because population, with the delays inherent in the age structure and the process of social adjustment, keeps rising. Population finally decreases when the death rate is driven upward by lack of food and health services. The exact timing of these events is not meaningful, given the great aggregation and many uncertainties in the model. It is significant, however, that growth is stopped well before the year 2100. We can thus say with some confidence that, under the assumption of no major change in the present system, population and industrial growth will certainly stop within the next century, at the latest.
>
> Is it better to try to live within that limit by accepting a self-imposed restriction on growth? Or is it preferable to go on growing until some other natural limit arises, in the hope that at that time another technological leap will allow growth to continue still longer? For the last several hundred years human society has followed the

second course so consistently and successfully that the first choice has been all but forgotten.

We would hope that society will receive each technological advance by establishing the answers to three questions before the technology is widely adopted. The questions are:

■ What will be the side-effects, both physical and social, if this development is introduced on a large scale?

■ What social changes will be necessary before this development can be implemented properly, and how long will it take to achieve them?

■ If the development is fully successful and removes some natural limits to growth, what limit will the growing system meet next? Will society prefer its pressures to the ones this development is designed to remove?

Man possesses, for a small moment in his history, the most powerful combination of knowledge, tools, and resources the world has ever known. He has all that is physically necessary to create a totally new form of human society – one that would be built to last for generations. The two missing ingredients are a realistic, long-term goal that can guide mankind to the equilibrium society and the human will to achieve that goal. Without such a goal and a commitment to it, short-term concerns will generate the exponential growth that drives the world system toward the limits of the earth and ultimate collapse. With that goal and that commitment, mankind would be ready now to begin a controlled, orderly transition from growth to global equilibrium.

Our conclusions are:

1 If the present growth trends in world population, industrialisation, pollution, food production, and resource depletion continue unchanged, the limits to growth on this planet will be reached sometime within the next one hundred years. The most probable result will be a rather sudden and uncontrollable decline in both population and industrial capacity.

2 It is possible to alter these growth trends and to establish a condition of ecological and economic stability that is sustainable far into the future. The state of global equilibrium could be designed so that the basic material needs of each person on earth are satisfied and each person has an equal opportunity to realize his individual human potential.

www.cluboframe.org

Activity

23 Study the details of the Club of Rome model and Simon's ultimate resource model.

a Suggest why they have been described as pessimistic and optimistic scenarios for the future of mankind.

b Which of the two theories is better supported by the discussions about global warming and climate change that are taking place at the moment?

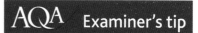

AQA Examiner's tip

Throughout your work in the core human geography section of the specification you should consider how Simon's ultimate resource model and the Club of Rome model apply. You ought to be able to discuss them in relation to

■ food supply issues

■ energy issues

■ health issues

as well as in relation to global population change.

People in cities

In this section you will learn:

- how and why cities grew in the past
- the reasons for the present-day growth of some cities
- to analyse the patterns caused by urbanisation in some cities
- to compare these patterns with cities in your area.

Most people in the UK live in cities. This has been the case since the mid-19th century, when migration from the countryside caused the proportion of the UK's population living in cities to pass 50 per cent.

Table 5.7 *London's population and population density, AD 60 to 2001*

Year	Population	Density (persons/hectare)
60	30,000	
200	45,000–50,000	
1100	14,000–18,000	
1200	20,000–25,000	
1340	40,000–50,000	
1600	200,000	
1650	350,000–400,000	
1700	575,000–600,000	
1750	650,000	
1801	1,096,784	1,764
1811	1,303,564	2,097
1821	1,573,210	2,530
1831	1,878,229	3,021
1841	2,207,653	3,551
1851	2,651,939	4,266
1861	3,188,485	5,129
1871	3,840,595	6,178
1881	4,713,441	7,582
1891	5,571,968	8,962
1901	6,506,889	10,466
1911	7,160,441	11,518
1921	7,386,755	11,882
1931	8,110,358	13,045
1939	8,615,050	13,857
1941	No census	due to war
1951	8,196,807	13,185
1961	7,992,443	12,856
1971	7,368,693	11,852
1981	6,608,598	10,630
1991	6,679,699	10,744
2001	7,172,036	11,536

Figures up to 1750 are estimates for an area that grew in size. No density estimates are available. The figures for 1801–2001 are from the census for Greater London.

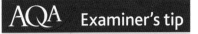

AQA Examiner's tip

When a question asks you to suggest reasons for something, it means that you cannot possibly be expected to know a definite correct answer. Instead you are being asked to use your geographical understanding and skills to work out sensible answers. You will be given marks for good reasoning, supported by facts. Try to fit your answers into the general body of geographical understanding that you have developed during your course.

Estimates suggest that the proportion of the whole world's population living in cities reached 50 per cent in the first few years of the 21st century.

London has been the biggest city in the British Isles for many centuries. At times during this period it was also the world's biggest city. London's growth can be seen in Table 5.7.

There were obviously several processes at work at the same time to cause this growth. Here are some examples:

- People were migrating from the countryside to the town, looking for work and opportunities.
- There was natural growth. Birth rates were high, partly because of the demand for labour.
- The area of London was growing, slowly until 1840 and much more rapidly after its mass transport systems began to develop.
- Densities were falling, but this fall in density was not uniform. Central areas generally had a denser population whereas the suburbs were less densely populated. Note that the main fall in density came in the first half of the 20th century as the suburbs spread rapidly. After 1951 there were stricter planning laws, including the setting up of the **green belt**, which restricted the outward spread.

It is hoped that some understanding of the reasons for urbanisation in the UK over the last few centuries will help in understanding the process of urbanisation that is taking place in many other parts of the world today and also help with an understanding of the processes of counterurbanisation and urban renewal that are taking place in more developed countries and particularly in the UK.

Table 5.8 *The world's top cities by population, 1800, 1900 and 1950*

1800	Name	Population
1	Beijing, China	1,100,000
2	London, UK	861,000
3	Guangzhou, China	800,000
4	Edo (Tokyo), Japan	685,000
5	Constantinople, Turkey (now Istanbul)	570,000
6	Paris, France	547,000
7	Naples, Italy	430,000
8	Hangzhou, China	387,000
9	Osaka, Japan	383,000
10	Kyoto, Japan	377,000

1900	Name	Population
1	London, UK	6,480,000
2	New York, USA	4,242,000
3	Paris, France	3,330,000
4	Berlin, Germany	2,707,000
5	Chicago, USA	1,717,000
6	Vienna, Austria	1,698,000
7	Tokyo, Japan	1,497,000
8	St Petersburg, Russia	1,439,000
9	Manchester, UK	1,435,000
10	Philadelphia, USA	1,418,000

1950	Name	Population
1	New York, USA	12,463,000
2	London, UK	8,860,000
3	Tokyo, Japan	7,000,000
4	Paris, France	5,900,000
5	Shanghai, China	5,406,000
6	Moscow, Russia	5,100,000
7	Buenos Aires, Argentina	5,000,000
8	Chicago, USA	4,906,000
9	Ruhr, Germany	4,900,000
10	Kolkata, India	4,800,000

Table 5.8 is a list of the 26 most populous cities in the world (those with a population over 8 million). All population figures for the world's largest urban areas are simply estimates. There is no way of knowing the exact population of such large places.

Activity

24
a Using Table 5.7, draw a line graph to show the two sets of data. The x-axis should show the independent variable, which is time. The y-axis needs to show three separate scales for total population density.

b Describe the patterns shown on your graph.

c Suggest reasons for the patterns you have described.

Key terms

Green belt: an area defined by Act of Parliament which surrounds a conurbation. It is very difficult to obtain permission for development on green belt. This acts to stop the sprawl of conurbations.

Link

This site has a huge amount of data on world cities:

www.demographia.com.

Activity

25 a Using Table 5.8 on page 183, mark the changing 10 biggest cities on an outline world map.

b Now mark the 26 cities of more than 8 million in 2005 (see Table 5.9) on a separate world map.

c Each member of the class should write down a list of statements about the changing pattern shown by the figures and the maps.

d Compare your statements and reach a set of group conclusions.

Table 5.9 *Cities with a population over 8 million, 2005*

1	Tokyo-Yokohama, Japan	33,200,000	14	Los Angeles, USA	11,789,000
2	New York, USA	17,800,000	15	Buenos Aires, Argentina	11,200,000
3	São Paulo, Brazil	17,700,000	16	Rio de Janeiro, Brazil	10,800,000
4	Seoul-Incheon, South Korea	17,500,000	17	Moscow, Russia	10,500,000
5	Mexico City, Mexico	17,400,000	18	Shanghai, China	10,000,000
6	Osaka-Kobe-Kyoto, Japan	16,425,000	19	Karachi, Pakistan	9,800,000
7	Manila, Philippines	14,750,000	20	Paris, France	9,645,000
8	Mumbai, India (formerly Bombay)	14,350,000	21	Nagoya, Japan	9,000,000
9	Jakarta, Indonesia	14,250,000	22	Istanbul, Turkey	9,000,000
10	Lagos, Nigeria	13,400,000	23	Beijing, China	8,614,000
11	Kolkata, India (formerly Calcutta)	12,700,000	24	Chicago, USA	8,308,000
12	Delhi, India	12,300,000	25	London, UK	8,278,000
13	Cairo, Egypt	12,200,000	26	Shenzhen, China	8,000,000

💡 What makes cities grow?

All urban growth is caused by a combination of natural population growth (an excess of births over deaths) and net migration (an excess of inward migration from rural areas to cities over outward migration away from the cities). Much urban growth, now and in the past, is due to migration from the countryside. There is often natural growth too, but it is a striking fact that birth rates almost always fall when people migrate to cities.

People move to the city for a variety of reasons:

■ the hope of jobs

■ the hope of being able to earn money to send back to the family in the rural area (village), and perhaps to be able to buy land in the village eventually

■ shortages of land, food and opportunities in the rural areas

■ the freedom from tradition that cities offer

■ the pull of the bright lights

■ war, natural disasters, etc. in rural areas

■ the hope that they will receive support from the state or from NGOs in the event of food shortages.

Activity

26 A useful way to sort and classify the causes of migration is to divide the causes into pushes which make people leave the countryside and pulls which attract people to the city. They can also be classified as voluntary or compulsory; permanent or temporary; or as local, national or international.

Study the list of causes of rural to urban migration given above. Try to add some other causes. Then classify your list using the three sets of criteria.

Birth rates usually fall in the city because:

- education levels are higher, especially for girls and women
- children, who were able to work on the farms in the countryside, are less of an economic advantage in the cities and may even be an economic liability as they can be expensive to feed, clothe and shelter
- large families can be a drag on the economic progress that migrants to the city hope to achieve
- in the cities there are not the same extended family structures that help with childcare in the rural areas.

Death rates in cities are affected by:

- the quality of housing – often poor when growth is rapid but often improving later
- the quality of water supply – as above
- the quality of sewage treatment and disposal – as above
- food supply – often better than in rural areas because cities are centres of storage and distribution
- health care – can be better than in rural areas.

All the above factors depend on wealth and there are often huge ranges of income, wealth and access to services in cities, especially in the fastest-growing cities.

AQA Examiner's tip

You will probably have come across the push–pull model of migration in your GCSE work. Now you are on an AS course the examiners are looking for more detailed, sophisticated answers. Don't fall into the trap of writing GCSE answers at A Level. You will not get an A level pass if you do!

Activity

27 Study Figure 5.21.

   a Note evidence from each photo of the range of wealth in the cities at different times and in different places.

   b What do the different cities have in common? How are they different?

Fig. 5.21 *Aspects of urbanisation:* **a** *Contrasts in present-day Mumbai urban area, India;* **b** *and* **c** *Contrasts in present-day London;* **d** *19th-century urban conditions in England*

Fig. 5.22 *Santa Marta, Colombia*

■ Case study

Colombia

Colombia lies in the north-west of South America. It has coasts on the Caribbean Sea and the Pacific Ocean. Approximately half of the country consists of the northern ranges and valleys of the Andes while the rest of the country lies in the Amazon basin. As with most countries in Latin America, Colombia underwent very rapid urbanisation in the second half of the 20th century. People moved from the countryside and here are some factors that pushed them:

■ mechanisation, which was removing opportunities for work on the large estates

■ land ownership laws that made it almost impossible for the poor to gain ownership or tenure of land

■ the insecurity involved in farming on land that the farmers had no long-term title to

■ soil exhaustion on many areas of farmland

■ lack of access to health care, education, clean running water, etc., in rural areas

■ political instability in the countryside, with conflict between guerrillas and the government, conflict between drug producers and the authorities, and the existence of government-backed militias and death squads.

They were pulled to the cities by many other factors, including:

■ work, or at least the prospect of possible work

■ education, or at least the prospect of possible education opportunities

■ freedom from the restrictive life in small rural communities

■ the opportunity to earn money to send back to support family members in the village

■ images of a glamorous life in the cities

■ a feeling that people concentrated in urban areas could exert more political power than those who were isolated in small rural groups.

Santa Marta has been the subject of an ongoing study since 1986 by Dr Peter Kellett of Newcastle University. He has followed the

Fig. 5.23 *Images from La Libertad settlement in Santa Marta*

growth and development of the settlement. Here are some of his observations.

- All cities in developing countries that are growing because of urbanisation are unique but many show some patterns that are similar.
- Santa Marta is a dynamic and rapidly changing city.
- People come here out of desperation and out of hope for something better.
- Housing changes as family circumstances change. Houses grow and develop as the family grows and as economic opportunities allow further construction to take place.
- The house is a major part of the economic life of many families. It is often used as a shop, workplace, store for equipment or goods for sale, space for renting out or for housing other family members in need, and so on.
- The building materials used in the house represent a capital investment. If the family falls on hard times, they might have to sell some of their building materials, perhaps to pay for emergency medical treatment.
- In this tropical area the land around the house is just as important as the house itself. It can provide living space, land on which to grow crops and rear animals (even in a city), a meeting place for neighbours, a storage area for the family business, etc.
- People who migrate to the city often retain very close links with the rural area that they came from. They may move back temporarily, more or less frequently. They may bring produce from the village to sell in the town. They often send money home to the family in the village, sometimes with an ambition of buying land in the countryside so that they can return 'home' eventually.
- People were forced by circumstances to occupy land that did not belong to them. However, they tried to formalise the occupation and make it legal as that would give them greater security. It would also add to the value of 'their' land and houses.
- People also thought that it was important to provide clean water, sewage disposal systems, electricity connections, schooling, policing and security, and they worked through community organisations to provide all these things and to formalise them with the authorities.

The urban patterns produced by migration

Cities grow because people migrate to them. Then, once they arrive, people often migrate within the city. Many geographers and social scientists have tried to look for patterns in the ways people finally settle in cities.

Why should geographers expect patterns to develop in cities? Surely, all the decisions about where to live are taken by individuals and families. Moreover, psychologists tell us that moving house is one of the most stressful events in any person's life, along with marriage, divorce, childbirth and death of a loved one. At a time like this, people are not going to obey rules, they are going to do what is best for themselves in their special circumstances. They are people with free will, so we ought to expect random distributions based on millions of individual decisions.

They are not inanimate objects obeying the laws of physics, yet each person's and each family's decisions have to be taken within sets of individual and family circumstances:

- income levels and affordability
- level of savings and the effect of this on decisions to rent or buy
- jobs
- schools
- desire for access to facilities such as transport, open space and shopping
- class, education, culture and the need to be near people of similar backgrounds and interests
- the balance between short-term needs and long-term plans.

They are also taken within the context of societal factors:

- planning regulations
- economic opportunities for landowners and builders
- wealth of the area
- physical factors, including flood risk, slope, stability of the ground
- historical factors from the previous development of the area
- competition for the more desirable locations
- transport links within the city and between the city and other areas.

Everyone makes individual decisions, but people with similar sets of circumstances often end up making similar decisions. This means that groups of people and families with particular characteristics end up living in the same area. What is more, similar sorts of areas can often be found in different cities. This has given rise to the patterns that geographers try to identify. In this section it is not necessary to look at urban structures or at rural settlements in detail. However, we consider four different areas in and around one major urban area: Newcastle upon Tyne. We will study and compare the characteristics of:

- an inner-city area
- a suburban area
- an area of rural/urban fringe
- an area of rural settlement.

You should then use them as comparisons for at least two similar areas in your own chosen place.

Case study

Tyneside

In this study we will look at five areas in and around Newcastle upon Tyne:

- **Wingrove ward** is an inner-city area just to the west of the city centre; this is covered by the statistical survey only.
- **Byker ward** an inner-city area just to the east of the centre.
- **Jesmond ward** is a suburb built mainly in the early 20th century.
- Gosforth is a suburb built mainly in the late 20th century and now expanding outwards. It includes **Castle ward**.
- **Longhorsley** is a village in Northumberland about 30 km north of Newcastle.

Skills

Using the National Statistics website

Your first task when studying an area like this is often to go to the National Statistics website:

http://neighbourhood.statistics.gov.uk/dissemination

You need to enter the name of the ward that you are researching. Alternatively you can enter the full postcode for any place within that ward.

If you are not sure what the names of the wards are that you need to research, you should consult someone in your local authority, search the authority's website, or go to the boundary committee website for the relevant information. There are boundary committees for England, Wales, Scotland and Northern Ireland.

www.boundarycommittee.org.uk/your-area

The National Statistics website offers a huge range of census data for your chosen area. You can look at key figures for the 2001 census where general summary tables offer about 60 different data sets (see Figure 5.24, Table 5.10 and Figure 5.25). You can also look for more specific data sets, including data sets for:

- age
- approximate social grade
- country of birth
- distance travelled to work
- ethnic group
- general health
- household composition
- tenure.

Age data is particularly useful for drawing population pyramids to compare age structures.

At the bottom of the web page there are also links to the primary care trust and the health authority, two further sources of data that might be invaluable for your study.

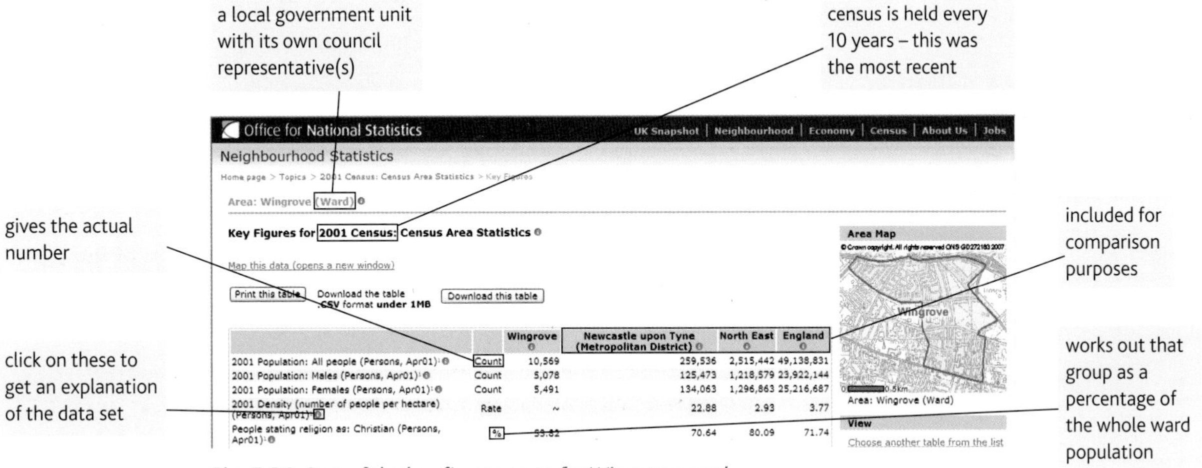

Fig. 5.24 *Part of the key figures page for Wingrove ward*

Table 5.10 *Selected data from the five areas*

		Wingrove	Byker	Jesmond	Castle	Longhorsley
2001 population	Count	10,569	8,220	11,849	11,436	1495
Ethnic group White	%	75.32	95.43	92.78	96.20	99.60
Ethnic group Mixed	%	1.81	0.73	1.47	1.75	0
Ethnic group Asian	%	19.81	2.62	3.92	2.11	0.20
Ethnic group Black	%	0.78	0.39	0.3	0.18	0
Ethnic group Other	%	2.28	0.83	1.53	0.75	0.20
General heath Good	%	69.98	55.71	78.51	70.18	74.72
General heath Fair	%	20.4	26.44	16.2	20.81	17.79
General heath Poor	%	9.62	17.85	5.28	9.01	7.49
With long-term illness	%	17.56	29.55	11.95	17.17	14.38
Aged 16–74; economically active; employees; full time	%	29.83	30.11	36.07	44.25	37.96
Aged 16–74; economically active; employees; part time	%	9.48	9.97	5.69	12.73	11.95
Aged 16–74; economically active; self-employed	%	6.69	2.99	7.64	6.17	16.79
Aged 16–74; economically active; unemployed	%	4.89	7.27	2.41	2.98	1.46
Aged 16–74; economically active; full-time student	%	19.46	7.54	35.28	6.28	5.20
Aged 16–74; economically inactive; retired	%	9.43	14.13	6.10	14.97	16.51
Aged 16–74; economically inactive; looking after home	%	7.77	7.51	2.43	5.11	5.66
Aged 16–74; economically inactive; permanently sick	%	7.07	15.05	2.64	5.46	2.92
Aged 16–74; no qualifications	%	29.86	47.59	6.28	25.34	18.80
Aged 16–74; highest qualification level 1	%	11.97	14.04	3.81	15.48	11.04
Aged 16–74; highest qualification level 2	%	14.76	14.16	9.31	20.68	21.62
Aged 16–74; highest qualification level 3	%	14.76	6.16	31.28	7.57	7.03
Aged 16–74; highest qualification level 4/5	%	24.05	11.68	47.46	24.48	35.68
All households	Count	3885	4171	4909	4708	593
Owner occupied; owns outright	%	21.26	7.89	22.92	30.52	35.08
Owner occupied; owns with mortgage	%	33.46	18.51	31.57	50.39	43.34
Owner occupied; shared ownership	%	0.31	0.84	0.53	0.15	0
Rented from council	%	14.67	58.33	1.96	12.76	5.73
Rented from housing association	%	5.05	4.96	5.68	1.00	1.35
Rented from private landlord	%	21.57	6.88	34.26	3.72	9.78
Rented – other	%	3.68	2.59	3.08	1.66	4.72

Fig. 5.25 *Location of each area*

Byker ward

In the 1960s, housing in Byker consisted almost exclusively of rows of small terraced houses dating from the late 19th and early 20th centuries. They had been built for the people who worked in the port, shipbuilding and engineering industries that lined the riverside. The housing had poor amenities and by the 1960s had fallen into a poor state of repair. There was little nearby open space.

Then a dramatic new housing scheme was designed to rehouse many of the people from the area. Some others were moved out from the inner-city area to new council estates on the edge of the city. The most obvious part of the redevelopment is the high-rise Byker Wall, but the Wall also shelters many low-rise housing areas.

The scheme has always been controversial. It has won many awards but it has also been the target of much criticism. However, it has continued to provide sound housing for comparatively poor people for over 30 years. Many of the original inhabitants were able to afford to buy their own homes, so generally they moved out and were replaced by other people in need of social housing. In the last few years this has included second-generation migrants and even asylum seekers, but the core population is still made up of white Newcastle people.

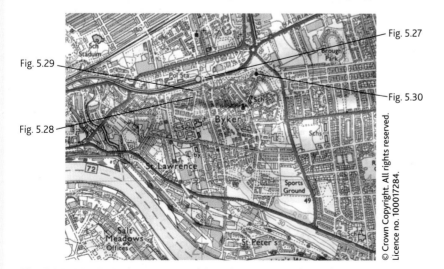

Fig. 5.26 *OS 1:25,000 map extract of the Byker area, part of map sheet 316*

Social housing in an inner-city area: Byker ward, Tyneside

The main Byker Wall housing scheme stretches along the top of the hill. The north-facing 'back' of the wall has only small windows so as to cut out the noise from the main road and the metro line.

The neighbourhood heating scheme is designed to provide cheap, efficient heating for all the homes in the Wall.

Dual carriageway to town centre. Planned when the wall was designed but only completed several years later. Runs in a cutting to reduce noise pollution.Crossed by footbridges to give access to the shops and services to the north.

Metro station. Provides rapid transit system to the city and to the coast.

Fig. 5.27

Some houses have been bought by the former tenants. One of the first signs of private ownership is the replacement of windows with double glazing and of the wooden cladding with PVC. Note the classical doorway, too. The rest of the houses and flats are now managed by Newcastle Housing, a housing association, and are not controlled by the council.

Parts of the Wall rise to 13 storeys high. From across the Tyne the Wall is said to look like the superstructure of one of the ships that used to be built on the banks of the river.

Fig. 5.29

Fig. 5.28

Well-lit walkways separate the houses and pedestrians from traffic.

Two-storey houses contrast with the flats in the Wall. Each has small private gardens to front and rear.

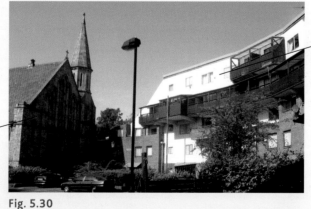

The church was here before the Wall was built and was incorporated into the structure.

A part of the Wall with medium-rise housing, five storeys high here. Note the balconies on flats above the ground floor to give views across the river.

Fig. 5.30

Jesmond ward

Although Byker was built to house workers in the heavy industry along the banks of the river, Jesmond was being built to house the owners and managers of factories and commercial premises and the clerical workers in better-paid jobs in the city centre. The richer people were able to build large family houses, with space for several servants, often on land overlooking the open spaces of Jesmond Dene or the Town Moor.

The lower middle classes had smaller houses, or Tyneside flats which were terraces with upstairs and downstairs flats. The two front doors were side by side but each flat was completely self-contained.

Around the middle of the 20th century, some of the families in the biggest houses were no longer able to run the houses. They were too big to manage without servants and people were no longer willing to accept the low wages and restrictions of servant life. Many of the big houses, especially those just outside the city centre, were taken over by businesses such as solicitors, dentists and other small firms. Then other houses, particularly those a little further from the centre, were sublet to the rapidly growing student population. In fact, **studentification**, almost the opposite of the better-known **gentrification**, has led to massive change in large parts of Jesmond over the last 25 years or so.

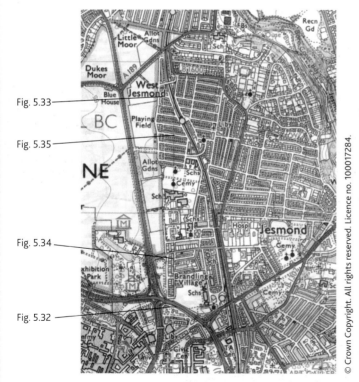

Fig. 5.31 *OS 1:25,000 map extract of the Jesmond area, part of map sheet 316*

Key terms

Studentification: when large family houses become too big and expensive to run, the inhabitants move out and the properties are subdivided and let to students. When several houses on a street become student lets, the nature of the area starts to change. There is more noise, gardens are less carefully tended, several old cars may be parked in the street, etc. Consequently, there is pressure on the remaining families to move out of the area, leaving more properties for student lets. The whole area deteriorates and moves downmarket.

Gentrification: a spontaneous and unplanned change by which individual families buy up run-down old property and improve it, adding to its value. Rewiring, adding central heating, replacing bathrooms and kitchens, adding extensions, and so on, all add to the value of the property. As more and more people do this in an area and it attracts a richer population, these richer people attract new shops and services, often also in renovated old premises. Thus the whole area improves and moves upmarket.

Housing in a suburban area: Jesmond ward, Tyneside

Some are still houses but many have been taken over by the university as offices and faculties. Others are offices for businesses which feel they benefit from the elegance of the buildings and their position on the edge of the central area.

Large Georgian-style houses, built in the 19th century. Then they were on the edge of the city; now they are just outside the city centre.

Although they are close to the centre, there is plenty of open space and well-planned, safe access for cyclists and pedestrians.

Fig. 5.32

Elaborate, large houses which are just far enough out from the centre to have avoided studentification.

The loft conversions were mostly done as these houses were turned into multi-occupance flats. They are aimed at a slightly wealthier market than the undergraduates who occupy smaller flats.

Fig. 5.33

Note the double depth of these houses.

Fig. 5.34 Large areas of big family houses were built in the early 20th century as the city grew. Most had access to the open space of Jesmond Dene or the Town Moor.

Fig. 5.35

At the end of one term or the start of the next there are many flats to let.

A street of Tyneside flats with pairs of doors side by side.

Gardens are not well kept in student areas.

Castle ward (Gosforth)

As Newcastle grew it absorbed surrounding towns and villages to become a **conurbation**. One of the places absorbed was Gosforth, a small town with its own services, beneath Newcastle in the urban hierarchy. Much of the area was a wealthy, middle-class commuter settlement with a wide range of housing types, but Gosforth also has areas of former miners' houses and some post-1945 council housing.

By 2000 housing had spread right up to the edge of the green belt to the north of Gosforth. Pressure grew to allow expansion onto the green belt, so the government finally passed a law allowing some of the green belt to be used for housing and modern, science-based industry on Newcastle Great Park. This has led to the construction of one major industrial unit – for Sage, a software company – and large areas of new housing, aimed at middle to high earners, continuing the spread of middle-class housing northwards from the CBD. Meanwhile, in Gosforth itself, **infilling** has taken place on any **brownfield sites** that become available.

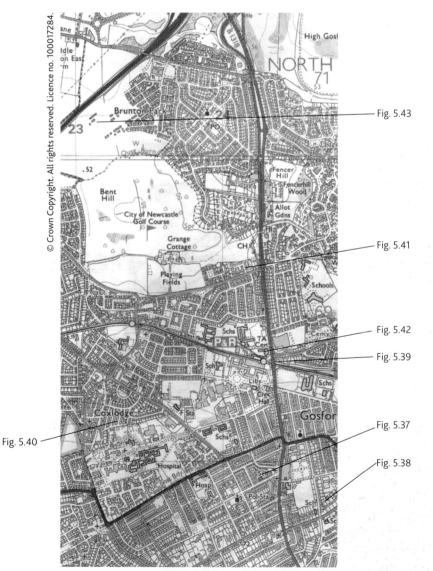

Fig. 5.36 *OS 1:25,000 map extract of Castle ward, part of map sheet 316*

Key terms

Conurbation: one large, more or less continuous area created as a city grows and spreads to absorb other cities, towns and villages in the surrounding area.

Infilling: the use of open spaces within a conurbation to build new housing or services, often close to where a green belt restricts outward growth.

Brownfield sites: sites that have been built on before but that have come available for new building because of demolition or redundancy of the old buildings.

Housing in an area of rural/urban fringe: Castle ward, Tyneside

Large, elaborate, family houses, close to Town Moor. Similar to better houses in Jesmond. No signs of subdivision yet.

Fig. 5.37

Large semi-detached houses built after the Second World War as the middle-class suburb expanded.

Fig. 5.38

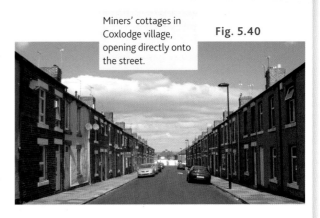

Estate of smaller houses, but planned with plenty of open space to be suitable for families. Also built after Second World War.

Fig. 5.39

Miners' cottages in Coxlodge village, opening directly onto the street.

Fig. 5.40

Recent infill on a brownfield site. Close to the quiet edge of the city, so designed as retirement housing.

Fig. 5.41

Recent infill on a brownfield site. Close to the main road and Metro station. Ideal for young single people and couples who commute into the city centre.

Fig. 5.42

Fig. 5.43

Housing on Newcastle Great Park on the edge of the city. Land should be cheaper here but the housing is designed with only minimal garden space. Car parking space is more important. A car is essential as there are few services on the estate – not very eco-friendly planning.

Longhorsley

Longhorsley lies in rural Northumberland north of Newcastle. The ancient peel tower in the centre of the village was built about 500 years ago. It was a defensive residence during the border wars between bands of English and Scottish reivers (cattle raiders).

In more peaceful times, Longhorsley was a stopping place for the drovers who led herds of cattle down from the hills of Scotland and north Northumberland for sale in the south. The large open spaces in the centre of the village were probably used to feed and rest the cattle overnight.

In the 1950s the village was a successful farming community with three farms, a number of smallholdings and around 500 inhabitants mainly working in agriculture. There were several shops, pubs and garages in the village to serve local people and passing trade.

Now all the farms are gone, although some of the farm buildings are still used by farmers from beyond the village. Others have been occupied by commuters and other non-agricultural workers who want land for keeping horses, etc. Some rural workers still live in the council estate but most residents of the estate commute to work elsewhere.

A number of estates of large private houses have been built on the edge of the village, housing commuters and retired people.

Fig. 5.60 *OS 1:25,000 map extract of Longhorsley, part of map sheet 325*

197

A rural settlement: Longhorsley, Northumberland

The peel tower converted to a house.

Fig. 5.45

Former farm buildings now residential. Note the conversion involving pointing and reconstructing walls, replacing windows with double glazing, converting the chimney to take the gas flue for central heating, etc.

' Fig. 5.46

Part of the village green, which was probably used by drovers as a pen for cattle. Surrounded by a mixture of old agricultural housing and non-farmworker housing from the interwar period.

Fig. 5.47

Part of the old service centre of the village along the main road. It shows the former garage and service station, the post office, the general store and a pub with B&B facilities. Longhorsley once had three pubs but now it has just one.

Fig. 5.48

Council housing estate, still with some agricultural workers.

Fig. 5.49

Private housing estate on the southern edge of the village. Note how this housing is much less crowded than many housing areas in the city.

Fig. 5.50

Question

1 From the statistics, photos and descriptions of the five wards in and around Newcastle, here are seven issues that suggest themselves for further study. Read the suggestions and think about how such studies could be carried out. Then consider how similar issues might be defined in your own local study areas, which illustrate the social, economical and political implications of population change. Also consider how you might carry out investigations of those issues.

- Wingrove and Byker are both inner-city wards, but Wingrove has a much higher proportion of non-white residents. How differently has this affected the environments of the two areas? Are the differences caused by council policy? Are the differences a result of the tendency of minority ethnic groups to live close to other members of their own community for support?
- Jesmond has a high proportion of student residents. How does the concentration of the student population change with distance from the university? Does the concentration of students in some parts of Jesmond lead to a concentration of particular types of services in those areas? What is the attitude of non-student residents to the presence of large numbers of students in the ward? Does their attitude vary with age or with distance from the studentified areas of the ward?
- The architecture and planning of the Byker Wall has always aroused controversy. What is the attitude of present residents of Byker to the unusual design? The Wall was designed, in part, to reduce noise pollution in the main residential area. Has this design been successful?
- In Castle ward there has been a lot of infilling in recent years. Map the extent of the infill in the last 20 years or so, and find out the attitude of the residents in the infill and of their close neighbours to the new developments. The development on former green belt land of Newcastle Great Park was meant to be built with respect for the environment. Has this happened? Many local residents were opposed to this development before it happened. What is their attitude to the development now?
- Longhorsley used to be an agricultural settlement but now it seems to be a commuter settlement. To what extent is this true? Do commuters from the village travel mainly to Newcastle or to the towns of south Northumberland? Has Longhorsley developed a tourist or leisure industry since it lost its farming? How else have farmers in the area diversified?
- There were big differences in the way people in the five areas viewed their general health when they were asked about it in the census. Is this reflected in the provision of health-care facilities in the different wards? Is it reflected in gym and health club membership?
- Can any of the differences in socio-economic characteristics shown in Table 5.10 be linked to the age structure of the populations in the wards?

Implications for social welfare

Note that **social welfare** means more than social security. It describes a much broader concept than access to state benefits. Social welfare is not spread equally throughout society. It can be more or less available:

- in different parts of a city
- to people from different social classes
- to different ethnic groups
- to different age groups
- to different genders or people of different sexual orientation.

As geographers we are most interested in spatial distributions of social welfare. However, the previous work on different urban and rural housing areas should have shown that social and ethnic groups and even age groups can become concentrated in particular areas. When certain groups become concentrated it can be good or bad for their social welfare.

It can be good when the people in the group are mutually supportive. This can happen when a concentration of students leads to provision of social and service provision for students, or when a concentration of old people in an area means there is a peaceful environment with good social services available for the elderly, or when a concentration of one ethnic group means that ethnic culture is strong and people can support each other in a new and strange society.

Key terms

Social welfare: the well-being of communities. It refers to the access that groups of people, or individuals, have to job opportunities, housing, health care, education, an unpolluted environment, a safe environment and freedom to practise one's culture, religion, etc.

However, concentration of groups can be damaging when areas of poor housing also have a shortage of good schools and medical facilities, or when separation of ethnic groups leads to lack of communication and growth in hostility between communities.

Activity

28 Discuss the following social welfare issues. In each case you should consider how geography and social welfare are linked. How do spatial differences between areas and the social groups have an impact on the welfare of the groups? Try to refer to specific areas that you are familiar with.

a In some places there is a tendency for wealthier families to move to particular areas because those areas have better schools. Does this lead to social segregation? Is this acceptable in society? Who benefits and who loses from this situation? Can anything be done to remedy any problems that might arise? Does this situation benefit society as a whole in the long term? Is the situation even more of a problem when social segregation of schools is also ethnic segregation?

b In our society some groups have more access to cars than others. Car-rich groups include the rich, men, the middle-aged, able-bodied and white. Car-poor groups include young adults, single mothers, the disabled and the elderly infirm. How does this affect the access of different groups to shops as large supermarket chains become more dominant? Does it have an even more serious effect on the rural poor? Does the lack of access to cars lead to a more dangerous environment for some groups, either because pedestrians and cyclists are vulnerable on the roads or because people are more vulnerable to attack when they are walking on the streets?

c In recent years it has been considered more efficient to concentrate medical services in large units. Only large regional hospitals can make efficient use of more modern, high-cost technology. Are medical services equally accessible in all parts of a city? Are they equally available to people living in rural areas? Are the large regional centres sufficiently supported by a network of local health centres?

d Some estates in some cities are seen as concentrations of crime and antisocial behaviour. Does the evidence support this? What are the possible causes of the problems? What solutions have been suggested? Are these solutions working to any extent?

☑ 💡 ⓘ *In this chapter you have learnt:*

- about the history and possible future of world population growth
- how population structure can vary from place to place and from time to time
- some of the causes of changes in population totals and structures
- that population depends on resources and that there are different models which try to explain how the balance between the two has varied in the past and might vary in future
- that the imbalance between population and resources is one factor that can lead to migration
- how migration and natural growth have led to rapid urbanisation, and that the rate of urbanisation has increased in the last 50 years or so
- that different housing areas develop in cities that can reflect differences in the socio-economic status of the population, and that resources may not be evenly distributed between different areas
- that patterns of housing areas can show similarities among cities in different regions.

Global patterns of food supply

In 1998 the United Nations (UN) Food and Agriculture Organization (FAO) published a map (see Figure 6.1) to show levels of nutrition and **malnutrition** in 177 countries of the world.

Figures 6.1 and 6.2 give dietary energy supply (DES) figures for 177 nations and 7 regional or socio-economic groups of countries. Topping the country list is Denmark with 3780 kcal available per person per day, more than double the 1580 kcal for Somalia.

In the world as a whole, enough food is produced to feed each person each day, but that does not happen because distribution is so uneven. It is access to food that is the real issue facing the world.

If the available food was distributed according to need, it would be sufficient to feed everyone in the world, providing 2720 kcal per person per day. But the reality is that 17 countries have severe food supply problems, with a DES of less than 2000 kcal. A further 37 have DES levels between 2000 and 2299 kcal.

Figure 6.1, which is based on data from the period 1994–96, does not reflect the effects of recent natural disasters, economic crises and

Key terms

Malnutrition: the lack of proper nutrition resulting from a poorly balanced diet.

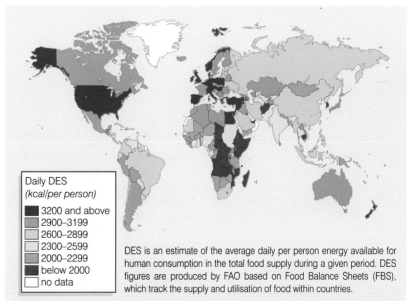

Daily DES
(kcal/per person)

- 3200 and above
- 2900–3199
- 2600–2899
- 2300–2599
- 2000–2299
- below 2000
- no data

DES is an estimate of the average daily per person energy available for human consumption in the total food supply during a given period. DES figures are produced by FAO based on Food Balance Sheets (FBS), which track the supply and utilisation of food within countries.

While DES does not indicate food consumption, it does identify: those countries in which people are more likely to have enough to eat (represented by shades of green ▮▮▯); those in which the daily DES is marginal (yellow ▯); those in which hunger and malnutrition are likely to be widespread (orange ▮). Those countries that face the most severe food supply shortages, with average daily DES below 2000 kilocalories per person per day, are coloured in red (▮).

Fig. 6.1 *World dietary energy supply (DES), 1994–96*

a Selected industrialised countries

b Selected sub-Saharan African countries

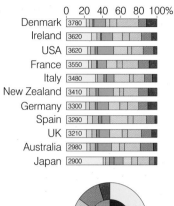

average for 25
industrialised countries

average for 46
sub-Saharan African countries

Fig. 6.2 *DES, 1994–96*

Link

An animated map showing how
the level of undernourishment has
changed over the last 40 years or so
can be seen at:

www.fao.org/es/ess/faostat/
foodsecurity/FSMap/flash_map.htm.

Key terms

Undernutrition: below the minimum
level of dietary energy (calorie)
consumption. The Department
of Health estimates this level at
1940 kcal per day for women and
2550 for men (average 2250),
but these figures can vary widely
depending on lifestyle and other
factors.

conflicts. Nor does it show inequity in the distribution of available
supplies *within* countries.

Nevertheless, national DES levels clearly indicate which countries have
food supply problems and a large proportion of the population suffering
from chronic **undernutrition**. Figure 6.1 shows the countries suffering
the severest shortages – with a DES of less than 2000 kcal – in red. They
are almost all in sub-Saharan Africa.

There are also large differences in the composition of the average diet in
industrialised and developing countries. Slightly more than a quarter of
the diet in industrialised countries is provided by cereals, another quarter
by meat, fish, eggs, milk and cheese.

In the countries of sub-Saharan Africa, on the other hand, nearly half
the diet (46 per cent) is made up of cereals and a further 20 per cent of
tubers. In the least developed countries, cereals, roots and tubers make
up nearly three-quarters of the daily diet.

Cereals and tubers provide food energy, but they do not contain adequate
levels of other essential nutrients, vitamins, minerals, proteins and fat.
Diets with over 75 per cent of calories from cereals are very unbalanced.
But diets can also be unbalanced in most industrialised countries. Fat
intake is often high and obesity widespread. Diet-related illnesses, such
as cardiovascular diseases and high blood pressure, are considered major
public health problems.

Trade in food

Figure 6.3 is also produced by the FAO. It shows the world trade in food,
indicating the countries that are either net importers or net exporters of
food.

On the map, countries are shown as net importers if they import more
food than they export. Then the net importers are shaded according to a
comparison between the country's net imports and its total consumption

Activities

1. Study Figure 6.1.

   a. Name the main countries with a severe shortage of food (i.e. DES of below 2000 kcal per person per day).

   b. Describe the distribution of these countries.

   c. Name the countries with a DES of over 3200 kcal per person per day.

   d. Describe their distribution.

   e. South and south-east Asia do not show up on this map as being areas of severe food shortages. Discuss possible reasons for this.

2. Search the internet, starting with the weblinks given here. Find out about one issue of food supply that is affecting the world today. Make a presentation on that issue. Your presentation should consist of:

   a. a dramatic headline that explains how the issue is affecting people in one or more parts of the world

   b. an analysis of the causes, particularly the geographical causes of that issue

   c. a commentary on the way the issue is being managed or might be managed in the future, to reduce its effects on people or the environment.

Link

The original map in Figure 6.1 can be found on the internet at:

www.fao.org/News/1998/img/NMpdfs/world-e.pdf.

Linked to the map is data about the average composition of diets in all the countries shown on the map. Some extracts from that linked data are shown in Figure 6.2.

The FAO has a huge website. It constantly provides new data and press releases. Search for the latest news on food issues here:

www.fao.org/newsroom/index.html.

Further information can be found at the Reuters Foundation AlertNet. Reuters is a major world news agency and the Reuters Foundation is a humanitarian charity which tries to alert the world to humanitarian crises. The AlertNet map is a GIS that shows details about emergencies such as food security crises, storms, earthquakes and health crises:

www.alertnet.org/map.

of food. For instance, in the UK we import 25 to 50 per cent of our total calorie consumption. Countries are shown as net exporters if they export more than they import. Note that the data is superimposed on a base map showing the countries where 20 per cent or more of the population is undernourished.

Compare Figure 6.3 with two further maps from the same series. Figure 6.4 shows the amount of food aid received per person and Figure 6.5 shows the proportion of the countries' total exports that consist of food exports.

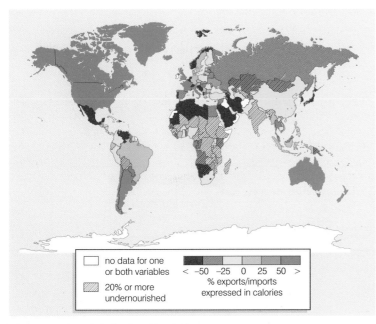

Fig. 6.3 *Net trade in food, 1999–2001*

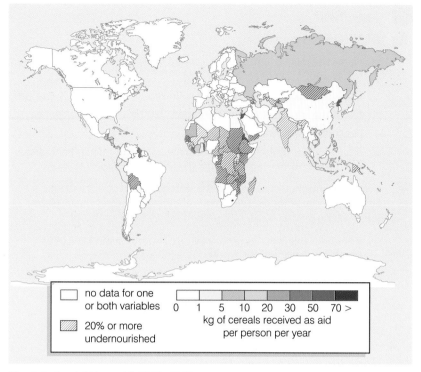

Fig. 6.4 *Food aid (cereals), 1999–2001*

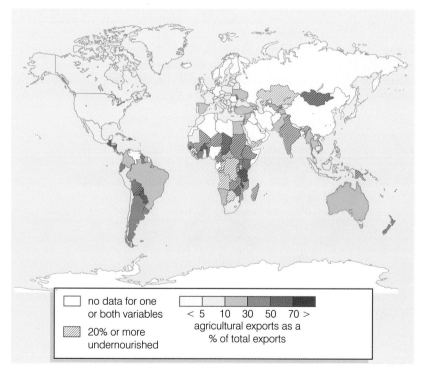

Fig. 6.5 *Food exports, 2001*

Activity

3

a Describe the main patterns shown on Figure 6.3 on page 203. In your description you should name some countries as examples but not too many. Concentrate on finding broad patterns, referring to continental or subcontinental areas and to major groupings of nations, such as the EU, sub-Saharan Africa and the rich North. Pay particular attention to countries that do not seem to match the overall patterns.

b Describe the patterns in Figure 6.4. Compare them with the patterns in Figure 6.3. Also compare the patterns of food aid (see Figure 6.4) and undernourishment (see Figure 6.2 on page 202).

c Make notes on the key points in Figure 6.5. Now you will have to deal with something that seems a real paradox at first. In many of the countries with a high rate of undernourishment, which receive a lot of food aid, agricultural exports make up a very large proportion of their total exports. Can this be true? Can it be morally justified? Can you discover the reasons for this apparent anomaly as you work through the rest of this chapter?

The geographical flow of world trade in food

The flows of trade in agricultural products are enormously complicated but some trends do stand out. The most important trend is the flow of food from rural areas to urban areas. This flow can be seen in every country and region with any trade in agricultural products.

Then there are the flows from the major grain-producing mid-latitude areas to the world's industrial areas. The former include the prairies of North America, the steppes of Russia, the pampas of South America and the downs of Australia (and, to a lesser extent, the lowlands of western Europe, particularly in France). The industrial areas include the industrial north-east and west coasts of the USA, the industrial conurbations of western and eastern Europe, and increasingly the cities of the newly industrialising countries (NICs) of south and east Asia, particularly China.

For many years there has been a flow of tropical produce (particularly plantation produce such as sugar, bananas, pineapples and coffee) from tropical regions to the temperate regions. Indeed this trade was one of the motivating forces behind the creation of the European empires of the 19th and 20th centuries. In recent years, with the development of cheap air transport, this flow has been joined by the flow of luxury products such as early vegetables and flowers to the supermarket chains of the industrialised countries.

A similar flow is the movement of meat and meat products from tropical regions to the industrialised countries. The most notorious example of this is the flow of meat from the cleared areas of the former Amazon rainforest to help provide the burgers and other meat products for North American and other world markets.

Less well known in the West, but absolutely vital, is the movement of rice from countries of south-east Asia – Thailand, Malaysia, Burma, etc. – to the major population centres further north, particularly India and China. India and China are the two biggest producers of rice in the world, but they still rely on imports to ensure their populations are fed.

The final flow generally takes the form of aid rather than trade. This is the movement of grain and other foodstuffs from North America and Europe to areas of acute malnutrition, mostly in Africa but also in some parts of South America and south Asia.

Fig. 6.6 *The modern global agribusiness food trade chain*

The business view of the world trade in agribusiness products

In order to understand the world trade in food, geographers need to look beyond the purely geographical, or place-based, factors and to consider who controls and manages the trade. For hundreds of years the trade in foodstuffs was rarely a simple transaction between the producers – farmers – and the consumers. Some kind of merchant or middleman has almost always been involved.

Many of you will know the story of Joseph in the Bible. After interpreting the dreams of the Pharaoh in Egypt, he became the chief planner of the food supply chain and ensured that surpluses from the seven good years were stored and saved for use in the seven lean years. Nearer our own time, the Mayor of Casterbridge in the Hardy novel of 19th-century Wessex made his fortune (and later lost it) as a dealer in corn – buying, selling and making a profit from the products of the local farms. Now, however, the trade is far more complex, stretching around the world and involving many more stages.

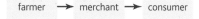

Fig. 6.7 *The pre-industrialised 'Mayor of Casterbridge' food trade chain*

Your own experiences will probably have made you aware of the dominance of the corporate sector – the supermarket chains – in the food supply industry in the UK and in other developed countries that you might have visited. However, this dominance is increasing in the developing world too. Indeed, the fastest-growing element in the food chain in developing countries is the supermarket sector, with sales growth rates of over 20 per cent per annum in some countries. In addition, food manufacturing and processing are on the rise, as urban consumers demand more processed foods. Industry increasingly looks at the millions of small farmers as customers of the input industry and as suppliers for the food processors and traders, and it increasingly looks at the poor consumers as customers.

■ The geopolitics of food

Two themes dominate the international **geopolitics** of food in the early 21st century:

- ▓ the issue of free trade in world food
- ▓ the issue of **food security** for developing countries, particularly those in sub-Saharan Africa.

Free trade in world food

From the 1970s to the present, the ideas of the free market and **globalisation** have increased their dominance of the world system of trade in all commodities, even in food. The simple theory behind free trade is that production of each commodity should be concentrated in areas where it has the greatest cost advantage. For instance, crops might be grown where the climate and soils are most suitable or where labour costs are lowest or where transport is cheapest and most efficient. In this way, prices will be reduced, production will increase and everyone will benefit.

However, this simple pattern has not been allowed to evolve in the two centuries of development in agricultural trade. Many countries have tried to protect what are seen to be the interests of their own farmers and their own citizens. This protectionism has been particularly common in the area of food production because countries think they need to ensure security of supply in case of war, natural hazard or world shortage. Countries and organisations like the EU have provided subsidies to help and encourage their own farmers to produce. They have also introduced **tariffs** to increase the price of imported food, which protects their farmers from cheaper competition.

The World Trade Organization was set up in 1995 (although it developed from the earlier GATT organisation). Here is an extract from one of its documents:

> The World Trade Organization (WTO) deals with the rules of trade between nations at a global or near-global level. But there is more to it than that.
>
> There are a number of ways of looking at the WTO. It's an organisation for liberalising trade. It's a forum for governments to negotiate trade agreements. It's a place for them to settle trade disputes. It operates a system of trade rules.
>
> Since GATT's creation in 1947–48 there have been eight rounds of trade negotiations. A ninth round, under the Doha Development Agenda, is now underway. At first these focused on lowering tariffs (customs duties) on imported goods. Now their scope has broadened.

Fig. 6.8 *Protestors at a rally in the Philippines against the WTO*

Key terms

Geopolitics: the way geography, demography, economics and the distribution of resources interrelate with the politics of nations and the relationships between nations.

Food security: the FAO says food security exists 'when all people, at all times, have access to sufficient, safe and nutritious food to meet their dietary needs and food preferences for an active and healthy life.'

Globalisation: a set of processes leading to the integration of economic, cultural, political and social systems across geographical boundaries. It refers to increasing economic integration of countries, especially in terms of trade and the movement of capital.

Tariffs: taxes charged on imports (foodstuffs in this case). They are designed to raise the price of cheap imports to allow home producers to compete.

Link

Go to the WTO website for more details:

www.wto.org.

Look at the page under 'What is the WTO?'

Some ideas of some WTO opponents can be seen at:

www.commondreams.org/headlines05/0127-02.htm.

Some people think that the WTO negotiations can operate unfairly against the poor and weaker countries. They think that the big industrialised countries hold such a powerful position in world trade that they can use the talks to insist that their goods are accepted by the poorer countries, even if it means destroying the livelihood of the poor farmers in developing countries.

💡 Food security for developing countries

At the start of the new millennium the United Nations adopted eight millennium development goals (MDGs) for all people to work towards achieving by 2015. The United Nations has set up a website to monitor the progress. Note especially the first goal.

1 Eradicate extreme poverty and hunger.

2 Achieve universal primary education.

3 Promote gender equality and empower women.

4 Reduce child mortality.

5 Improve maternal health.

6 Combat HIV/Aids, malaria and other diseases.

7 Ensure environmental sustainability.

8 Develop a global partnership for development.

In order to achieve the MDGs, the following strategies are being developed by members of the United Nations:

▓ Increase aid and debt relief to the poorest countries. At the turn of the millennium, the total development aid to all poor countries was just over $1 billion. In particular, ensure that the aid goes to farmers and agricultural communities to enable them to invest in technology that will help them to increase production without losing control over their land and way of life.

▓ Reduce the subsidies paid to farmers and food processors in the developed countries. At the turn of the millennium over $350 billion was paid to subsidise agriculture in the major industrialised countries. Moreover, the markets in developed countries are often protected by tariffs that make it more expensive to import produce from abroad. These subsidies and tariffs then create a distorted market, so it becomes impossible for producers from developing countries to take advantage of their lower production costs and to compete in the world market for agricultural products. Loss of access to markets means loss of production, loss of income and increased reliance on food aid in the poor countries.

▓ The International Model for Policy Analysis of Agricultural Commodities and Trade (Impact) is a scheme which suggests that child malnutrition could be reduced by half for nearly all of the developing countries through investments in five key drivers of food and nutrition security: rural road construction, education, clean water provision, agricultural research, and irrigation. If developed in a planned and coordinated way in the key agricultural areas, Impact could improve agricultural production and allow that increased production to be marketed at a profit, so it can be invested in further production increases.

▓ Link

More details on the MDGs can be found at the UN website:

http://unstats.un.org/unsd/mdg/default.aspx.

Unfortunately, any moves to improve conditions for food producers in less developed countries have been held back by the changes in prices for some of the major commodities traded on the world market. Many prices of agricultural products have increased very slowly or have fallen. This has been due to increasing competition as developing, tropical and subtropical countries have tried to break into world markets. This has meant that the more developed countries have been able to move their purchasing to the country offering the lowest prices. At the same time, the prices of machinery, oil, fertilisers, insecticides, etc., have risen steadily. The producers have been squeezed between rising costs and steady or falling income.

■ Contrasting agricultural systems

Some of these key terms can be combined. Some farms are intensive, commercial mixed farms; others are extensive, subsistence pastoral farms; and so on.

■ Key terms

Types of farming

Commercial: farming for sale and profit. It can range from a small family farm in the UK up to the huge corporation-owned farms in the US Midwest. A plantation is a specialised form of commercial farm. Plantations are usually owned by large firms because big investments are needed in growing, processing and transporting crops. Most plantations are in tropical and subtropical areas and grow tree crops for export. Coffee, tea, sugar, bananas, palm oil, rubber and pineapples are typical plantation crops.

Subsistence: growing food for the family. It was once widespread when people lived in small, isolated communities but it has become rare now that transport is so much easier and trade is more common. Some farmers in remote parts of poor countries are probably best described as near-subsistence farmers, but even they often sell surpluses when they are produced.

Intensive: when the land is farmed with a high rate of inputs so that a high rate of outputs can be produced.

Capital-intensive: uses a lot of machinery, fertilisers and pesticides, buildings with heating and ventilation systems, irrigation, etc.

Labour-intensive: has a big input of work per area of land.

Extensive: uses a large area of land with low inputs and low outputs per hectare.

Arable: originally meant land that is fit to cultivate. However, in geography it is used to describe farming crops. Wheat, rice, barley, soya and cotton are typical arable crops. They can be grown as monoculture when a farm (or even a whole region) concentrates exclusively on a single crop.

Livestock: keeping mainly animals. They can be kept mainly for meat, mainly for milk or mainly for wool, leather, etc. Examples of livestock are cattle, sheep, pigs, goats, camels and poultry.

Mixed: growing crops and keeping animals. It has many benefits as the crops can provide fodder for the animals and the animals can provide manure for the soil.

■ Activity

4 Classify a variety of farming types using the key terms given above. Combine key terms to create a more complex classification.

■ Link

For a detailed example of subsistence farming, see the Sahel case study on pages 148–51.

■ Did you know?

Types of farming: further information

Capital-intensive and labour-intensive
Grain farming in the US Midwest is capital-intensive.

Growing padi rice in the Ganges delta of India and Bangladesh is labour-intensive.

Family-run dairy farms in England are both capital- and labour-intensive.

Extensive
Ranching in Wyoming and hill sheep farming in the highlands of Wales and Scotland are forms of extensive farming.

Arable
Most farms in East Anglia are arable farms growing wheat, barley and sugar beet as their main crops.

Livestock
Hill sheep farming and dairy farming in the UK are forms of livestock farming. So is the nomadic pastoralism of tribes such as the Maasai in Kenya.

Mixed
Most of the farms in the Midlands of England used to be mixed farms. However, this became much less common in the UK during the 20th century as farmers moved towards greater capital intensity and more specialisation.

Managing the food supply

Link

Read all about the theory of supply and demand at:

http://en.wikipedia.org/wiki/Supply_and_demand.

People have always had to manage food supply and that is why farming took over from hunting and gathering and why farmers and the scientists, planners, merchants, etc., who support them have always tried to find ways of increasing productivity and improving storage of the food that has been produced.

Increased production can lead to problems, however. When farming and food supply are run as a commercial enterprise the laws of supply and demand operate. If supply increases and demand does not increase, the price of the food produced will fall.

However, farmers cannot just change their whole production systems immediately in response to changes in prices. Their businesses are run on a long-term basis and are not as flexible as factory systems of service providers. Also, they depend to a large extent on climate and soil conditions in the area and this too makes it difficult to adapt to the market.

At the same time, many governments feel that they cannot afford to let farming suffer too much from wildly fluctuating market prices. Farming and food production is so important that there has to be some planning to protect farmers from fluctuating prices if that will help to guarantee the country's food supply and ensure food security.

As a result of this complex set of forces and the importance of trying to achieve food security, different systems in different parts of the world try to manage food supply by increasing and decreasing food production, sometimes both at the same time.

Strategies to increase food production

It is possible to imagine the first farmers looking at their crops and thinking, 'These plants produce the best yields. Let's save them and use them as seed for next year. That will give us even bigger yields.' Then, one year, someone must have concluded, 'We bred a cow that produces a lot of milk with the biggest bull and the calf is even better – lots of milk and plenty of meat too.'

Plant and animal breeding technology have always been with us, as long as farmers have taken notice of what goes on in their crop fields and their animal herds. One of the periods of most rapid development of agricultural methods and of technology linked to farming came during the so-called agricultural revolution in England during the 18th and 19th centuries. During this period, farming moved away from the old three-field system and its land enclosures. Individual management of farms became more important than the village-based sharing that preceded it.

Once farmers owned their own patches of land, they became keen to improve it and improve yields and profits. Mechanisation, improved plant and animal breeding, improved rotation systems, and more efficient marketing all followed. These changes took place alongside the industrial revolution that was helping the country move from small-scale craft manufacturing to large-scale factory manufacturing in cities. It was these urban populations that needed the increased agricultural surplus.

💡 The green revolution

The green revolution is the worldwide transformation of agriculture that led to significant increases in agricultural production between the 1940s and the 1960s. It occurred as the result of programmes of agricultural research, extension, and infrastructural development, instigated and largely funded by America's Rockefeller and Ford Foundations and other agencies from the developed countries. It helped food production to keep pace with and even overtake worldwide growth.

The term 'green revolution' was first used in 1968 by the director of USAID, William Gaud, who noted the spread of the new technologies and said, 'These and other developments in the field of agriculture contain the makings of a new revolution. It is not a violent Red Revolution. I call it the Green Revolution.'

There were four main components of the green revolution:

- increased use of fertilisers
- increased use of irrigation
- increased use of pesticides
- development of the new HYVs.

The first three involved applying technologies that had already been developed and were widely used in developed countries of the temperate latitudes. It was the fourth point that was revolutionary. Essentially the new seeds were developed using laboratory-based plant breeding techniques. The new plants were generally able to absorb more nitrogen from the soil and so produce higher yields. However, this increased absorption had to be channelled into increased grain content, producing a heavier plant. To avoid the risk of the larger plants collapsing under the weight of grain, shorter, thicker stems were bred into the new varieties.

The Rockefeller and Ford Foundations jointly established the International Rice Research Institute (IRRI) in the Philippines in 1960. High-yielding varieties (HYVs) spread throughout the Philippines, Indonesia, the Indian subcontinent and countries throughout Latin America, Asia and North Africa. USAID became involved in subsidising rural infrastructure development and fertiliser shipments. The Indian government collaborated with USAID to import a huge amount of wheat seed. India then began its own programme of plant breeding, irrigation development and financing of agrochemicals. By the late 1970s, the green revolution had raised rice yields in India by 30 per cent and given India vital time to curb its population growth without suffering a recurrence of the devastating famines of the 1940s.

The transition from traditional agriculture, where inputs were generated on-farm, to green revolution agriculture, which required the purchase of inputs, led to the widespread establishment of rural credit institutions. Smaller farmers often went into debt then often lost rights to their farmland.

The increased level of mechanisation on larger farms made possible by the green revolution removed an important source of employment from the rural economy. Many landless labourers lost their traditional sources of employment and were forced to migrate to the towns, increasing urbanisation.

▮ Did you know?

The green revolution: further information

Better performance

HYVs significantly outperform traditional varieties in the presence of adequate irrigation, pesticides and fertilisers. In the absence of these inputs, traditional varieties may outperform HYVs.

Buy seeds every year

One criticism of HYVs is that they were developed as F1 hybrids, meaning they need to be purchased by a farmer every season rather than saved from previous seasons, thus increasing a farmer's cost of production.

Yields doubled

Cereal production more than doubled in developing nations between 1961 and 1985. Yields of rice, maize and wheat increased steadily during that period. This can be attributed roughly equally to irrigation, fertiliser and seed development, at least for Asian rice.

Energy inputs

The ratio of crops produced to energy input has decreased over time. Green revolution techniques rely on chemicals from fossil fuels. If we have reached peak oil production, we could be heading for a decline in food production or even a Malthusian catastrophe.

Did you know?

In the most basic sense, the green revolution was a product of globalisation, as shown by the creation of international agricultural research centres that shared information, and with transnational funding from groups like the Rockefeller Foundation and USAID. Additionally, the inputs required in green revolution agriculture created new markets for seed and chemical corporations, many of which were based in the USA.

Link

See page 146 for more on salinisation.

Did you know?

The spread of green revolution agriculture affected biodiversity. The green revolution acted to reduce agricultural biodiversity, as it relied on just a few varieties of each crop. This has led to concerns about the susceptibility of a food supply to pathogens that cannot be controlled by agrochemicals, as well as the permanent loss of many valuable genetic traits bred into cereal varieties over thousands of years. To address these concerns, massive seed banks such as Bioversity International have been established.

Link

Read the paper by Dr Peter Hazell in full at:

www.ifpri.org/pubs/ib/ib11.pdf.

Because wealthier farmers had better access to credit and land, the green revolution increased class disparities. Because some regions were able to adopt green revolution agriculture more readily than others (for political or geographical reasons), interregional economic disparities increased as well.

The increase in food production led to a decrease in food prices for urban dwellers, and the increase in urban population increased the potential for industrialisation. However, industry was unable to absorb all the displaced agricultural labour and some cities grew at unsustainable rates.

Green revolution agriculture increased the use of pesticides, which were necessary to limit the high levels of pest damage that inevitably occur in monocultures. Organochlorides, which spread with the green revolution, do not easily break down in the environment and therefore accumulate through the food chain and spread throughout ecosystems. Problems with pesticides include the poisoning of farm workers, the contamination of water, and the evolution of resistance in populations of pest organism.

Irrigation projects have created significant problems of **salinisation**, waterlogging, and lowering of water tables in certain areas. In addition, the construction of dams has led to the forced removal of people – often among the poorest groups in the country – from land they have traditionally lived on.

India's success

The green revolution resulted in a record grain output of 131 million tonnes in 1978–79. This established India as one of the world's biggest agricultural producers. No other country in the world which took part in the green revolution recorded such a level of success. India also became an exporter of food grains around that time.

- Yield per unit of farmland improved by more than 30 per cent between 1947, when India gained political independence, and 1979, when the green revolution was considered to have delivered its goods.
- The crop area under HYV varieties grew from 7 per cent to 22 per cent of the total cultivated area during the 10 years of the green revolution. More than 70 per cent of the wheat crop area, 35 per cent of the rice crop area and 20 per cent of the millet and corn crop area used the HYV seeds.
- The demand for fertiliser, pesticides and fungicides spurred the growth of manufacturing industry.
- The increase in the demand for irrigation water led to dam construction, which in turn led to the production of hydroelectric power, again stimulating industrialisation.

The green revolution, however impressive, has not succeeded in making India totally and permanently self-sufficient in food. In 1979 and 1987, India faced severe drought conditions due to a poor monsoon season; this raised questions about whether the green revolution was really a long-term achievement. However, in today's globalised economy, 100 per cent self-sufficiency is not considered as vital a target as it was when the world political climate was more dangerous due to the Cold War.

In 2002 the International Food Policy Research Institute published a paper by Dr Peter Hazell, a development economist. In it, he discusses the achievements and the problems associated with the green revolution. Then he looks for a way forward. Here is an extract:

Real per capita incomes almost doubled in Asia between 1970 and 1995. The absolute number of poor people fell from 1.5 billion in 1975 to 825 million in 1995 ... much of this steady decline is attributable to agricultural growth and associated decline in food prices.

Development practitioners now have a better understanding of the conditions under which the Green Revolution and similar yield-enhancing technologies are likely to have equitable benefits among farmers. These conditions include:

1   a scale-neutral technology package that can be profitably adopted on farms of all sizes

2   an equitable distribution of land with secure ownership or tenancy rights

3   efficient credit and product markets so that farms of all sizes have access to modern farm inputs and information and are able to receive similar prices for their products

4   policies that do not discriminate against small farmers and landless labourers (for instance no subsidies for mechanisation).

These conditions are not easy to meet. Governments must make a concerted effort to ensure that small farmers have fair access to land, knowledge and modern inputs.

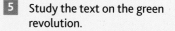

Activity

5   Study the text on the green revolution.

a   Make a list of all the benefits brought by the green revolution

b   Make a second list of all the problems caused by the green revolution.

c   What can be learned from the green revolution experience about how to manage innovation in agriculture in developing countries in future?

Genetically modified crops

What are genetically modified (GM) crops? What is genetic modification? Are GM foods safe? Can genetic modification lead to the creation of Frankenfoods? Can GM crops finally abolish hunger and ensure food security?

As explained in the section on the green revolution, humans have modified their crops ever since farming began. However, genetic modification of crops really began in 1977, when scientists discovered they could inject genes from one plant into another to give the resulting plant some desirable characteristics. Since then a whole series of GM plants have been produced. The most common modifications have produced plants that are resistant to diseases, pests or herbicides. Herbicide resistance means that a field can be sprayed to kill weeds and the spray will not harm the crop.

Other adaptations have included vitamin A-boosted rice, protein-enriched potatoes, drought- or salt-resistant crops that can flourish in poor conditions, insect-repelling crops that protect the environment by minimising pesticide use, and plants with improved flavour, increased shelf life, increased hardiness, and so on.

GM tomatoes, as purée, first appeared on British supermarket shelves in 1996 (a different fresh GM tomato first appeared in the USA in 1994), but the consumer furore that surrounded GM technology did not erupt until February 1999. This was because a controversial study suggested that a few strains of GM potatoes might be toxic to laboratory rats. This was followed by a European anti-GM food campaign led in the UK by environmental groups. It culminated in an unofficial moratorium (suspension) on the growth and import of GM crops in Europe and led to a trade dispute with the USA.

Link

One place to start to answer some of the questions posed in this section on GM Crops is on the *New Scientist* website:

http://www.newscientist.com/channel/opinion/gm-food.

Read the 'Instant Expert' column, which is constantly updated.

Also search for GM information here:

http://www.guardian.co.uk/theissues.

This is also an interesting article:

http://www.ncbe.reading.ac.uk/NCBE/GMFOOD/menu.html.

AQA Examiner's tip

If you are ever asked to refer to a website in an examination or in coursework, you should always be prepared to comment on its reliability.

GM crops are rare in Europe, and strict labelling laws and regulations are in place for food. Public opinion towards the technology remains largely negative. Several UK government reports have offered qualified support for GM crops and produce, although they note that the economic benefits of the technology are currently small. GM produce has been taken up with far less fuss in the USA, India, China, Canada, Argentina and Australia.

Critics fear that GM foods could have unforeseen adverse health effects on consumers, producing toxic proteins (and allergens) or transferring genes for antibiotic resistance and perhaps for other characteristcs that could have harmful effects in humans. But there has been little evidence to back up such risks so far.

More plausible threats are that modified crops could become insidious 'superweeds', or that they could accidentally breed with wild plants or other crops, genetically polluting the environment. This could be a potentially serious problem if pharm crops, engineered to produce pharmaceutical drugs, accidentally cross-breed with food varieties.

Large numbers of field trials, carried out by the UK government and others, reveal that gene transfer does occur. One study showed that transgenes had spread from the USA to traditional maize varieties in Mexico. A second revealed that conventional varieties of major US food crops have also been widely contaminated, and a third proved that pollen from GM plants can be carried on the wind for tens of kilometres. Many experts agree that insect-repelling plants will also speed the evolution of insecticide-resistant pests.

Genetic modification of crops may offer the largest potential benefits to developing nations. However, the growing globalisation of agriculture is a trend that worries some. Activists and disgruntled farmers worry that the agricultural biotech industry is encouraging reliance on their branded herbicide-resistant plants to create monopolies and control the market.

Companies such as Monsanto and Syngenta protect their GM seeds with patents. Companies have also investigated technology protection systems (TPS). One type of TPS, dubbed the Terminator by its critics, is a genetic trick that means GM crops fail to produce fertile seeds. This prevents the traditional practice of putting seeds aside from the crop to replant the following year, forcing farmers to buy new seed every year.

Activity

6   a   Study at least two of the sites named in the Link box. Write a report on the reliability of each site. Then summarise the main arguments of each site.

b   Consider the organisation that runs the site. Do they appear to present a fair and balanced view? Do they support their statements with references that you can check? Can you check any of the statements from elsewhere or from your own knowledge?

c   Write a summary of the main arguments of the best site. You could do this by cutting and pasting, but you ought to edit your summary to make it manageable.

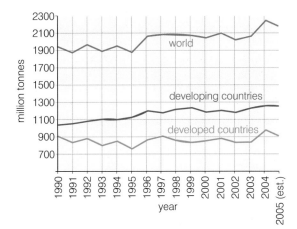

Fig. 6.9 *World cereal production, 1990–2005*

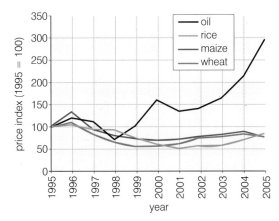

Fig. 6.10 *Food and energy prices, 1995–2005*

Activity

7　a　Describe the changes shown in Figure 6.10.

　　b　How can the data from Figure 6.9 help to explain the changes in cereal prices in Figure 6.10?

　　c　Describe the changes in oil prices between 1995 and 2005. How will this affect farmers trying to modernise and mechanise their production?

　　d　How and why will this affect the prices of fertilisers, insecticides and herbicides?

　　e　Discuss the implications of Figures 6.9 and 6.10 for the long-term future of food production.

Non-high-tech solutions to food supply problems

Read this extract from a recent policy statment by ActionAid India:

act:onaid

Very high levels of poverty stubbornly persist in India, despite the fact that the Indian State implements some of the largest and most ambitious public works and micro-credit programmes designed to combat rural poverty. Even after five decades of planned development, India remains home to the largest population of poor people in the world.

It is estimated that one-third of the world's poor reside in India, and there are more poor people in India than even in all of sub-Saharan Africa. Although official estimates of the Government of India says that every third Indian is poor, according to the estimate of internationally recognised poverty which is a dollar a day, one of every two persons in India is poor. Official data, assuming a calorie adequacy of 2400 calories a day, indicates that two out of three are malnourished or under-nourished.

Poverty is an extremely complex phenomenon, which manifests itself in a dense range of overlapping and interwoven economic, political and social deprivations. These include lack of assets, low income levels, hunger, poor health, insecurity, physical and psychological hardship, social exclusion, degradation and discrimination, and political powerlessness.

However, policy instruments are themselves designed to address poverty mainly as low income and consumption issues, to the fatal neglect of its larger and complex social and political dimensions, and of the aspirations of the poor. On the basis of empirical research, it has been established that the actual aspirations of the poor are in fact for 'survival, based on the stable subsistence; security, based on assets and rights; and self-respect, based on independence and choice'.

Fig. 6.11 *ActionAid works to alleviate poverty*

In the years since ActionAid issued this statement, poverty levels in India have fallen and fewer people are undernourished. However, the problem is still enormous, and the gap between rich and poor is widening. There are still large numbers of subsistence farmers, landless rural people, low-caste people and members of tribal groups who still do not enjoy food security, despite the increases in food production that have taken place. Women are disproportionately represented in this group of poor people.

Across India and in other areas where members of the 'poorest billion' are concentrated, ActionAid and other groups like them are working on a multi-target approach to development which recognises that a number of criteria have to be met if the very poor are to be raised out of poverty. These criteria are that everyone has the right to:

- food through sustainable livelihood
- education for all children, with full respect for girls' rights
- health through free and accessible primary care
- housing with legal security and provision of basic services
- security and freedom from violence and coercion, whether domestic or otherwise.

Here are two case studies on projects run or supported by ActionAid in India and Bangladesh.

Case study

Land rights and tea production in Chembakolli

Chembakolli lies in the Nilgiri Hills in southern India, an area of tropical monsoon rainforest. In the 1990s it had been designated as a conservation zone by the Indian Forestry Commission.

The inhabitants of the area are Adivasi, tribal people who traditionally lived as hunters and gatherers in the forest. In the last 50 years or so, they worked as temporary day labourers for Hindu farmers who had settled on the floodplains within the hills. However, in recent years mechanisation has reduced the demand for their labour. At the same time, the Forestry Commission has made it more and more difficult for the Adivasi to follow their traditional way of living in the forest. Areas that had formed part of their traditional land for generations were placed out of bounds and efforts were made to force the Adivasi into towns.

ACCORD, a local NGO supported by ActionAid, originally tried to help the people by bringing health care, improving the water supply and helping set up schools in the villages, but soon realised that this was not enough without major structural change. So the organisation began supporting the people to take action through the courts to gain rights to the land that their families had lived on for as long as they could remember.

Fig. 6.12 *Tea production in Chembakolli*

As they negotiated, they also began to develop tea planatations on the hills in their neighbourhood, again with advice and support. The area was ideally suited to this form of farming, but the Adivasi were encouraged to grow and sell their own tea rather than working for companies owned and run by outsiders. Although they had to use the tea-processing factories on local plantations, they kept control of the sale of their own tea. At first, they sold to a fair trade organisation in Germany, but now they are selling a proportion of their tea through a cooperative of unemployed people in Luton, north of London.

Fig. 6.13 *Adivasi people from Chembakolli visit the cooperative in Luton. Here they are showing local school students how they build their houses in the forest*

The theory behind this development is that the fair trade organisation pays the Adivasi a better price than they would receive if they sold through middlemen to a supermarket chain in Europe. Selling through the cooperative allows the growers (in Chembakolli) and the retailers (in Luton) to deal directly with each other. They can keep control of the trade and they gain maximum benefit from their work and investments.

Link

Land colonisation is also discussed on pages 98–99.

Key terms

Char: an island formed from silt deposited in the delta. The land is at about sea level. It is very fertile, so it attracts settlers desperate for land. However, it can easily be washed away by monsoon floods or by cyclones. Even if the cyclones do not destroy the chars, they flood them with salt water, which reduces their fertility.

Colonisation: the spread of settlement onto previously uninhabitable land. One example is the colonisation of the chars. Another example is the spread of cultivation into desert margin areas by using irrigation water or new farming techniques (e.g. crops genetically engineered to be drought resistant).

Case study

Small-scale enterprises for women in Kukri Mukri

Kukri Mukri is an island in the delta region of the Ganges-Brahmaputra, in Bangladesh. Much of the land is **char** land that has been **colonised** by landless people. People live on the chars, and many do not have formal title to the land because they have only recently colonised the newly formed land. They grow subsistence crops of rice and vegetables, catch fish in the delta or even venture into the Bay of Bengal. Any surplus is taken to local markets for sale, but travel to and from the markets is difficult because of the poor infrastructure.

The small areas of land available to most families, the constant threat of flooding or insufficient water for the crops during the monsoon season, and the constant threat of dispossession, all mean that food security is poor. When there is a surplus, prices at the market fall; when there is a poor crop the area is so isolated that it is difficult to obtain relief supplies. Most families have a poorly balanced diet. Women are more or less confined to the house by their religion and by tradition.

ActionAid worked through local partners to set up credit organisations for local women. The women could take out loans to start small enterprises which they could run on their own terms. Projects included:

- duck breeding
- literacy classes
- introducing new crops, such as red cabbage
- **intermediate technology** pumps.

Partners drilled tube wells for villages that did not have reliable access to fresh water. Once the wells are drilled down to unpolluted groundwater layers, the technology to raise the water is simple and robust. The pump can be run without expensive energy supplies and maintenance can be done by local people. Spares are cheap. Having the clean water supply improves health, especially for babies and young children, and allows irrigation to be used in the dry season, increasing the crop yield from the land.

Fig. 6.14 *Kukri Mukri island, Bangladesh*

Key terms

Intermediate technology: also called appropriate technology, this is a way to introduce technology to people who have not used it before. It has to be more efficient than the simple, traditional technology but it must not be too expensive to run and maintain. It ought to be manageable and repairable by the people who use it without relying on outside technicians.

a

Women want to be able to read so they can keep up with their children in school. Note the use of maps and symbols in the literacy class. This helps people to discuss and negotiate land rights with officials.

b

Ducks can feed on and around the paddy fields. They do not damage the rice but eat pests like insects and snails. The women can run the business from home. They produce eggs and meat – important protein sources – and the eggs can be sold to make more money so that other women start similar enterprises.

c

Red cabbage is high in B vitamins, which are low in the traditional diet. The cabbage adds variety and makes the diet more balanced.

Fig. 6.15 *Some of the ActonAid projects on Kukri Mukri*

■ The CAP and food supply management

Governments often try to protect their farmers from wildly fluctuating food prices. This is a way of trying to ensure food security as fluctuations that are too great could put farmers out of business and reduce the national food supply. Probably the best-known and most complex system of controlling food supply has been the Common Agricultural Policy (CAP) of the European Union (EU). Part of the CAP strategy has been to reduce food production in some circumstances so as to reduce gluts, keep prices high and ensure continued profits for farmers.

The CAP was set up soon after the end of the Second World War. During the war, much of Europe had suffered very severe food shortages and famine was quite a serious problem in some parts of central Europe in the late 1940s. The CAP was designed, in the late 1950s, to plan production and increase food security by maximising production. To do this, tariffs were raised against imports and guaranteed prices were paid to producers within the EU. In addition, small-scale peasant farmers were encouraged to amalgamate their farms to make larger units which were more suitable for mechanisation.

The CAP was spectacularly successful in increasing food production. By the mid-1970s there were huge surpluses of wheat, butter, wine, olive oil and other products. It was costing an enormous amount to (a) produce and (b) store all this surplus food. Some of the surplus was used for famine relief in poor countries, sold to poor countries at **subsidised** prices or **dumped** on poor countries even when there was no famine.

Strategies to reduce food production

By the 1990s, the CAP had to be reformed. However, there was much political opposition to any reform, particularly from small farmers in the Mediterranean regions of France, Spain, Portugal, Italy and Greece. A much higher proportion of the population is engaged in agriculture in these areas than in the UK, so the farmers there had a lot of political power. They were able to use this power to exert strong pressure on their governments and on the EU. However, CAP reforms were made.

- Growers of low-quality wine and olive oil were paid to reduce the areas under crop and to increase the quality of their produce from the remaining areas.
- Subsidies to dairy and livestock farmers were reduced so farmers were no longer encouraged to produce as many animals. This reduction in stock levels was designed to reduce overgrazing, which was leading to soil erosion in some upland areas.
- Arable farmers were paid to set aside up to 10 per cent of their land and not to grow crops on it, so as to reduce the grain mountains.
- The total amount of subsidies paid to farmers through the CAP was gradually reduced.
- Subsidies were more widely distributed as countries from eastern Europe joined the EU and needed payments to help their small farmers reorganise production to fit market economy.

Perhaps the most important change to the CAP payments in the UK were linked to conservation measures and **stewardship**. In 2006 the Department for Environment and Rural Affairs (Defra) set up Natural England to work with farmers and other landowners. This extract sets out its aims:

■ Key terms

Subsidy: a payment to a producer to help cover the costs of production so that the product can be sold at a price lower than the true cost. This means that the producer can compete against foreign imports.

Dumping: the sale of products that have been produced with the aid of subsidies and then are sold in another country at a price that is cheaper than the cost of production. This might seem generous but it undercuts farmers in the receiving country. This can make their farms uneconomic, put them out of business and increase dependence on the country that dumped its produce.

Stewardship: taking responsible care of the environment, based on the premise that we do not own resources, but are managers and are responsible to future generations for their condition.

Natural England will work for people, places and nature, to enhance biodiversity, landscapes and wildlife in rural, urban, coastal and marine areas; promoting access, recreation and public well-being, and contributing to the way natural resources are managed so that they can be enjoyed now and in the future.

Natural England is working towards the delivery of four strategic outcomes, which together deliver on our purpose to conserve, enhance and manage the natural environment for the benefit of current and future generations.

1   **A healthy natural environment:** England's natural environment will be conserved and enhanced.

2   **Enjoyment of the natural environment:** more people enjoying, understanding and acting to improve the natural environment, more often.

3   **Sustainable use of the natural environment:** the use and management of the natural environment are more sustainable.

4   **A secure environmental future:** decisions which collectively secure the future of the natural environment.

www.naturalengland.org.uk

Link

For further details of stewardship schemes, see the Natural England website:

www.naturalengland.org.uk.

Look up the 'About us' section.

Natural England helps to administer Defra funding for farmers involved in environmental conservation projects. Further details about the schemes can be found on the Natural England website and on the Defra site:

www.defra.gov.uk.

Look up 'Grants & funding'.

Defra has produced a booklet that outlines the stewardship schemes:

www.defra.gov.uk/erdp/pdfs/es/es-promotional-booklet.pdf.

Changes in demand for food

In this section you will learn:

- about changing demands for food in developed countries like the UK

- how some of these changes are environmentally friendly and may be more sustainable

- how some changes may not be sustainable

- that production of luxury vegetables in developing countries can have pros and cons for the producer countries.

Key terms

Organic food: food produced to certain production standards. Crops are grown without the use of conventional pesticides, artificial fertilisers, human waste or sewage sludge, and are processed without ionising radiation or food additives. Animals are reared without the use of antibiotics or growth hormones and must not be genetically modified.

Link

For a detailed study of Aviaries Farm, an organic mixed farm in Somerset, go to:

www.face-online.org.uk.

Look up 'Farm profiles', 'Aviaries Farm'.

Organic food

Organic food production is regulated in the UK by several bodies, including the Soil Association. Currently, the USA, the EU, Japan and many other countries require producers to obtain organic certification in order to market their food as organic.

Supporters of organic farming claim that organic farms have a smaller environmental impact than conventional farms. Several surveys and studies have attempted to examine and compare conventional and organic systems of farming and there is general agreement that organic farming is less damaging because:

- organic farms do not release synthetic pesticides into the environment, some of which have the potential to harm local wildlife

- organic farms are better than conventional farms at sustaining diverse ecosystems – populations of plants and insects, as well as animals

- when calculated per unit area or per unit yield, organic farms use less energy and produce less waste, such as packaging materials for chemicals.

In addition, organic farming has health benefits:

- Farmers and their families are not as exposed to pesticides which can cause stomach upsets and may contain carcinogens (cancer-causing chemicals).

- There are far fewer pesticide residues in organic products on sale in shops. Although residues in conventionally produced foods are generally closely monitored and are considered safe, some studies have shown that organic crops are marginally safer. However, this point is still not proven.

Some people claim that organic food tastes better. However, this has not been proved in any reliable tests.

On the other hand, organic food is almost always more expensive because of the higher production costs. The higher production costs are mainly caused by the more intensive use of labour.

The appearance of organic vegetables is less uniform than the appearance of conventionally grown produce that is sold by the supermarkets. Organic farmers say that, without using chemicals to control growth, it is difficult to meet supermarket standards for appearance. Organic fruit and vegetables can appear to be oddly shaped, vary in size and even be slightly blemished. However, none of these things affects the nutritional value of the products.

One big unanswered question is whether organic farming could ever be developed on a big enough scale to feed more than just a small section of the population. (Maybe the reference to Cuba in the Did you know? box goes some way to answering that question.)

💡 Food miles and seasonal food

In early September, home-grown seasonal fruit and vegetables like apples, onions, carrots and green beans were available throughout the country. But so too, in three central London supermarkets, were apples bought 4700 miles from the USA, onions over 12,000 miles from Australia and New Zealand, carrots from South Africa (5100 miles) and beans from Kenya (3600 miles).

In 2004 Defra commissioned a report into the costs of food transport for all food brought into and moved around the UK. Figure 6.16 shows some of its conclusions.

Food transport has significant and growing impacts
Food transport accounted for an estimated 30 billion vehicle kilometres in 2002, of which 82 per cent were in the UK.

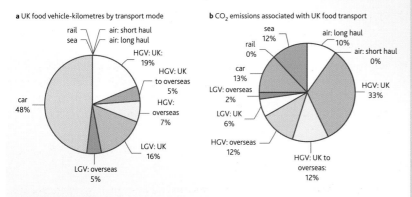

Food transport accounts for 25 per cent of all HGV vehicle kilometres in the UK

Food transport produced 19 million tonnes of CO_2 emissions in 2002

Transport of food by air has the highest CO_2 emissions and is the fastest-growing mode
It produces 11 per cent of the food transport CO_2 emissions

Environmental, social and economic costs
The environmental, social and economic costs of food transport are over £9 billion each year and are dominated by congestion costs.

Fig. 6.16 *Extract from Defra report, 2004*

■ Activity

10 The Defra report in Figure 6.16 also analysed the cost to the public of food transport. It estimated the social and environmental costs per year (£ million) of the transport under a number of headings. Here are the results:

CO_2	Air quality	Noise	Congestion	Accidents	Infrastructure	Total
364	439	283	5187	2036	815	9124

a   Use these figures to construct a pie chart (see below).

b   Comment on the figures in the table and the pie chart.

c   Suggest how the total cost of food transport could be reduced.

d   Refer to the planning of food production, the planning of transport networks and the structuring of communities.

■ Skills

How to draw a pie chart

A pie chart shows how a total is divided into its constituent parts. A circle is made up of 360°, so 3.6° represents 1 per cent of the total. Therefore you need to work out the percentage that each part of your data set contributes to the total (100 per cent) of your data set. Set out your table like this:

Cost type	Cost in £ millions	Fraction of total (%)	Angle of pie chart (°)
CO_2 pollution	364	4[1]	14[2]
Air quality	439	5	18
Noise	283	3	11
Congestion	5187	57	205
Accidents	2036	22	80
Infrastructure	815	9	32
Total	**9124**	**100**	**360**

1   To work out CO_2 pollution cost as a percentage of total cost:
$$\frac{\text{Cost value}}{\text{Total cost}} \times \frac{100}{1} = \frac{364}{9124} \times \frac{100}{1}$$
$$= 4\%$$

2   To work out the angle in the pie slice for CO_2 pollution:
Percentage of total cost × 3.6 = 4 × 3.6
$$= 14°$$

1   Choose a convenient radius for your pie.

2   Draw a radius from the centre of the circle straight up to 12 o'clock.

3   Start filling in the sections of the pie from 12 o'clock.

4   Start with the largest section of the pie.

5   Place your protractor with the 0° line at 12 o'clock.

6   Measure off 205°. Mark the end of that sector.

7   Complete your sectors in order of size. Finish with the smallest, which should take you back to 12 o'clock.

8   Shade. Add a key and title. Label as necessary.

■ Local food sourcing

In French supermarkets there is often a separate section for regional specialities or products of the region. This is an attempt to build on and continue the French pride in their local products. This used to be a very important part of French food culture, although it has become less so with the advance of the hypermarket and the growth of fast food and convenience food.

However, this attempt to preserve the local specialities does reduce the distance travelled by food, helps local farmers, allows local supermarket managers some autonomy from central control and makes profits for the supermarket. Maybe the local markets and specialist local shops are a more important way of sourcing local foods but these sections in the supermarkets are an interesting development. People in the UK are taking some steps towards local sourcing of foods.

Farmers' markets

Farmers' markets have been set up across the UK to try to provide a new outlet for farmers to sell directly to the public in their own neighbourhoods. There are currently around 500 farmers' markets in the country. The box shows the criteria that farmers' markets must meet to gain certification.

■ Link

A complete directory of the markets certified by the National Farmers' Retail Markets Association (FARMA) can be found at:

www.farmersmarkets.net/findafmkt.htm.

National Farmers' Retail & Markets Association Core Criteria

1 **Locally produced**
Only produce from the defined area shall be eligible for sale at a farmers' market. Producers from the area defined as local must be given preference.

2 **Principal producer**
The principal producer, a representative directly involved in the production process or a close family member, must attend the stall.

3 **Primary, own produce**
All produce sold must be grown, reared or caught by the stallholder within the defined local area.

4 **Secondary, own produce**
All produce must be brewed, pickled, baked, smoked or processed by the stallholder using at least one ingredient grown or reared within the defined local area.

Local labelling and traceability

Many restaurants now run source labelling schemes, by which they name the farm or group of farms that produced the meat and vegetables that they use. In order to make this work, they have to build up close contacts with local farmers and food processors so they can ensure consistency in the product. In these schemes 'local' has a link to quality as well as to geography. Labels which say 'local' and 'seasonal' imply that the food is fresh and special.

Some supermarkets have similar schemes, although they are often national rather than local. The chief executive of food retail for the Co-operative Group has said: 'We are committed to supporting British farmers and all Co-operative fresh meat and poultry is now British. We

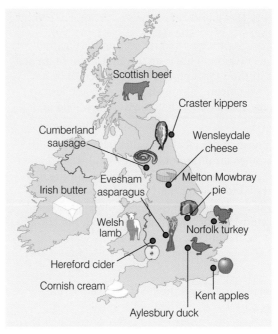

Fig. 6.17 *Food produce specialities in the UK*

Fig. 6.18 *The Red Tractor logo*

know this is important to Co-op customers, who are also increasingly interested in the seasonality and provenance of the food they buy. By working closely with British farmers, including many small local producers, we are providing the opportunity for our customers, whether they live in Scotland, Wales, England or Northern Ireland, to enjoy and take pride in the best foods sourced from their nation.'

The Red Tractor scheme is another development that tries to assure consumers about the quality and production methods of food that carries the logo. The scheme inspects farmers and processors to make sure that their businesses are run with high quality controls. This ensures that food safety and hygiene standards are maintained as well as standards for animal welfare and the environment.

Activities

10 a Find out details about the location, times and types of stall at your nearest farmers' market.

   b Find out some of the local specialities of your region and other regions of the country. Try to discover how they are marketed to appeal to particular sections of the market.

   c Suggest why that local environment is particularly suited to the speciality.

11 a Local specialities can sometimes be more expensive than imported alternatives, despite the added costs of transport for the imports. Suggest why.

   b List and explain some of the advantages of buying local that might offset the increased costs.

Worldwide food sourcing and the ghost acres

Much of the food that is eaten in the UK is imported from elsewhere. These imports include produce that cannot be grown in our climate (such as bananas, pineapples and oranges). Since the 19th century we have also imported produce that we cannot produce in sufficient quantities by using the space in the UK, or that can be grown more cheaply elsewhere (such as wheat from the plains of North America, lamb from New Zealand and beef from Argentina).

In recent years, though, some new types of import have grown in importance:

- fresh vegetables airfreighted from subtropical regions
- beef produced on cleared rainforest areas of Brazil and other equatorial regions
- cereals and high-protein foods imported to feed livestock.

In all three cases the food is imported at considerable cost in food miles (although the cost to the environment is not always reflected in the price paid in the shops) and is imported from countries where food for local people is often in short supply and where food security is not good. In fact, the term 'ghost acres' (which was originally used in India about land used for growing produce for export to Britain) is now widely used in poor countries to describe land used for export crops.

Airfreighted vegetables

Ferry Fast, a company based in Pershore, Worcestershire (originally set up to transport locally grown produce) states on its website that it imports fruit, flowers and vegetables from 17 countries, many of them developing countries in tropical and subtropical regions.

From Kenya it imports baby corn, chillies, green beans, extra-fine beans, okra, mangoes, mangetout, sugar snap peas, passion fruit and flowers. Some of these items cannot be grown in the UK, but peas and beans certainly can. However, the market now demands that these vegetables are available all year round, so land in Kenya that was formerly used for subsistence crops is now used for producing luxury crops for export.

What is more, many of the crops need irrigation water to grow economically and this reduces the water supply available for local food supplies. On the other hand, production of these crops does offer work to a growing number of Kenyans and some of the farms producing the crops are Kenyan-owned. Wages and profits from the production are taxed, which provides revenue for the government.

> ■ **Link**
>
> To find out more about Ferry Fast, its history and full details of the foods it imports and the countries it deals with, go to:
>
> www.ferryfast.co.uk/sales_main.htm.

> ■ **Activity**
>
> **12** **a** Consider the advantages and disadvantages of Kenya's production of vegetables, fruit and flowers for export from the viewpoints of some of these people:
> - farm owner in Kenya
> - subsistence farmer in Kenya who now works as a casual farm labourer in Kenya
> - manager of an airfreight company
> - scientist studying global warming
> - supermarket manager in the UK
> - commercial vegetable grower in the UK
> - Portuguese migrant working for commercial vegetable grower in the UK
> - you, the consumer.
>
> **b** Does cultural or ethnic background affect your answers? Discuss this with the rest of your class.

Beef from Brazil

George Monbiot is a leading environmental campaigner. Here is what he said in one of this articles for the *Guardian* newspaper:

Until 1990 Brazil produced only enough beef to feed itself. Since then its cattle herd has grown by some 50 million, and the country has become, according to some estimates, the world's biggest exporter: it sells 1.9 m tonnes a year. The United Kingdom is its fourth-largest customer, after Russia, Egypt and Chile. One region is responsible for 80% of the growth in Brazilian beef production. It's the Amazon.

The past three years have been the most destructive in the Brazilian Amazon's history. In 2004, 26,000 sq km of rainforest were burned: the second-highest rate on record. This year could be worse. And most of it is driven by cattle ranching.

Cattle ranching, if it keeps expanding in the Amazon, threatens two-fifths of the world's remaining rainforest. This is not just the most diverse ecosystem but also the biggest reserve of standing carbon. Its clearance could provoke a hydrological disaster in South America, as rainfall is reduced as the trees come down.

www.guardian.co.uk, 18 October 2005

Choices magazine is published by the American Agricultural Economics Association (AAEA). It covers the economic implications of food, farm, resource and rural community issues directed toward a broad audience. Have a look at this extract from *Choices*:

Major factors that explain the improvement of the productivity of the cattle industry in Brazil were:

- Improvement in animal genetics mostly through the use of cross breeding programs. Cattlemen are using imported bull semen, such as Red Angus, Angus, Simmental, and Limousin, to cross with the domestic Nelore breed.
- (Cheap loans under the MODERAGRO programme). MODERAGRO includes funds for soil erosion and conservation of lands and is expected to reach approximately US$390 million at a subsidised interest rate of 8.5% per year. Each producer may borrow up to US$50,000.
- The Agriculture and Livestock Plan expects to allocate US$19.2 billion of rural credit, of which US$5.1 billion is designated for the beef sector.

Also significant has been the aggressive marketing efforts of ABIEC (Brazilian Beef Processors and Exporters Association), an association of the largest beef processors, packers, and exporters. They emphasize the product as natural (grass-fed beef as opposed to grain-fed beef), environmental, and healthy.

ABIEC targets markets worldwide, but their primary focus is the European Union. For the last two decades, the cattle industry has moved towards the Center-West region. It is now home to over one-third of Brazil's herd. But recently, cattle production has begun to move North (into Amazonia) because of the expansion of soybean production, which has raised land prices in the Center-West. Raising cattle in the North is 10% more profitable than in other regions in Brazil because of lower land prices. Once timber is harvested, there is competition from other land uses such as crop production.

www.choicesmagazine.org, 12 February 2006

High-protein food imports for livestock

World livestock production exceeds 21 billion animals each year. The Earth's livestock population is more than three and a half times its human population. The raising of livestock takes up more than two-thirds of the world's agricultural land. In 1900 just over 10 per cent of the total grain grown worldwide was fed to animals; by 1950 this figure had risen to over 20 per cent; by the late 1990s it stood at around 45 per cent. Over 60 per cent of US grain is fed to livestock.

There are 44 million ghost acres in Thailand alone (an area about the size of Ireland) devoted to supplying manioc for European cattle. Export commodities such as these distort a developing country's agricultural economy, encouraging small farmers to participate in growing cash crops for export rather than food crops for local needs. Brazil has become a major supplier of soyabeans for European animal feed, but to do this it has had to cut down a quarter of its Cerrada Plateau forest, some 12 million acres, causing immeasurable damage.

These are typical examples of the ghost acres. In the UK we exploit two of these ghost acres abroad for every one acre we farm at home. We can do this only because the true costs of exploiting Brazil and Thailand, and the true costs of shipping the animal feed to Europe, are not reflected in the price of the food that consumers buy.

This land contributes to developing world malnutrition by driving impoverished populations to grow cash crops for animal feed, rather than food for themselves. Intensive monoculture crop production causes soils to suffer nutrient depletion and reduces opportunities for local food security and sustainable development.

In addition, the rearing of cattle takes a lot of water. According to UNESCO figures, producing 1 kg of beef uses as much water as 40 baths. or 300 toilet flushes, or as is needed to produce 16 kg of wheat flour.

Activities

13 Refer back to Activity 12. Consider the issues linked to imports of Brazilian beef and imported protein for UK animals from a similar range of viewpoints.

14 a Is the UK's food supply sustainable and secure?

b Are we paying the real price for the food that we eat when the environmental and social costs of our food are taken into account?

c Can it ever be acceptable to reduce the intensity of agricultural production in order to conserve the environment when there are still people in the world who are undernouirished?

d If more of the world's agricultural area is to be used for producing biofuels, what will happen to the price and availability of food supplies?

e Many parts of the developing world do not enjoy food security at present. Should the governments of those countries follow a policy of developing agricultural productivity whatever the cost?

AQA ■ **Examiner's tip**

The specification states, at the end of the section on food supply issues, that 'two contrasting approaches to managing food supply and demand must be studied'.

After studying this chapter carefully, you will realise you have already done at least two such studies that can be adapted to fit examination questions:

■ The geopolitics of food (pages 206–209) looked at free trade in food and the MDGs to try to manage world food production to better suit the needs of the poor.

■ The green revolution and other high-tech solutions (pages 211–213) looked at examples from India.

■ Non-high-tech solutions (pages 216–219) looked at examples from India and Bangladesh; this could be supplemented with a study of land reform in India.

■ Strategies to reduce food production (pages 220–221) looked at the CAP in Europe and stewardship schemes in the UK.

■ Worldwide food sourcing (pages 226–229) included case studies of Brazil and Kenya.

Make your case studies work for you. Adapt your knowledge to fit the demands of questions under different headings in the specification.

✔ ♀ 𝒊 *In this chapter you have learnt:*

■ some of the main patterns of world food production, malnourishment and trade in foodstuffs

■ some of the factors affecting the world trade in food, including major geopolitical factors and the influence of the food transnational corporations

■ how countries and individuals try to ensure their own food security through high-technology solutions (including the green revolution and genetic modification) and appropriate technology solutions

■ about the strengths and weaknesses of those proposed solutions

■ how, in some places at some times, there have been attempts to improve food security by limiting food production and keeping food prices high

■ how the EU countries are now moving towards encouraging more environmentally friendly sustainable farming

■ about conflicting pressures to produce and market foods that are locally produced and foods that are globally produced and marketed.

7 Energy issues

Types of energy sources and national energy mixes

Key terms

Renewable resources: resources that will not run out and which are continuously being created. They include solar, wind, tide, hydro-electric and geothermal power.

Flow resources: the result of a continuous flow like wind or tide.

Non-renewable resources: finite or limited resources, which will run out sooner or later. They include fossil fuels like coal, oil and natural gas and also nuclear, because it uses mined uranium. Breeder reactors, which create their own fuel, are theoretically possible but are not sufficiently developed.

Stock resources: there is a stock of each resource and when that stock is gone it is gone forever.

💡 The fundamental division between different types of energy source is between **renewable** (or **flow**) **resources** and **non-renewable** (or **stock**) **resources**. Fossil fuels are the main non-renewable resources.

What are fossil fuels?

Coal

Coal is a fossil fuel. It was created when forests growing in shallow swamps during the Carboniferous period died and were covered by sediments. The organic material in the trees could not rot away and so it was preserved. Layers of rock on top compressed the organic material and squeezed out the moisture. The coal formed as seams of rock in between layers of sandstone and shale.

If the coal is buried deep below ground, shaft mines have to be dug down to reach the coal. If it is fairly close to the surface it can be recovered by opencast methods where the overburden is stripped away by great mechanical diggers and then the coal is quarried out. The overburden is eventually replaced and the landscape can be restored.

Oil

Oil is also a fossil fuel. It was formed below the sea from the remains of microscopic sea creatures that died and fell to the sea floor. They were covered by layers of sediment, and again this trapped and compressed the organic remains. Heat and pressure slowly turned the organic content of the rocks into oil. This percolated through pores in the rock and travelled upwards towards the surface. If it was trapped by a layer of impermable rock above, it formed an oil reservoir.

Natural gas

Natural gas is often formed at the same time as oil. It is usually lighter and so lies on top of the oil. Both oil and natural gas are extracted using wells which are drilled down to the reservoir. Usually the oil and gas are initially forced out by their own pressure in the reservoir but later on the reservoir pressure falls and pressurised fluids have to be forced down the well to push up the oil. The oil and gas that are extracted are replaced by mud, which fills the old reservoir.

Why do fossil fuels cause problems?

Hydrocarbons

The plant and animal remains that form fossil fuels are chemicals called hydrocarbons. They are compounds that contain hydrogen atoms and carbon atoms. The carbon was taken from the atmosphere by photosynthesis, then used to build the structures of the plants or animals.

When the fuel is used, the carbon combines with oxygen and produces heat plus carbon dioxide. This carbon dioxide is a waste product that escapes into the atmosphere.

Coal, oil and natural gas contain impurities. Natural gas contains fewer impurities than coal and oil. The impurities can lead to the formation of acid rain.

■ The UK's energy mix

Until recently the UK was largely self-reliant for energy, producing significant quantities of oil, coal and gas. The gradual depletion of oil and gas reserves and a reduction in domestic coal production have led to a growing dependency on imports.

The UK is still the largest producer of oil and natural gas in the EU. Proved oil reserves were 4 billion barrels and natural gas reserves were 0.53 trillion m^3 at the end of 2005. However, UK production has passed its peak. Although the UK is still a net exporter of oil, the next decade will almost certainly see a decline in domestic oil and gas production and an increase in imports.

The UK still has large reserves of coal but domestic production is declining and imports are increasing because:

- much of the remaining coal is deep and in geologically complex formations, making it difficult and expensive to mine
- much of the reserve of coal has a high sulphur content, which means it contributes strongly to the formation of acid rain, or the waste fumes from power stations need to undergo expensive cleaning
- there are restrictions on mining some of the cleaner deposits because they are only suitable for opencast mining, which is seen as more damaging to the environment, and these deposits are often found close to settlements
- imports from South Africa and Australia are cheaper because of easier conditions for mining, and they are lower in sulphur than most UK coal, which makes them more environmentally friendly or less environmentally damaging.

Table 7.1 *Energy mix for the UK, 2004*

Million tonnes of oil equivalent	Primary energy supply[1]	Domestic production[2]	Net imports[3]
Solid fuels	38.3	15.6	22.6
Oil	81.6	96.9	–12.8
Gas	87.4	86.4	1.5
Nuclear	20.6	20.6	
Electricity			0.6
Renewables	3.7	3.5	0.5
Other	0.6		
Total	**232.1**	**223.1**	**12.1**

[1] The energy consumed in the country
[2] The energy produced in the country
[3] The total energy imported less the total exported
Note: 1 does not always equal 2 + 3 because supplies can be put into and taken out of storage.

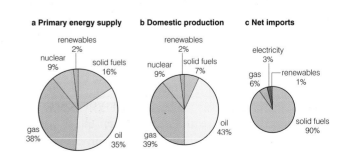

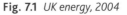

Fig. 7.1 *UK energy, 2004*

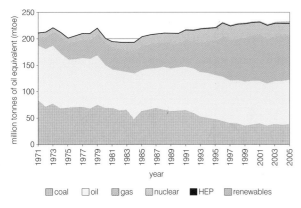

Fig. 7.2 *Changes in the UK's energy mix, 1971–2005*

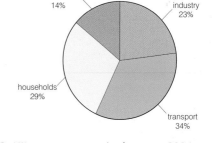

Fig. 7.3 *UK energy consumption by sector, 2004*

The key figures for the UK's **energy mix** are shown in Table 7.1. These figures are given in million tonnes of oil equivalent (mtoe). A toe of coal is the amount that would be needed to generate as much energy as a tonne of oil. Using toes is a useful way of comparing different parts of the energy mix.

Figure 7.1 shows supply, domestic production and net imports as pie charts; the pie charts compare percentages of the different components, not totals. Pie charts like these are very useful for seeing how the different parts of a country's energy mix contribute to the total. The areas of charts (a) and (b) are also drawn to show the comparative size of domestic production and domestic supply, but chart (c) is not drawn to the same scale.

Figure 7.2 shows how the energy mix has changed over time and Figure 7.3 shows which sectors of the economy use most of the energy. Note that total energy use has remained fairly constant over the last 10 years or so, whereas transport and household uses have both increased (transport by 18 per cent between 1990 and 2004) and industrial use has declined.

Activity

1 When you have carefully studied the data on the UK's energy mix (Table 7.1 and Figures 7.1 to 7.3), choose the energy mix of another EU country. Germany and France are shown on pages 234–5. Write a comparison between the energy mix of that country and the UK. Try to explain the differences between the two countries.

Figures 7.10 to 7.13 on page 235 show the changing energy supply in one industrialising country (China) and one poor country of sub-Saharan Africa (Kenya), for contrast with the EU countries.

Note that in both these countries the section labelled 'renewables' consists largely of wood and other biomass used for domestic heating and cooking in rural regions.

Note also that in 2006 Kenya's population was estimated at 35 million and its growth rate was 2.5 per cent. China's population was estimated at 1.29 billion and its growth rate was 1 per cent.

Key terms

Energy mix: the different sources of energy used by households, industry and commerce, and in the electricity generation industry.

Link

Further information about the data shown here can be found at:

http://ec.europa.eu/energy/ energy_policy/doc/factsheets/mix/ mix_uk_en.pdf.

If you wish to research more details about the country you have chosen (or about any other EU country), go to:

http://ec.europa.eu/energy/energy_ policy/facts_en.htm.

Click on 'Energy Mix' for details about that country.

Did you know?

You can try to plan the country's future electricity supply by using the BBC's interactive Electricity Calculator at http://news.bbc. co.uk/2/shared/spl/hi/uk/06/ electricity_calc/html/1.stm.

Table 7.2 *Energy mix for Germany, 2004*

Million tonnes of oil equivalent	Primary energy supply	Domestic production	Net imports
Solid fuels	85.8	58.3	27.7
Oil	125.4	5.7	121.3
Gas	78.7	14.7	65.9
Nuclear	43.1	43.1	
Electricity			−0.2
Renewables	13.8	13.8	
Other	1.0	1.2	
Total	**347.7**	**136.8**	**214.7**

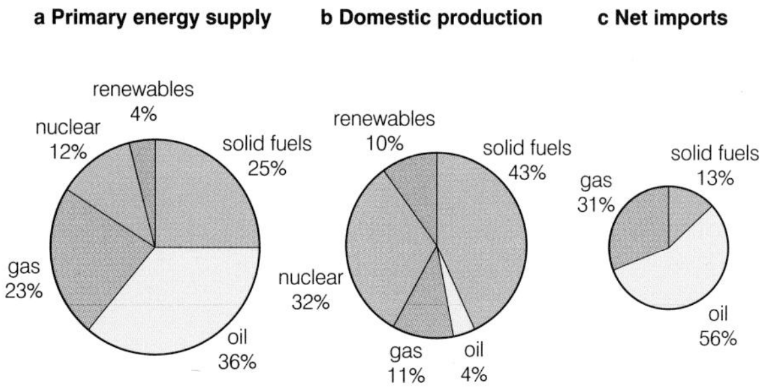

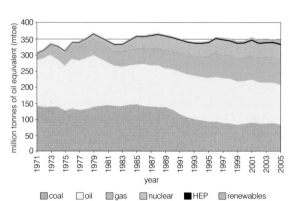

Fig. 7.4 *Germany's energy, 2004*

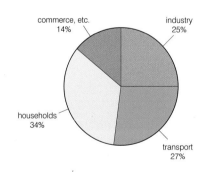

Fig. 7.5 *Changes in Germany's energy mix, 1971–2005*

Fig. 7.6 *Germany's energy consumption by sector, 2004*

Table 7.3 *Energy mix for France, 2004*

Million tonnes of oil equivalent	Primary energy supply	Domestic production	Net imports
Solid fuels	14.1	0.5	13.3
Oil	92.8	1.7	94.1
Gas	39.2	1.1	37.8
Nuclear	115.6	115.6	
Electricity			−5.3
Renewables	17.3	17.4	−0.1
Other	−5.3		
Total	**273.7**	**136.4**	**139.8**

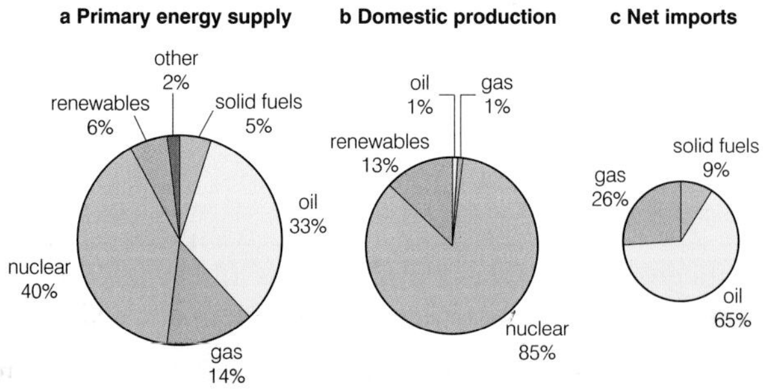

Fig. 7.7 *France's energy, 2004*

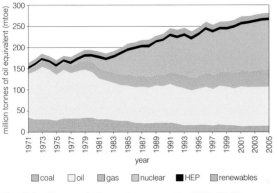

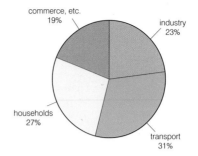

Fig. 7.8 *Changes in France's energy mix, 1971–2005*

Fig. 7.9 *France's energy consumption by sector, 2004*

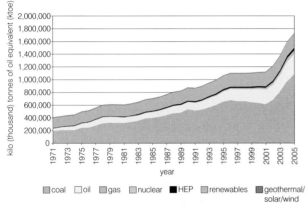

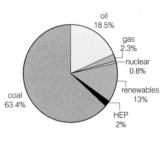

Total: 1,717,153 ktoe

Fig. 7.10 *Changes in China's energy mix, 1971–2005*

Fig. 7.11 *China's share of total primary energy, 2005*

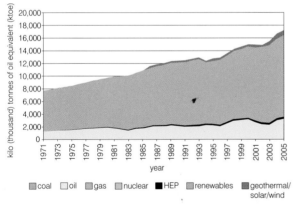

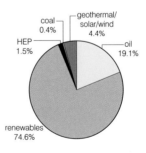

Total: 17,246 ktoe

Fig. 7.12 *Changes in Kenya's energy mix, 1971–2005*

Fig. 7.13 *Kenya's share of total primary energy supply, 2005*

Activity

2　**a**　Compare the changing energy mix in China and Kenya with the changing mix in the UK or with any other EU country.

　　b　Suggest reasons for the differences that you observe.

　　c　Suggest what the consequences of these differences might be.

　　d　Suggest how the energy mix in each country might change over the next 20 years or so.

World energy trade

Activity

3 Compare Figures 7.15 and 7.16.

a Which areas are the largest producers?

b Which areas show increasing production and which are declining?

c If these trends continue, what may be the future of the world trade in oil?

AQA Examiner's tip

When there is so much data in a source, it is useful to cut out the data that is not relevant to your purpose. You are unlikely to remember more than a small amount of what a complex data source shows and you will not have time in your exam to write about all the data. Concentrate on the big picture.

Trade in oil

Figure 7.14 shows the distribution of proved oil reserves in the world. Notice the predominance of the Middle East. It has much more oil in its reserves than the rest of the world combined. Less obvious is the importance of Russia and the southern parts of the former Soviet Union around the Caspian Sea, such as Azerbaijan. These countries make up most of the reserves shown in Europe and Eurasia.

Figure 7.15 shows the present levels of production in the different regions and how this pattern has evolved over the last 25 years.

Figure 7.16 shows the consumption of oil in each major region and the changes during the last 25 years. It is drawn to the same scale as Figure 7.15 and very clearly illustrates the imbalance in supply and demand.

Figure 7.17 shows the major movements of oil around the world in 2006 from several major producing regions to other regions. It does not show internal movements within countries (so it does not show movements from Alaska to mainland USA, for instance). This is a very complex map, so select a small part and study that, then move on to a new part and study that. You will gradually build up a picture.

Note that on Figure 7.17, and only on this map in this series, North America has been divided into three – USA, Mexico and Canada – and the USA is an importer from each of the other two. In Europe the North Sea area has been separated from Russia and its neighbours. Japan, China and Australia are all big importers and all are included in the Asia-Pacific region. That is why some oil is shown as flowing from south Asia to China, Japan and Australia. A lot of oil is shown as flowing into the region as a whole but the amounts going to the big consumers are not separated out.

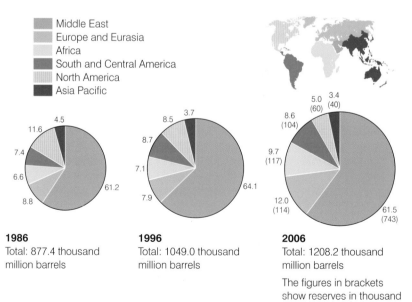

Legend:
- Middle East
- Europe and Eurasia
- Africa
- South and Central America
- North America
- Asia Pacific

1986
Total: 877.4 thousand million barrels

1996
Total: 1049.0 thousand million barrels

2006
Total: 1208.2 thousand million barrels

The figures in brackets show reserves in thousand million barrels

Fig. 7.14 *Distribution of oil reserves, 1986, 1996 and 2006*

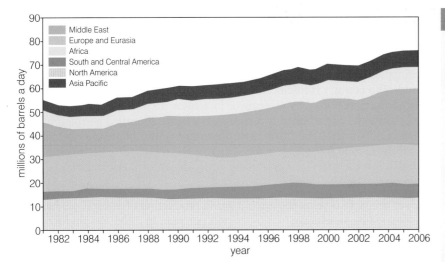

Fig. 7.15 *World oil production*

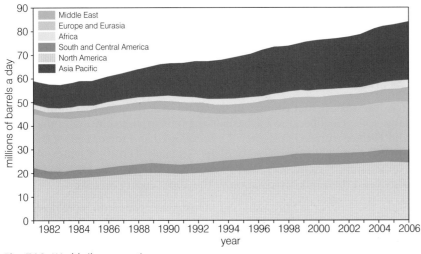

Fig. 7.16 *World oil consumption*

Activities

4 Compare Figures 7.15 and 7.16.

   a Briefly describe the changing patterns of consumption in each major region.

   b Summarise the trend in world consumption.

   c How well does consumption match production?

   d What conclusions can you draw about the world trade in oil at present? Check your conclusion against Figure 7.17.

5 Study Figure 7.17.

   a List the biggest flows (say over 50 million tonnes) giving source, destination and quantity.

   b Comment on the pattern revealed by your list.

   c List all the flows into the USA in order of size.

   d Comment on the pattern revealed by the list. In particular, refer to the economic and geopolitical consequences of this pattern.

Link

If you need to check any of the numbers or find out about the precise destinations of the flows in Figure 7.17, check the 2006 BP Statistical Review of World Energy at:

www.bp.com.

Type 'Statistical review' into the website's search engine (page 20 has details of the flows).

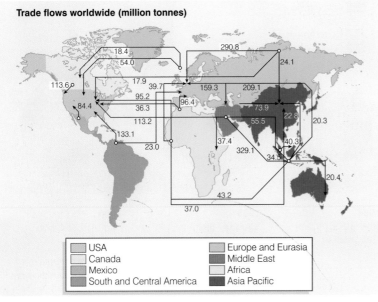
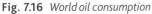

Fig. 7.17 *Major oil trade movements, 2006*

■ Link

The Oil Depletion Analysis Centre has very useful information about the future of oil:

www.odac-info.org.

■ Trade in gas

When oil was first discovered, the gas that was found in the same fields was thought to be worthless. It was too difficult and expensive to transport safely and so it was just flared, or burnt off. However, by the mid-20th century it had been developed as an economic fuel. It could either be transported by pipeline or by tanker. To move it by tanker the gas had to be cooled until it turned into a liquid (liquified petroleum gas or LPG). Now it is the third most important source of energy worldwide and the second most important source of electricity generation, after coal. It also has the benefit of producing far fewer atmospheric pollutants than either coal or oil.

Over the last 10 years the annual world production of natural gas has increased by an average of 2.5 per cent per year. In 2005–06 production increased by 3 per cent. Increasing production in the USA and Russia is the most important trend, although the biggest reserves and the biggest new discoveries are in the Middle East.

Figure 7.19 is similar in some ways to Figure 7.17 but the trade in gas is on a smaller scale than the trade in oil. Note that no single area dominates gas exports like the Middle East dominates oil exports, and no single area dominates gas imports like the USA dominates oil imports.

■ Trade in coal

The UK was the first country in the world to develop its coal mining on a large scale. Coal became the basis of the industrial revolution in the 18th and 19th centuries. Later the UK was followed as a major user of coal by other European countries, particularly Germany, France, Belgium, the Netherlands, Luxembourg, and then eastern Europe. The USA and Japan also based their industrialisation in the 20th century on coal.

Since the 1950s the European coal industry has gone into rapid decline. Deep mining of coal has almost completely ended in the UK, France and

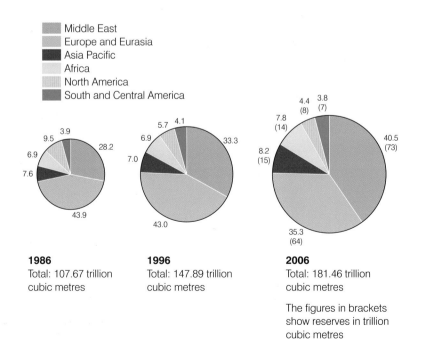

Fig. 7.18 *Proved reserves of natural gas, 1986, 1996 and 2006*

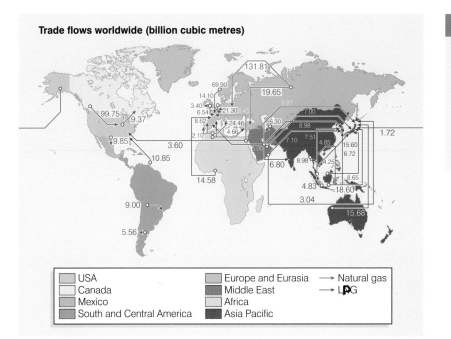

Fig. 7.19 *Major natural gas trade movements*

Activity

6 Study Figure 7.19.

a List the biggest flows (say over 15 billion m³) giving source, destination and quantity.

b Comment on the pattern revealed by your list.

Belgium, and is much reduced in Germany. However, eastern Europe still mines significant quantities.

The main reasons for the decline of coal mining in the UK were:

- all the easily accessible coal had been mined
- remaining deposits are too deep and faulted to mine economically at present
- most deep coal contains a high proportion of impurities, particularly sulphur, which cause acid rain
- labour costs were much higher than in countries like South Africa
- mechanisation was more difficult with the deep and faulted coal seams
- government policy, arguably politically motivated, was to wind down the coal mining industry in the 1980s and 1990s.

Did you know?

According to the World Coal Institute, coal reserves are available in almost every country worldwide, with recoverable reserves in around 70 countries. At current production levels, proven coal reserves are estimated to last 147 years.

In contrast, proven oil and gas reserves are equivalent to around 41 and 63 years, at current production levels respectively. Over 68 per cent of oil and 67 per cent of gas reserves are concentrated in the Middle East and Russia.

Total world primary energy consumtion (% by fuel, 2005)

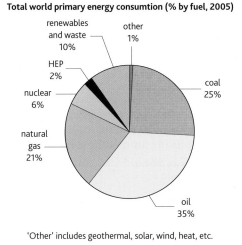

'Other' includes geothermal, solar, wind, heat, etc.

Total world electricity generation (% by fuel, 2005)

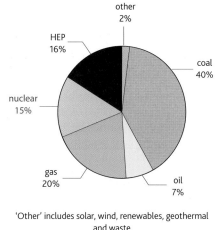

'Other' includes solar, wind, renewables, geothermal and waste

Fig. 7.20 *World energy consumption and electricity generation*

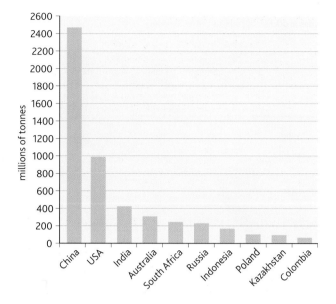

Fig. 7.21 *The world's top 10 coal producers, 2006*

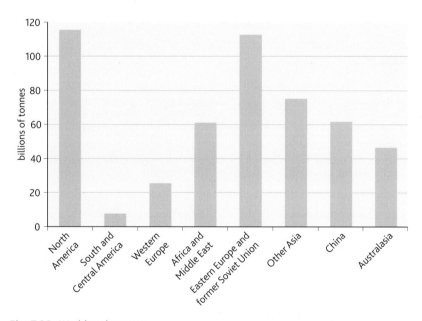

Fig. 7.22 *World coal reserves*

However, despite the run-down of coal mining in western Europe, coal is and will remain important as a world source of energy.

Almost 5000 million tonnes of coal were mined worldwide in 2006 – a 78 per cent increase over 25 years. This is predicted to increase to 7000 million tonnes by 2030, with China accounting for half the increase. Most of the coal produced is used close to where it was mined. Only 16 per cent of coal production enters into world trade (see Figures 7.21 and 7.22).

Coal and electricity

Coal is the major fuel used for generating electricity worldwide. Table 7.4 shows some countries that are heavily dependent on it.

Table. 7.4 *Dependence on coal for electricity*

Poland	93%	Israel	71%	Czech Rep.	59%
South Africa	93%	Kazakhstan	70%	Greece	58%
Australia	80%	India	69%	USA	50%
China	78%	Morocco	69%	Germany	47%

Coal and steel

Approximately 13 per cent of total hard coal production is currently used by the steel industry and almost 70 per cent of total global steel production is dependent on coal.

Table 7.5 *Top coal exporters (left) and importers (right), million tonnes, 2006*

Country	Total	Steam	Coking	Country	Total	Steam	Coking
Australia	231	111	121	Japan	178	105	73
Indonesia	129	104	25	South Korea	80	60	20
Russia	92	82	10	Taiwan	64	58	6
South Africa	69	68	1	UK	51	44	7
China	63	59	4	Germany	41	33	9
Colombia	60	60	–	India	41	22	19
USA	45	20	25	China	38	29	9

What is striking when studying these figures for coal exports and imports is the change in the countries listed since the early and middle years of the 20th century. The UK and Germany were among the world's main exporters in the early 20th century; then they were overtaken by the USA as the main exporter in the middle of the century. The main importers in the early 20th century were other industrialised countries in Europe.

Now, however, the southern hemisphere countries dominate world exports and, except for Germany and the UK, the top importers are mostly in Asia. Four of the top seven importers are newly industrialised countries (NICs). These changes are indicative of the massive changes that took place in the pattern of world industry, especially the world's heavy industry, in the late 20th and early 21st centuries.

The geopolitics of energy

In 1989 the American commentator, Francis Fukuyama, wrote an essay called 'The End of History?'. In it he argued that the end of the Cold War and the collapse of **communism** in eastern Europe signalled the end of the progression of human history:

> What we may be witnessing is not just the end of the Cold War, or the passing of a particular period of post-war history, but the end of history as such: that is, the end point of mankind's ideological evolution and the universalization of Western liberal democracy as the final form of human government.

From 'The End of History?', 1989

Activity

7 Study all the resources in this section on coal.

a Coal is and will remain important as a world source of energy. Suggest why this statement is true.

b How might this continued importance affect the environment?

Key terms

Communism: a system of government in which the state plans and controls the economy and owns the means of production. The goods and services produced are then divided between the people in the way that the state considers best for everyone.

Democracy: a political system in which the people have the power to elect their government by the vote of a majority. They also have the power to vote to change the government.

Ideology: a set of beliefs that form the basis of a political, economic or other system.

Since then the world has seen two major wars in Iraq; the growth of Islamic fundamentalism and the clash between its supporters and the Western liberal **democracies**; major diplomatic crises over developments of the nuclear industries in North Korea and in Iran; the reassertion of Russian nationalism and Russia's growing economic power; the emergence of communist China as a world power; and so on. This hardly seems like the domination of the world by a single form of government. It does seem that the old confrontation between two superpowers has been replaced by a complex geopolitical situation with several changing **ideologies** struggling for power.

Throughout the world, one of the main driving forces of this struggle for power is competition for energy supplies. Here are two examples:

Steep decline in oil production brings risk of war and unrest, says new study

Output peaked in 2006 and will fall by several per cent a year.

Decline in gas, coal and uranium also predicted.

World oil production has already peaked and will fall by half as soon as 2030, according to a report which also warns that extreme shortage of fossil fuels will lead to wars and social breakdown.

www.guardian.co.uk, 22 October 2007

Canada flexes its muscles in scramble for the Arctic

Eight countries lay claim to oil-rich, unspoilt region.

Global warming opens up fabled North-west Passage.

www.guardian.co.uk, 11 July 2007

■ Case study

Russian oil and gas exports

Through large parts of the 20th century the world's geopolitical system was dominated by two superpowers, the USA and the USSR. They were fairly well matched in terms of area, population size, resource base, level of industrialisation, military might, alliances with other countries and nuclear armaments. Their political systems were very different, though, with the USA's free-market, capitalist democracy being opposed in many ways to the USSR's centrally planned, state capitalist, communist system.

Then, in the late 1980s and early 1990s, the communist system in Russia and eastern Europe collapsed. This is what Francis Fukuyama saw as marking the 'end of history'. Following this collapse, Russia went through a period of political and economic turmoil. Many former state-owned enterprises, including the oil and gas industries, were privatised (and some of the profits found their way into football clubs in the UK). Foreign transnational companies (TNCs) were also allowed to enter the country to search for and exploit gas and oil fields.

When Putin became president in 2000 he quickly brought in powers to bring oil and gas back into state control and to curb the TNCs.

By 2007 Russia's economy had become heavily dependent on oil and natural gas exports, making it vulnerable to fluctuations in world oil prices. According to an International Monetary Fund (IMF) study, a

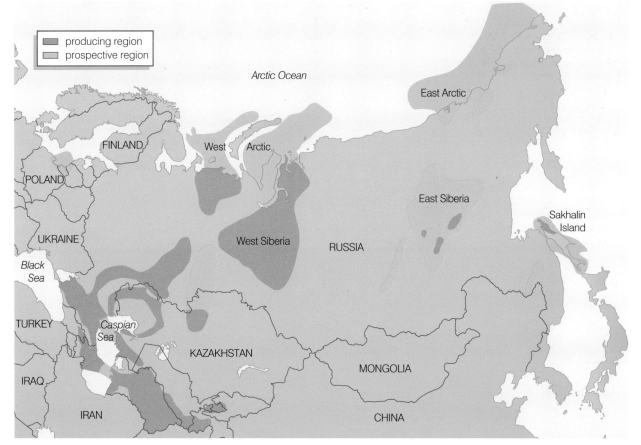

Fig. 7.23 *Oil and gas production: existing and prospective regions*

$1 (about 51p) per barrel increase in oil prices for a year is estimated to raise federal budget revenues by 0.35 per cent of gross domestic product (GDP), or $3.4 billion (about £1.74 billion). A large part of the profits was put into a stabilisation fund in 2004 to help the country plan for the future. By the end of 2006, the fund was worth almost $80 billion (about £41 billion), or about 7 per cent of the country's GDP. Raw materials such as oil, natural gas and metals dominate merchandise exports and account for over two-thirds of all Russian export revenues.

Although estimates vary widely, the IMF and the World Bank suggest that in 2005 the oil and gas sector represented around 20 per cent of the country's GDP, generated more than 60 per cent of its export revenues (64 per cent in 2007), and accounted for 30 per cent of all foreign direct investment (FDI) in Russia.

The govenment continues to advance the state's influence in the energy sector. Taxes on oil exports and extraction are still high, and Russia's state-influenced oil and gas companies are obtaining controlling stakes in previously foreign-led projects. State-owned export facilities have grown at breakneck pace, while private projects have progressed more slowly or have met with obstructions by state-owned companies or by various government agencies. For instance, Shell had been investing in the development of the Sakhalin oil and gas fields but was accused of causing environmental damage. Then political pressure was put on the company, which was more or less forced to reduce its holdings in the new developments so that state-controlled firms could take them over.

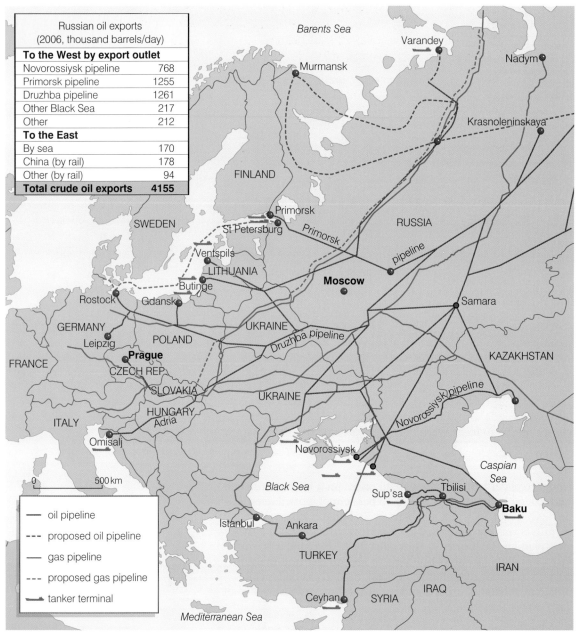

Russian oil exports (2006, thousand barrels/day)	
To the West by export outlet	
Novorossiysk pipeline	768
Primorsk pipeline	1255
Druzhba pipeline	1261
Other Black Sea	217
Other	212
To the East	
By sea	170
China (by rail)	178
Other (by rail)	94
Total crude oil exports	**4155**

Legend:
— oil pipeline
--- proposed oil pipeline
— gas pipeline
--- proposed gas pipeline
⇀ tanker terminal

Fig. 7.24 *Oil and gas pipelines to Europe*

Questions

1 Kazakhstan and its neighbours in central Asia were very keen to build pipelines through Azerbaijan and Georgia to the south of Russia. The countries of western Europe supported them in this project. Explain why these could be strategically important.

Ukraine/Russia gas dispute threatened Europe's central heating

Ukraine was part of the USSR until it gained independence in 1991. However, the country remained economically and politically closely linked to Russia until 2005. Then a new government with western sympathies was elected. Soon after this a major dispute about gas prices emerged.

Whilst the two countries had been allied, Ukraine received gas from Russia at prices well below the world market price. Once there was a threat to the previously close relationship Gazprom, the Russian state gas supply company, threatened to raise prices and, on 1 January 2006, Gazprom shut off gas supplies to Ukraine. As a result supplies to Europe were also affected. Even though Russia has used the threat of a cutoff to demand higher natural gas prices in recent years, this was the first time that a supply disruption affected flows to Europe. After negotiations with Ukraine, Gazprom agreed to a sell its natural gas to the Ukraine at the market price.

It is now clear that the developments in oil and gas, and particularly their growth in exports, have helped Russia to re-establish some of its power and influence on the world stage. This is illustrated in Figures 7.24 and the newspaper article on page 244.

Trade, between countries or between people, works best when both partners gain in approximately equal measures and neither side becomes too dependent on the trade. In the case of Russia's oil and gas exports, the balance of benefits varies from country to country.

It is clear that Russia gains a huge part of its GDP from the trade and also gained a great deal of TNC capital and expertise at a time when the economy was changing rapidly.

Countries in the West gain vital energy supplies. The UK is now starting to import gas from Russia as North Sea supplies run low. The Russian trade has also allowed the West to reduce its dependence on Middle East suppliers.

However, the purely economic relationship can become complicated by the geopolitical situation, as was shown by the Ukraine gas crisis. No country wants to become too dependent on a trade partner that could use the trade to exert political influence. This could happen in the UK if Russia tries to regain some of its old superpower status.

Questions

2 **a** List the different outlets for Russian oil and gas that lead towards western Europe.

b Suggest where production from the eastern Siberian and Sakhalin fields might be exported to.

c Which of these export routes are most likely to be disrupted by:

■ severe weather conditions

■ political unrest?

Transnational corporations and the oil trade

There are huge profits to be made from the oil industry. However, large investments of capital are also needed by the industry for:

■ exploration
■ drilling
■ extraction
■ transport
■ storage
■ refining
■ distribution and sales
■ training and workforce development.

Only very large corporations can afford the long-term investment that is needed in the main parts of the industry. However, the wealth and expertise that the corporations have developed gives them great economic and political power.

Table 7.6 on page 246 shows the world's top economic entities in 2006. Fifty-one of the top 100 are corporations and eight of them are oil or gas TNCs. One characteristic of all these oil corporations is their level of integration of the different aspects of the oil business, from exploration through to forecourt sales. Many also have interests in the chemical industries that use refinery products. Fortunately, the companies are all keen to build up good public relations with customers, shareholders and the general public, so they provide very detailed websites. The two corporations with the strongest British links are BP and Shell.

Table 7.6 *The world's top economic entities*

Rank	Country*/corporation	GDP revenue ($ millions)
1	USA*	11,667,515
2	Japan*	4,623,398
3	Germany*	2,714,418
4	UK*	2,140,898
5	France*	2,002,582
21	Austria*	290,109
22	Wal-Mart Stores	287,989
23	BP	285,059
24	Exxon Mobil	270,772
25	Royal Dutch/Shell Group	268,690
26	Indonesia*	257,641
27	Saudi Arabia*	250,557
33	General Motors	193,517
42	Iran*	162,709
43	General Electric	152,866
44	Total	152,610
45	Argentina*	151,501
46	Chevron	147,967
47	ConocoPhillips	121,663
50	Malaysia*	117,776
79	Sinopec	75,077
98	China National Petroleum	67,724

Link

Look at the site map on the Shell website:

www.shell.com.

Go to 'About BP' and 'What we do' on the BP website:

www.bp.com.

Activity

10

a Use the internet to explore one of the major oil TNCs.

b Use the information that you find to create a flow diagram showing different stages in the company's operations.

c Add details of countries where the company is exploring and producing.

d Find out the nature of the company's involvement in the transport of oil by tanker and/or pipeline.

e Locate some of the major refineries.

f Add details about marketing of petrol and about involvement in the chemical industry.

g Use the company websites to see how and why the company is involved in the development of alternative energy resources.

h Research some of the issues associated with the company. For example, you might look at the way Shell has had issues with the environment in its Sakhalin oil developments, or BP has had environmental issues in Alaska. Both companies have issues with minority rights and the environment in Nigeria.

The environmental impact of energy production

In this section you will learn:

- about acid rain, fuelwood use and nuclear power

- how they are being managed at present

- how they might be better managed in future.

AQA Examiner's tip

Global warming and the greenhouse effect are probably the greatest problems linked to the use of energy. They will be dealt with in detail in the A2 book. You will not be tested on this topic at AS Level.

Link

See pages 88–9 for more on acid rain.

You should now have looked at some of the issues in oil production by one of the major TNCs. You might have looked at the TNCs' impact on the environment. However, all energy production has some impact on the environment and it is essential that you:

- understand how the impact occurs
- consider what can be done (including what you can do) to minimise the harmful impacts
- consider how the benefits and drawbacks of each form of energy production can be balanced out so that decisions about energy are based on rational grounds.

Acid rain

In the 1980s **acid rain** was seen as a major crisis confronting Europe and eastern North America and causing loss of forests, deterioration of fish stocks in rivers and lakes and damage to buildings and health. The problem was made worse because the areas that suffered most were usually not the main sources of the problem. Much of the acid pollution that originated in the UK ended up damaging Scandinavia and western Germany. However, concerted international action seems to have brought the problem under much better control, at least in western Europe and the eastern parts of the USA and Canada.

What is acid rain?

Sulphur dioxide (SO_2) and nitrogen oxides (NO_x) are the primary causes of acid rain. In the USA, about two-thirds of all sulphur dioxide and one-quarter of all nitrogen oxides come from electric power generation that relies on burning fossil fuels like coal. Coal accounts for most US sulphur dioxide emissions and a large portion of nitrogen oxide emissions. Sulphur is present in coal as an impurity, and it reacts with air when the coal is burned to form sulphur dioxide. In contrast, nitrogen oxide is formed when any fossil fuel is burned.

Acid rain occurs when these gases react in the atmosphere with water, oxygen and other chemicals to form various acidic compounds. Sunlight increases the rate of most of these reactions. The result is a mild solution of sulphuric acid and nitric acid. Prevailing winds can blow the compounds that cause acid deposition for hundreds of kilometres.

Effects of acid rain

Acid rain causes acidification of lakes and streams and can damage or kill trees. In addition, acid rain accelerates the decay of building materials and paints. Before reaching the earth, gaseous sulphur dioxide and nitrogen oxide can reduce visibility and harm people's health, particularly by causing breathing problems. Figure 7.25 shows how prevailing westerly and south-westerly winds carry the worst pollution from its main source regions towards the Baltic states.

Fig. 7.25 *Acid rain in western and central Europe*

Managing acid rain

There are several options for reducing sulphur dioxide emissions:

- using coal containing less sulphur
- washing the coal before it is burned
- using devices called scrubbers to chemically remove the sulphur dioxide from the gases leaving the power station
- burning other fuels in power stations, such as natural gas
- using other sources of electricity besides fossil fuels.

Catalytic converters, which are similar to scrubbers in power plants, reduce nitrogen oxide emissions from cars. There are also alternative energies available to power cars, including natural gas and batteries that store electricity.

Things can be done to restore the quality of lakes and streams more quickly. In particular, lime (a basic compound) can be added to acidic lakes to neutralise the acidity. This process, called liming, has been used extensively in Norway and Sweden. Liming is expensive and is considered a short-term remedy in only specific areas. It does not solve the broader problems of soil chemistry, forest health and human health. However, it often helps fish to remain in a lake.

Far more important than reducing the effects was dealing with the causes. The most important legislation aimed at curbing atmospheric pollution in Europe was the 1988 EU Large Combustion Plants Directive. This stated that total emissions of sulphur dioxide across Europe had to be reduced by 58 per cent by 2003, and nitrogen oxide and particulate emissions reduced by 40 per cent by 1998. Since the signing of these agreements there has been a substantial reduction in sulphur dioxide

Link

This site has an animation that explains the causes and effects of acid rain very clearly:

www.epa.gov/acidrain/education/ site_students/acid_anim.html.

emissions in western Europe. This is reflected in the measurements of sulphur concentrations in the air and rainfall in southern Norway recorded by the Norwegian Institute of Air Research (NILU). Between 1980 and 1996, the reduction in sulphur emissions in Norway was as much as 75 per cent, a trend reflected in the gradual improvement of water quality in lakes in southern Norway. Emissions of nitrogen oxides in Europe continued to increase until the mid-1980s. Since then, however, emissions have been reduced by around 20 per cent.

The UK and Germany used to be the main sources of acid rain but Figure 7.24 shows that there are now few major sources in western Europe. Now, the main problem region in Europe is found in the east, particularly in Poland and Ukraine, as their many power stations burn coal with a high sulphur content.

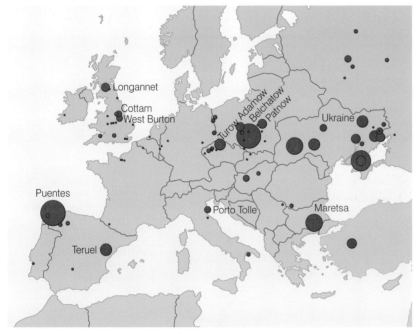

Fig. 7.26 *Major sources of acid rain pollution in Europe*

Fuelwood

Burkina Faso, like other countries of the Sahel, is confronted by a fuelwood crisis. Over 90 per cent of the energy used for cooking there comes from wood. The consumption of wood is greater than the rate of new growth, so there is no ecological sustainability. At the same time, alternative fuels are so expensive that there is no economic sustainability. For a family to cook with containers of liquid costs 72 francs a year, which is more than the average income of 45 per cent of the population.

One writer studying the area wrote: 'Will we – in a not too distant future – have to organise a system of energy aid just as we did with regard to food aid? Will there be an energy famine in the Sahelian countries?'

This fuelwood crisis began to emerge during the oil crisis of the 1970s and has been aggravated by agricultural policies that aim at making African countries self-sufficient in food production. Self-sufficiency has been achieved at the expense of existing forest lands, which are the main sources for fuelwood. National programmes tend to overlook this relationship between food and forest, so the focus has been on producing

Did you know?

Deforestation is affecting many rural people, who have been accused of being the cause of deforestation. More often these people produce fuelwood from their own food farms, secondary forests or fallow lands and supplement it by burning waste such as corn husks. Deforestation is caused by the need to obtain fuelwood for the curing of tobacco and tea, by excessive felling of timber for export, by agricultural production, by bushfires and most significantly by demand for wood as a fuel from urban households.

more food at the expense of forest. This means that wood energy is not being exploited in a manner that is sustainable in African countries, but a more acceptable means for safe and sustainable energy production is yet to be found.

Table 7.7 and Figure 7.27 show the dependency on biomass as a source of energy in Africa as a whole, and in sub-Saharan Africa in particular.

Table 7.7 *Energy consumption in Africa*

Fuel	World	Africa	Africa as a percentage of world
	Million tonnes of oil equivalent (mtoe)	Million tonnes of oil equivalent (mtoe)	
Oil	1610	25	1.6
Gas	2740	85	3.1
Coal	3180	86	2.7
HEP	630	14	2.2
Biomass	600	140	23.4
Total	8760	350	4.0

Fuel	North Africa	Sub-Sahara Africa (excl. South Africa)	South Africa
	Million tonnes of oil equivalent (mtoe)	Million tonnes of oil equivalent (mtoe)	Million tonnes of oil equivalent (mtoe)
Non-biomass	80	47	83
Biomass	10	126	4
Total	90	173	87
Percentage of total	26	49	25

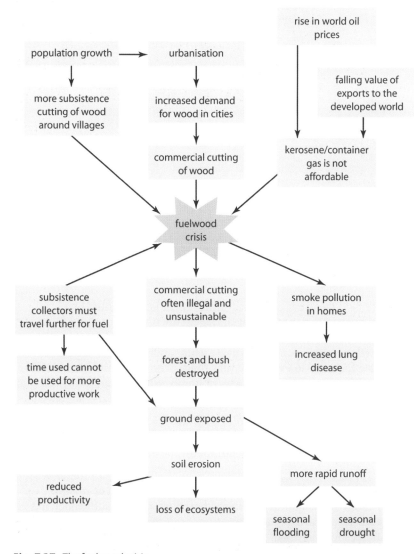

Fig. 7.27 *The fuelwood crisis*

One solution to the fuelwood crisis has been the use of solar cookers across sub-Saharan Africa. **Solar cooking** is an excellent example of a sustainable solution to an ecological and economic problem.

Solar Cookers International has compiled a list of countries with the highest potential for solar cooking (see Table 7.8). Criteria for this ranking include annual average sunlight, cooking fuel scarcity and population size. Of the estimated 500 million people who have abundant sunshine and suffer from fuel scarcity, 85 per cent of them live in just 10 countries. Many of these countries are also suffering the fuelwood crisis.

Fig. 7.28 *Solar cooking in Uganda*

Nuclear power

The UK relies on atomic energy for 20 per cent of its electricity but current estimates suggest that, apart from Sizewell B, all existing power stations will be closed by 2023. No reactors have been built since the 1980s. The Chernobyl accident, rapidly rising **decommissioning** costs and the problems of storing or disposing of nuclear waste, combined to put expansion plans on hold. However, the current energy crisis, rising costs of fossil fuels and concerns about global warming mean that nuclear power has to be considered seriously again.

Arguments in favour of nuclear power development

According to estimates, fossil fuels will be used up within 50 years. There are large reserves of uranium, and the breeder reactors that the industry hopes might be developed will be far more fuel-efficient than the present generation of reactors. Unfortunately, this doesn't mean we can have an endless supply of fuel. Breeder reactors need a feedstock of uranium and thorium, so when we run out of these two fuels (in about 1000 years), breeder reactors will cease to be useful. However, this is still a more long-term solution to the power supply problem than the current burning of coal, gas and oil.

Because nuclear power plants need little fuel, they are less vulnerable to shortages because of strikes, natural disasters or international tensions.

Link

Solar Cooking International, a charity based in California, has a superb website at:

http://solarcookers.org.

Here is an excellent slide show that explains how one type of cooker is made in Darfur refugee camps:

www.csmonitor.com/slideshows/2007/chadsolar.

Lots of solar resources, from good to eccentric, are listed at:

www.solarcooking.org.

Click on the link 'Audios and Videos'.

BBC News has produced a well-balanced, guide to nuclear power. It can be found at:

http://news.bbc.co.uk.

Type 'Guide to UK nuclear power' into the search box.

Table 7.8 *Countries with the highest potential for solar cookers*

1	India
2	China
3	Pakistan
4	Ethiopia
5	Nigeria
6	Uganda
7	Sudan
8	Afghanistan
9	Tanzania
10	South Africa

Note that many of the countries of sub-Saharan Africa have populations that are too small for inclusion on this list, even though they have long sunshine hours and suffer from fuel scarcity.

Key terms

Solar cooking: uses the rays of the sun, often concentrated by reflection off aluminium foil, to heat a box in which food is kept. The heat makes the box act as a slow cooker for the food.

Decommissioning: closing down a nuclear reactor and disposing of the contaminated material safely.

Uranium is comparatively evenly deposited around the globe, so no country or small group of countries can dominate the market as can happen with oil and gas. On the other hand, nuclear power plants could be vulnerable to terrorist attack if excellent security is not in place.

Perhaps the strongest point in favour of nuclear power in the minds of many people is the low output of greenhouse gases produced. They still produce carbon dioxide, particularly during the construction period, but this form of pollution is much less than with the burning of fossil fuels. However, it is still more than from most forms of renewable energy. Nuclear power produces almost no sulphur, and sulphur is an important cause of acid rain.

Arguments against nuclear power development

Many people think that nuclear power stations are dangerous because of damaging radiation. The worst case of a nuclear disaster was in 1986 at the Chernobyl facility in Ukraine. A fire ripped apart the casing of the core, releasing radioactive isotopes into the atmosphere. Thirty-one people died as an immediate result. An estimated 15,000 more died in the surrounding area after exposure to the radiation. However, that accident was caused in part because of poor maintenance and human errors that should have been avoided. Most nuclear power stations built before Chernobyl, and all built since then, have far better management and safety systems to avoid such a catastrophe.

A stronger argument against nuclear power is that a satisfactory, long-term solution to the problem of dealing with nuclear waste has not yet been developed. The by-products of the process remain radioactive for thousands of years, requiring safe disposal away from society until they lose their significant radiation values. Some of the world's nuclear waste has been buried but much is in temporary storage. Transportation of the waste is risky, as many unknown variables may affect the containment vessels. If one of these vessels were compromised, the results could be deadly.

Managing waste disposal

The government set up the independent Committee on Radioactive Waste Management (CoRWM) to look at nuclear waste disposal in the UK. It reported in 2006 and here is an extract:

> CoRWM is recommending geological disposal as the end point in the long-term management of radioactive waste.
>
> Geological disposal in an underground repository is the waste management option that is currently favoured by many countries for spent fuel, including Belgium, France, Finland, Germany, Japan, Sweden, Switzerland and the United States. No country is yet operating a geological repository for these materials but some have identified sites.
>
> Geological disposal is based on the concept of the retention of the waste within a geological repository behind a buffer of crushed rock, clay and grout.
>
> Excavation would typically be to a depth of 200–1000 metres in a variety of rock types including crystalline rocks, clays and salt. The British Geological Survey estimates that approximately 30 per cent of the land surface may lie above suitable rock formations.

■ Link

The full CoRWM report can be seen at:

www.corwm.org.uk/content-1092.

However, it is likely that underground investigations will not begin for at least 15–20 years and a decision on the detailed repository design will not be needed until then.

The delay will allow time for further research, discussion and agreement with potential host communities.

[Meanwhile] the Government will need to take account of the issues raised by requirement for interim storage:

i   The design and engineering of new stores to take account of the security of their contents and protection against attack.

ii The design lifetime of new stores should cover a period of at least 100 years.

www.corwm.org.uk

Link

In 2005 *New Scientist* published a list of 10 possible nuclear waste disposal sites in the UK. Go to:

www.newscientist.com.

Type 'Secret nuclear waste disposal sites revealed' into the search box.

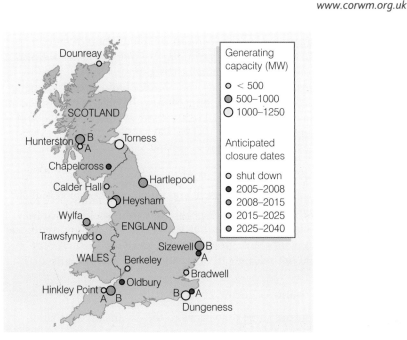

Fig. 7.29 *Nuclear power stations in the UK*

Activities

11 a Study Figure 7.29. Describe the location of the present-day UK nuclear power stations.

   b Suggest how their locations were planned.

   c Estimate when new generating capacity will need to be built to replace the nuclear power stations as they close.

12 There has been little public discussion of possible sites for any new nuclear stations that are built. If new building does go ahead:

   a Try to find out where it is planned to build the new stations.

   b Make your own suggestions for future sites, and justify your suggestions.

13 a What criteria, apart from stable geology, should be used to choose nuclear waste disposal sites?

   b Suggest one or more possible sites for the long-term disposal of nuclear waste. Justify your suggestions.

The potential for sustainable energy supply and consumption

i Renewable, flow resources include:

▨ biomass energy

▨ solar power

▨ wind power

▨ tidal power

▨ wave power.

Biomass fuels

For many years Brazil has led the world in the production of fuel for cars and lorries using biomass. In particular, it produced ethanol from sugar. In the last 15 years or so, many other countries have started to show a keen interest in ethanol and other similar biofuels and, perhaps unsurprisingly, it is the USA and China, two of the biggers consumers of petroleum, that have led the way. Here are some of the reasons behind this rush to biofuels:

▨ The price of oil is rising.

▨ There is an impending shortage of oil.

▨ A wide variety of crops can be used, and much crop and food industry waste can also be converted.

▨ Biofuels only release carbon that has been collected by photosynthesis as the producer plants have grown. Unlike fossil fuels, when they burn biofuels do not release carbon accumulated over millions of years.

▨ Biofuels allow countries greater energy security.

Unfortunately, there are some drawbacks to the expansion of ethanol production:

▨ Land is being lost from food production as it is turned to production of crops like corn (maize) and oilseed rape, which are grown in increasing quantities. This could lead to increased food prices or even food shortages. In this case it is likely to be poor people and poor countries that suffer first.

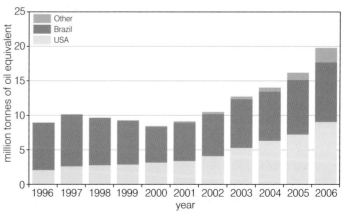

Fig. 7.30 *World ethanol production, 1996–2006*

- Production can lead to monocultures and loss of traditional countryside.
- Production on the necessary scale will almost certainly demand big inputs of fertiliser and pesticides which, at present, are mainly produced from oil-based chemicals.

Solar power

Read this extract from the website of a company that fits solar power systems:

> Solar photovoltaic (PV) cells convert light into electrical energy. The amount of electrical energy produced depends on the amount of light that falls on the PV material. PV requires only daylight, not direct sunlight, to generate electricity although the output from a PV cell will vary with the intensity of the light.
>
> PV cells come in all shapes and sizes and can be connected to the national grid or simply to a battery bank. In any event, they will significantly reduce the running costs of any building in which they are fitted.
>
> PV cells generally come in the form of rectangular panels of variable sizes, or in the form of individual solar slates, which are installed on the roof in very much the same way as roof tiles.

www.solarpaces.org

Fig. 7.31 *A photovoltaic barrier near Chur, Switzerland*

Link

Further details of solar power systems can be found at:

www.solarpaces.org.

Details of a photovoltaic barrier at Munich airport can be found at:

www.isofoton.com/corporate.

Search under 'Isofoton around the world'.

Did you know?

PVPS is the Photovoltaic Power Systems Programme of the International Energy Agency (IEA).

Installed PV capacity base is concentrated in a relatively small number of countries. Between them, Japan, Germany and the USA accounted for 90 per cent of installed capacity in PVPS member countries at the end of 2005.

The growth in German-installed capacity has been especially dramatic, rising by an average of more than 55 per cent annually over the past decade. Spain's installed capacity is set to rise rapidly by 2010.

Concentrating solar power

Solar concentrating power systems use concentrated solar radiation as a high-temperature energy source to produce electrical power and drive chemical reactions. These clean energy technologies are appropriate for areas in the tropics and subtropics with long hours of sunshine where direct solar radiation is high. The first commercial plants have been in operation in California since the mid-1980s. Some of the most important developments in Europe are taking place in Spain, at Sanlucar la Mayor, west of Seville.

Here the experimental PS10 solar concentrating plant has been developed with EU support and funding. The idea is to concentrate reflected sunlight on a tower where water is heated. The heated water produces steam and the steam drives a turbine to generate electricity. First results are promising and the technology is already being used at other sites in Spain.

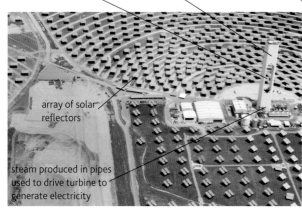

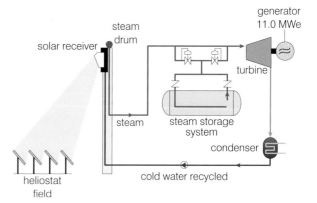

Fig. 7.32 *An experimental solar power plant near Seville, Spain*   **Fig. 7.33** *How the PS10 works*

■ Wind power

In 2006, 60 per cent of the world's wind power generation was installed in Europe, with two-thirds of that capacity in Germany and Spain. Among developing countries, India has the biggest amount of installed wind power generation, but China is quickly developing capacity.

In total, wind power capacity trebled between 2001 and 2006 and now accounts for 0.8 per cent of global electricty generation. It is expected that capacity will increase by around 22 per cent per year between 2006 and 2011. Nuclear power still produces 20 times as much electricty as wind does, but wind power is increasing far more rapidly than nuclear power.

There are three main factors slowing down the development of wind power:

■ the high capital costs of installing equipment

■ the unreliability of much of the equipment for long-term operation, although reliabilty is improving

■ the sporadic nature of the wind and the need, therefore, to provide backup plant.

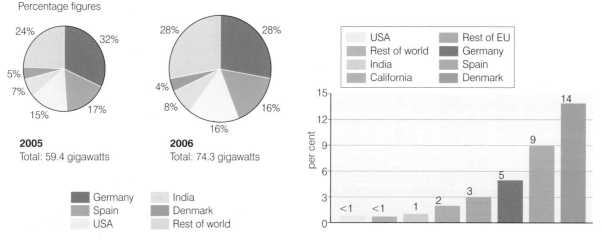

Fig. 7.34 *Installed wind generation capacity*   **Fig. 7.35** *Wind generation as a percentage of total electricity generated*

The UK has built many small onshore windfarms, but they do not yet produce a large amount of electricity. Moreover, the areas that have suitable wind for generating electricity are mainly in remote highland regions where building, maintenance and grid connection costs are high. Also there tends to be strong opposition to the construction from local people and environmentalists. Therefore, it seems as though the future for UK wind power lies offshore.

In the first round of developments, the government approved a comparatively small number of offshore sites. The biggest operating at present (Barrow and Kentish Flats) have a capacity to generate 90 MW (megawatts) of electricity. The second-phase sites are going through the planning process at present. The biggest, Triton Knoll, will have the capacity to generate 1200 MW. London Array is the second biggest site. In total, the second-phase sites should generate over 7000 MW and meet 70 per cent of the government's 2010 target for renewable energy.

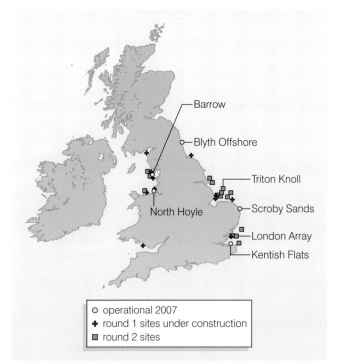

Fig. 7.36 *Offshore wind farm sites in the UK*

Key elements of the London Array project are:

- up to 341 turbines, installed over a four-year period
- associated offshore and onshore substations
- cabling (between turbines and to shore).

The wind farm would be constructed in phases, and when fully complete would generate up to 1000 MW of electricity. This is enough to meet the electricity needs of 750,000 homes – around a quarter of Greater London or all of the homes in Kent and East Sussex.

The project would contribute significantly to the government's target for renewable energy – providing around 10 per cent of its target for 2010. It would also prevent the emission of 1.5 million tonnes of carbon dioxide each year – the amount created by a fossil fuel power station producing the same amount of electricity.

■ Link

Find out more about UK offshore developments at:

www.bwea.com.

Find out more about the London Array site at:

www.londonarray.com/about.

Ormonde is a dual-use gas/wind development. Read more at:

www.reuk.co.uk.

Type 'Ormonde' into the quick search box.

■ Activities

14 Study Figure 7.36.

   a Describe the location of the main areas of offshore wind development in the UK.

   b Suggest why these areas were chosen.

15 Industry sources say that building offshore is more economically viable than building onshore. Suggest why.

16 Offshore development has to be carefully planned to reduce environmental damage. Suggest what problems might arise and how they might be avoided.

www.londonarray.com

Link

For further details of the Severn barrage proposals go to:

www.reuk.co.uk/Severn-Barrage-Tidal-Power.htm.

An alternative way of developing the estuary is suggested at the Friends of the Earth website:

www.foe.co.uk.

Type 'Severn barrage' into the search box.

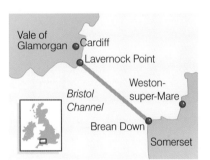

Fig. 7.37 *Proposed site of the Severn barrage*

Link

The Islay site is described at:

www.wavegen.com.

A trial site called Wavehub is based in Cornwall. It is designed as a plug-in system to test various designs of wave generator:

www.wavehub.co.uk.

One system that is being tested off the coast of Portugal is called Pelamis:

www.reuk.co.uk.

Type 'Pelamis' into the quick search box.

Alderney in the Channel Islands has its own scheme:

www.are.gb.com.

Finally, look up the Manchester Bobber project:

www.reuk.co.uk.

Type 'Bobber' into the quick search box.

Tidal and wave power

Tidal and wave power are at an experimental or design stage in the UK (although one tidal generation plant has been running successfully at La Rance in Brittany, France, since the 1970s) but they offer huge potential for power generation in the UK. If developed successfully, there would be potential to sell the technology and skills to other countries.

Tidal power

The Severn barrage is a proposed tidal power station to be built across the Bristol Channel (Severn estuary). The River Severn has a tidal range of 14 metres – the second highest in the world – making it perfect for tidal power generation.

The £15 billion barrage would stretch 16 km (10 miles) between Lavernock Point and Brean Down. It would act as a bridge between England and Wales and have an operational lifetime of up to 200 years. A total of 214 turbines would be built into the barrage. Trapped water would return through the turbines at high pressure when the tide turns, generating electricity. An enormous set of shipping locks would allow shipping to pass through the barrage.

The tidal turbines along the barrage would generate the same amount of electricity as three of the latest nuclear power stations – 8.6 MW during flow and 2 MW on average. This would be sufficient to provide 5–6 per cent of the current electricity usage of England and Wales. It would cut the UK's carbon emissions by 16 million tonnes each year (assuming Severn barrage electricity replaced electricity from coal-fired power stations) – equal to 3 per cent of total current emissions.

Wave power

A number of wave power experiments have been set up around the coast of the British Isles and a scheme on the Isle of Islay is successfully feeding electricity into the national grid. Details of some of these experiments can be found via the Link boxes.

Designing for energy-use reduction

Have a look at this extract which compares the cost of protecting oil supplies by military operations and the cost of insulating people's homes so they use less energy:

> Nearly a fourth of US dwellings completely lack insulation, and most others have old windows that radiate away energy, just plain holes and gaps through which energy escapes, etc. If the government had given tax breaks for putting in insulation and for conservation, the US would have saved millions of barrels a day, replacing everything Iraq or Venezuela produces.
>
> Insulation is better than war.

www.energybulletin.net

'Insulation is better than war' could become the slogan for the 2000s, like 'Make love not war' was during the 1960s and 1970s. Perhaps 'Think global, act local' is a better slogan.

Case study

Woking

Woking in Surrey is a beacon authority for sustainable development. That means it has been recognised by the government as having excellent policies for sustainable development and it lights the way for other local authorities to help achieve a sustainable future. The council's statement of aims says that sustainable development is about 'integrating and balancing the often competing needs of economic, social and environmental issues. It involves thinking about the future, caring for the environment, improving quality of life and encouraging greater community participation.'

Table 7.9 lists some of the items on the council's sustainability checklist.

Table 7.9 *Woking Council's sustainability checklist*

Checklist item	Comment
Use of energy, water, minerals and materials	Find case studies at www.woking.gov. uk/environment/Greeninitiatives/ sustainablewoking
Waste generation/sustainable waste management	Well-planned strategies reduce waste and reduce energy demands
Pollution to air, land and water	Between 1990 and 2006 Woking Council cut its own carbon emissions by 81%. Emissions fell by 21% across the borough
Factors that contribute to climate change	See the extract on pages 259–60
Protection of and access to the natural environment	
Travel choices that do not rely on the car	Reduce use of fuel for travel to work, shops, leisure
A strong, diverse and sustainable local economy	Cut costs of transport of parts, finished products and services
Meet local needs locally	Think global, work local
Contribute to Woking's pride of place	Pride in sustaining the environment, pride in beacon status

Climate change strategy

Planning and regulation

The way in which developments are regulated, planned and built and the way in which resources are used to do this can determine whether or not they are sustainable. Simply by re-evaluating how and where we build things we can reduce emissions and help to adapt to some of the issues climate change will bring about.

Essentially there are four main elements of sustainable development that can be taken into account in the local planning system.

Location

Average car use generates over three tonnes of CO_2 emissions a year. Nearly half of the households in Woking have two or more

Link

Here is a website that asks visitors to commit to reducing their own energy footprint. It is worth a visit:

www.energysavingtrust.org.uk/ commit.

To find out how the government is trying to get developers to follow good practice when they build new houses or refurbish old ones, visit this professional, interactive site. It is often technical, but does give an idea of what can be done:

www.energysavingtrust.org.uk/ housingbuildings.

Click on 'Visit our interactive house'.

Question

1 When you have used the excellent resources on the Woking Council website, make a summary of two or three initiatives that the council has taken.

2 Find out what is being done to reduce carbon emissions or to plan for climate change in your local area. Compare this with Woking. Suggest what else could be done in your area to reduce or manage climate change.

■ Link

Further details of Woking Council's initiatives can be found at:

www.woking.gov.uk/environment/sustain.

AQA Examiner's tip

The Woking Council website lists many more initiatives but two or three examples, explained and described clearly in your examination, will be plenty.

cars. The location of new development, in respect of the need to travel to places of work, shops, schools and entertainment, can have a significant impact on CO_2 emissions.

Layout

The layout of a site and its buildings can be devised so that it is more sustainable. For example, buildings or windows can be positioned to take advantage of passive solar gain (warmth from sunlight). Terraced housing and flats are more sustainable than detached housing because heat loss through walls and roofs is minimised.

Landscape

The landscape around a development can help to reduce energy use. For instance, trees, hedges and shrubs can create shelter from the wind, reducing heat loss; or they can create heat traps reducing the need for heating and provide shade in summer to reduce the need for air conditioning.

Sustainable construction methods

Energy use providing services like water, heating and lighting in buildings equates to 50 per cent of the UK's carbon emissions.

www.woking.gov.uk

✓ *i* 💡 *In this chapter you have learnt:*

■ about the different ways of producing energy from renewable and non-renewable sources

■ how different countries have different energy mixes and that the nature of the energy mixes has important consequences for countries' economic and geopolitical interests

■ about the world trade in oil, gas and coal

■ how the demand for energy can cause international tensions and conflicts

■ about the role of the transnational corporations in the world trade in and supply of energy

■ about some of the environmental issues associated with the exploitation, transport and use of energy resources, how these issues are being managed and how they might be better managed in future

■ that there are many potential sources of sustainable energy, and about the technical issues involved in developing these resources on an economic and sustainable basis

■ about the contributions that individuals can make towards a future with sustainable use of energy resources.

8 Health issues

Global issues in health care

In this section you will learn:

▪ about the geography of health

▪ about the geography of infectious diseases, including bird flu and HIV/Aids.

Key terms

Palliative: a drug or other treatment designed to reduce symptons and/or ease pain without dealing with the conditions that cause the problem.

Link

Navigate to the WHO website:

www.who.int/en.

Go to 'About WHO', then the 'WHO agenda'.

Link

See the millennium development goals on pages 208 and 281.

💡 The world's population is increasing and life expectancy is getting longer in most parts of the world (although it is being reduced in some), so it is clear that health care is improving in many areas.

However, people still fall ill and die. Doctors and scientists continue to seek new cures or **palliatives** for illnesses, some of which appear to be new illnesses. Many of the new cures are expensive and so too is the training of doctors and other health workers. Inevitably, the supply of health workers and the supply of drugs and equipment are limited. Equally inevitably, some people have better access to those limited supplies.

Some of the key issues in health lie in the provision of more equal access to health care between countries and within countries.

ℹ️ Is there a geography of health?

The World Health Organization (WHO) is the directing and coordinating authority for health within the United Nations system. The WHO has two major health objectives: to promote development, and to foster health security. They are explained in some detail on the WHO website.

1 Promoting development

During the past decade, health has achieved unprecedented prominence as a key driver of socio-economic progress, and more resources than ever are being invested in health. Yet poverty continues to contribute to poor health, and poor health anchors large populations in poverty. Health development is directed by the ethical principle of equity: Access to life-saving or health-promoting interventions should not be denied for unfair reasons, including those with economic or social roots. Commitment to this principle ensures that WHO activities aimed at health development give priority to health outcomes in poor, disadvantaged or vulnerable groups. Attainment of the health-related Millennium Development Goals, preventing and treating chronic diseases and addressing the neglected tropical diseases are the cornerstones of the health and development agenda.

2 Fostering health security

Shared vulnerability to health security threats demands collective action. One of the greatest threats to international health security arises from outbreaks of emerging and epidemic-prone diseases. Such outbreaks are occurring in increasing numbers, fuelled by such factors as rapid urbanization, environmental mismanagement, the way food is produced and traded, and the way antibiotics are used and misused. The world's ability to defend itself collectively against outbreaks has been strengthened since June 2007, when the revised International Health Regulations came into force.

Activities

1 Having read the statement of the WHO's first two objectives, do you think there is a geography of health?

   a Can aspects of health be linked to place?

   b Can aspects of health be linked to the connections between places?

   c Can aspects of health be studied at different scales – local, regional, national and global?

   d Do the aspects of health mentioned above interrelate with other topics that are regularly studied as part of the geography syllabus?

   If you can answer yes to any of the questions a–d then there is a geography of health and it is a valid area for study as part of the A level course.

2 Work as a class to draw up a list of ways in which health issues affect world affairs at this point in history. The WHO objectives on page 261 might give you some ideas to start the discussion.

Key terms

Health: the overall condition of an individual at a given time in regard to soundness of body or mind and freedom from disease or abnormality.

Public health: the aspect of medical activity directed towards improving the health of the whole community. Public health addresses the health of the population as a whole rather than medical health care, which focuses on treatment of the individual ailment.

Morbidity: the state of being ill or diseased, or the occurrence of a disease or condition that damages health and quality of life. It can also be used to mean the relative incidence of a particular disease in a society.

Mortality: death. The term is often accompanied by the cause of death (a specific disease or condition or injury).

What is good health?

It is very important to distinguish between **health** as it applies to an individual and as it applies to society as a whole. The latter is usually known as **public health**.

Individuals are ultimately responsible for their own and their family's health and good public health depends to a large extent on making all members of society fully engaged in their own good health. However, individuals need the help and support of government in:

- making good decisions about their own health and welfare
- having access to the best possible facilities to receive health care
- having support in maintaining good health as well as trying to improve bad health.

Good health is being able to function in an efficient and productive way. It involves good functioning of both mind and body. Bad health is sometimes referred to as **morbidity**. It is important to distinguish between morbidity and **mortality**.

The link between individual health and public health

In 2007 the Department of Health published a document called 'Creating Healthier Communities'. It included the diagram shown in Figure 8.1.

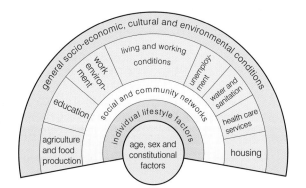

Fig. 8.1 *The main determinants of health*

At the centre of the diagram is the individual with the given factors that influence his or her health – age, sex and constitution (genetic make-up). Surrounding each individual are layers of influence that can – in theory – be modified. These layers interact with each other and with the individual throughout his or her life. It is these layers – the physical, economic and socio-cultural factors, and the living and working conditions – that bring the study of health issues into the field of geography.

One part of any government's public health policy must be to consider how to change public attitudes to their own health and to aspects of their lifestyle that influence their health. The government tries to act as a 'catalyst for change'. Figure 8.2 shows how attempts have been made to catalyse changes in smoking. This has been a long-term change and has been developed on four different fronts:

▪ **enable** – put policies in place to help people to help themselves

▪ **engage** – get people to think about changing

▪ **exemplify** – show how it is done

▪ **encourage/enforce** – legislate to change the behaviour of individuals or organisations.

Smoking – public attitude is changing following the example of other countries' smoking policies and by increasing the profile of the harm that cigarettes cause

■ NHS therapy and treatment for smokers
■ nicotine replacement therapy (NRT) on prescription and over the counter
■ medical advice on smoking
■ banning smoking at work and in public places
■ helplines and websites
■ markets for anti-smoking products

■ taxation on tobacco
■ banning on advertising, sponsorship and promotion
■ increased health warnings
■ legislation allowing smoke-free policies
■ tackling black markets

enable

encourage/ enforce

Catalyse

engage

■ publicity/ communications campaigns
■ no-smoking day
■ obligations on GPs to address
■ increased warnings
■ banning misleading 'light' branding

exemplify

■ no smoking in public sector estate
■ smoke-free NHS
■ other government departments redirected tax-take to anti-smoking

Fig. 8.2 *Attempts to catalyse changes in smoking*

You will be aware from your work on population in Chapter 5 that there is a great variation in the vital rates of population around the world. Birth, death, infant mortality and life expectancy rates vary enormously from country to country. Your work should have shown you that these rates are closely linked to the level of development of countries. As countries' economies develop, the vital rates can change quickly.

Activities

3 Study Figure 8.1.

a For each of the seven sections in the layer 'living and working conditions', discuss how that factor can affect an individual's health.

b Suggest some factors that might be included as individual lifestyle factors and suggest how each factor can affect an individual's health.

4 Study Figure 8.2. Draw a 'catalyse' diagram for any other aspect of public health, such as childhood obesity, increasing exercise, reduction of road traffic accidents, breast cancer awareness or Aids awareness. It could show what you know has been done, what you think should be done, or both.

5 Study the map of the world rates of life expectancy provided at www. worldlifeexpectancy.com.

a Describe the general patterns shown on the map. Look at the patterns closely and see if there are any anomalies (i.e. countries that have a higher or lower life expectancy than you might have expected).

b Click on any country listed in the column at the right of the page. Then, on the left side, you will see a list of the causes of death in that country, comparing that country with the rest of the world. Describe the main features revealed in this column.

c Click on up to six more countries to see causes of death in those countries too. Select countries at a range of different levels of development and compare their causes of death.

Link

Go to the BBC News website for more information and a good interactive map that shows how bird flu has spread to the UK:

http://news.bbc.co.uk.

Enter 'Bird flu' into the search box.

Activity

6 a The BBC website has an interactive map showing how far bird flu had spread by January 2004. Study this map online to see how it spread from that point onwards, and how its spread was linked to bird migration patterns.

   b Describe the pattern of spread shown on the map. Refer to places and dates. Refer to core areas and leaps.

   c How and why was the spread of the virus linked to the migration patterns of birds?

   d In most EU countries the spread of the virus was slowed down by mass culling of domestic birds and by movement controls on domestic birds in infected areas. Suggest why such policies would be less effective in:

      ▪ most African countries

      ▪ areas on desert margins and in arctic and subarctic areas.

   e If the health authorities around the world ever see that this type of flu is spreading among humans, what actions could they take to fight a major pandemic of the virus?

Infectious diseases: bird flu

There are many different strains of avian flu or bird flu. The strain currently causing concern on a worldwide basis is known as H5N1 and it was first identified in Hong Kong in May 1997. It spread to other parts of south-east Asia, with many outbreaks among bird populations and occasional infections of people – almost always those working closely with poultry.

Infectious diseases: HIV/Aids

'Healthy life expectancy in some African countries is dropping back to levels we haven't seen in advanced countries since Medieval times,' says the Coordinator of the WHO statistics team.

According to WHO, life expectancy in several countries in southern Africa is now 15–20 years lower than it would have been without HIV.

Aids is now the leading cause of death in sub-Saharan Africa, far surpassing the traditional deadly diseases of malaria, tuberculosis, pneumonia and diarrhoeal disease. Aids killed 2.1 million Africans in 2006.

Aids: key dates

The latest scientific studies suggest that Aids first appeared in central Africa in about **1959**. However, it did not come to general notice until **1979** when gay men in parts of the USA and heterosexuals in Tanzania and Haiti began to develop symptoms of the disease that were noted by doctors and epidemiologists. Epidemiologists study the prevalence of infections among the population. The term 'Aids' was first used in **1981**.

In **1983** the Institut Pasteur in France isolated HIV. In **1987** the first anti-Aids drug was approved in the USA. By **1991** it was estimated that 10 million people worldwide were HIV-positive.

In **1997** the number of Aids deaths in the USA fell for the first time since the outbreak started. However, the total number of infections worldwide had risen to 22 million, with 6.4 million deaths. Most of the infections and deaths were in sub-Saharan Africa.

In **2006** there were about 40 million infections worldwide, with over 60 per cent of them in sub-Saharan Africa. Around 20 per cent of all cases are in south and south-east Asia.

Activities

7 Study the Aids key dates and compare them with your study of the spread of avian flu. The scales of the outbreaks are very different so far.

   a Although they are very different, are there any similarities in the patterns of spread – core areas and leaps?

   b Are there any similarities in the speed of spread in more developed and less developed areas?

8 Study Figures 8.3 to 8.5.

   a Draw a table from the maps to show three sets of data. Show the region with most infections at the top and the one with the fewest at the bottom. Put total infections in the first column, then deaths, then new infections.

   b Describe the patterns shown in your table and suggest reasons for these patterns.

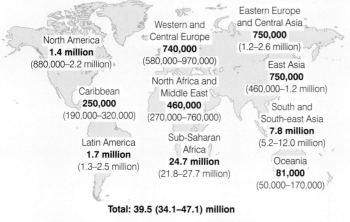

Total: 39.5 (34.1–47.1) million

The **bold** figures are the best estimates. The figures in brackets show
the lowest and highest estimates using different ways of measuring.

Fig. 8.3 *Estimated number of adults and children living with HIV in 2006*

Total: 4.3 (3.6–6.6) million

The **bold** figures are the best estimates. The figures in brackets show
the lowest and highest estimates using different ways of measuring.

Fig. 8.4 *Estimated number of adults and children newly infected with HIV during 2006*

Total: 2.9 (2.5–3.5) million

The **bold** figures are the best estimates. The figures in brackets show
the lowest and highest estimates using different ways of measuring.

Fig. 8.5 *Estimated number of adult and child deaths from Aids during 2006*

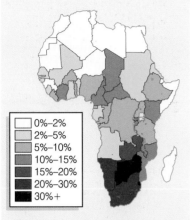

☐	0%–2%
	2%–5%
	5%–10%
	10%–15%
	15%–20%
	20%–30%
■	30%+

HIV infection is wipespread in most of sub-Saharan Africa (about 7%, as opposed to 1% worldwide), with incidences above 30% in Botswana, Zimbabwe and Swaziland.

Fig. 8.6 *HIV in Africa*

■ **Link**

The graph in Figure 8.7 was widely published. Here is one blogger's response to it:

www.ethanzuckerman.com/blog/?p=43.

■ **Key terms**

Antiretroviral (ARV) drugs: designed to protect the immune system from the damaging effects of the HIV virus.

Opportunistic infections: illnesses that strike people whose immune systems have been damaged by HIV.

HIV/Aids in southern Africa

HIV/Aids is devastating southern Africa (see Figures 8.6 and 8.7).

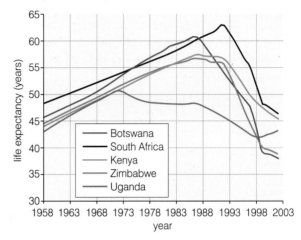

Fig. 8.7 *Life expectancy in southern Africa*

Southern Africa remains the epicentre of the global HIV epidemic: 32 per cent of all people with HIV live in this region and 34 per cent of all HIV deaths occur there. Several factors have helped the spread of the epidemic:

- a very mobile population with a lot of men working away from home in the mines of South Africa, on farms, in casual work in the cities or driving lorries
- lack of education about sex and hygiene
- problems of distributing condoms, of affording them and of overcoming reluctance among men to use them
- traditional taboos about discussing sex
- traditions of older men initiating young girls into sex.

The high proportion of people infected with the virus who develop the symptoms and die from them is due to:

- the lack of **antiretroviral (ARV) drugs** at affordable prices
- the late onset of treatment, even when it is available, because people are reluctant to be tested
- the poverty of many people which means they have a poor diet and so lack resistance to the **opportunistic infections** that often result when the immune system is damaged by the HIV virus
- the poor living conditions of the people, which make them more vulnerable to tuberculosis (TB) infection often the principal cause of death for people who are HIV-positive.

HIV/Aids is particularly damaging to the economies of countries in southern Africa because:

- it strikes mature adults at an age when they are potentially most productive, so much of their potential contribution to the economy can be lost
- it strikes all types of people, not mainly the poor and undereducated – this often means a waste of investment in education and training
- many children are left orphaned and unable to continue with their education, reducing their value to the workforce

■ the costs of treatment and/or palliative care are huge in relation to the health-care budgets of poor countries.

Zimbabwe is the only country in the region where there appear to be signs of a decline in the rate of infections. The observed declines seem to be related to a combination of factors associated with behaviour changes that began in the late 1990s, especially reductions in casual sexual encounters along with an increase in condom use and later first sexual experiences than had been normal.

In South Africa the data gathered in the country's extensive antenatal clinic network showed that the trend was still upwards in 2005. However, the trend among younger women seems to have reached a plateau.

As in the rest of sub-Saharan Africa, the epidemic in South Africa disproportionately affects women. Young women (15–24 years) are four times more likely to be infected than young men (17 per cent of the age group compared with 4.8 per cent of young men).

One of the most worrying aspects of the epidemic in southern Africa is the reluctance to admit to the possibility of infection. This is partly due to a lack of education about HIV/Aids, partly due to the lack of facilities for testing, but also partly because it is often felt that it is better not to know. Anyone who does have Aids is still likely to suffer prejudice from employers and from the community, so if drugs are not available at affordable prices, there is no point in knowing because there is no hope of any improvement of the condition.

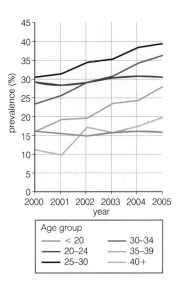

Fig. 8.8 *HIV prevalence by age group among antenatal attendees in South Africa, 2000–05*

Fig. 8.9 *Aids activists in South Africa work to get better treatment, to publicise and to reduce the stigma of the disease*

Treating HIV/Aids

It has been shown that the most effective way to combat HIV is to take a combination of different antiretroviral drugs. It is usually best to take three at the same time.

The drugs have been made widely available in the developed world. However, they are expensive and difficult to distribute in countries with underdeveloped infrastructures, so they are often unavailable to millions of people in the developing world.

Many of the big pharmaceutical companies have been reluctant to lower the price of their products, arguing that they need the high profits to research and develop new alternatives. However, concerted international pressure has forced a rethink, and cheaper generic versions of expensive **patented drugs** are now being made available.

UNAIDS and the G8 group of the world's eight major industrial nations are also trying to help provide treatment for Aids sufferers and to slow down the spread of HIV. Figures 8.9 and 8.10 show some of the things that are being done and suggest how more could be done.

Fig. 8.10 *Zambia World Aids Day poster*

Can poor countries tackle HIV/Aids?

The impact of Aids is devastating to the economies of low and middle income countries with high HIV prevalence. These countries, already suffering from heavy debt burdens, low productivity and weak infrastructure, are being further impoverished by the scourge of Aids. There is strong evidence that investment in HIV-related treatment and care can reduce hospitalisations and other direct and indirect costs of HIV/Aids. Brazil has completed a number of economic analyses demonstrating significant cost savings since the introduction of universal coverage of HIV-related treatments, including ARV, in 1997.

In addition to prolonging the lives of countless teachers, health workers, farmers, students and other precious human capital, it makes sense for countries to invest in health care in general and HIV treatment specifically because access to care and treatment is a human right.

Different approaches are being used to fund access to care and treatment in low and middle income countries. These include universal, free-of-charge access to treatment programmes through the public sector (e.g. Brazil), direct government subsidies to patients (e.g. Mali, Romania, Trinidad) and purchasing by patients after large-volume purchases at low prices by the government (e.g. Uganda). It is clear, however, that the vast majority of people living with HIV and in need of treatment will not be able to afford to cover the costs of their care.

HIV care will need to be provided at a price that is proportionate to local purchasing power – and for many people in many communities that means HIV care and treatment must be free.

■ Key terms

Patented drugs: medicines that have been developed by a company that has claimed rights to their production. No other company can produce them without permission and a licence bought from the patent holder. This means that the company can charge high enough prices to earn back the costs of developing the drug.

Intellectual property rights: the ideas behind the patents. The patents make sure that people and the companies they work for are paid for their efforts.

This year's G8 Summit in Heiligendamm, Germany, was a time for civil society to hold governments accountable to the promises they made. While climate change and international security dominated media attention on the G8, AIDS campaigners focused mainly on the lack of AIDS financing, weak health systems, **intellectual property rights** and lack of accountability on AIDS promises.

They also failed to deliver ambitious enough treatment targets by committing to provide treatment for only 5 million people in Africa 'over the next few years'. Current estimates indicate the real treatment need in Africa by 2010 could now be up to 11 million people. Steve Cockburn, Campaign Coordinator of the Stop AIDS Campaign was there at the summit and found the whole process frustrating. 'If actually delivered, the money promised will save lives, yet ultimately this outrageous poverty of ambition shown by the G8 will cost many more. By falling scandalously short of what the UN says is needed to fight HIV and AIDS, and by setting treatment targets well below actual need, they have capped ambition at a level which will be fatal for many'.

There were some positive outcomes in that leaders re-affirmed the goal of universal access to AIDS prevention, treatment, care and support by 2010. However, they did little to explain how it will be achieved. There was no mention of a working group to monitor G8 AIDS promises, something that campaigners, led by the Global Unions, have been working for.

'Clearly campaigners all around the world need to work even harder, more closely, be more coordinated and take leadership in order to have a more effective voice and to make sure that leaders, at the G8 and beyond, keep their promises on AIDS' stated Linda Hartke, Coordinator for the Ecumenical Advocacy Alliance, an international network of over 100 churches and Christian organisations.

From www.ua2010.org, the website of a group that protested at the G8 summit

At the G8 summit in Germany in 2007 the host country pledged:

to provide an additional US$60 billion a year over the coming years to fight HIV/AIDS, malaria and tuberculosis, especially for prevention programmes and to strengthen health systems in the least developed countries (LDCs). Germany has pledged €4 billion by 2015.

From www.g-8.de, the German government's website

The role of transnational corporations in health care

In this section you will learn:

- how transnational corporations (TNCs) can bring benefits and cause problems for the world's health

- how pharmaceutical and tobacco corporations have huge influence on health issues but in very different ways.

Key terms

Lobbying: presenting a case to the government and legislators on behalf of a client. Legislators in the UK are MPs; legislators in the USA are representatives and senators.

Off-patent medicines: medicines where the patent no longer applies. Other companies are allowed to produce copies of that drug and can charge lower prices. Drugs produced by a variety of different companies are called generic drugs.

Link

For more detail on the views of the APG go to:

www.apg.uk.com.

Select 'News & Papers', 'Position Papers' then click on 'Ensuring Access to Essential Medicines in Least Developed Countries and Sub-Saharan Africa'.

Pharmaceutical corporations

Are the pharmaceutical corporations heroes or villains? Or are they just ordinary corporations operating in a market and making reasonable profits for their shareholders by developing and selling drugs that prolong people's lives and make their lives better? They often make huge profits (see the section on GSK). They also have to test their new products and occasionally there are problems with the tests or problems when drugs cause side effects that were not predicted and are not even recognised at first. On the other hand, the drugs they produce save millions of lives every year and make millions of other lives better.

Here are just a few reasons why it is expensive to develop new drugs:

- Scientists need to be trained then paid for their work.
- Laboratories and research facilities need to be equipped and managed.
- Only a small proportion of the drugs developed will ever be deemed sufficiently safe and effective to be sold for profit.
- Drugs have to be tested before use and monitored in use.

The American Pharmaceutical Group

The American Pharmaceutical Group (APG) represents American transnational drug companies that work in the UK. It acts as a public relations and **lobbying** body for the drugs industry. It is clearly concerned at some of the negative publicity that the big pharmaceutical TNCs have received in recent years over the cost of medicines for poor people in poor countries. It is doing a lot to try to counteract this negative publicity. Here is an extract from its website:

Interest Areas
Access to Medicines in Developing Countries

'Pharmaceutical companies in the UK and abroad have made clear progress in getting medicines to the poorest in the world.'
Prime Minister Blair, 30 March 2005

The APG does not accept that basic healthcare should depend upon where people live.

Clearly, low prices and the absence of patents do not provide universal access to medicines. Out of the World Health Organization's Essential Medicines List, 90%–98% are **off-patent** and can be produced at low cost by other manufacturers.

The truth is that without the right infrastructure, the initiatives taken by the pharmaceutical industry and others will not work. Governments have a responsibility to minimise corruption and the diversion of resources, and provide investment in education. In health, there must be adequate transport, so that medicines are sent regularly to the correct areas, with professional staff to supervise their application to patients.

The APG is working in partnership with the Department for International Development, and individual companies are:

- Contributing to the affordability of essential medicines by differential pricing (i.e. lower prices) where still necessary, and by donation programmes.
- Supporting broader health and development goals in developing countries, working with national governments and voluntary organisations.
- Increasing investment in R&D for diseases disproportionately affecting such countries.

www.apg.uk.com

Table 8.1 *Top 10 pharmaceutical TNCs by share value, 31 December 2006*

Company	Base	Value (£ million)
Johnson & Johnson	USA	97,661
Pfizer	USA	95,281
Roche	Switzerland	80,157
GlaxoSmithKline	UK	77,362
Novartis	Switzerland	77,066
Sanofi-Aventis	France	64,166
Merck	USA	48,294
AstraZeneca	UK	42,036
Amgen	USA	40,656
Abbott Laboratories	USA	38,144

GlaxoSmithKline

GlaxoSmithKline (GSK) is the biggest UK-based pharmaceutical TNC. Here is an extract from its home page:

GSK at a glance

- Our mission is to improve the quality of human life by enabling people to do more, feel better and live longer.
- We are a research-based pharmaceutical company.
- Every hour we spend more than £300,000 (US$562,000) to find new medicines.
- We are the only pharmaceutical company to tackle the three 'priority' diseases identified by the World Health Organization: HIV/AIDS, tuberculosis and malaria.
- Our business employs over 100,000 people in 117 countries.
- We make almost four billion packs of medicines and healthcare products every year.
- Over 15,000 people work in our research teams to discover new medicines.

- We screen about 65 million compounds every year in our search for new medicines.
- We supply one quarter of the world's vaccines and by the end of February 2007 we had 23 vaccines in clinical development.
- In 2006 we donated 155 million albendazole tablets to help eliminate lymphatic filariasis (elephantiasis), making almost 600 million treatments in total.
- In 2006 we shipped 206 million tablets of preferentially-priced Combivir and Epivir (our HIV treatments) to developing countries – including 120 million tablets supplied by generics manufacturers licensed by GSK.
- In 2006 our global community investment was £302 million, 3.9% of profit before tax.
- Many of our consumer brands are household names: Ribena, Horlicks, Lucozade, Aquafresh, Sensodyne, Panadol, Tums, Zovirax.

www.gsk.com

█ Link

GSK states the aims of its work in developing countries at:

www.gsk.com/responsibility.

Select 'Developing countries'.

For more detail about GSK's work with HIV/Aids-infected people in poor countries go to:

www.gsk.com/community.

Select 'Positive Action Programme'.

A video called 'The Journey' briefly describes the development of GSK's involvement with HIV/Aids. It can be accessed at:

www.gsk.com/infocus.

Select 'World Aids Day'.

For GSK's work on malaria go to:

www.gsk.com/infocus.

Select 'The menace of malaria'.

GSK describes its work with HIV/Aids sufferers in both developed and underdeveloped countries. Its website outlines the different strands of its work:

HIV/Aids: the pandemic in perspective

The global community is aware of the scale of the problem. For its part, the pharmaceutical industry is working hard to find new and more effective treatments for HIV, the viral infection which can lead to AIDS.

A lot of emphasis is placed on anti-retroviral treatments. These medicines are specifically designed to block the action of retro-viruses, a type of virus, of which HIV is the most well-known.

However, viral resistance to existing drugs continues to be one of the biggest challenges in effectively treating HIV. Consequently the emphasis is currently on expanding the number of anti-retroviral drugs available with different modes of action or improved efficacy, tolerability and ease of use.

GlaxoSmithKline is helping with an array of initiatives including improving the convenience of delivering anti-retroviral therapy, developing molecules that address drug-resistant HIV. In addition the company is carrying out research into a vaccine against HIV infection.

The search is on for a cure, but that is not the whole story. The consequences of HIV/AIDS are such that they demand a local, as well as an international, response.

Various community-based groups provide a wide range of information, counselling, care and other support services. These groups form the backbone of the fight against HIV/AIDS in many countries where governments are unable or unwilling to combat the effects of the epidemic.

GSK works with these groups through its Positive Action programme.

www.gsk.com

█ Tobacco corporations

Throughout this chapter there are references to smoking and health. Time and time again smoking has been shown to damage the health of passive and active smokers, and it is known to be highly addictive. It has been estimated that tobacco smoking is responsible for 6 million deaths per year worldwide and seriously damages the health of many millions more.

But the tobacco industry is big business. Major parts of it are controlled by a small number of TNCs. It is interesting for geographers look at the distribution of these corporations and to see how they deal with the damage caused by their products.

The tobacco industry produces more than 5000 billion cigarettes a year globally. Tobacco is smoked by around 1 billion adult customers around the world every day. The biggest market is China, where 350 million smokers consume around 1800 billion cigarettes a year, or 35 per cent of the global total. The industry in China is state-owned. Outside China, stock market quoted international tobacco companies compete and account for more than 51 per cent of the global market (see Table 8.2).

Table 8.2 *Market shares of individual tobacco corporations*

Company	Base	% market share
Phillip Morris	USA	18.7
British American Tobacco (BAT)	USA/UK	17.1
Japan Tobacco	Japan	7.7
Imperial Tobacco	UK	3.5
Gallaher	UK	3.1
Altadis	Spain	2.1

British American Tobacco

The following extract describes British American Tobacco (BAT) in the company's own words. It comes from the BAT website:

Tobacco leaf

Our Group purchases some 460,000 tonnes of tobacco leaf a year, over 80 per cent of it by volume from farmers and suppliers in emerging economies. We aim to ensure that we only purchase leaf from responsible and sustainable sources.

Our Social Responsibility in Tobacco Production programme addresses the social and environmental issues associated with tobacco growing and processing and reaches around 250,000 farmers who supply all the leaf we buy.

The programme covers good agricultural practices for improving soil and water conservation, appropriate use of agrochemicals, and environmental, occupational health and safety. It is also active in eliminating exploitative child labour and promoting afforestation initiatives for the farmers who require wood for tobacco curing to obtain it from sustainable sources.

As a very large international business, British American Tobacco's supply chain is made up of around 250,000 farmers. With growing expectations that businesses should encourage good standards of corporate responsibility in their supply chain, British American Tobacco has developed a supply chain programme. Its supply chain programme includes BEST, their Business Enabler Survey Tool, which sets out in detail the standards they expect of the suppliers from whom they buy raw materials, including leaf.

Social Responsibility in Tobacco Production (SRTP) is a significant programme that aims to ensure that they only purchase tobacco leaf from responsible and sustainable sources, by working to address the agricultural, environmental and social issues associated with tobacco leaf growing and processing.

BEST assesses suppliers across 102 performance criteria, covering, for example, suppliers' business ethics; environment, occupational health and safety (EHS) management; employee rights; procedures for quality production; effective cost controls and the supplier's ability to trace the sources of raw materials, including sourcing wood from certified forestry.

Manufacturing

Manufacturing tobacco products is a large-scale global operation and we have factories all over the world. Our Group companies produce some 689 billion cigarettes through 52 cigarette factories in 44 countries and have four other factories in four countries manufacturing only cigars, roll-your-own tobacco and pipe tobacco.

Marketing

Successful marketing is the bedrock of growth for any fast moving consumer goods (FMCG) business and we are no exception. But when we talk about growth, there's a big point to make clear. By growth, we don't mean 'selling smoking' to boost the number of people in the world who smoke or the amount they smoke. We mean growing our share – more specifically, the value of our share – of the large number of adults who choose to be tobacco consumers.

As Jimmi Rembiszewski, our Marketing Director, puts it: 'Ours is a mature market – one where everyone already knows what tobacco is. There would be no commercial sense in trying to promote tobacco products to people who know what they are and have decided they don't want them.

'We invest in positioning our high quality brands competitively for the adults who've decided they do want to buy tobacco. And we've shown that through focus, intelligence, responsiveness and a high priority on responsibility, we can successfully build the brand loyalty of adults who have chosen to be tobacco consumers and win consumers away from competitor brands.'

▶

Sales by our subsidiary and associate companies account for just over 17 per cent of the global cigarette market and our share of the value of the global market is higher. Our share is a lot more than it was a decade ago and we have set our sights firmly on growing it yet more.

Global drive brands

Our global drive brands – Kent, Dunhill, Lucky Strike and Pall Mall – are at the forefront of our innovations, product refinements and trade engagement, with each brand differentiated and given a special focus within our 'win-win-win' approach. Over recent years, we've grown our global drive brands by more than 80 per cent – while at the same time obeying strict laws on tobacco marketing and adopting tight voluntary marketing standards of our own, that in several countries go beyond the law.

British American Tobacco has a very broad geographic base and is well placed to meet the changing environment. We are not overly reliant on markets with high profit margins but declining volumes and are well represented in markets where profit margins are currently lower but volumes are set to rise and strengthening economies allow

people to 'trade-up' to better quality, higher margin international brands.

Although our products pose risks to health and our industry can be seen as controversial, our products are legal, calls for prohibition are exceptionally rare and about a billion adults globally choose to smoke. We work continuously to manufacture and sell our products responsibly.

We have been one the FTSE 100's most successful companies – delivering an average total shareholder return over the past five years of 26 per cent per year compared to 7 per cent for the FTSE 100.

Are you exploiting developing countries to compensate for the decline in smoking in the western world?

No. We have been in the developing world since our company was formed more than 100 years ago. Put simply, our presence in a market has typically meant that smokers can choose between cigarettes made by a local (sometimes state-owned) manufacturer or from an international company. As disposable income grows in developing countries, so smokers often want to trade-up to higher quality, international brands.

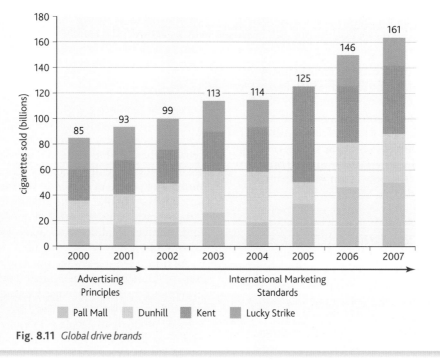

Fig. 8.11 *Global drive brands*

www.bat.com

However, there are alternative views about BAT and the other tobacco TNCs. For instance, the major American TNCs are being sued in the USA by a group of smokers who claim that their health has been damaged because of misleading advertising:

Leading tobacco firms in the US, including British American Tobacco, are to face a class action lawsuit seeking punitive damages of up to $200bn relating to the alleged fraudulent promotions suggesting 'light' branded cigarettes are safer, or less addictive, than regular ones.

Judge Jack Weinstein, sitting in a New York district court, certified the claim as a class action yesterday. The judge's ruling means the industry can be sued by 'light cigarette' smokers as a whole, rather than forcing each claimant separately to prove a case against the industry. The number of potential claimants could run into tens of millions.

Judge Weinstein summarised the claim, which is known as the Schwab case after the lead claimant Barbara Schwab, by saying: 'The claim is that the carcinogenic and other adverse effects smokers sought to avoid were not reduced by smoking "light" rather than other cigarettes; that defendants knew this was the case; that they concealed this fact; that they urged plaintiffs – through advertising and other public statements – to smoke these "lights" knowing smokers were being misled.'

Judge Weinstein's ruling comes a month after the US federal government won a ruling from federal judge Gladys Kessler. She found that America's largest tobacco firms had violated racketeering laws in a conspiracy stretching back to the 1950s, during which they had sought to maximise profits while deceiving smokers about the extent of their research into health risks associated with cigarettes.

Action on Smoking and Health (ASH) and Greenpeace produced a report which tried to show, using BAT's own words, how the company had used a variety of different strategies to promote its brands and gain access to markets. These strategies were mainly concerned with using corporate responsibility claims and green issues to improve the environment for sales of its cigarettes. Here are three passages from that report:

The recent award to BAT's Managing Director in Hungary demonstrates the group's sympathetic handling of local aspirations. Among the projects are a clinic for the diagnosis of disease; accommodation for the homeless, as well as arts and educational projects. For BAT, such programmes not only win allies in local markets but open the doors of politicians and regulators.

After BAT's 1992 donation of HK$300,000 to repair the Haizhou Bridge in the Guangzhou province of China '[this is] the sort of gesture to which officialdom will be obligated, and can benefit BAT in more ways than advertising alone'.

Support of growers [tobacco farmers in developing countries] will be invaluable in our continued battle with critics of the industry. Indeed we have already used them to help us brief both delegates to the WHO and to the FAO. The only hope of them being able to operate effectively is with funding help.

■ Link

The full report by ASH and Greenpeace can be seen at:

www.newash.org.uk/ash_bezns5bm.htm.

www.newash.org.uk

In 2004 researchers in London produced a paper based on research into tobacco smuggling in Asia. Using documents from BAT's own library, the report claims to show how BAT and other companies have tried to expand their sales in Asia through encouraging tobacco smuggling. Cigarettes are sold in countries where they are legal and the corporations use various methods to encourage (or at least not to discourage) their

■ Link

Researchers at the London School of Hygiene and Tropical Medicine have written 'Complicity in Contraband: BAT and Cigarette Smuggling in Asia'. You can read it at:

www.lshtm.ac.uk.

Enter 'Complicity in contraband' into the search box.

movement to neighbouring countries where they are illegal. By these methods it is claimed that the company can gradually build a demand for its products that eventually forces the target countries to open their markets. Obviously China is the biggest target in the long term.

■ Activities

9 Use the text and various websites cited in this section to write a summary of the international activities of BAT. Make reference to tobacco growing, cigarette manufacturing and marketing.

10 The BAT website refers to 'markets with high profit margins but declining volumes and markets where profit margins are currently lower but volumes are set to rise'. Suggest what these references mean on a global scale.

11 In the past 20 years BAT has closed a number of cigarette factories in richer, more developed countries and opened new ones in poorer, less developed countries. Suggest why.

12 a Produce a list of methods that BAT uses to expand its sales in new markets.

b Explain why these methods are necessary.

c Suggest how they work.

Health issues in rich and poor countries

In this section you will learn:

- how rich countries and poor countries have different health problems

- how health-care systems have to be adapted to meet different needs and different funding possibilities in countries at different stages of development.

Key terms

Diseases of affluence: diseases that are thought to be a result of increasing wealth in a society.

Obesity: excess of body fat that is 20 per cent or more over a person's ideal weight. Obesity strains the cardiovascular system and increases the risk of diabetes, hypertension, etc.

Diseases of proverty: diseases that result from impoverishment.

Link

Look at Activity 5 on page 263 based on life expectancy measures. Visit the website again at www.worldlifeexpectancy.com. Compare the main killers in more developed countries with the main killers in less developed countries.

Diseases of affluence

Diseases of affluence generally include type 2 diabetes, coronary heart disease, **obesity**, some forms of cancer, alcoholism, depression and possibly a range of other psychiatric illnesses.

Some of these illnesses are interrelated. For example, obesity is thought to be a partial cause of many other illnesses. They are mostly non-communicable diseases, whereas the diseases of poverty tend to be largely communicable through infection, poor public health provision or poor hygiene.

The trend is for these diseases of affluence to occur more as starvation and **diseases of poverty** decline, and as people live longer. Policy makers are sometimes criticised for failing to deal with the fact that development could be seen as self-defeating if it means exchanging one set of diseases for another. On the other hand, it is clear that it is impossible to stop people from becoming ill and dying, so it becomes ever more expensive to deal with all the diseases that affect people as they live longer.

Factors associated with the increase of these illnesses appear to be, paradoxically, things that many people would regard as improvements in their lives. They include:

- increased use of the car
- less strenuous physical exercise
- easy accessibility to large amounts of low-cost food
- more high-fat and high-sugar foods in the diet
- more foods which are processed, cooked and commercially provided (rather than seasonal, fresh foods prepared locally at time of eating)
- increased leisure time
- prolonged periods of inactivity or sedentary work and leisure
- greater use of alcohol and tobacco
- longer lifespans because of:
  - reduced exposure to infectious agents throughout life
  - greater use of antibiotics and vaccines.

Type 2 diabetes in the UK and worldwide

Type 2 diabetes is a typical disease of affluence. It is part of an interrelated set of causes and consequences, often linked to lifestyle:

Urgent action is needed to defuse the 'diabetes timebomb', with more than 3 million people in the UK now estimated to have the condition, a leading health charity said in November 2007.

The number of people in Britain diagnosed with diabetes shot up by 100,000 in the year 2006/07 and a total of 2.3 million Britons are now diagnosed diabetics. The vast majority have the type 2 disease. A further 750,000 are believed to have type 2 diabetes without knowing it.

Key terms

Balanced diet: the overall dietary pattern of foods consumed that provide all the essential nutrients in the appropriate amounts to support life processes, such as growth in children without promoting excess weight.

What is diabetes?

There are two main types of diabetes. Type 1 diabetes is an autoimmune condition which occurs when the body's immune system attacks the cells in the pancreas that produce insulin. It often begins in childhood or adolescence. This disease can be controlled but little can be done to prevent its onset. Type 2 diabetes develops when the body becomes resistant to insulin. The pancreas responds by producing more insulin and the liver, where glucose is stored, releases more glucose to try to increase the amount available.

Who is likely to suffer type 2 diabetes?

Type 2 diabetes usually develops in people over the age of 40, and the risk of getting it increases with age. However, it is becoming increasingly common among overweight children in the UK. Type 2 diabetes runs in families, and it is more common in men. It is also particularly common among people of African-Caribbean, Asian or Hispanic origin.

People who are overweight or obese and who aren't physically active are more at risk of developing type 2 diabetes. In particular, people who are an apple shape – with lots of fat around the abdomen – are at a greater risk of developing the condition.

Type 2 diabetes has long been linked with behavioural and environmental factors such as being overweight, physical inactivity and dietary habits. Major lifestyle changes resulting from industrialisation are contributing to a rapid rise in diabetes worldwide, especially in industrialising countries. An estimated 135 million people worldwide had diagnosed diabetes in 1995 and this number is expected to rise to at least 300 million by 2025 (according to K. M. V. Narayan, a leading researcher into the condition). Between 1995 and 2025, the number of people with diabetes will increase by 42 per cent (from 51 million to 72 million) in industrialised countries and by 170 per cent (from 84 million to 228 million) in industrialising countries.

What problems are caused by diabetes?

Untreated type 2 diabetes can also lead to a number of long-term complications.

- Over time small blood vessels become damaged. This can cause irreversible damage to the eyes and kidneys, leading to blindness and kidney failure if left unchecked.
- Nerves can be damaged, which can affect the ability to feel sensations and pain, especially in the hands and feet.
- Larger blood vessels can be damaged and make heart disease and stroke more likely.
- Damage to the circulation can also increase the risk of leg or foot ulcers, which can lead to gangrene and even amputation.

How is diabetes treated?

In many cases, type 2 diabetes can be controlled by lifestyle changes alone.

- A healthy diet is essential. This is the **balanced diet** recommended for good health: low in saturated fat, sugar and salt; high in fibre, vegetables and fruit.
- Carbohydrates (starchy foods) should be spread throughout the day to prevent high blood sugar levels after a meal.
- Keep weight under control to help reduce the risk of cardiovascular disease.

■ Regular physical activity can increase the body's response to insulin.

■ Smoking damages the circulation and it is especially important that people with diabetes do not smoke.

■ Alcohol can be consumed in moderation but should not be taken on an empty stomach.

If lifestyle changes don't reduce glucose levels, patients may be prescribed medicines to increase insulin production.

■ Diseases of poverty

There are clear links between good diet and good health. There are equally clear links between poor diet and poor health.

Famine

Famines persist in the 21st century. Why? New famines are unexpected, unprecedented and highly politicised. It is a paradox that the increasing potential to eradicate famines goes hand in hand with an increasing potential to cause them.

Many people believe that famines are caused by a shortage of food. However, detailed studies are now showing that people suffer in famines not because of food shortages, but because they lack the resources or other entitlements needed to obtain food. Even in poor and hungry regions, there are always a few rich landowners who can afford to buy food, who control a disproportionate amount of land and who often continue to export agricultural produce during times of famine.

Famine is largely a function of the failure of institutions, organisations and policies, not just the failure of markets and farmers. Central, local and community governments play key roles in causing famine as well as preventing it, and the absence of effective systems of government can be a cause and a consequence of famine.

Famines in Africa must be explained in a long-term context. They occur where and when poverty – often concentrated on a fragile, degrading resource base – interacts with economic, agricultural, social and demographic policies. These interactions make some segments of society and some regions vulnerable to even minor climatic and manmade shocks.

The region of the world that has been most prone to repeated and widespread famine in the late 20th and early 21st centuries is the Sahel region of Africa. Major international crises affected the region in 1973–74 and 1984–85.

Then in 2005 serious famines affected Niger and Chad. Lesser problems also affected Mauritania, Guinea Bissau, Cape Verde and Senegal. However, 2005 also saw food surpluses in Gambia, Mali and Burkina Faso and there was a food surplus in the region as a whole.

Unfortunately, many people in the area were not able to buy food when their own crops and livestock failed. All nine of the Sahelian countries are classed as least developed countries and, for instance, 61 per cent of the people of Niger have less than $1 per day to live on. Over half the country's wealth is owned by 20 per cent of the population while the poorest 20 per cent own less than 5 per cent of the wealth.

Most of Niger's poor live in rural areas and depend on subsistence farming. The main constraint on their farming is an unreliable water

Activities

13 a Explain why type 2 diabetes is becoming more common.

b Suggest some of the lifestyle changes that people can make to reduce the risk of developing type 2 diabetes.

c Why are better-off and better-educated people more likely to be able or willing to make these changes than other people in society?

14 Look back at Figure 6.1 on page 201.

a Describe the distribution of countries in the lowest two categories on the map, where hunger and malnutrition are likely to be widespread.

b Describe the distribution of countries in the highest two categories, where hunger should not occur but where there might be more problems related to overeating.

AQA Examiner's tip

If you are not sure where the countries listed here are, look them up in an atlas.

Link

Some schemes to try to improve productivity of farming and increase food supply in the Sahel are described on pages 148–153.

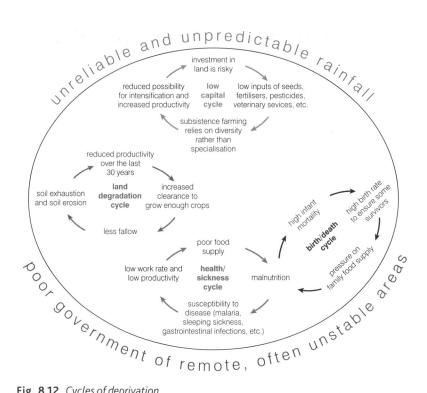

Fig. 8.12 *Cycles of deprivation*

supply or no water supply. Where irrigation can be made available the productivity of the land is high, but rainfall is seasonal and it appears that the region has been suffering from decreasing rainfall since the 1970s. Some of the interlinked cycles of poverty are shown in Figure 8.12.

To break the cycles of poverty and produce real development in Niger and other countries of the Sahel, it will require a multipronged attack on the problems of the area. This would have to include:

- improvements in farming productivity
- development of irrigation so it is affordable and manageable by people in rural communities
- improved marketing so that food can be distributed efficiently to increase farmers' incomes and to improve food security
- incentives to encourage farmers to invest surpluses in improving agriculture
- improved childcare to reduce the infant mortality rate
- inoculation and immunisation programmes
- improved hygiene to reduce the risks of transmission of infections
- simple rehydration medicines to reduce deaths from gastrointestinal infections
- access to birth control advice and affordable condoms – but people must *want* to practise birth control, so they must first be sure that the children who are born will survive
- education, particularly of women, to ensure that they can read and understand instructions for health care, hygiene, etc.
- improved access to modern ways of cooking to reduce fuelwood collection, which is time-consuming and cuts time for family care
- reduction in the use of wood for cooking, which reduces respiratory problems caused by smoke.

Link

Solar cookers are explained on page 251.

Activity

15 Simply providing food aid can never be seen as a solution to the problems caused by the famine in Niger, or in the wider Sahel region, or in less developed rural areas generally. Explain why this is so and suggest how development of medical care services is also needed.

Health-care systems that suit the needs of poor communities

Clearly it is extremely difficult to provide modern Western-style health-care facilities in the least developed countries of the world. In many countries this has been accepted and governments try to set up low-cost services that provide all parts of the country with basic medical services. The millennium development goals (MDGs) recognised the most important needs of the developing countries. It is striking that three of them are primarily health-care goals and several of the others are closely linked to health care.

Here are the eight MDGs agreed at the United Nations Millennium Summit in September 2000:

1 Eradicate extreme poverty and hunger.

2 Achieve universal primary education.

3 Promote gender equality and empower women.

4 Reduce child mortality.

5 Improve maternal health.

6 Combat HIV and Aids, malaria and other diseases.

7 Ensure environmental sustainability.

8 Develop a global partnership for development.

Link

The home page of Health-e is at:

http://health-e.org.za.

But there is a long way to go. Have a look at this extract from Health-e, a website concerned with health matters in southern Africa:

Infectious diseases and complications of pregnancy and delivery cause at least 10 million deaths worldwide each year, according to a recent WHO report.

Better access to health workers could prevent many of those deaths. The report shows clear evidence that as the ratio of health workers to population increases, so does infant, child and maternal survival.

At least 1.3 billion people worldwide lack access to the most basic healthcare, often because there is no health worker. The shortage is global, but the burden is greatest in countries overwhelmed by poverty and disease where these health workers are needed most.

Shortages are most severe in sub-Saharan Africa, which has 11 per cent of the world's population and 24 per cent of the global burden of disease, but only 3 per cent of the world's health workers, according to the report.

To meet the growing need in South Africa, the HR plan focuses much attention on training healthcare workers. By May, it wants a high level agreement on targets for production of health workers. This will include doctors and nurses but also people trained in basic healthcare, hygiene and disease prevention techniques. Such workers can be trained more cheaply and in far greater numbers than the university educated doctors whom they support.

But will South Africa simply be using taxpayers' money to train professionals who leave for greener pastures? After all in 2001, 23,407 South African born health workers were working in Australia, New Zealand, Canada, Britain and the USA. Almost 9000 of these (8921) were doctors, yet at the same time back in South Africa the public sector only had 11,332 doctors.

To prevent a post-graduation exodus, one of the important pillars of the HR plan is a staff retention policy based on better pay, a package of incentives and improved conditions of service.

But government remains lukewarm about recruiting foreign health workers to fill the gaps. It says it will pursue foreign workers primarily through government-to-government agreements as it had with Cuba, and it will not actively recruit people from African countries.

http://health-e.org.za

Did you know?

The DfID website gives the following information:

Spending on health per person per year

UK average: £1400

Sub-Saharan Africa: £5

World Health Organization's (WHO) recommended minimum: £17

Health workers

WHO's recommended minimum is five health workers per 2000 people

In some countries there is only one health worker per 1000 people

In Europe there are 10 per 1000 people

Global shortage of health workers will be 4 million by 2015

20% of UK direct aid to countries goes in health – £515 million a year

Health and aid: IHP

To try to ensure that aid which goes to improving health care and working towards the MDGs is used efficiently, the UK government recently helped to set up the International Health Partnership (IHP); it was launched on 5 September 2007.

Downing Street
05.09.07

A new international partnership was launched today that will help build national health systems in some of the poorest countries in the world. It will mean healthier people, living longer lives. Prime minister Gordon Brown, ministers from developing countries and donor countries, and leaders from all of the major health agencies and foundations, launched it today at 10 Downing Street.

The International Health Partnership (IHP) aims to improve the way that international agencies, donors and poor countries work together to develop and implement health plans, creating and improving health services for poor people and ultimately saving more lives.

Seven 'first wave' countries in Africa and Asia today announced that they would join the new International Health Partnership. They are Burundi, Cambodia, Ethiopia, Kenya, Mozambique, Nepal and Zambia. These countries have agreed that they would benefit from closer donor and international partner coordination as they work to improve the health of their people.

Donor countries and agencies that signed today's partnership agreement are the United Kingdom, Norway, Germany, Canada, Italy, Netherlands, France, Portugal, World Health Organization, UNAIDS, Bill and Melinda Gates Foundation.

The IHP is part of a renewed global push to meet the health Millennium Development Goals – cutting child deaths, improving maternal mortality and fighting major diseases. It aims to make health aid work better for poor countries by doing three things:

- focusing on improving health systems as a whole and not just on individual diseases or issues
- providing better coordination among donors
- and developing and supporting countries' own health plans.

The key objective is to ensure that collective efforts back 'comprehensive, country-owned and developed health plans which produce tangible and measurable results'. There need to be 'sustainable health systems' and 'sustainable and fair structures for health systems financing'. This means 'strengthening and using existing systems of coordination, coordinating support to implementation of sector plans and shared accountability for achieving results'.

In this context, developing countries commit themselves to produce comprehensive health plans, in a participatory way and with accountability to their citizens for delivery; and donors commit themselves to working together to support these plans.

The challenges facing developing countries' health systems are numerous and vary from access to medicines to the availability of clinics and the availability of trained health workers to predictable health budgets. The IHP aims to address some of the major issues that can influence the effectiveness of aid to poor countries.

www.dfid.gov.uk

Health and aid: Cuba

Cuba has adopted a rather different approach to health care not only in Cuba itself but also in other countries across the less developed world. From the time of the socialist revolution in 1959 it has tried to develop a health-care system that provides excellent services for all its people and this has been a priority almost above all others.

From the outset of the revolution, Fidel Castro made the health of the individual a metaphor for the health of the nation. Therefore, he made the achievement of developed country health indicators a national priority. Rather than compare Cuban health indicators with those of other countries at a similar level of development, he began to compare them with those of the USA, particularly their infant mortality and life expectancy rates. To achieve these aims, Cuba has had to tackle a number of linked issues, most importantly sanitation, nutrition, medical services, education, housing, employment, equitable distribution of resources, and economic growth.

In 2006 Cuba's infant mortality rate was 5.6 per 1000 live births, lower than the US figure of 7.0 per 1000 live births. Life expectancy at birth in Cuba today is the same as for US citizens, 77 years. These achievements make Cuba a model and therefore make possible its policy of medical diplomacy – sharing its experience of developing health care for all the people in a poor country.

In the past 35 years Cuba has tripled its number of health-care workers. Cuba went from one doctor for every 1393 people in 1970, to one doctor for every 159 people in 2005. This was part of Fidel's 'put a doctor on every block' policy. Having accomplished this in urban and rural areas, even isolated areas, Cuba is now exporting this model through its medical diplomacy initiatives.

Cuba's accomplishments in health realms are not just in primary care or in the production of doctors. There was a simultaneous development of high-tech medicine and biotechnology. Cuba shares its expertise through numerous international medical conferences that it holds every year, and through scientific exchanges.

Despite economic hardship during the 1990s after the loss of the support of the Soviet Union, Cuba continually increased its spending on domestic health as a percentage of total government spending, in order to shield the most vulnerable section of the population from the worst effects of the crisis. As a result, the initial deterioration in the population's health status was short-lived and the health indicators quickly improved.

Having suffered a post-apartheid brain drain dubbed the 'white flight', South Africa began importing Cuban doctors in 1996. In 1998 there were already 400 Cuban doctors practising medicine in South African townships and rural areas. By 2004 there were about 1200 Cuban doctors working in countries across Africa, implementing a comprehensive health programme modelled on Cuba's own.

Today Cuba has 130,000 health-care professionals with a university education, 25,845 of whom are serving as volunteers in international missions in 68 different countries. Of these, 17,651 are doctors, 3069 are dentists and 3117 are health-care technicians working in areas such as optics.

Activities

16 Read the text on the IHP and on Cuba's Healthcare Diplomacy.

  a Describe the main aims of each programme. Refer to the stated aims and to any 'hidden' aims that the UK and Cuban governments might have.

  b Compare the strengths and weaknesses of the two programmes from the viewpoint of the countries receiving the help with their health care. Think about short-term and long-term benefits from each programme. Refer to sustainable health care in your answers.

17 Draw up a table to compare health care in Cuba and the UK. You should include headings such as:

  ▪ Priorities in the system.
  ▪ Access for all.
  ▪ Public and private provision.
  ▪ Measuring success (use internet research to find the latest figures for infant mortality rates, life expectancy, etc.)
  ▪ Training programmes for health workers.
  ▪ Links with developing countries, including the supply of health workers.

  Use references at the start of the chapter to South Africa. Contrast the health-care systems of Cuba and South Africa in terms of their problems and solutions. The link to the Health-e website on page 281 will be useful here.

Regional variations in health and health care in the UK

In this section you will learn:

- about the variations in health in regions of the UK
- how health and health care are linked to other measures of well-being
- how the government is trying to improve the nation's health
- how to research more local details about health and health care.

Link

If you do not know where any of these authorities are, go to the National Statistics site at:

http://neighbourhood.statistics.gov.uk/dissemination.

Type in the name of the authority that you wish to locate, then press the search button.

🔢 The Office for National Statistics gives a variety of information about health and related matters in the UK. Among the data it publishes is life expectancy data for each local authority in the UK. The local authorities are ranked to produce Table 8.4.

Table 8.3 *The highest and lowest life expectancies for men (left) and women (right)*

a Males		
Rank order	Local authority	Years
Highest life expectancy		
1	Kensington and Chelsea	82.2
2	East Dorset	80.9
3	Hart	80.2
4	Uttlesford	80.0
5	Wokingham	80.0
6	South Norfolk	80.0
7	Chiltern	80.0
8	Horsham	79.9
9	Brentwood	79.8
10	Crawley	79.8
Lowest life expectancy		
432	Glasgow City	69.9
431	West Dunbartonshire	71.0
430	Inverclyde	71.1
429	Comhairle nan Eilean Siar (Western Isles)	72.1
428	Manchester	72.5
427	Renfrewshire	72.6
426	North Lanarkshire	72.7
425	Dundee City	73.0
424	Blackpool	73.2
423	Clackmannanshire	73.2

b Females		
Rank order	Local authority	Years
Highest life expectancy		
1	Kensington and Chelsea	86.2
2	Epsom and Ewell	84.5
3	East Dorset	84.1
4	South Cambridgeshire	83.9
5	Rutland	83.8
6	Purbeck	83.7
7	Guildford	83.6
8	New Forest	83.6
9	North Dorset	83.5
10	Horsham	83.4
Lowest life expectancy		
432	Glasgow City	76.7
431	West Dunbartonshire	77.5
430	North Lanarkshire	77.6
429	Inverclyde	77.9
428	East Ayrshire	78.0
427	Liverpool	78.1
426	Renfrewshire	78.2
425	Halton	78.3
424	Hartlepool	78.3
423	Manchester	78.3

Activity

18 a Study Table 8.3. On an outline map of the UK, mark each of the top 10 and bottom 10 local authorities for female life expectancy. Do the same for male life expectancy.

b Describe the patterns.

Table 8.4 *Life expectancy at birth in the USA by race and sex, 1930–2004*

	All races		White		Black	
Year	Male	Female	Male	Female	Male	Female
2004	75.2	80.4	75.7	80.8	69.8	76.5
2000	74.3	79.7	74.9	80.1	68.3	75.2
1995	72.5	78.9	73.4	79.6	65.2	73.9
1990	71.8	78.8	72.7	79.4	64.5	73.6
1985	71.1	78.2	71.8	78.7	65.0	73.4
1980	70.0	77.4	70.7	78.1	63.8	72.5
1970	67.1	74.7	68.0	75.6	60.0	68.3
1960	66.6	73.1	67.4	74.1	–	–
1950	65.6	71.1	66.5	72.2	–	–
1940	60.8	65.2	62.1	66.6	–	–
1935	59.9	63.9	61.0	65.0	51.1	55.2
1930	58.1	61.6	59.7	63.5	47.3	49.2

■ Activities

19 Watch the animations (see the Link box) for male and female life expectancies. Try to print at least the most up-to-date map for each sex.

a Does the pattern continue the one that you saw in the top 10s?

b Overall life expectancy – how is it changing?

c Are the patterns of areas with short and long life expectancy changing? If they are changing, are they getting more or less marked?

d Suggest reasons for the differences between the regions.

20 Use the statistics in Table 8.4 to draw a line graph. Describe the pattern shown by the data. Suggest reasons for the patterns. Compare the figures with those for the UK.

■ Link

Go to a superb animated map showing changing life expectancy rates in the UK over the last 14 years:

www.statistics.gov.uk/life-expectancy.

For the full data for Table 8.3, go to:

www.dh.gov.uk.

Enter 'Health Profile of England 2007 'into the search box. You can click on the links at the bottom of the page to download the full document or parts of it.

For information about Wales go to:

www.wales.nhs.uk.

Enter 'Pictures of health for local authorities'.

For information about Scotland go to:

www.scotpho.org.uk.

Click on 'Community profiles: introduction'.

■ Health profiles of England

The Department of Health (DH) has a section called the health improvement monitoring team. Its job is to provide the department with the data it needs to show how the state of the nation's health varies from region to region and over time. It has published 'Health Profile of England 2007', which can be seen in full on the internet.

One of the most useful sections for geographers is the table of health indicators by region. It shows a huge range of factors that directly and indirectly measure the health of people in each region. A traffic light scheme is used to show which regions are better than, worse than or around the national average.

Note that each health indicator is based on a different set of data. The full document explains the data sets and how they were constructed.

Some of the data from the table for England's regions can be seen in far more detail on another page of the DH website. This shows information for every local authority. It is possible to compare the local authority score with the national score for each of the indicators in Table 8.5.

Table 8.5 *Health profile of England*

Indicator	Period	Unit[1]	England	North East	North West	Yorks & the Humber	East Mids	West Mids	East of England	London	South East	South West
Our communities												
1 Income deprivation	2003	%	12.9	17.3	15.9	14.1	11.5	14.6	9.6	16.9	8.4	9.9
2 Ecological footprint	2001	ha per capita	5.47	5.2	5.4	5.3	5.4	5.3	5.5	5.5	6.1	5.2
3 Homelessness	2004/05	%	7.8	8.9	8.6	5.9	6.6	10.2	7.8	8.7	6.9	7.4
4 Children in poverty	2001	%	21.3	27.8	25.3	23.0	19.0	22.9	15.6	29.9	14.2	16.1
5 Education – GCSE achievement (5 A*–C)	2005/06	%	57.5	57.4	56.6	54.5	55.4	56.4	59.3	58.3	59.7	58.2
6 Violent crime	2005/06	cr per 1000	19.8	18.2	21.1	22.2	18.6	19.4	15.0	26.5	17.3	17.0
Giving children and young people a healthy start												
7 Smoking in pregnancy	Note[2]											
8 Breastfeeding	Note[2]											
9 Obese children	2005	%	14.3	18.3	15.0	11.4	14.5	15.8	14.1	18.2	13.4	14.0
10 Physically active children	2005	%	69	70	68	67	70	70	73	68	69	74
11 Teenage pregnancy (under 18)	2002–04	cr per 1000	42.1	51.2	45.3	47.0	40.8	46.4	33.6	50.4	33.6	34.6
The way we live												
12 Adults who smoke	2000–02	%	26.0	30.3	27.4	28.0	26.6	24.6	24.7	26.0	23.7	25.0
13 Binge-drinking adults	2000–02	%	18.2	25.1	23.0	21.5	17.8	15.9	16.7	15.4	15.5	15.8
14 Healthy eating (5 a day)	2001–02	%	23.8	16.8	22.2	20.4	22.6	22.8	23.9	27.6	28.9	23.3
15 Physically active adults	2005–06	%	11.6	11.4	11.1	11.1	11.6	10.5	11.3	11.6	12.5	12.6
16 Obese adults	2000–02	%	21.8	23.9	21.6	22.6	25.1	24.2	20.9	20.3	20.4	19.2
How long we live and what we die of												
17 Life expectancy at birth – males	2003–05	years	76.9	75.4	75.4	76.2	76.9	76.2	78.0	76.9	78.1	78.1
18 Life expectancy at birth – females	2003–05	years	81.1	79.8	79.9	80.6	80.9	80.8	81.8	81.4	82.0	82.2
19 Deaths from smoking	2003–05	easr	234.4	296.0	279.3	258.3	229.7	237.7	206.0	236.7	204.7	199.9
20 Early deaths – circulatory disease	2003–05	easr	90.5	108.5	108.6	95.9	91.4	97.2	77.4	96.8	75.9	74.7
21 Early deaths – cancer	2003–05	easr	119.0	136.2	132.6	124.9	117.6	120.7	110.9	116.9	111.2	109.7
22 Infant deaths (under 1 year)	2003–05	cr per 1000	5.1	4.7	5.7	5.8	5.2	6.8	4.2	5.2	4.0	4.4
23 Road injuries and deaths	2003–05	cr per 100,000	59.9	46.0	59.5	68.2	69.1	53.2	69.3	58.3	58.3	53.1
Health and ill health in communities												
24 Feeling 'in poor health'	2001	%	7.8	10.4	9.6	8.9	7.8	8.4	6.4	8.2	5.9	6.8
25 Mental health	2005	cr per 1000	27.4	41.4	40.4	29.0	24.1	28.3	20.0	26.6	19.1	25.9
26 Alcohol-related hospital stays	2005/06	easr	247.7	390.8	397.8	243.4	212.3	232.5	164.9	227.7	196.0	253.5
27 Drug misuse	2004–05	cr per 1000	9.9	9.5	11.4	11.7	8.2	10.6	6.5	14.4	6.4	9.4
28 People with diabetes	2006	%	3.7	3.8	3.9	3.7	3.9	4.0	3.4	4.0	3.3	3.5
29 Children's tooth decay (5 year olds)	2005/06	mean no.	1.5	2.0	2.0	1.8	1.3	1.0	1.1	1.7	1.1	1.6
30 Sexually transmitted infections (gonorrhoea)	2005/06	Note[3]	35.3	21.7	35.2	35.5	24.8	34.3	17.1	88.9	18.9	19.1
31 Older people: hip fracture	2005/06	easr	565.3	567.1	530.1	533.8	589.4	570.0	576.3	502.6	558.7	657.8

= significantly higher 'performance' than national average or target rate
= indistinguishable from or consistent with national average or target rate
= significantly lower 'performance' than national average or target rate
NO SHADE = significance not calculated

ha per capita = hectares per person
cr = crude rate of reference population (varies by indicator)
easr = European age standardised rate
1 See website for fuller description of indicators. See column 'LHP Definition' in annex C for definition of target unit.
2 Data not available.
3 New episodes per 100,000 population.

Activity

21 Use a copy of Figure 8.13.

a Map at least one set of data from Table 8.5. You could use a shading map, located proportional circles or located bars. If you use either of the last two methods, you could place them against a background shaded using the traffic light scheme.

b Compare maps of different data sets, your own or other people's. Discuss the patterns that the maps reveal.

c Suggest explanations for the patterns.

d Suggest what links exist between the different data sets. Try to suggest whether any correlation is because one set of data *causes* another set, or whether the two sets are both influenced by the same cause or causes.

Fig. 8.13 *The English regions*

Link

Go to:
www.communityhealthprofiles.info.

Click on 'Find profiles' and search for your local authority. Then select your local authority and click on it.

It is also possible to view the death rates from particular conditions and to compare them with national averages.

Some data is even broken down for individual wards in the authority Figure 8.14 shows data for Newcastle upon Tyne from the DH website. Figure 8.15 shows various measures of health for Newcastle and compares them with nationwide averages. Newcastle was chosen because the data can be linked to the case study in Chapter 5.

This map shows variation in the percentage of people on low income, between small areas *within this local authority* (2003).

Local income groups

☐ 1 Least income-deprived fifth of areas in this local authority

☐ 2

▨ 3

▨ 4

■ 5 Most income-deprived fifth of areas in this local authority

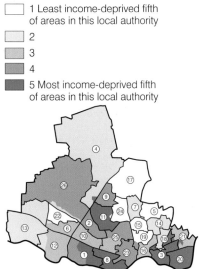

Ward boundaries have changed since 2001, so differ from Figure 5.25.

Wards

1 Benwell and Scotswood
2 Blakelaw
3 Byker
4 Castle
5 Dene
6 Denton
7 East Gosforth
8 Elswick
9 Fawdon
10 Fenham
11 Kenton
12 Lemington
13 Newburn
14 North Heaton
15 North Jesmond
16 Ouseburn
17 Parklands
18 South Heaton
19 South Jesmond
20 Walker
21 Walkergate
22 Westerhope
23 Westgate
24 West Gosforth
25 Wingrove
26 Woolsington

Health inequalities

This chart shows inequalities in life expectancy (2001–05) at birth for men and women for the five local income groups presented on the map on the far left.

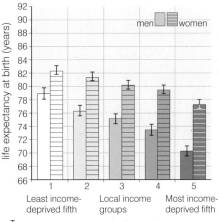

⊺ 95% confidence interval. These indicate the level of uncertainty about each value on the graph. Longer/wider intervals mean more uncertainty. When two intervals do not overlap it is reasonably certain that the two groups are truly different.

Fig. 8.14 *Income and health inequalities in Newcastle*

Domain	Indicator	Local no. per year	Local value	Eng. avg	Eng. worst	England range	Eng. best
Our communities	1 Income deprivation	54,130	20.3	12.9	31.1		3.3
	2 Ecological footprint	n/a	5.426	5.470	6.430		4.904
	3 Homelessness	906	6.9	7.8	35.8		0.0
	4 Children in poverty	16,963	35.0	21.3	58.8		5.2
	5 Education – GCSE achievement (5 A*–C)	1,600	55.8	57.5	33.6		81.9
	6 Violent crime	5,289	19.6	19.8	41.1		5.0
Giving children and young people a healthy start	11 Teenage pregnancy (under 18)*	278	57.5	42.1	95.3		12.8
The way we live	12 Adults who smoke*	n/a	32.2	26.0	37.3		15.5
	13 Binge-drinking aduls	n/a	29.2	18.2	29.2		8.8
	14 Healthy eating (5 a day)	n/a	17.4	23.8	11.4		38.1
	15 Physically active adults	n/a	12.3	11.6	7.5		17.2
	16 Obese adults	n/a	21.8	21.8	31.0		14.6
How long we live and what we die of	17 Life expectancy at birth – males*	n/a	74.9	76.9	72.5		82.2
	18 Life expectancy at birth – females*	n/a	80.2	81.1	78.1		86.2
	19 Deaths from smoking	581	312.1	234.4	366.5		147.6
	20 Early deaths – circulatory disease	289	108.8	90.5	151.3		44.9
	21 Early deaths – cancer	383	144.8	119.0	168.0		81.6
	22 Infant deaths (under 1 year)	15	5.1	5.1	9.9		1.2
	23 Road injuries and deaths	115	42.5	59.9	214.1		20.2
Health and ill health in our community	24 Feeling 'in poor health'	29,695	10.9	7.8	15.4		4.2
	25 Mental health	7,990	44.1	27.4	72.0		8.5
	26 Alcohol-related hospital stays	1,207	440.4	247.7	652.4		85.6
	27 Drug misuse	2,740	15.0	9.9	34.9		1.3
	28 People with diabetes	9,804	3.5	3.7	5.9		2.1
	29 Children's tooth decay (5 year olds)	n/a	2.3	1.5	3.2		0.4
	31 Older people: hip fracture	261	489.4	565.3	936.8		259.7

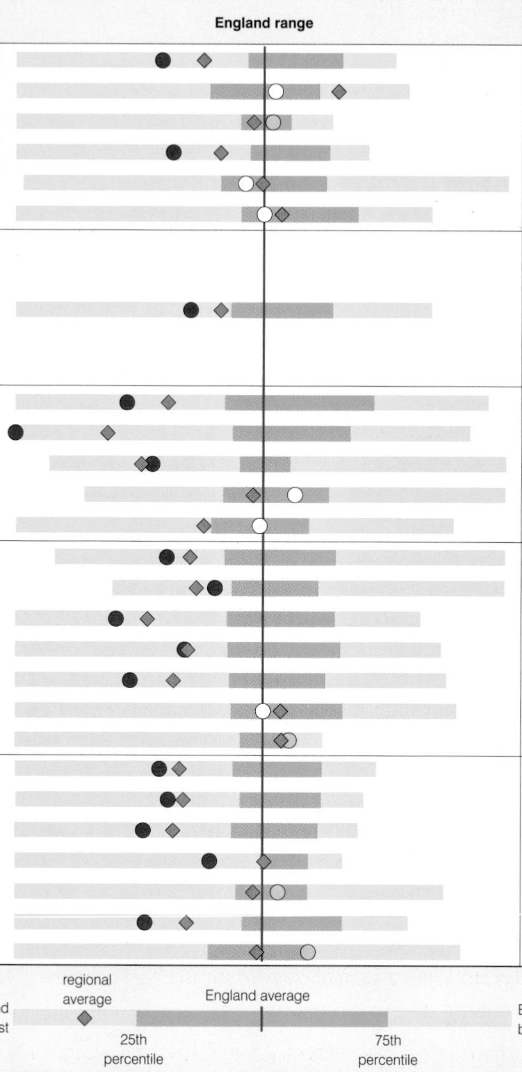

Legend:
- ◐ significantly better than England average
- ● significantly worse than England average
- ○ not significantly different from England average
- * PSA target measure, 2005–08

England worst — regional average — England average — England best
25th percentile — 75th percentile

Fig. 8.15 *Health summary for Newcastle*

Link

Look at the Tyneside case study on pages 188–99.

Activity

22 Re-read Activity 21 on page 287.

a Carry out its steps for a single health authority. Use the Newcastle figures here or your own example taken from the DH website.

b Suggest some of the geographical issues that the detailed figures for the health authority raise. Suggest how you might carry out further studies to investigate these issues.

Factors affecting access to health care

Many factors that affect access to health care are worthy of investigation by geographers. They include variations in:

■ age

■ gender

■ wealth

- occupation type
- education level
- environment
- pollution levels.

In the UK many aspects of health provision are closely linked to age. For instance, antenatal, maternity and post-natal services through GPs, midwifery services, hospital maternity units and health visitor services are age related. So are health services linked to schools. There are specific services linked to old people and the geriatric stages of life.

Other health services, such as contraceptive clinics, sexually transmitted disease clinics and breast screening services are aimed more or less at specific age groups, and some are aimed at one sex. However, health facilities must be considered more widely than just medical facilities. Under-16s who may have lost access to school playing fields are just the same group that find it difficult to gain access to private health and fitness clubs. Even local authority facilities may have age restrictions which stop or limit access for young people.

Opportunities for young people to exercise are further restricted by the increase in traffic on the roads in many places. Until recently many more children used to walk or cycle to school, but a variety of pressures have reduced that exercise possibility. In particular, the increased traffic on the roads and the heightened concern about stranger danger and bullying mean that more parents drive their children to school. This increses traffic on the roads and congestion around schools, which increases the danger to children and adds more pressure not to walk or cycle.

There have been some local initiatives to develop school access plans, where certain routes are recommended. Some schools have also set up walking bus schemes, where groups of parents and children agree to meet and walk to school together so that everyone has company and a degree of protection from traffic. Unfortunately, the school run in cars has become even more common.

It is not just children who find it difficult to access to exercise facilities and other health facilities. The elderly are less mobile than young adults; more women now own cars yet access to cars is still more common for men than for women; the wealthy own more cars than the poor; and more and more facilities are more accessible to car users than to public transport users, pedestrians or cyclists. For many years there has been increasing pressure to own cars as they have become more of a necessity and less of a luxury. This has created a vicious circle as increased car use means that more and more facilities are designed to suit car users.

Access to facilities is easier for the rich, the educated, the two-parent family, people between about 20 and 65, men and the employed. It is more difficult for the young, the old, the poor, the single-parent family, the unemployed, recent migrants and women. Low education levels are often associated with some of these disadvantaged groups, which means they are less able to understand and negotiate their way through complex bureaucratic systems which give access to health care and they are less well equipped to argue for their full rights from the system. Cultural factors may also play a part. Some women find it difficult to use gyms and swimming pools because of traditions of dress and separation of the sexes.

■ **Did you know?**

Access to exercise opportunities also varies from place to place and from group to group. An example is the recent loss of playing fields in some areas, particularly in some inner cities and suburbs of expanding cities, where school and local authority facilities and land have been sold off for housing and commercial development. The profits from these sales are often ploughed back into new education facilities, but at a cost to fitness, particularly for young people.

■ Link

The Department for Transport publishes a database of articles. Many relevant documents can be accessed through:

www.dft.gov.uk/prg/sustainable/schooltravel.

Also try the Sustrans website at:

www.sustrans.org.uk.

If there is to be equal access to health and fitness facilities for all, a big effort has to be put into redesigning facilities and their locations to make them accessible to all, and into ensuring that all groups (by age, sex, culture, etc.) can make good use of what is provided. Public transport has to be improved and made more attractive and affordable. If local and national governments are to play a full role in improving the health of the nation and in reducing differentials in life expectancy and fitness, they must build these factors into their planning.

■ The Wanless Report

In February 2004 a report was produced for the Treasury by Derek Wanless, called 'Securing Good Health for the Whole Population'. It considered ways of better organising and financing aspects of health care to allow better access for all. The whole of the report is available on the internet but most of it is only marginally relevant to geographers. Some sections can be accessed separately.

■ Link

The home page for the Wanless Report is at:

www.hm-treasury.gov.uk.

Enter 'Securing Good Health for the Whole Population'. There are various PDFs that form this report. It is worth reading the summary and the case studies.

The case studies are probably the most useful section for geographers. There are sections on:

■ smoking

■ health inequalities and strategies to reduce them

■ obesity and physical exercise.

The section on smoking examines the links between smoking and social class and looks at ways of reducing smoking.

■ Activities

23 Read at least one of the sections of Wanless Report in the Link box. Summarise the arguments in that section, with particular reference to what it says about:

■ spatial distributions of aspects of health care and well-being

■ links between different aspects of health and well-being.

24 The Wanless Report set out national strategies and targets. Examine how well health care is provided in local areas. The NHS Services Directory can be found at:

www.nhs.uk/servicedirectories.

This geographical information system (GIS) allows the user to find information about many different health-care facilities in any part of the country.

The information on each type of facility can be seen as a list or a map.

Compare the map of facilities with maps of population distribution, or different social class distributions, to see how well the needs of different groups are served and how easily they can gain access to the facilities.

More details about the availability of different types of exercise facilities can be found at:

www.thefitmap.co.uk.

This allows you to search for the following:

- health clubs
- personal trainers
- fitness centres
- physiotherapists
- yoga teachers
- personal fitness trainers
- fitness venues.

This is a commercial site and is not as detailed or as unbiased as the NHS site. Despite its name, it does not provide a map of facilities so it is less useful for geographers.

25 Use what you have learnt in this chapter, and your local knowledge, to identify issues in your local community. Then search the NHS Service Directory site to find information to analyse those issues. You may be able to extend your analysis further, using the skills of data collection, presentation and analysis that you have developed.

✔ 💡 *In this chapter you have learnt:*

- about the nature and meaning of the geography of health, and about why this is an important area for study by geographers

- about the nature of infectious diseases, how they can spread, the consequences of their spread and the measures that can be taken to control their spread

- about the issues linked with the spread of HIV/Aids in southern Africa

- how different diseases can affect societies at different stages of their economic development and how societies have to continue to seek cures for new diseases

- how the activities of transnational corporations can improve and damage people's health

- that health and well-being and the conditions that affect well-being differ from one region to another within the UK

- how the UK government is trying to adopt policies to improve health-care facilities and the general level of fitness of the population

- how to research into health and health care in local areas.

In this section you will find examination questions for each of the eight chapters covered in this book, in the style you can expect in your Unit 1 examination.

Chapter 1 Rivers, floods and management

1 (a) Outline how a river can erode its wetted perimeter. *(4 marks)*

(b) When a river is flowing round a bend, it is more likely to erode on the outside of the bend rather than on the inside. Explain why. *(4 marks)*

(c) Study Figures 1 and 2. The maps show Boscastle, a village on the north Cornwall coast that was affected by severe flooding in August 2004.

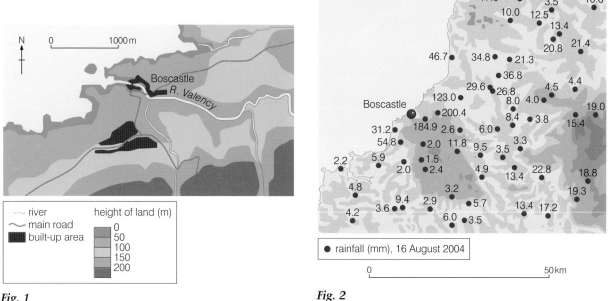

Fig. 1

Fig. 2

Suggest why the nature of the landscape and precipitation may have combined to cause flooding. *(7 marks)*

(d) Explain how rejuvenation can affect both the long and the cross profiles of river valleys. *(15 marks)*

2 (a) (i) What is the wetted perimeter of a river? *(2 marks)*

(ii) Suggest how and why the wetted perimeter of a river might change with distance from the source and changes of the season. *(6 marks)*

(b) Study Figure 3, which shows the effect of urbanisation on river discharge.

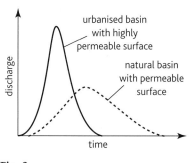

Fig. 3

Suggest why storm hydrographs in urban and rural drainage basins may show different responses to similar rainfall events. *(7 marks)*

(c) With reference to one or more examples that you have studied, discuss alternative ways of managing drainage basins to reduce the risk of flooding. *(15 marks)*

Chapter 2 Cold environments

1 (a) **(i)** Describe the main features of a corrie. *(4 marks)*

(ii) Explain how a corrie is formed. *(6 marks)*

(b) Study Figure 2.33 on page 70. Describe the map evidence that suggests that this area has been affected by periglacial processes. *(5 marks)*

(c) 'Antarctica is a unique physical and ecological environment and so it should be conserved at all costs with no economic development allowed.' Discuss this statement and assess its validity. *(15 marks)*

Chapter 3 Coastal environments

1 (a) In the context of coastal erosion, what is meant by the following terms?

(i) abrasion

(ii) attrition. *(4 marks)*

(b) Study Figure 3.12 on page 92. Explain how rock type and structure have influenced the development of the coastal features shown. *(6 marks)*

(c) Using a labelled map or diagram **only**, show how wave action can produce a spit. *(5 marks)*

(d) For one example of a scheme of coastal management, explain why the scheme was needed and how the scheme attempts to achieve its main aims. *(15 marks)*

Chapter 4 Hot desert environments and their margins

1 (a) How does the following contribute to the development of desert climates? Descending air producing high pressure and cold currents off the west coasts of continents. *(6 marks)*

(b) Study Figure 4.26 on page 142. Outline the evidence that shows that water has played an active part in the formation of this desert landscape. *(5 marks)*

(c) Explain why salt lakes are found in many of the world's deserts. *(4 marks)*

(d) Describe how farmers in more developed countries have tried to use arid and semi-arid lands and discuss the potential of such schemes for sustainability. *(15 marks)*

💡 Chapter 5 Population change

1 (a) Study Table 1.

Table 1

Population by age group, 2005	Kenya (thousands)	Hungary (thousands)
0–19	19,398	2,217
20–59	14,802	5,141
60+	1,399	2,099

(i) What do you understand by the term 'dependency ratio'? *(2 marks)*

(ii) Compare the dependency ratios for Kenya and Hungary. *(4 marks)*

2 Study Table 2.

Table 2

Indicator, 2005	Kenya	Hungary
Birth rate (‰)	39.2	9.3
Death rate (‰)	11.8	13.2
Life expectancy at birth (years)		
Males	53.0	69.2
Females	55.2	77.4

(a) Suggest reasons for the differences in the vital rates for Kenya and Hungary. *(4 marks)*

(b) Suggest how the differences in the vital rates might affect the dependency ratios in the two countries. *(5 marks)*

(c) Choose areas that you have studied that represent two different types of settlement from the following list:

- an inner-city area
- a suburban area
- an area of rural/urban fringe
- an area of rural settlement.

  - Name each area and state which type of settlement it represents.
  - Assess how the age structure in each of your chosen areas has implications for social welfare in those areas. *(15 marks)*

Chapter 6 Food supply issues

1 (a) Describe the major technological change which led to the green revolution that affected many developing countries in the late 1960s and 1970s. *(4 marks)*

(b) **(i)** What do you understand by the term 'intermediate or appropriate technology'? *(2 marks)*

(ii) For one or more examples of the use of intermediate or appropriate technology to increase food production in a less developed country, discuss the results of the use of this technology. *(9 marks)*

(c) Study Figure 4, a photograph taken in the Yorkshire Dales National Park.

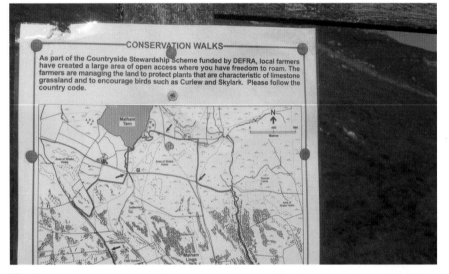

Fig. 4

List the groups and individuals with an interest in the way the land around here is farmed. Discuss how environmental stewardship schemes can encourage farmers to manage the land in a way that encourages conservation of the environment. *(15 marks)*

Chapter 7 Energy issues

1 (a) **(i)** What is meant by the term 'fossil fuels'? *(2 marks)*

(ii) Many geographers fear that fossil fuels may become exhausted at some point in the future. Why might this happen? *(2 marks)*

(iii) Study the energy mix for China and Kenya in Figures 7.10 to 7.13 on page 235. Compare the energy mixes of the two countries. *(5 marks)*

(b) Describe the environmental impact from the gathering of fuelwood in one country that you have studied. *(6 marks)*

(c) Analyse how the geopolitics of energy has led to conflict in world affairs. *(15 marks)*

Chapter 8 Health issues

1 (a) Study Figure 8.3 on page 265. Outline the global distribution of HIV/Aids and discuss the factors that influence its pattern of distribution. *(8 marks)*

  (b) Name a disease of affluence that you have studied. Explain why this disease is most common in more developed countries and wealthier communities. *(3 marks)*

  (c) With reference to a named area, suggest how age and gender can influence people's access to health-care facilities. *(4 marks)*

  (d) Referring to both pharmaceutical and tobacco companies, explain how transnational corporations can influence the health of people in countries at different stages of development. *(15 marks)*

Glossary

Ablation: the process of wastage of snow or ice, especially by melting.

Abrasion/corrasion: the wearing away of the shoreline by sediment carried by the waves.

Accumulation: the net gain in an ice mass. The sources of accumulation are direct snowfall and avalanching from higher slopes.

Acid rain: a broad term used to describe several ways that acids fall out of the atmosphere. A more precise term is acid deposition, which has two parts: wet and dry.

Aids: acquired immune deficiency syndrome; a group of infections, including pneumonia, TB and skin cancers, that strike people whose immune system has been damaged by the HIV virus.

Antiretroviral (ARV) drugs: designed to protect the immune system from the damaging effects of the HIV virus.

Arable farming: originally meant land that is fit to cultivate. However, in geography it is used to describe farming crops. Wheat, rice, barley, soya and cotton are typical arable crops. These can be grown as monoculture when a farm (or even a whole region) concentrates exclusively on a single crop.

Attrition: the reduction and rounding of particles of sediment carried in water by repeated collision with each other and the shore.

B

Balanced diet: the overall dietary pattern of foods consumed that provide all the essential nutrients in the appropriate amounts to support life processes, such as growth in children without promoting excess weight.

Baseflow: water that reaches the channel largely through slow throughflow and from permeable rock below the water table.

Birth rate (BR): the number of live births per thousand population per year, expressed as births per thousand (‰).

Brownfield sites: sites that have been built on before but that have come available for new building because of demolition or redundancy of the old buildings.

C

Capital-intensive farming: uses a lot of machinery, fertilisers and pesticides, buildings with heating and ventilation systems, irrigation, etc.

Carrying capacity: the largest population of people or animals that a particular area or ecosystem can support at a given level of technological development.

Channel flow: the movement of water within the river channel.

Char: an island formed from silt deposited in the delta. The land is at about sea level. It is very fertile, so it attracts settlers desperate for land. However, it can easily be washed away by monsoon floods or by cyclones. Even if the cyclones do not destroy the chars, they flood them with salt water, which reduces their fertility.

Colonisation: the spread of settlement onto previously uninhabitable land. One example is the colonisation of the chars. Another example is the spread of cultivation into desert margin areas by using irrigation water or new farming techniques (e.g. crops genetically engineered to be drought resistant).

Commercial farming: farming for sale and profit. It can range from a small family farm in the UK up to the huge corporation-owned farms in the US Midwest. A plantation is a specialised form of commercial farm. Plantations are usually owned by large firms because big investments are needed in growing, processing and transporting crops. Most plantations are in tropical and subtropical areas and grow tree crops for export. Coffee, tea, sugar, bananas, palm oil, rubber and pineapples are typical plantation crops.

Communism: a system of government in which the state plans and controls the economy and owns the means of production. The goods and services produced are then divided between the people in the way that the state considers best for everyone.

Compressional flow: also known as compressing flow, this is the type of glacier flow whereby a reduction in velocity leads to an increase in thickness of a glacier.

Condensation: the process by which water vapour is converted into water.

Conurbation: one large, more or less continuous area created as a city grows and spreads to absorb other cities, towns and villages in the surrounding area.

Corrosion: includes the dissolving of carbonate rocks (e.g. limestone) in sea water and the evaporation of salt crystals which expand on formation and help the rock to disintegrate.

Cross-sectional area: the total length of the bed and the bank sides in contact with the water in the channel.

D

Death rate (DR): the number of deaths per thousand population per year, expressed as deaths per thousand (‰).

Decommissioning: closing down a nuclear reactor and disposing of the contaminated material safely.

Democracy: a political system in which the people have the power to elect their government by the vote of a majority. They also have the power to vote to change the government.

Dependency ratio: shows how many young people (under 16) and older people (over 64) depend on people of working age (16 to 64). The dependency ratio is worked out with this formula:

$$\frac{(\% \text{ under } 15) + (\% \text{ over } 65)}{\% \text{ between } 15 \text{ and } 64} \times 100$$

Countries that have a high dependency ratio have more people who are not of working age, and fewer who are working and paying taxes. The higher the number, the more people who need looking after.

Desertification: the making of deserts or the spreading of a desert into new areas around its margins.

Discharge: the volume of water flowing in a river per second, measured in cumecs (m³/s).

Diseases of affluence: diseases that are thought to be a result of increasing wealth in a society.

Diseases of poverty: diseases that result from impoverishment.

Diurnal range: the difference between the lowest temperature and the highest temperature in a 24-hour period.

Dumping: the sale of products that have been produced with the aid of subsidies and then are sold in another country at a price that is cheaper than the cost of production. This might seem generous but it undercuts farmers in the receiving country. This can make their farms uneconomic, put them out of business and increase dependence on the country that dumped its produce.

Dynamic equilibrium: rivers are constantly changing over time to reach a state of balance with the processes that determine their form. As the flows of energy and materials passing through a river system vary, the river changes to move towards this equilibrium.

E

Endoreic: this type of drainage occurs where rivers flow into the desert area but dry up and terminate in inland seas (like the River Jordan in the Dead Sea) or salt flats.

Energy mix: the different sources of energy used by households, industry and commerce, and in the electricity generation industry.

Ephemeral: these streams are most common in the desert. They flow intermittently after rainstorms, or seasonally in desert margin areas.

Erosion: the wearing away of the surface of the land. It includes the breakdown of rock and its removal by wind, water or ice.

Eustatic: changes in sea level induced by variations in the amount of water in the oceans.

Evaporation: the transformation of water droplets into water vapour by heating.

Evapotranspiration: the loss of water from a drainage basin into the atmosphere from the leaves of plants.

Exogenous: these desert rivers rise in rainy, mountain regions outside the desert and continue flowing across the desert. Two examples are the Colorado and the Nile.

Extensional flow: also known as extending flow, this is the extension and related thinning of glacier ice in those zones where velocity increases.

Extensive farming: uses a large area of land with low inputs and low outputs per hectare.

F

Famine: a time when there is so little food that many people starve.

Flood: a temporary excess of water which spills over onto land.

Flow resources: the result of a continuous flow like wind or tide.

Food security: the FAO says food security exists 'when all people, at all times, have access to sufficient, safe and nutritious food to meet their dietary needs and food preferences for an active and healthy life.'

Frequency: how often floods occur.

G

Genocide: the deliberate and systematic destruction or killing of an entire people who belong to one racial, political, cultural or religious group.

Gentrification: a spontaneous and unplanned change by which individual families buy up run-down old property and improve it, adding to its value. Rewiring, adding central heating, replacing bathrooms and kitchens, adding extensions, and so on, all add to the value of the property. As more and more people do this in an area and it attracts a richer population, these richer people attract new shops and services, often also in renovated old premises. Thus the whole area improves and moves upmarket.

Geopolitics: the way geography, demography, economics and the distribution of resources interrelate with the politics of nations and the relationships between nations.

Glacial: a period of time when masses of ice develop and advance into lower altitudes due to a sustained decline in temperature. Extensive continental ice sheets form during such periods.

Globalisation: a set of processes leading to the integration of economic, cultural, political and social systems across geographical boundaries. It refers to increasing economic integration of countries, especially in terms of trade and the movement of capital.

Green belt: an area defined by Act of Parliament which surrounds a conurbation. It is very difficult to obtain permission for development on green belt. This acts to stop the extended sprawl of conurbations.

Groundwater flow: the deeper movement of water through underlying rock strata.

Groundwater storage: the storage of water underground in permeable rock strata.

H

Health: the overall condition of an individual at a given time in regard to soundness of body or mind and freedom from disease or abnormality.

HIV: human immunodeficiency virus, which attacks the immune system of people who are infected. Infection is caused when body fluids from an infected person are passed into the body of another. This can happen through unprotected sexual intercourse, blood transfusions, sharing of needles, or from mother to baby during childbirth.

Hydraulic radius: the ratio of the cross-sectional area of the channel and the length of its wetted perimeter.

Hydrograph: a graph showing for a given point on a stream the discharge, stage (depth), velocity, or other property of water with respect to time; a graphical representation of stream discharge (volume/time) during a storm or flood event.

I

Ideology: a set of beliefs that form the basis of a political, economic or other system.

Infant mortality: a measure of the number of infants dying under one year of age, usually expressed as the number of deaths per thousand live births per year.

Infilling: the use of open spaces within a conurbation to build new housing or services, often close to where a green belt restricts outward growth.

Infiltration: the downward movement of water into the soil surface.

Intellectual property rights: the ideas behind the patents. The

patents make sure that people and the companies they work for are paid for their efforts.

Intensive farming: when the land is farmed with a high rate of inputs so that a high rate of outputs can be produced.

Interception: prevention of rain from reaching the Earth's surface by trees and plants.

Interception storage: the total volume of water held on the surface of vegetation.

Interglacial: a period of time, such as the present day, when ice still covers part of the Earth's surface, but has retreated to the polar regions.

Intermediate technology: also called appropriate technology, this is a way to introduce technology to people who have not used it before. It has to be more efficient than the simple, traditional technology but it must not be too expensive to run and maintain. It ought to be manageable and repairable by the people who use it without relying on outside technicians.

Isostatic: changes in sea level resulting from the rise and fall of land masses.

L

Labour-intensive farming: has a big input of work per area of land.

Life expectancy: the average age to which the population lives. It is expressed in terms of years. Male and female life expectancy figures are often given separately.

Livestock farming: keeping mainly animals. They can be kept mainly for meat, mainly for milk or mainly for wool, leather, etc. Examples of livestock are cattle, sheep, pigs, goats, camels and poultry.

Lobbying: presenting a case to the government and legislators on behalf of a client. Legislators in the UK are MPs; legislators in the USA are representatives and senators.

M

Magnitude: the size of the flood.

Malnutrition: the lack of proper nutrition resulting from a poorly balanced diet.

Mixed farming: growing crops and keeping animals. It has many benefits as the crops can provide fodder for the animals, and the animals can provide manure for the soil.

Morbidity: the state of being ill or diseased, or the occurrence of a disease or condition that damages health and quality of life. It can also be used to mean the relative incidence of a particular disease in a society.

Mortality: death. The term is often accompanied by the cause of death (a specific disease or condition or injury).

N

Natural increase/decrease: the difference between the numbers of births and deaths for every hundred people per year expressed as a percentage.

Non-renewable resources: finite or limited resources, which will run out sooner or later. They include fossil fuels like coal, oil and natural gas and also nuclear, because it uses mined uranium. Breeder reactors, which create their own fuel, are theoretically possible but are not sufficiently developed.

O

Obesity: excess of body fat that is 20 per cent or more over a person's ideal weight. Obesity strains the cardiovascular system and increases the risk of diabetes, hypertension, etc.

Off-patent medicines: medicines where the patent no longer applies. Other companies are allowed to produce copies of that drug and can charge lower prices. Drugs produced by a variety of different companies are called generic drugs.

Opportunistic infections: illnesses that strike people whose immune systems have been damaged by HIV.

Optimum population: the population at which the quality of life of the people of a country or a region is the highest possible, at a given level of technological development.

Organic food: food produced according to certain production standards. Crops are grown without the use of conventional pesticides, artificial fertilisers, human waste or sewage sludge, and are processed without ionising radiation or food additives. Animals are reared without the use of antibiotics or growth hormones and must not be genetically modified.

Overland flow: the movement of water over the surface of the land, usually when the ground is staturated or frozen or when preciptiation is too intense for infiltration to occur.

Overpopulation: when any increase in population reduces the average quality of life of the population.

P

Palliative: a drug or other treatment designed to reduce symptons and/ or ease pain without dealing with the conditions that cause the problem.

Patented drugs: medicines that have been developed by a company that has claimed rights to their production. No other company can produce them without permission and a licence bought from the patent holder. This means that the company can charge high enough prices to earn back the costs of developing the drug.

Percolation: the gravity flow of water within soil.

Population structure: the breakdown of a country's population into groups defined by age and sex.

Precipitation: all forms of moisture that reach the Earth's surface (including rain, snow and dew).

Pressure melting point (PMP): the temperature at which ice under pressure will melt.

Public health: the aspect of medical activity directed towards improving the health of the whole community. Public health addresses the health of the population as a whole rather than medical health care, which focuses on treatment of the individual ailment.

Q

Quaternary period: the latest period in geological time spanning the last 2 million years. It is sub-divided into the Pleistocene epoch (the most recent ice age) and the Holocene epoch (the post-glacial period of the last 10,000 years).

R

Recurrence interval: the interval at which particular levels of flooding will occur.

Renewable resources: resources that will not run out and which are continuously being created. They include solar, wind, tide, hydroelectric and geothermal power.

S

Salinisation: the process whereby soluble salts accumulate in the soil. It happens naturally when rainwater sinks into the soil, dissolves salts and is then evaporated, precipitating the salts near the surface. However, if irrigation water is drawn up from below ground, it can cause even more rapid salinisation. This can be toxic to many crop plants.

Sinuosity: the curving nature of a meander, described as:

Actual channel length

Straight-line distance.

Social welfare: the well-being of communities. It refers to the access that groups of people, or individuals, have to job opportunities, housing, health care, education, an unpolluted environment, a safe environment and freedom to practice one's culture, religion, etc.

Soil moisture: the total amount of water, including the water vapour, in an unsaturated soil.

Solar cooking: uses the rays of the sun, often concentrated by reflection off aluminium foil, to heat a box in which food is kept. The heat makes the box act as a slow cooker for the food.

Solution: the dissolving action of water on rocks, particularly carbonate rocks such as limestone.

Starvation: a state of extreme hunger resulting from lack of essential nutrients over a prolonged period.

Steady state: when the amounts of accumulation and ablation are equal over the course of a year. As a result, the snout of the glacier will remain stationary.

Stewardship: taking responsible care of the environment, based on the premise that we do not own resources, but are managers and are responsible to future generations for their condition.

Stock resources: there is a certain stock of each resource and when that stock is gone it is gone forever.

Storm flow: water that reaches the channel largely through runoff. This may be a combination of overland flow and rapid throughflow.

Studentification: when large family houses became too big and expensive to run, the inhabitants moved out and the properties are subdivided and let to students. When several houses on a street become student lets, the nature of the area starts to change. There is more noise, gardens are less carefully tended, several old cars may be parked in the street, etc. Consequently, there is pressure on the remaining families to move out of the area, leaving more properties for student lets. The whole area deteriorates and moves downmarket.

Sublimation: a transition from the solid state (ice) to gas (water vapour) with no intermediate liquid stage (water).

Subsidy: a payment to a producer to help cover the costs of production so that the product can be sold at a price lower than the true cost. This means that the producer can compete against foreign imports.

Subsistence farming: growing food for the family. It was once widespread when people lived in small, isolated communities but it has become rare now that transport is so much easier and trade is more common. Some farmers in remote parts of poor countries are probably best described as near-subsistence farmers, but even they often sell surpluses when they are produced.

Surface storage: the total volume of water held on the Earth's surface in lakes, ponds and puddles.

Surge: a short-lived phase of accelerated glacier flow.

T

Tariffs: taxes charged on imports (foodstuffs in this case.) They are designed to raise the price of cheap imports to allow home producers to compete.

Throughflow: the movement of water downslope within the soil layer.

Topography: the arrangement of the natural and artificial physical features of an area.

U

Undernutrition: below the minimum level of dietary energy (calorie) consumption. The Department of Health estimates this level at 1940 kcal per day for women and 2550 for men (average 2250), but these figures can vary widely depending on lifestyle and other factors.

Underpopulation: when an increase in population could increase the average quality of life.

Urbanisation: an increase in the proportion of a country's population living in urban areas. It is sometimes used to mean the process of moving from rural to urban areas.

V

Velocity: the speed and the direction at whcich a body of water moves.

W

Wave crest: the highest point of a wave.

Wave energy: $E \propto$ (is proportional to) LH^2 where L is wavelength and H is wave height. A small increase in wave height will result in a large increase in energy.

Wave frequency: the number of waves per minute.

Wavelength: the distance between two successive crests.

Wave period: the time taken for a wave to travel between one wave length.

Wave steepness: the ratio of the wave height to the wave length (note that this cannot be steeper than 1:7 as this is when the wave breaks).

Wave trough: the lowest point of a wave.

Weathering: the breakdown of rocks in situ (in their original location, without them being moved away). This produces finer particles that can then be moved away by agents of erosion such as wind and running water.

Wetted perimeter: that portion of the perimeter of a stream channel cross-section that is in contact with the water.

Index